(THE) LATE NIGHT
GUIDE
TO C++

THE LATE NIGHT GUIDE TO C++

NIGEL CHAPMAN

JOHN WILEY & SONS

Chichester • New York • Brisbane • Toronto • Singapore

Copyright © 1996 Nigel Chapman
Published in 1996 by John Wiley & Sons Ltd,
        Baffins Lane, Chichester,
        West Sussex PO19 1UD, England

        National   01243 779777
        International (+44) 1243 779777

Illustrations by Jenny Chapman

e-mail (for orders and customer service enquiries): cs-books@wiley.co.uk
Visit our Home Page on http://www.wiley.co.uk
                or
        http://www.wiley.com

Other Wiley Editorial Offices

John Wiley & Sons Inc., 605 Third Avenue,
New York, NY 10158-0012, USA

Jacaranda Wiley Ltd, 33 Park Road, Milton,
Queensland 4064, Australia

John Wiley & Sons (Canada) Ltd., 22 Worcester Road,
Rexdale, Ontario M9W 1L1, Canada

John Wiley & Sons (Asia) Pte Ltd, 2 Clementi Loop #02-01,
Jin Xing Distripark, Singapore 0512

5-1-97

Library of Congress Cataloging-in-Publication Data

Chapman, Nigel P.
   The late night guide to C++ / Nigel Chapman.
      p. cm.
   Includes bibliographical references and index.
   ISBN 0 471 95071 8 (alk. paper)
   1. C++ (Computer program language)   I. Title.
QA76.73.C153C47 1996
005.13'3 – dc20   96-28029
                                              CIP

British Library Cataloguing in Publication Data

A catalogue record for this book is available from the British Library

ISBN 0 471 95071 8

Produced from PostScript files supplied by the author
Printed and bound in Great Britain by Bookcraft (Bath) Ltd
This book is printed on acid-free paper responsibly manufactured from sustainable forestation,
for which at least two trees are planted for each one used for paper production.

SIR TOBY BELCH ...Not to be a-bed after midnight is to be up betimes, and *"deliculo surgere"*, thou know'st—

SIR ANDREW AGUECHEEK Nay, by my troth, I know not; but I know, to be up late is to be up late.

Twelfth Night II.iii
Wm. Shakespeare

Contents

x

Begin

Did you ever stay up late into the night, working on a computer program? Not because you were getting paid to, or because you had to have a demonstration ready for a marketing meeting the next morning, or because you wanted to get it finished before you went on holiday, but just because you couldn't stop? Because there was something fascinating about making that program work that was just...worth staying up for?

If you are going to program computers, it seems to me that you need that sort of excitement, because it's a pretty miserable business without it. Too often, people with a job to do seem to have lost touch with what can make it interesting. One way to get back in touch is by finding out about new developments—but that's not so easy. Unless you are a student, or like books that patronize you with shallow explanations and feeble jokes, you are, for the most part, stuck with the reference manuals. If your days are full of coding and maintenance, you won't feel much like spending your evenings in the company of such dry companions. So, inevitably, people who, only a few years ago, were eager young programmers right at the edge of the technology are finding it hard to adapt and keep up. They have begun to feel alienated and defensive and they are losing their touch.

I am on a mission to restore fun and excitement to jaded programmers, and the *Late Night Guides* are my way of going about it. "Late Night" because you've got a job to do during the day; "Late Night" because their mood and attitude belong to the night; and "Late Night" because this is no time for children and young persons. This is the time for anybody who is smart, and who has been around a time or two.

Accordingly, I don't pretend to be impartial, objective or balanced, and I try not to hide behind the passive voice, the scientific style, or the authorial "we". ("We" in this book is you and me.) There is plenty of room in the margins for you to write *So you say*, or *Oh yeah??!* (or even *How true!!*).

Don't do this to a library book

This book contains no exercises for the student, no self-assessment checkpoints and no ten minute workouts. I assume you have work to do and will want to apply what you learn here to that, instead of having me set up hoops for you to jump through.

This, then, is the *Late Night Guide to C++*. It's not an attempt to teach programming, still less design. It does aim to show you what C++ is like, and what it's like to program in it. By the end, you should be able to write quite sophisticated C++ programs. I have included details of some excellent books on advanced C++ programming for your further reading, when you are ready to move on to the truly hard task of writing good re-usable software.

This book is aimed at people who already know how to write non-trivial programs in some language, and who know their way around computers. This includes professional programmers and software engineers, teachers of programming, and people working in other areas who need to use a programming language as a tool. It may also appeal to some students, particularly mature ones, whose pre-university experience leads them to find programming courses aimed at undergraduates with little programming knowledge unsuitable. I assume you've heard of C++ and have a vague idea of what it is for. One thing I don't assume is that you either know or like C.

C++ is a big, complex language, and all attempts to describe it by starting at the beginning and working through its features in sequence seem to be doomed to get bogged down early on, and to be plagued with forward references. Therefore, I have adopted a treatment that is best described as a spiral. Starting with the simplest features, I begin to circle round C++. Each circuit goes into greater detail about some features already seen, and introduces some new ones. These are then taken up again as the spiral widens and returns. There is one exception to this scheme. I am sure that by the time they have finished chapter 6, many readers will feel I should have said something more than a few tantalizing hints about constructors earlier on. I decided to defer their introduction until I had covered enough of the rest of C++ to give a full account, because I have seen too many people led astray by a simplified introduction to constructors. If my caution is exaggerated, it is probably because I have been led astray myself.

The example programs turn in a spiral, too. An example may be introduced to illustrate a specific feature being described at that point in the text, but it will usually be a more or less complete program that also uses previously described features, not a specially tailored fragment that only shows one thing. Later, the same example may reappear in a more elaborate version, which is often improved by incorporating extra language features. In this way, examples reinforce earlier material and emphasize that language features are not used in isolation. The price for this organization is that you start out with an incomplete picture that, in some cases, is only really finished at the book's end, and some initial versions of programs which, while correct, are less than perfect. Nevertheless, I have attempted to minimize forward references and to defer details to a point where they can be fitted in to a suitable context. I have done my best to supply a useful index and a few suggestions for further reading. Although I have omitted some features which I consider unimportant, I do describe advanced features and recent additions.

Presentation.

Some aspects of presentation deserve note.

Programs are mostly presented with commentary interspersed in the text; the code is easily identifiable by being in a fixed-width teletype style font `like this`. In some cases, remarks on the code are presented in parallel with it, set off to one side, but I prefer to take advantage of the typographical possibilities of a book instead of including comments in the technical sense. All the code has been taken from programs that have been compiled and tested, but it is possible that errors have been introduced during their incorporation into the text. Responsibility for all errors is mine. The programming style is also entirely my very own—I call it neo-classical post-retropunk, but other people have a different name for it.

Sometimes, C++ constructs are presented with the aid of pseudocode, in which italicized words such as *statement* are used to stand in for occurrences of other constructs. Generally, syntax is described using an extended BNF meta-notation: italicized words again stand for C++ constructs—nonterminals, if you like the jargon—with symbols that stand for themselves in a bold version of the teletype font. Curly brackets enclose items that may occur zero or more times, square brackets enclose optional items, round brackets are used for grouping and a vertical bar separates alternatives. Watch out for the difference between { and **{** and so on.

Because I believe that you can learn from mistakes, I sometimes give examples of errors or things I consider bad practice. These are identified by a large
! black exclamation mark in the margin, like the one you see here.

▷ You will also see indented passages like this set in smaller type than the surrounding text, with triangles at the beginning and end. Apart from this one, these passages are either somewhat tangential or highly detailed; one or two will probably only make sense if you have a computing degree. In all cases, except this one, they may
◁ be omitted at first without great loss.

Who is Bjarne Stroustrup and what are the ARM and the draft standard?

You will find frequent references to all of these throughout the book. Stroustrup is the inventor, chief developer, first implementor and general *grand fromage* of C++. Praise and blame him. The ARM is the *Annotated C++ Reference Manual*, which forms the base document for the proposed ANSI/ISO C++ standard. (A full reference can be found on page 345.) The first "committee draft" of this standard was circulated at the end of April 1995, and has been used as the basis of the description of C++ found in this book. A final ratified standard is not now expected before 1998.[1] In the meantime, the ARM provides a relatively accessible reference. However, some of the differences between it and the draft standard are significant and I have noted them in the relevant places.

---

[1] Although I refer to the April 1995 committee draft as the "draft standard", it is probably worth emphasizing that it does not have the status of an ISO Draft International Standard.

Opening Time

Before we settle in to the serious business of the night, let's take the opportunity to spend a little time to consider what sort of programming language this book is about.

C++ Considered

1

I have known a programmer go to extraordinary lengths to avoid using C++. The person I have in mind even took up theoretical computer science for a while, writing TEX macros and Awk scripts to keep his spirits up. It isn't difficult to sympathize with him. Despite its considerable power and flexibility, C++ is an easy language to dislike on a superficial acquaintance. Only after making an effort to understand how C++ came to be like it is and what it can do did this programmer come to respect C++ and use it effectively. But no, he never did come to love it. Not much, anyway.

It's probably easiest to dislike C++ if you were schooled in the Structured Programming movement. C++ seems to defy all the tenets of that discipline. It is a language riddled with side-effects, packed with features impossible to bring under the discipline of invariants and weakest preconditions; it even lets you do arithmetic on pointers and characters. Worst of all, for structured programmers, it is bound up with a new programming methodology that looks suspiciously bottom-up, whose aficionados seem intent on throwing away all the lessons of top-down program construction that took so long to learn.

C programmers and assembly language enthusiasts find it easy to dislike C++ too. What this group of programmers values most is the ability to manipulate machine resources more or less directly, without interference from a programming language or its designer. C++ is seen as taking that ability away. It is strongly type checked, the epitome of the "bondage and domination" languages machine-oriented programmers are so disparaging about. The C++ compiler is well known to insert function calls for you without your explicit instruction. This loss of control over the fine detail of program execution, together with the suspicion that this *must* imply a loss of efficiency, can make C++ hard to swallow.

Other groups of programmers have their own objections to C++. For the increasing number of novices faced with learning to program by learning C++, it is simply too big and full of difficult and apparently unnecessary features, which are just there to make programming harder than it need be and to make programming teachers appear cleverer than they are. To application programmers with a real job to do—business programmers working with a fourth generation data processing language or scientists getting their numbers out of a Fortran program—C++ looks like another in the long line of computer scientists' toys, too concerned with programming for its own sake.

Lisp programmers dislike C++ because it isn't Lisp.

Everybody can find something to object to in the idiosyncratic syntax of C++, whether it's the need to use *two* equals signs to test equality, the abstruse syntax of declarations, the host of superficially unconnected uses of the keywords `static` and `virtual` or any one of a hundred other peculiarities and infelicities. To cap things off, the C++ community seems to make special efforts to use its very own jargon. Even experienced programmers who have mastered the notoriously esoteric vocabulary of computing can feel shut out by this private language with its "virtual functions", "abstract base classes", "public inheritance", "protected members" and many other opaque terms.

This is a lot of criticism, and most of it is justifiable. Given which, it's easy and tempting to turn your back on C++ and wait for the bubble to burst. This would be foolish.

For a start, there *are* good things about C++, as the host of enthusiastic C++ programmers bears witness. Chief among these is that it offers support for programming in an object-oriented style. You could be forgiven for greeting this announcement with a yawn. So much trumpeting of the virtues of object-oriented programming has gone on and so much of it has been exaggerated or ill-informed that it has become hard to distinguish between marketing, the self-aggrandizing of bandwagon followers and the real merits of the methodology. But it does have some, as we will see.

C++ isn't the only programming language providing support for object-oriented programming. It doesn't even provide the best support for it. It does, however, combine that support with other, easily appreciated, advantages. High on many people's list of these is its efficiency. It is true that efficiency is less important than correctness, that the really significant gains in efficiency are made by improvements to algorithms, and that the easiest way to get linear speedups is to buy a faster computer ... but sometimes the overhead you incur by using an inefficient language can matter. Even useful and civilized computer applications have to perform very rapidly sometimes. Any program that does a lot of interaction with its users must be fast enough to live up to people's expectations of machines. Many specialized systems, such as telecommunications switching software, must be fast enough to keep up with events in the outside world.

The need for efficiency is sometimes seen as an obstacle to object-oriented programming. Support for object-oriented features in some programming languages does incur an overhead. For example, it is sometimes convenient to represent every object in a program as a pointer to its stored value, even for objects that are directly representable in a machine word. This means that there is an extra memory access performed every time an integer variable is used, for example. However, it has been a design principle of C++ that it should offer efficiency comparable to that of C, and that, where a particular feature necessarily imposes a performance penalty, C++ programmers who do not use that feature will not pay the penalty.

Another major advantage of C++, which is often taken for granted, is that it is *just* a programming language. It is used in a manner familiar to anyone who has used any major programming language of the last thirty years: you make a source file with your favourite editor, compile it, usually link it with other separately compiled pieces and libraries, and then run the resulting executable program like any other program on your system. There is no need to learn a special C++ editor (although there are such things and you can use them if you like) or to go into a special C++ environment to run the program. Although integrated programming environments can be extremely good, there is too much useful software already available for it to be realistic to expect anyone to work exclusively with such an environment. Most programmers find the consequent need to work in a schizoid way, with a programming environment for one set of tasks and a general-purpose environment for another set, unacceptable. C++ fits in as part of any general purpose computing environment, which makes using the language and any programs written in it much more convenient and comfortable.

For many experienced programmers, C++'s huge advantage over other object-oriented programming languages is simply that it has developed from C. *A lot of programmers know C.* ISO C is nearly a subset of C++, so it is comparatively easy for C programmers to move to C++. This can be done gradually, first taking advantage of the small improvements offered within the C subset and then moving on to the use of object-oriented features. Much of the syntax is familiar and the underlying model of program execution is basically the same. Whereas the real difficulties in mastering C++ stem from a need to change your way of thinking about programming, the similarities between C and C++ ease the initial transition by minimizing superficial distractions. In contrast, mastering some other object-oriented programming language means learning a new syntax for the familiar constructs as well as mastering new ideas and often a new semantic model. A high degree of compatibility with C also makes it easy to incorporate existing code into new programs or to produce new C++ versions of old C programs.

Above all, though, *C++ is here.* To ignore it is to confine yourself to an impoverished little enclave. It means cutting yourself off from the wealth of libraries and application frameworks written in and for C++. It also means cutting yourself off from much of the important contemporary debate about programming language design and programming methodology. Acknowledging the supremacy of C++ does not imply embracing it wholeheartedly or uncritically, but denying it is denying reality.

▷ It's instructive to glance at the history of C++'s rise to power, starting with a look at its genealogy.

C++ contains very few original ideas. The source of most of its syntax and semantics is C. C itself is often described as a successor to BCPL, a machine-oriented high-level language developed at Cambridge University[1] primarily for systems programming tasks such as compiler writing. BCPL in turn was developed from a subset of CPL, an elegant general purpose high level language that was too ambitious for its

---

[1] If you want to be really accurate, developed by Martin Richards *of* Cambridge University while he was at MIT.

time and never fully implemented. The subset which became BCPL was a drastically stripped down version of CPL (the B stands for Basic; what the CPL stands for is a complex tale that doesn't belong here) used to write a prototype CPL compiler. BCPL retained much of CPL's syntactic elegance but dispensed with most of its high level semantic features. Most radically, BCPL threw out CPL's type system completely, replacing it with the idea that every value is of the same type, the word. You could do anything you wanted to a word—just as you can in assembly language—including treat it as an address, that is, a pointer. Doing arithmetic on pointers to traverse data structures is quite a natural thing to do in this setting. So are all sorts of other low level tricks. However, you gain the ability to do these tricks at the expense of losing all type checking. Errors resulting from treating things that aren't pointers as pointers or calling functions with inappropriate arguments were commonplace in the life of a BCPL programmer. The way BCPL linkage was usually done, it was even possible to call functions that weren't there, with exciting results at runtime.

Not much of the BCPL legacy is actually visible in C. The syntax is changed radically, incorporating ideas from Algol68 and PL/I, as well as innovatory notations undreamt of in any other language. More importantly, a type system is reintroduced. This also was innovatory, being designed to reflect the different types available in machines of the time, rather than the mathematical abstractions usually used as the basis of types in a high level language. The most obvious link with BCPL is the retention of full frontal pointers, with pointer arithmetic and all, but in the context of a typed language—however half-hearted the type checking actually performed by C compilers—this took on a new character. For example, the precise effect of adding one to a pointer depends on what the pointer is supposed to be pointing at.

C has been described as a weed: it's scruffy and ugly but it has taken root everywhere. It has also been described as the ultimate computer virus. The agent of its propagation was the UNIX operating system.[2] UNIX was written in C and a C compiler came free with every copy of UNIX, which was itself distributed for only a nominal fee, and therefore eagerly snapped up by impecunious academic institutions. The UNIX system calls were available as C library functions; if you wanted to write programs that used the facilities of the operating system in an effective way, or interacted with the tools available under UNIX, you had to write C, or put up with a good deal of awkwardness.

Use of C spread with the use of UNIX and it expanded with the explosive growth in PC use, helped by the early availability of C compilers for PCs. Even though, on paper, Pascal is a better designed language, programmers found that the ease of system programming in C, together with its freedom from the irksome restrictions of Pascal's crude, but strongly enforced, type system, made C a better tool for doing real programming.

By the end of the 1970s, although the use of C was still to reach its height, ideas about programming language design had moved on and C was beginning to look rather old-fashioned, its shortcomings for certain types of programming, especially on a large scale, becoming obvious. At that time, a great deal of research was going on into the incorporation of abstract datatypes—user-defined types with their own operations—into programming languages. The origin of this concept is usually

[2]Larry Wall, perpetrator of the Perl language, is putting it about that programmers switched to C because they found lower case easier to read than upper. He may have something.

traced back to Simula67, a special-purpose extension of Algol60, designed originally for writing simulation programs. In simulation, the idea of defining a class of objects to which you can do certain specific things is a natural and useful one. Once it had been implemented as part of a programming language its wider implications as the basis of an approach to programming began to be appreciated. A host of experimental languages incorporating abstract datatypes was designed, including Alphard, CLU, Euclid, Mesa and Model. None of these ever got much further than the laboratory.

However, Simula67, in its original guise as a simulation language, was the second major influence on C++. Bjarne Stroustrup, working at AT&T Bell Labs, needed to write software to simulate the performance of a planned distributed version of the UNIX kernel. He had previous experience of simulation using both Simula and BCPL. He had found that Simula's facilities for modularization and type checking, based on the use of classes, made writing this sort of program a relatively easy task, but that its performance was not acceptable. Rewriting in BCPL produced the necessary improvement in speed, but at the cost of seriously increased programming difficulty. Thus the idea of adding classes—the structuring device—to C—an efficient language—was born.

Stroustrup's first language was called *C with Classes*. It was considered as an extended dialect of C, not as a language in its own right. It was used within Bell Labs for network and machine simulations, and also distributed on a small scale to some universities. At the time, classes were considered to be an abstract data type facility; the object-oriented bandwagon had yet to start rolling. *C with Classes* was redesigned and renamed C++ to provide a proper language. Its first commercial release was available in 1985. By mid 1986, it was estimated that there were about two thousand C++ users in the world. Alternative compilers appeared first in 1987; in June 1989, "Release 2.0" of the AT&T compiler provided a solid implementation and rounded off C++ with some additional features. Compilers for the PC appeared between 1988 and 1990. It is estimated that the number of C++ users doubled every seven and a half months, with an estimated four hundred thousand by 1991. After that, nobody could keep count.

Since 1990, a committee has been working under the auspices of the American National Standards Institute (ANSI) to produce a standard definition of C++. In 1991, a C++ working group of the International Standards Organization (ISO) was convened; the two organizations are working together to produce a joint standard. During the standardization process, the committee has incorporated further extensions into the language, as well as clarifying details of existing features. The standard will ◁ include a definition of a standard C++ library.

C++ has evolved since its first release and continues to evolve. Again and again, its designer has emphasized that the language has evolved to meet the needs of its users. He also insists that the language should be judged as a tool, not as an intellectual achievement. It is noteworthy that Stroustrup was not a programming language expert; his original interests lay in operating systems and distributed computing. His responsiveness to and awareness of the needs of users may ultimately be the key to C++'s continuing success and the best reason to adopt it.

OBJECT-ORIENTED PROGRAMMING

Because of the impact object-oriented ideas have had on the design of C++ and on its use, it is necessary to devote some space to them.

There are two distinct ways of looking at object-oriented programming; I call them the classical and romantic views. Generalizing and simplifying wildly, we can say that the classical view of things is primarily concerned with structure and underlying principles, while the romantic is more concerned with surface and appearance. From a classical viewpoint, then, the important aspects of object-oriented programming are *abstract data types, inheritance* and *dynamic binding.* From the romantic viewpoint, it is the *object metaphor* that is the essence of object-oriented programming.

The object metaphor seems to have wide appeal as a way of thinking about programs, even though, in truth, it is something of a mixed metaphor. It likens a program to a collection of objects which communicate with each other by passing messages. How many sorts of objects do you know that pass messages to each other? In this aspect, object-oriented programming is *anthropomorphic* programming. Objects are considered to know various things about their own state and to be able to perform certain actions, which they do in response to messages. The repertoire of actions an object can perform depends on the class it belongs to. The organizational principle here is that objects can be classified according to the actions they perform. Any program is thought of as a model of some real world situation or mathematical abstraction. A program can be designed by thinking about the *sorts of things* that it models. These sorts of things are then characterized by their behaviour, and this leads to a specification of some classes. A particular program will perform a task by creating some objects belonging to these classes, which will then carry out the desired computation by exchanging messages which cause them to carry out actions (possibly including the creation of further objects).

Classes are not, in general, independent. They are related, in particular, by the principle of inheritance, whereby a class can be defined as a refinement of an existing class. It inherits the properties of the old class and adds some new ones of its own. If the division of objects into classes corresponds to our normal habit of classification of things into sorts of things, then inheritance corresponds to the habit of arranging these sorts of things into a hierarchy, based on the notion that a class may encompass several special sorts of things, each of which is itself a class. We use this sort of organization of classes all the time in our ordinary affairs. For example, in a café at night we will see many people; a few of these will be distinguished by the way they are dressed and the fact that, if we ask them for a cup of coffee they will go and get one and, some time later, demand payment from us. Waiters, as they are known, are people: they walk, talk, sleep and all that, but they are distinguished from other people by these special properties. In some contexts, a waiter can be treated like any other person—you could ask anybody the time, for example—but in others you deal with then in special ways. We can say that the class of people includes the class of waiters. Similarly, the class of computer programs includes the classes of text editors, operating systems, games, compilers, screen savers, word processors, and so on. The class of compilers includes that of C++ compilers and also Pascal compilers. Each of these is a computer program, and shares characteristics, such as the ability to be executed on a computer, but each has its own peculiar characteristics. For example, word processors can do paragraph formatting, but compilers cannot.

The final important aspect of the object metaphor is that the action performed in response to a message will depend on the class of the object receiving it. Metaphorically, the receiver interprets the message according to the understanding built into its class. This sort of behaviour can be seen in both the examples in the previous paragraph. If you ask a waiter for a cup of coffee, he'll bring it for you. If you ask someone else, either they'll ask a waiter or they'll tell you to get lost.[3] Things are even more clear cut with computer programs. On, for example, a Macintosh computer, just about every program responds to the "message" sent by pressing the command and Q keys at the same time (command-Q) by "quitting", or terminating execution. On the other hand, whereas an editor might respond to the message command-F by trying to find a search string in the file being edited, the operating system will respond by trying to find a particular file on disk.

▷ The object metaphor is most closely associated with the Smalltalk programming language. The original Smalltalk project was concerned with the development of a programming language to support a concept that was radical at the time, that of a personal computer. The project started from the premise that its users would not be conventionally trained programmers and a lot of the early work on Smalltalk focussed on young children as computer users. (This may well be the source of the anthropomorphism of objects—small children readily ascribe personalities to ◁ almost anything.)

In a language based on the object metaphor, we might design a class called, say, `charstring` of character strings. One of the actions an object belonging to this class can perform is sticking a further string of characters on to the end of itself. So, if `s1` and `s2` are `charstring`s, somehow initialized, you would cause `s2` to be attached to the end of `s1` by sending the message `append` to `s1`, with `s2` as an argument, something like

```
s1 append s2
```

(not using any particular language's syntax). The `charstring` object `s1` sees the message `append` and responds by carrying out its appending action, which causes it to obtain the following value, `s2`, and stick it on the end of its present string of characters.

To the classical view of object-oriented programming, all this is mere concrete syntax, a potentially misleading analogy. What can it possibly matter whether we write an operation's name after its first operand, as if it were a "message", or put the operation name first, followed by all its operands in brackets, as if it were a function, like `append(s1, s2)`? If you wrote in Lisp, you'd put the whole lot in brackets as `(append s1 s2)`. What matters is that

---

[3]It has been pointed out to me that it is possible that some people might suggest you come round to their place where they will make you a cup. This sort of thing never happens to me.

the operations that can be applied to that object are syntactically restricted to the ones that have been declared to belong to its class.

A class here is seen as a *datatype*. I find it easiest to understand this use of "datatype" at first by going back down to the machine code level where all data (and instructions) are actually stored as bit patterns in memory locations. Thus, the same thirty two bit pattern might be an integer, four characters, a floating point number, or an address. The bits themselves are not any of these things (at least, not in conventional machines). What determines "what" they "are" is what you do to them. If you use an integer add instruction, the bits are treated as a twos complement integer. It's best to think of integers as abstract mathematical things (whatever that means); bit patterns are a possible *representation* of integers; so are decimal or roman numerals. But computationally, the "integerness" lies not in the bits but in the operations you apply to them. Hence, we think of abstract datatypes as comprising a set of values and a set of operations. To say that "x is of type T" means that x can take on the values of T and you can perform the operations of T on x.

By defining abstract datatypes, a programmer is able to hide the representation of values and make sure that only operations that make sense, in the context of the concepts they are supposed to represent, can be applied to them. Using abstract datatypes imposes a type discipline and structure on the data manipulated in a program. Inheritance is now seen as sub-typing: a means of constructing new specialized types from old, more general, ones. A problem may arise when a sub-class inherits operations but needs to redefine some of them. If you like, an object of a sub-class does the same things as objects of its parent class, but in a different way. Or, more in keeping with the classical view, a class may need to inherit an interface (what it does) but not the implementation (how it does it). This creates a problem if we want to write functions that take as their arguments objects of a particular class or any of its sub-classes and behave in an appropriate way for any argument.

Don't suppose it will catch on

For example, suppose I was writing a program to simulate the economic activity of a city. I would certainly want a class of buildings, but buildings come in different sorts: dwellings, offices, shops, monasteries and so on. For any building, the operation `calculate_local_tax` makes sense, but for each of these sub-types the calculation is done in a different way. In this country, at the time of writing, dwellings incur a Council Tax, computed as a bizarre function of the number and status of its inhabitants and its supposed market value, whereas commercial buildings are charged a Business Rate, computed in a thoroughly obscure way, and the inhabitants of monasteries pay nothing at all. If I wanted to simulate the collection of local taxes, I might wish to do it by writing a function that took as its argument the set of buildings of all types and computed the total revenue by applying the `calculate_local_tax` operation to each in turn. The set will be composed of objects of type `building`, which is OK, since any object of a sub-type of `building` is also considered to be a `building`, reasonably enough. But then the `calculate_local_tax` operation of the class `building` will be called for each building, and this is wrong—in fact, the operation doesn't make any sense for buildings in general. What I need to be able to do is bind the `calculate_local_tax` operation *dynamically* at the time it is called, to the actual type of each object, not statically to the type each object appears to have from the program text.

Dynamic binding is the most difficult aspect of object-oriented programming to understand in the abstract, and a proper account of it will have to wait until we get on to the relevant feature of C++, virtual functions. Once mastered, though, this ability to inherit interfaces, not implementations, greatly enhances the usefulness of inheritance. Indeed, it is sometimes claimed to be the most important aspect of object-oriented programming.

I have described object-oriented programming in two different ways. The two different views of object-oriented programming are complementary. Debate about which view is correct is crass and unhelpful, but failure to appreciate that there are two different views leads to misunderstandings. There may be occasions on which one or the other is more helpful—for example, the romantic view is often found useful in program design, while the classical view is more helpful for language design—but the success of object-oriented programming is due to a large extent to the coexistence of the two views. Without the rigorous underpinning of the theory surrounding abstract datatypes the object metaphor would be little more than whimsy. On the other hand, abstract datatypes have been around for a long time but have only been widely used since the object metaphor supplied an intuitive framework for thinking about them informally.

But... so what?

ABSTRACTION AND PROGRAMMING

Real programs are too big to be understood all in one piece. Actually, just about *everything* is too big to be understood in one piece. We cope by using abstraction. Abstraction is the mental process by which we separate things from specific associations and attributes. For example, I can think of the colour red independently of the red shirt I am wearing or the red car passing by. It is a process of generalization—from particular red things to the idea of red—and of ignoring irrelevant details—the shirt's material and the car's speed. Abstraction is a habitual process we use to make what sense we can of the world. It occurs in a more formal guise when we have to solve simple mathematical problems. For example, when we approach the sort of problem that begins "A projectile is launched from a point..." we start by drawing a diagram showing the flight of the projectile, with the launch angle (usually θ) and velocity (v) indicated. The problem and the diagram abstract away from the details of a particular projectile. Everything—whether it's the sounds of battle and men dying in the mud as an artillery shell is fired, or the summer sun and the sound of waves breaking on a beach as a little girl throws a brightly coloured beach ball—everything except the angle and velocity is ignored. Both problems are reduced to an abstract diagram and a set of equations that will enable us to calculate the point of impact.

We abstract away details by giving something a name and then using the name instead of the complex thing it refers to. In mathematics we also abstract by *parameterization*: we use variables like θ and v to represent a potentially infinite number of different values in the same expression. The names of variables don't matter. Velocities can be u and angles ϕ, because they aren't the names of any particular velocity or angle but stand in for any values.

In programming, we desperately need to abstract away from implementation details—how a particular computation is carried out or a particular value is stored—in order to be able to write and think about programs big enough to carry out useful tasks. Writing programs mostly consists of defining and combining abstractions. Programming languages can help by providing features for building abstractions.

All programming languages provide a way of breaking the sequence of instructions in a program into more manageable pieces. In C++ the pieces are called functions; elsewhere, the names routine, subroutine and procedure are used equivalently. When you define a C++ function, you are giving a name to one or more statements, the function body. Elsewhere in the program, this name can be used as a statement, referred to as a call of the function, which causes the function body to be executed, after which, control passes to the statement following the call ("the function returns"). Alternatively, the function body may compute and return a value, in which case the function can be called within an expression, a bit like a mathematical function.

Like mathematical functions, C++ functions usually take arguments. The function definition specifies the names and types of some formal arguments, which can be used within the function body like any other variables. When the function is called, the calling program supplies some values, the actual arguments, which are used to initialize the formal arguments before execution of the function body begins.

This obviously relates to my earlier general description of abstraction. Functions provide abstractions over expressions (if they return a value) and statements (if they don't). That is, they allow us to suppress the details of a computation and refer to it by name only. More than that, functions with arguments provide abstraction by parameterization: they let us describe an infinite number of computations by using the formal argument names to stand in for arbitrary values.

Because of the way computers work, it is easy to think of a program as a set of instructions manipulating stored data in memory. The abstraction of functions manipulating arguments is a natural step from there. This leads us to concentrate on the task being performed by the program. We're quite good at organizing the computational component of large programs in this way, and designing them by breaking the task into successively smaller sub-tasks, until we end up with simple functions that can be coded directly. Although this can be an effective way of designing programs, it has two unfortunate consequences. First, the structure of a program is based on the decomposition of the particular task it performs, and so the functions we write will probably be specific to that task. Second, functional abstractions give us little help with organizing data. Abstract datatypes allow us to abstract over data and organize it in an effective way that can be used in more than one program, just as functions allow us to abstract over instructions and build function libraries.

To see what this means, think about organizing the data in the absence of abstract datatypes. Older languages, such as C or Pascal, allow programmers to define their own types in the form of structures (also called records). A structure consists of a collection of named fields, each of a specified type, so structures let us define types that are collections of items. Now, suppose I was writing a program that had to manipulate dates, perhaps a calendar or diary (not a dried fruit inventory—the other sort of dates). A date comprises a day, a month and a year, so I could define a structure with these three components, let us say all integers. I would soon discover that I needed to do various things to my dates, for example, print them out or calculate the date a certain number of days after a given one. That is, "date" is a datatype—a set of values and a set of operations. In a language that only lets me define structures, I would have to write functions to carry out these operations. With the structure I have described, addition of a number of days to a date would be a complicated procedure involving the numbers 28, 29, 30, 31, 4 and 400, so naturally I would define a function to carry it out and whenever I wanted to perform the addition operation I would call that function. However, if I wanted to add a number of years to a given date I simply need to add it to the year member of the date structure, so I might be tempted not to bother wrapping that operation up in a function and incurring the overhead of a call. Instead I might just write the appropriate addition wherever I needed to carry out this operation. I could then be in serious trouble if I changed my mind and decided that a better way of storing dates was as the number of days since some base date. I would have to find every operation adding a year and change it. On the other hand, I would only have to change my function to add a number of days once.

The use of functions to access data is something that good programmers have been doing for a long time, but it is only a discipline. The language and compiler do nothing to enforce it. By the same token, there is nothing to prevent me (or, more likely, someone else maintaining my code) from doing arithmetic directly on the day and month fields of a date structure, whether or not the result respects the way in which dates work. The trouble is that the logical connection between the data in the structures and the operations on it in the functions is lost. Languages which incorporate support for abstract datatypes restore this connection. Reverting to the romantic view of object-oriented programming, it is often said that the object metaphor allows us to invert the relationship between data and computation. Instead of having functions working on passive data, we think of the data as a set of active objects that carry out the computation by performing the actions characteristic of their class. This provides a way of thinking about programs which encourages and systematizes a disciplined approach to data.

As well as providing an intellectual tool for organizing the data aspects of a program, object-oriented programming provides an immediate practical advantage in the form of *encapsulation*. This means that the representation of an object is hidden from its users. Romantically, we would say that the object manages its own state; classically, that the state can only be altered by the operations defined as part of the object's abstract datatype. Either way, provided the operations behave the way they are supposed to, the designer of a class is free to choose any representation she likes. Furthermore, if the choice of representation turns out to have been a bad one, it can be changed without any change to programs that use the class.

The most widely touted merit of object-oriented programming is that it makes extensively re-using existing code a feasible proposition. Each of the three aspects identified as making up the classical view of object-oriented programming contributes to this. First, the encapsulation following from the use of abstract datatypes makes it possible to write code that uses objects of a class which is independent of the way the class is implemented. Without abstract datatypes, it may be difficult to separate the implementation of some potentially re-usable abstraction from the surrounding code that manipulates it. Second, inheritance provides a way of customizing an existing class, to produce specialized versions of it. A general purpose class may then be re-used in a variety of applications by producing such variants. The code that is common across the range of applications is re-used—only the necessary variation need be added. Finally, dynamic binding provides interface inheritance and additional flexibility without sacrificing the advantages of type checking. Proponents of object-oriented programming claim that it makes it possible to design software components that can be taken from a library, possibly customized, and then assembled to make a system to perform some required task. The analogies of software integrated circuits and software factories are frequently employed to describe this mode of software production. The hope is that substantial increases in productivity will result. The fear, rarely expressed but contributing to some programmers' hostility to object-oriented programming, is that programmers will be reduced to the state of assembly line workers, apart from a few privileged component designers.

These claims and fears need to be put in perspective. There is nothing new about re-using software. Function libraries have been around as long as assemblers. Typically, though, because functions only provide abstractions of computation, but not of data, only small parts of a program can be isolated and put in a library. The majority of the code that makes up a program is concerned with manipulating data and is intimately bound up with the particular data structures devised for that program. This is not to say, though, that re-use of code doesn't happen without object-orientation—it just isn't done through linguistic mechanisms.

Those who would put forward the proposition that object-oriented programming is a revolution in programming sometimes claim that, before objects, every new project was written from scratch. This simply is not true. The first reaction of most programmers when given a new system to build is to look at an old one and see whether it can be adapted. Adaptation may mean extreme re-structuring, patching and extending, but it does result in the re-use of large pieces of existing code. Furthermore, all experienced programmers have a repertoire of data structures at their disposal, and writing a linked list insertion function or a table lookup is usually done by reproducing one they've done before, with the minor changes needed to fit in to the new context. You can probably do it as fast as you can type. The ideas, algorithms and form of the code are being re-used, just not the physical code itself. Obviously, there's some scope for introducing (or re-introducing) errors, and it is necessary to compile the new version, but it is still probably quicker than finding a component in a library, reading its documentation to make sure it will be suitable, and perhaps refining it somewhat.

To understand the excitement about re-usable code, you have to scale things up. Don't think about re-using a stack, think about re-using the code for inter-acting with a window in a graphical user interface. All windows are generically similar, but each application needs to create and control its own particular win-dows. The code for this is not stuff you want to write twice: all that moving and zooming and clipping and detecting mice is, frankly, a pain if you have to get right down to the level of display primitives. You don't even want to write it once: what you want to do is have somebody else write it all and provide you with a window library, so you can get on with writing some interesting code to sit behind the window and do something useful. The rub here is that just putting a bunch of functions into a library won't answer. In order to keep track of the size, position, status, colour and whatnot of your window, you need a data structure. It is inviting chaos to leave the responsibility for creating and maintaining that data structure with the application programmer—clearly, the responsibility belongs with the data structure, and if that is in a library, then that is also where the code to look after it should be. It won't help to use your programming language's scope rules so that the library can build a data structure and keep it hidden inside a library module, because in any realistic application you will want to be able to have more than one window. You will want to be able to create a window data structure for each one, and apply win-dowing operations, and no other sort, to it. In short, you want to be able to create window objects, belonging to a window class. When you consider that there are different sorts of windows, you will see that you will also want to have a collection of different window classes, hierarchically arranged so that they share common operations by inheritance.

Object-oriented programming languages provide tools for making this sort of code re-use possible. The scale and complexity of the computer applications that are being demanded by users these days make it necessary. Virtuoso pro-grammers can simulate objects and classes in any language that lets you store functions (or pointers to them) in data structures, but why do all the work your-self when a compiler can do it for you? C++ provides a sufficient set of language facilities to enable you to define classes and create objects, and use inheritance and dynamic binding. Not elegantly, not in the way that some object-oriented purists think it must be done, but effectively.

APPROACHING C++

C++ is becoming the dominant programming language of the 1990s and a great many programmers will end up using it, at least some of the time. Many of them will find the power and flexibility of the language enable them to write bigger and better programs than ever before—the experience of the existing C++ community testifies to the truth of this statement, however much like an advertising claim it may sound. Others are going to be intimidated and con-fused by the size and complexity which are the reverse side of this power and flexibility. And others are always going to find the untidiness of C++'s syntax and semantics hard to bear.

There is going to be a lot of pressure on programmers adopting C++ to adopt object-oriented programming methods at the same time. This may take the form of explicit management pressure, or more subtle peer group pressure, or it may be the effect of the way C++ is presented in texts (including this one). It's worth remembering that C++ isn't a language that requires you to do everything in an object-oriented way. You can write programs based exclusively on functional abstractions, very much like C programs. You can use classes as abstract datatypes without necessarily using inheritance. The real benefits from using the full range of object-oriented techniques come when you are constructing libraries of re-usable software components, and C++ has all you need to do this in a fully object-oriented way. In fact C++'s facilities for object-oriented programming aren't even the end of the story. The development of C++ beyond its original release has emphasized the provision of further facilities for the construction of re-usable software—facilities such as exception handling to deal with unexpected events and templates to provide generic classes—that can be added to your repertoire if you find you need them, or not, depending on your programming experience, level of skill and the sort of programs you are developing. C++ accommodates a whole range of programming styles and lets you use whatever suits both you and the task in hand.

The design of C++ is concerned with *enabling* you to do certain things, not *forcing* you to do them. Nor is it concerned with preventing you from doing other things: for example, it is actually very easy to subvert the information hiding provided by classes, if you really want to. What C++ does provide is help in avoiding doing certain things accidentally. It has been observed[4] that a programming language's contribution to software quality can take one of two forms. Either it can make it hard to write bad programs, or it can make it easy to write good ones. Unlike many languages designed under the influence of the Ada exercise, C++ does little to stop you writing bad programs. Its design aim has been more in keeping with making it easier to write good ones. But, in order to write good C++ programs, you not only need to be a good programmer and willing to accept C++ on its own terms and not as an imperfect attempt to be something else—you need to know a lot about C++.

---

[4]By Robert Dewar, of the Courant Institute, NYU.

The C++ Happy Hour

To entice you in, I'm going to pretend that C++ can be made simple. It can't, but if we start with a simplified description we will be in a better position to understand what's really going on when we get to the full story, later.

Fundamentals

2

C++ is a hybrid between a 'pure' object-oriented language—one in which *every-thing* is an object—and a procedural language. It includes object-oriented features allowing programmers to define classes, specify inheritance relationships between classes, create objects and pass messages to them. It also includes procedural features providing facilities for manipulating variables and values of a few built-in types, for organizing control flow with sequencing, selection and iteration, and for defining and calling procedures.

This hybrid arrangement is not unique to C++; it was shared by Simula67, and Modula-3 and Oberon-2 are other, contemporary, examples. In all such languages, the relationship between the object-oriented and procedural features has a twofold, almost paradoxical, nature. On the one hand, the object-oriented features provide a framework for putting together small pieces of program, the actions that each sort of object can perform. These small pieces can be written with conventional techniques for small scale programming, using the procedural part of C++, so the procedural features are *inside* the classes. On the other hand, a class defines a datatype, and objects of user-defined types can be manipulated, like objects of built-in types, using the procedural features of the language as a combining framework, so these features are also *outside* the classes. Since user-defined types can make use of other user-defined types, we find an alternation of procedural and object-oriented programming features, with pure procedural programming with built-in datatypes at the bottom of a set of layers of abstraction, which are built up as user-defined types in an object-oriented way.

The procedural subset of C++ is almost, but not quite, the same as ISO C; Stroustrup described it as "a better C", a phrase that has become a cliché. While devotees of C might wonder how it could be bettered, others might be forgiven for wondering whether anything could be much worse. Indeed, as we'll see, most of the weaknesses and infelicities of C++ derive from its designer's insistence on maximal compatibility with C, and its legacy of a low-level, machine-oriented philosophy of system programming. At the same time, it has to be recognized that compatibility with C is C++'s major strength and accounts for most of its popularity.

Two sensible ways of beginning to program in C++ are by writing in your established procedural style to become familiar with the syntax and semantics of C++'s procedural subset, or by making use of pre-existing classes in a C++ library relevant to some problem domain of interest to you—graphical interface objects, perhaps. In either case, you will need to become familiar with the procedural subset in order to put together a program, whether it manipulates low-level built-in objects or high-level user-defined ones.

Since the facilities available for procedural programming in C++ are essentially the same as in most other languages, their treatment in this section is fairly rapid. Experienced programmers might do well to skim it and pass on as quickly as possible to the racier material in the next chapter and beyond.

VALUES AND EXPRESSIONS

Underlying *everything* in C++ is the idea of storage. Storage corresponds to the main memory of a conventional late twentieth century digital computer: it consists of a collection of locations, each with an address. At any time, each location can hold a value; the value held in a location can be updated so the location holds a new one. This probably seems utterly banal, but so much follows from it that it's worth emphasizing here.

The ARM makes the bald statement that "an object is a region of storage", for example. Objects can be of different sizes and the interpretation of the bit patterns stored in them depends on their type. There is a variety of fundamental types, corresponding closely to the types wired into the hardware of mainstream computers. More complex types can be defined by programmers, and objects of these types can then be created and manipulated.

Objects can be given names (we'll see how, shortly). A named object is usually called a variable. Unlike mathematicians' variables, C++ variables actually vary in value. The lexical rules about what constitutes a legal name are much what a world-weary programmer might expect: a name is an arbitrarily long sequence of upper- and lower-case letters, digits and underline characters. It must begin with a letter or an underline. The same letter in upper- and lower-case forms is different. (So you can use n and N as two different names, which you might find appealing if you are mathematically trained.) You probably wouldn't want to use names that begin with _ (or would you?), but you shouldn't anyway—such names are supposed to be kept for internal use by the standard library, as are names containing a double underline, which should also be avoided. Most programmers just use _ to separate words in names that are really phrases, like the_symbol_table. Some syntactically legal names are still not permitted, because they are reserved words, having a special meaning as part of C++. These will be noted as we come across them.

Simple Declarations and Types

Every name that you use in your program must be introduced explicitly by means of a declaration. These come in a number of varieties; we'll start with the simplest, which has the form

```
type name ;
```

where *type* is the name of a type, and *name* is the name you are declaring. The semicolon is required.

So what types are available? Most of the time, you'll be using types that you've either defined yourself or taken from some library, but in the end, everything is built from a few fundamental types.

There is a plethora of arithmetical types corresponding to different varieties of integer and floating point numbers. Most of the time you can confine yourself to just two of these: `int` and `float`, which correspond to integer and floating point numbers occupying the "natural" number of bits on your machine. We can now see some examples of declarations using these types.

```
int i;
int j;
float current_interest_rate;
```

The *name* in a declaration can be replaced by a list of *name*s, separated by commas, if you want to declare several variables of the same type in a single declaration:

```
int number_of_rows, number_of_columns;
```

Another useful fundamental type is called `char` (short for character). Objects of type `char` are "large enough to store any member of the implementation's basic character set", says the ARM, and `char`s are usually used to hold characters, but they don't have to be. They are also used for small integers, and you can perform arithmetic on them.

The declarations shown so far do not just introduce a name into the program, they also cause the name to be associated with an object, which will be created at runtime when the declaration is executed. Not all declarations do this—later on we'll have to be more precise in our use of the word "declaration". For now, assume that the declaration introduces the names, so that the C++ compiler can keep track of their use, and also causes storage to be reserved for objects. By default, when most objects are actually created at runtime, their values are undefined. You can, however, provide an initial value by adding an initializer to the declaration. For the simple types we are considering at the moment, a declaration with an initializer takes the form

```
type name  = value { ,  name  = value } ;
```

as in

```
int i = 0, j = 0;
```

Here the variables are initialized with constant values. Constants of integer type are written as conventional numbers, those of floating point type as decimal fractions optionally followed by an **e** and an exponent (to base 10):

```
float pi = 3.14159;
float c = 2.998e8 ;
```

The variable c is initialized to (an approximation to) 2.998×10^8 (physicists for the use of). Character constants are written as single characters enclosed in single quotes:

```
char y_or_n = 'y';
```

Initializing all your variables when you declare them is a good idea, since uninitialized variables are a common source of errors. C++ does not, however, require you to do it.

Having declared some variables, what can you do with or to them?

Assignment

Because C++ is based on the underlying idea of mutable storage, the most momentous (not necessarily the most useful) thing you can do to a variable is change its value. You can do this by means of an assignment statement. In its simplest form, this is written

name = *value* ;

Yes, the assignment operator is written as an equals sign. Zillions of C and Fortran[1] programmers won't see anything remarkable about this. Anyone raised on Pascal or BCPL,[2] or who is more comfortable with mathematics than with programming, might have some trouble getting rid of the idea that = means "is equal to". You do get used to it. After all, if programmers can get used to writing 2*x instead of $2x$, why make a fuss about = instead of := (itself a compromise substitute for ←)? Just keep reminding yourself it's only a notation.

While we're on the subject of notation, notice the semicolons. In C++, the semicolon is a statement *terminator* not a separator, as it is in most of the Algol and Pascal families. The syntax is such that you almost never need to put two of them the way you sometimes did in PL/I. BCPL and Awk hacks will be disappointed to learn that you can't leave the semicolons out at the end of lines.

Here's a fragment of code that actually does something.

```
int x = 0, y = 1;      declare and initialize two variables
int temp;      declare another without initializing it
tmp = x;      exchange the values of x and y so x = 1 and y = 0
x = y;
y = temp;
```

Not very exciting, and not a complete C++ program. Below is the same code with the boilerplate necessary to make it compile and run and produce some output. There is an important thing to be noted: the programs and code fragments in this book do not have any proper comments; the commentary is for the most part in the surrounding text, and where it is included with the code it has been set off to the side in a special font, as in the example just shown. Real programs, though, will have to use comments for their documentation. The convention in C++ is that comments are introduced by a pair of slash characters //, and extend to the end of the line. I do not intend to tell you how to comment your programs; doubtless you or the organization you work for will have your

---

[1] and Basic and PL/I and Perl and...
[2] or Algol68 or Modula2 or Ada or...

own conventions. Similar remarks apply to other aspects of program layout. The conventions I have adopted here are designed to make the best use of a book page and to harmonize with the rest of the book's design. Different criteria will apply to production code intended for editing on a screen or printing on a lineprinter. Organizations often impose style guidelines about such things as indentation and layout of particular constructs, which you would be well advised to follow when you are asked to. It does seem worth mentioning that a far more satisfactory approach to program presentation and documentation is offered by the various literate programming systems that are available. Several of these work with C++.

▷ There is an alternative convention for comments. They may be bracketed between the character pairs /* and */. This is the old C convention, which has been retained in C++ for the sake of compatibility. Its use is discouraged, since it is more error-prone—missing */s can not only throw a compiler off track and lead to misleading error messages, they can also, occasionally, transform a program into another legal but different one... with hilarious results, as the programmer it happens to will be ◁ the first to agree, no doubt.

Just this once, the next example has real comments as well as all the other extras necessary to turn the preceding fragment into a legal program. A minor illuminating modification has also been made to the code.

```cpp
#include <iostream>      // Treat this line as necessary
                         // red tape.  It makes available
                         // the output facilities used below.

int main()               // More red tape
{
   int x = 0, y = 1;
   cout << "x = " << x              // These two lines send
      << " y = " << y << endl;      // output to the standard
                                    // output stream.
   int temp = x;                    // temp is initialized,
                                    // not assigned to

   x = y;
   y = temp;
   cout << "x = " << x              // Output the new
        << " y = " << y << endl;    // values
   return 0;              //  Last piece of red tape
}
```

The #include <iostream> line is needed in any program that uses the standard input and output facilities of the C++ iostream library, which will be described as we go along. A tiresome practical consideration in this context is too important to be ignored, so *take heed*. The precise wording of the red tape needed to access standard input and output (and any other facilities of the standard library) may well be different on your compiler from that used in this book. I have followed the conventions used by the particular compiler I am using at present, but these conventions and others in wide use predate the draft standard's recommendations on this subject. Since the latter depend on a relatively new feature of C++ which is not presently universally available, many compilers still use their own conventions. You may find that the name in angle brackets is `iostream.h` or `iostream.hxx`, or some such variant, or you may find that an extra line

```
using namespace std;
```

is needed after `#include <iostream>`. You will have to check your local documentation or experts. The arrangement of the standard library as specified by the current draft standard is described in chapter 12.

Returning to the example, every C++ program also needs (to get ahead of ourselves) a definition of a function called `main`—this is what the line `int main()` provides, the curly brackets delimiting the extent of `main`. Execution begins with the first statement inside these curly brackets, and, in the normal course of events, finishes with the last. The value following the keyword `return` at the end of `main` may be passed back to the operating system to be used as a return code, where that makes sense. It is used to indicate success or failure of a computation, with zero defined as denoting success, and minus one, failure; other values may have implementation-dependent meanings.

The name `cout` is a special one and refers to the standard output—usually your terminal—and the `<<` is an operator that sends things to the standard output. The characters written between double quotes (") are printed literally on the standard output by `<<`; `endl` is a rather complicated sort of object, of a kind we'll look at in detail later, but for now it is enough to know that it has the effect, when sent to `cout`, of producing a new line. When you compile and run this program it produces the output:

```
x = 0 y = 1
x = 1 y = 0
```

The two innovations introduced by the modification to the code are that `temp` is initialized with something other than a constant, and that its declaration follows an executable statement. This may come as a surprise unless you know Algol68 (or certain obscure Scottish descendants of Algol). In C++, declarations are considered as statements, so they can appear among other statements—you don't have to segregate the declarations somewhere at the beginning. This is nice, because you don't have to declare a variable until you need it, and it is usually the case that by then you can usefully find a value to initialize it to.

Sometimes you may want to ensure that once a variable has been initialized its value should never be changed. The reserved word `const` can be put in front of any declaration to establish that no changes can be made to the value of the variable being declared (so a declaration with `const` must have an initialization). This is useful for giving symbolic names to constants, as in

```
const float pi = 3.14159;
const float deg_to_rad = pi/180;
```

As you can see, a variable declared with `const` need not be initialized to a simple constant. This means that `const` can also be used by the more sophisticated programmer to establish invariants on the values of variables.

Arithmetic Expressions

Cheerfully permuting the values of variables by assignment offers only limited rewards to most programmers. We need to do computation on the values to get anywhere. Unremarkably, C++ lets you write expressions to do arithmetic calculations. Cheap pocket calculator arithmetic is done with the operators +, −, * (multiplication), / and % (remainder—what else?), which can be applied to constants and variables of all the three types we have seen so far, although arithmetic on char values is only sometimes sensible. The precedence of operators is conventional and brackets can be used for grouping. The order of evaluation of an operator's operands is undefined.

'Mixed-mode' arithmetic—with operands of different types—is allowed. It is important to realize that if one of the operands is of the type float then the operation will be carried out using floating point arithmetic and will give a floating result. And if not, not: division of two integers gives an integer result, which is truncated if the division isn't exact. This allows for classic traps like this:

```cpp
#include <iostream>

int main()
{
    float x = 100.0, y = 100.0, z = 100.0;
    cout << "x = " << x
         << " y = " << y
         << " z = " << z << endl;
    x = x * (1/2);
    y = 1/2 * y;
    z = z * 1/2;
    cout << "x = " << x
         << " y = " << y
         << " z = " << z << endl;
    return 0;
}
```

which produces the output

```
x = 100 y = 100 z = 100
x = 0 y = 0 z = 50
```

...exactly as it should.

The sign of the remainder of an integer division given by the % operator is implementation-defined if one of the operands is negative and the other positive. This is an improvement on the old chestnut "the usual rules of arithmetic apply"—there aren't any covering this situation. The effect of division by zero is undefined, as is the handling of arithmetic overflow.

▷ About that "plethora of arithmetical types"...These are: char, signed char, unsigned char, short int, int, long int, unsigned short int, unsigned int, unsigned long int, float, double and long double. This multitude of sorts of numbers allows you to exercise considerable control over the possible range and precision of the numbers in your program. The actual sizes of these objects are implementation-dependent. There are few guarantees, but a `long int` is no smaller than an `int`, which is no smaller than a `short int`, and so on for all the families. The header file `limits` provides details about the range of values representable in objects of each arithmetic type with any particular implementation of C++.

The ARM gives lots of rules about conversion between different arithmetic types. Some of these conversions are dangerous, in the sense that they might lose significant information or do unexpected sign extension. On the whole, it's wise to confine yourself to `int`, `char`, `unsigned int` and `float`, unless you have a good reason not to, and to avoid conversions between arithmetic types unless you know exactly what you're doing.

◁ C programmers should note that the rules for arithmetic conversions in C++ are not identical to those of C.

In C++ the assignment operator is treated as an arithmetic operator that can be used within expressions, its use is not reserved for a special assignment statement. Actually, any expression can be used as a statement in C++, though only ones with side-effects, like an assignment, make much sense. An expression of the form

```
name = value ;
```

has the same value as its right hand side, but, as a side-effect, it updates its left hand side in the way previously described. A common way of making use of this behaviour is to set several variables to the same value:

```
x = y = z = p = q = a;
```

Apart from this, most uses of assignments within expressions are tricky and obscure.

The simple assignment operator is only one of the available assigning operators. Notationally, you can put just about any binary operator symbol in front of the = sign, to form a compound assigning operator symbol, like +=, *=, -=, %= or /=. The meaning of an expression like `i += j + 1` is the same as `i = i + j + 1` *except* that `i` is only evaluated once. This is only important (apart from a trivial gain in speed that is often optimized away by the compiler) if evaluation of the left hand side has side-effects—not possible in the cases we have looked at so far, but the left operands of assigning operators can be more complex than a variable. Generally, side-effects should be avoided; assigning operators can just be thought of as an attractive shorthand for operations that update a particular value.

An even shorter hand is available for the common case of incrementing an integer variable by one: `++i` is equivalent to `i += 1`, that is, to `i = i + 1`. Like all other assignments this has a value—the updated value of `i`—as well as performing the action. It's often the case that you want to take the value of a variable and *then* increment it. For this, you can use the ++ operator in postfix form: `i++` has as its value the original value of `i` and adds one to `i` as a side-effect. (So—as many have observed before me—C++ should really be ++C.) The operator -- can also be used in both prefix and postfix forms to perform decrements by one.

An Introduction to Strings

You can't do anything very interesting with numbers alone, unless you're a numerical analyst, so let's look at another datatype, the string. Strings are different from `int`, `float` and `char` because they are not part of the C++ language, they are defined in the standard library.[3] (C programmers please note: a string is not the same as an array of `char`—there'll be things to be said about *those* in a later chapter.) As well as letting us write programs that manipulate text a bit, strings also demonstrate how easy it is to use classes taken from a library. We will only be looking at a subset of the facilities offered by the string class.

Since strings are not part of the C++ language, you need to include their definition in any program that uses them. This is done by putting the incantation

```
#include <string>
```

at the top of your program. (As with `iostream`, the actual text you need to include the necessary definitions may be slightly different on your system.)

Strings can be declared using the same syntax as for numerical types, and they can be initialized with string constants: sequences of characters enclosed between (teletype-style) quotation marks ("). For example:

```
string lower_case = "abcdefghijklmnopqrstuvwxyz";
string upper_case = "ABCDEFGHIJKLMNOPQRSTUVWXYZ";
string digits = "0123456789";
```

A string can be printed out in the same way as a number can by "sending" it to `cout`:

```
cout << lower_case;
```

causes `abcdefghijklmnopqrstuvwxyz` to be printed on the standard output.

Individual elements of the string are of type `char` and can be accessed using the notation

```
string [ index ]
```

where *string* stands for any expression yielding a string and *index* is an integer between 0 and $n - 1$, where n is the number of characters in the string; so, for example, `lower_case[5]` is equal to `'f'`. Such subscripted strings can be used on both the left and right hand sides of an assignment; when used on the left they provide a way of changing individual elements, so

```
lower_case[5] = 'F';
```

turns `lower_case` into `abcdeFghijklmnopqrstuvwxyz`.

You can build a new string by sticking two strings together end to end. This operation is known as concatenation and is denoted by the + operator— operators in C++ are not restricted to a single meaning. The expression

```
lower_case + upper_case
```

would have the value

---

[3] At the time of writing, the library standard is still a draft, and not all C++ vendors can be relied on to supply a string class exactly the same as the one described here, although you have a right to expect something very similar—check your system documentation.

```
abcdeFghijklmnopqrstuvwxyzABCDEFGHIJKLMNOPQRSTUVWXYZ
```

if it was evaluated after the assignment to `lower_case[5]` shown above. You can also use the += assigning operator to perform the concatenation in place. For example

```
lower_case += upper_case
```

would update the string stored in `lower_case` to the concatenated value a...Z. The allocation of storage to accommodate the expansion is done behind the scenes inside the string class.

Evidently, if such updates are intended, the name `lower_case` was ill-chosen. If, on the other hand, they were not intended, then the variable should have been declared with `const` to prevent them:

```
const string lower_case = "abcdefghijklmnopqrstuvwxyz";
```

You may be wondering how you include a " character inside a string. The answer is that you precede it by a \. Several such "escape combinations" are available. The commonest is \n, which stands for a newline character (whatever that means on your machine). Other combinations will be introduced as and when they are needed.

CONTROL STRUCTURES

This is all very well, but so far we can do no computation worthy of the name. This is because, of the three control structures of Structured Programming—sequencing, selection and iteration—we only know how to do the first: statements are executed in sequence in the order they are written. We need selection and iteration to alter this simple sequential flow of control if we are ever to do anything interesting.

Both selection and bounded iteration adumbrate the idea of testing whether some condition holds. A test can only have one of two possible outcomes: either it succeeds or it fails. C++ has a rather neurotic attitude to tests. In its formative years, a machine-oriented approach was taken, with all tests yielding an integer value that was accounted as failure or success according to whether it was zero or not. That was fine for most purposes, but the draft standard has introduced a datatype `bool` (short for Boolean, after the algebra) with two values, denoted by the constants `true` and `false`, more consistent with an abstract approach to Boolean algebra. Any integer not equal to zero is automatically converted to the `bool` value `true` when it is used as a test, while zero is converted to `false`. Conversely, a `bool` value can be used whenever an integer is required: `true` is converted to one, `false` to zero. Hence, to a first approximation, any code that worked under the old rules works under the new one (but `true` and `false` are now keywords and can no longer be used as variable names). You can use `bool` just like any other datatype, for example to declare variables and function arguments and result types. The convertibility to and from integers is unusual, but it does permit some useful idioms.

▷ If you have an old compiler that doesn't implement `bool`, you will almost certainly be able to find a header `<bool.h>` containing declarations that simulate it, if not in

◁ a library, then in the directory of a fellow programmer. You will need to be aware, when we consider overloading in chapter 7, that simulated `bool` is not a separate datatype, whereas `bool` proper is.

Selection

The two-branched conditional takes the form

```
if ( expression ) statement₁ else statement₂
```

Both `if` and `else` are reserved words. Syntactically, note that the test is written in brackets and there is no explicit `then` keyword, as there is in most other programming languages; note also the absence of any ; following either statement: this is because simple statements already carry their own terminator and we don't want to have to write two of them in a row. Semantically, if the expression's value is `true` (or any integer but zero) the first statement is executed, if its value is `false` (or zero) the second. The expression will usually be some sort of comparison, written using the infix operators >, <, <=, >=, with the obvious interpretation, and == and != with the rather less obvious interpretation of equals and not equals, respectively. If the comparison succeeds, the value is `true`, otherwise `false`.

The == operator takes a bit of getting used to, but = has already been used for assignment, and therein lies a trap. Because an assignment is an expression yielding a value, and because the expression in a test can be anything that evaluates to an integer, things like

!
```
if (x = 0) ...
```

are legal. The test always fails and sets x to zero as a side effect, to the programmer's great amusement. Luckily, most modern compilers will issue a warning if you use an assignment as a test in this way.

Here are a couple of examples of selections done properly, both of which will be comfortingly familiar.

```
int magnitude;        This sets magnitude to the absolute value of x...
if (x < 0)
  magnitude = -x;
else
  magnitude = x;
int maximum;          ...while this sets maximum to the greater of x and y or
if (x > y)            their mutual value if x is equal to y.
  maximum = x;
else
  maximum = y;
```

Often, you will want to execute more than a single statement in either branch. This is no problem. A sequence of statements enclosed in curly brackets { and } is a compound statement, which is treated syntactically as a single statement. It's sometimes the case that you don't want to do anything if a test fails. In that case, `else` and the statement (or compound statement) following it can be left out. Here is an example of both these embellishments.

```
if (x > y)                 Ensure x ≤ y by swapping the values of x and y, if
{                          necessary.
  int temp = x;
  x = y;
  y = temp;
}
```

In the conditional *statement* just described, one of two actions is performed, depending on the outcome of the test. There is also a conditional *expression*, where one of two expressions is evaluated, depending on the outcome of a test. The whole conditional expression can be used syntactically anywhere any other sort of expression can. (It's usually necessary, and never does any harm, to put brackets round it to make sure all the operators bind the way you want them to.) The syntax is not pretty:

```
test? expression₁: expression₂
```

The *test* is evaluated and converted to `bool` if necessary; if it is `true`, *expression₁* is evaluated, otherwise *expression₂* is. Only one of *expression₁* and *expression₂* is evaluated. Whichever is is used as the value of the whole conditional expression. It follows (does it not?) that both *expression₁* and *expression₂* must be present and that they must both be of the same type. (Which rather suggests the question "What if only one of them is of the same type?", but...let it pass, let it pass.)

The absolute value example given previously could be written as well, if not better, as

```
int magnitude = x < 0 ? -x : x;
```

It's a matter of taste.

Boolean values, in particular the results of comparisons, can be combined using the operators `&&` (logical AND) and `||` (logical OR), which can be defined as follows ($\equiv$ denotes equivalence):

```
exp1 && exp2 ≡ exp1 ? exp2 : false
exp1 || exp2 ≡ exp1 ? true : exp2
```

That is, `exp1 && exp2` is `true` if both `exp1` and `exp2` are `true`; `exp1 || exp2` is `true` if either or both of `exp1` or `exp2` is. Note the implication of the equivalent conditional expressions that the evaluation of these operators is "lazy", that is, it proceeds from left to right only as far as it has to. This means that constructions like

```
if (y < INT_MAX || y+1 > limit)
```

where `y` is an `int` and `INT_MAX` denotes the largest possible `int` value, will not cause overflow.

▷ The single `&` and `|` operators exist and are *not* lazy: they evaluate both their operands and then combine them bit by bit. Their use should be confined to man-◁ ipulating bit masks.

You can also invert conditions. ! is the logical NOT operator.

```
!exp ≡ exp? false : true
```

There is one more selection statement. It is a strictly redundant notation for expressing a particular pattern of tests. This pattern comprises a sequence of equality comparisons between an integer value and a series of constants, like this:

```
int val = exp;
if (val == const₁)
  statement₁
else
  if (val == const₂)
    statement₂
  else
    if (val == const₃)
      statement₃
    else

        .
        .
        .

      if (val == constₖ)
        statementₖ
      else statement_d
```

The effect, as you can see, will be to execute *statement_i* if and only if *exp* evaluates to *const_i*, and to execute *statement_d* if *exp* is not equal to any of the *const*s. As usual, any of the statements may be compound. This whole sequence can be expressed as a single *switch statement*.

```
switch (exp)  {
case const₁:
  statement₁;
  break;
case const₂:
  statement₂;
  break;
case const₃:
  statement₃;
  break;

    .
    .
    .

case constₖ:
  statementₖ;
  break;
default:
  statement_d;
  break;
}
```

This has exactly the same meaning: the value yielded by the expression in brackets is compared with each of the constant values following the keyword `case`, and the statement corresponding to the case that matches is executed; if none of them does, the default case is executed instead.

Multi-branched conditionals like this are common in imperative programming languages. C++'s switch statement (really C's) is a particularly poor realization of the idea. Although insisting that each case be a constant integer is a common restriction in mainstream imperative languages, and makes it easy for a good compiler to optimize the switch statement so that something more efficient than a linear sequence of comparisons is generated, it seriously limits the usefulness of the construct as a multiple choice, in the style of guarded commands. A further weakness is concealed by the fact that, in reality, the switch command isn't quite as I've explained it. Each of the cases is considered a label, and control is passed to the label that matches the expression, but this is simply a jump, and control continues sequentially from that point. You may have been wondering what those `break`s were. A break is another control statement that passes control to the end of the enclosing switch, so, with the breaks as shown, the effect is as described.

This "jump to the case and then jump out when you see a break" semantics means that if any of the statements corresponding to a case is compound, you don't need to put curly brackets round it. You'd do better not to, because their presence might deceive you into thinking that they delimited the extent of the code executed for that case. Not so: you must put in the explicit break to cause control to pass to the end of the switch. Accidentally omitting a break is a common mistake, particularly for Pascal programmers. Deliberately omitting one sometimes lets you share code between cases in a superficially pleasing manner. However, code that depends on this device can be obscure to anyone who didn't write it and is easily upset by changes to the program. I wouldn't tell anyone never to do it; there may be, for all I know, occasions when you are so pressed for space that you need all the code sharing you can get, or when you want to keep a sequence of code small enough to fit into an instruction cache. However, any code that relies on falling through a case should certainly bear a prominent comment:

```
case 'X':
  xflag = 1;
// LOOK OUT: fall through to the next case
//           because xflag implies yflag.
case 'Y':
  yflag = 1;
  break;
```

Two final points: any statement may be labelled with more than one case (or any case may label an empty statement and fall through, if you prefer), and the default may be omitted. In that case, if the expression fails to match any of the cases given, control just passes straight to the end of the whole switch.

The switch statement is a mainstay of a certain style of programming, popular since the 1970s. Often, the value being switched on is either a tag field, distinguishing some variant of a data structure, or it is a character read from the input. In C++ the former case is rare, since dynamic binding provides a better way of achieving the same end. The latter case is also less common than it was, since the handling of command lines if being increasingly superseded by graphical interface programming. Even lexical analysers are usually table driven.

Loops

Theory tells us that we only need one form of iteration, the while-loop, which executes some statements (the loop body) repeatedly until some condition ceases to hold. For this to achieve anything, the condition must involve some variables that are modified in the loop body. In C++, the syntax for such a loop is

```
while ( expression ) statement
```

where *expression* is evaluated as a test, just as it is in a conditional statement, and *statement* may be compound if necessary; `while` is a reserved word. The *statement* is the loop body. It is executed repeatedly as long as the expression does not evaluate to `false`. The possibility that the expression evaluates to `false` the first time it is evaluated is not ruled out. In that case, the loop body is never executed.

At last, we can do some computation. But here's a fatuous example instead (Figure 2.1 on the following page).

For the first time, in this example, we do some input. Input and output aren't really symmetrical, but the iostreams library tries to make them appear as much so as possible. Instead of sending objects to `cout` to be output, we take them from the standard input stream `cin`. The input operator is >>. It might help to think of >> and << as traffic signs, like the chevrons on sharp bends, directing objects from the input into variables and from variables to the output respectively. Thus the statement `cin >> n;` has the effect of sending the next value from the input stream into the variable n, or, in other words, of reading an integer into n.

The streams `cin` and `cout` are "tied" together, so that output to `cout` is always completed before the following input operation from `cin`. The prompts therefore appear when they should. I only mention this in case experience with other languages has made you worried that they might not.

▷ If you find that prompts only appear when a newline is sent to `cout` you have a non-standard stream library. You can force output to happen straight away by sending an object called `flush` to the output stream, for example,

```
cout << "how many?  " << flush;
```

◁

▷ In a while-loop, the condition is tested before the loop body so that sometimes the body of the loop may never be executed. Occasionally, you encounter a situation when you want the body to be executed at least once, no matter what the initial condition. This can be achieved using a loop where the test is performed after the body. In C++, it has the form

```
#include <iostream>        These lines are necesary since we will use library
#include <string>          classes to do i/o and to store strings
int main()
{
  int n;
  cout << "how many?  ";                              Prompt for a
  cin >> n;                                           number and
  if (n < 0)                                          read it into n,
    cout << "negative values don't make sense"        ensuring that it
              << endl;                                 is positive
  else
  {
    int i = 0;              Set up a counter and an empty string
    string s = "";
    while (i < n)           Loop adding n asterisks to the end of s
    {
      s += "*";
      ++i;
    }
    cout << s << endl;      So now write a line of n asterisks
  }
  return 0;
}
```

Figure 2.1   Writing Stars

```
do statement while ( expression ) ;
```
Experience tells me that at least 90% of the time, this is the wrong thing to do—a do-while loop causes the body to be executed one or more times, but inexperienced programmers often try to use it in circumstances where you need to do something once, and then something almost the same, zero or more times after it. Trying to make your code neater with a do-while can either make you overlook that "almost", or tie yourself into convolutions accommodating it. Of course, if "one or more times" really is what you need, you should use do-while.

◁

Although while-loops are adequate to specify any iterative computation, another form of loop is provided: the for-loop. Most imperative programming languages provide some construct for repeatedly executing a statement while the value of some variable takes on successive values in some range. The C++ for-loop is usually used for loops of this sort, but it is actually more general. It has the form

```
for ( start; condition; increment ) statement
```

Here, `for` is a reserved word, *start* is a statement or declaration without its semicolon, *increment* is an expression (usually with side-effects) and *condition* is a test expression.

The meaning is the same as the following compound statement:

```
{
  start;
  while (condition)
  {
    statement
    increment;
  }
}
```

The simple numeric for-loop, which increments a loop counter variable from some initial value to a final one, is exemplified by a re-writing of the loop part of the stars program.

```
for (int i = 1; i <= n; ++i)
  s += "*";
```

You would probably be wise to confine yourself to loops of this general form, i.e., ones with headers obeying the pattern

```
for (int cntr = init; cntr <= final; cntr += incr)
```

where the counter variable `cntr` starts with the initial value *init* and is incremented by *incr* each time round the loop until it reaches the value *final*. More elaborate for-loops with different types of loop variable constitute a characteristic idiom of C programming. They can be neat and compact, they can also be tricky and obscure. At the risk of attracting the scorn of C experts, I will tend to prefer while-loops to for-loops in this book, except for numerical iterations. However, you should not let me dictate your style: choose the formulation of your computation which makes most sense to you (or work within the style guidelines of your organization), always remembering that the most important thing is to be correct.

Any of the components inside the for loop brackets may be left out: if the test is omitted, it is taken to be always `true`. The most commonly seen use of this is

```
for (;;)
```

which is an idiom for an infinite loop (`while (true)` is another.)

The fact that you can declare a variable in the loop header should make you ask whether such a variable can still be used outside the loop. The equivalent while-loop provides the answer: no, because a for-loop constitutes a scope, like a compound statement. However, this is a recent change in C++ and many compilers still use the old rule where the answer was yes.

This does, somewhat belatedly, raise the issue of scope. The scope of a variable is the region of program text in which it can be used. (Scope is a static property of the program text.) Until we get on to functions, classes and separate compilation, scope questions are trivial. The only unit of scope we know about is a block, the program text enclosed between a pair of curly brackets or making up the header and body of a for-loop. The scope of a name extends from its declaration to the end of the smallest enclosing block. Thus, a name cannot be used before it has been declared. (You guessed that, I imagine.) It is illegal for the same name to be declared as a variable more than once in the same block.

(Unless. . . But leave the 'unless' until page 51, it isn't very important.) However, a block may contain inner blocks. A name declared in an outer block may be redeclared in an inner block, and inside the inner block the new declaration takes precedence. This is the "block structure" found in many programming languages since Algol60. If you're not already familiar with it, just make it a rule never to re-use variable names in the same block. You won't be missing anything that's fun.

▷ I omitted to mention that a condition in an if, switch, for or while statement can take the form of a declaration. Its value is that used to initialize the variable being declared; the variable remains in scope until the end of the statement being controlled by the condition. ◁

▷ Within an inner block, the scope resolution operator :: can be used to provide access to a global variable whose declaration has been hidden in this way. If a variable, `orinoco` say, is declared globally and then re-declared in an inner block, inside the inner block, `::orinoco` refers to the global variable. Although this may sound like a travesty of the principles of block structure, the feature does have its uses. ◁

Because a variable declared in a for loop's header only remains in scope to the end of the loop body, you can have two for loops in the same block both declaring the same loop variable. Hence, the understandable habit of calling all your loop variables `i` is conveniently supported.

Abrupt Transfers of Control

We have already seen `break` used to jump out of a switch statement. It has a similar use in loops: within a loop, the statement

```
break;
```

causes immediate exit. Furthermore, the statement

```
continue;
```

causes the next iteration to be started. (Both `break` and `continue` are reserved words.) Both these statements should be used with discretion. Even if you don't believe in predicate transformers and weakest preconditions and all that, it is easiest to reason about (and debug, if you will) structures with a single entrance and exit.

Although the best way of terminating a program's execution is to allow control to reach a `return` in `main`, sometimes, especially when errors have been detected, you may prefer to give up completely without doing so. You can abandon execution using the statement

```
abort();
```

However, you should treat this as a drastic expedient. It may leave some sort of mess, for example, by not releasing locks, and, in some environments, may cause a post-mortem to be produced or a debugger to be invoked. A more satisfactory response to runtime errors will be described in chapter 11.

Any program that uses `abort`, which is actually a library function, must have the magic incantation `#include <stdlib.h>`. This will also make available to you two constants, `EXIT_FAILURE` and `EXIT_SUCCESS`, which may be used as the values passed back by return statements in `main` to indicate failure or success in a standard and perspicuous manner.

You can attach a label to any statement and use a `goto` statement to jump to it unconditionally (subject to some restrictions). Don't.

Abstractions

As any serious programmer knows, the art of programming consists of more than implementing algorithms using the facilities described in the previous chapter. Programming on a small scale, where the emphasis is on algorithms, *is* important, despite a recent tendency among methodologists to disparage it. Such programming may require the exercise of considerable expertise, talent and ingenuity. However, as people write larger programs, the art of devising and combining abstractions becomes more and more important, as coping with the complexity of the program itself becomes more and more difficult.

C++ supports both kinds of abstraction—procedural and data—which, by consensus, are considered necessary for modern programming. These should not be thought of as competing forms of abstraction, belonging to competing schools of programming. They are complementary and inter-dependent. C++ functions can take arguments of user-defined types, so the principle of procedural abstraction extends to abstraction over statements and expressions involving objects of these types. User-defined types are implemented as C++ classes, within which the operations of the type are C++ functions of a slightly special sort. Once again, we see a two-fold relationship between the procedural and object-oriented features of this hybrid language.

FUNCTIONS

The facilities for defining and using functions in C++ are much the same as those provided by any other high level imperative language, and quite straightforward in themselves. Some of the more advanced detail gets rather murky, though, and the introduction of functions will force us to take a proper look at scope, especially in the context of separately compiled functions.

Function Definitions

A function definition consists of a function header followed by a compound statement (a sequence of statements between curly brackets). The header has the form

```
return-type name ([arg-type name {,arg-type name }])
```

(Notice the absence of a semicolon at the end.) The *return-type* and *arg-types* are type names, specifying the type of the value returned by the function and the types of each of its arguments. There is no special construct for defining a function that doesn't return a value; what you do in this case is specify that the return type is `void`. In this context, you can think of `void` as meaning "no type".

A trivial example of a void function is

```
void out_twice(int n)
{
  cout << n << endl;
  cout << n << endl;
}
```

Such a function can be called by using its name as a statement, and supplying expressions for the actual arguments (see the discussion in chapter 1). A call

```
out_twice(4+1);
```

will produce

```
5
5
```

If the function takes no arguments, there will be no formal argument names. However, the brackets in the function header are still required:

```
void function_with_no_args()
{
  cout << "I cannot argue" << endl;
}
```

They are also needed in the function call:

```
function_with_no_args();
```

Now you realize that the examples of complete programs we have seen all include a definition of a function `main`, taking no arguments and returning an `int` result, and that execution of a program is a call of this function.[1]

A function with a return type other than void (conveniently, if inelegantly, called a non-void function) should include a statement of the form

---

[1]It should be noted that the type of `main` is not uniquely specified by the draft standard. In many implementations it takes arguments which are picked up off the command line, where there is one.

```
return expression;
```

where the expression's type is the same as the return type. The return statement causes a return from the function, yielding the value of *expression* as the value of the call. A function may have more than one return statement, perhaps on different branches of a conditional. If no return statement is reachable in the function body the behaviour is undefined—always bad news. A void function normally returns when control passes the last statement in the function's body, but you may use an explicit return statement with no expression to return from other points.

The following is the definition of a little function that takes a single character as its argument and returns `true` or `false` according to whether it is a lower-case vowel or not:

```
bool is_vowel(char c)
{
    return c == 'a' || c == 'e' || c == 'i'
        || c == 'o' || c == 'u';
}
```

Argument Passing

Although it's not the real truth, it's simplest to believe at first that C++ supports two mechanisms for passing the values of arguments into functions: call by value and call by reference. Which of the two is used is determined by the way arguments are declared in the function header.

What we've seen so far is call by value, where the formal arguments are initialized with a copy of the actual arguments. After that, there is no connection between formals and actuals. In particular, if you assign to a formal within the function body, this will have no effect on the value of any variable used as an actual argument. In contrast, with call by reference the formal argument is made into a pseudonym for the actual: they are just two names for the same variable and any assignment to the formal argument made in the function body also updates the actual.

Call by reference is specified by putting an ampersand (&) on the end of the *arg-type* of each argument you want called that way. The calling mechanism is specified for each argument, so it is possible to mix value and reference in the same function definition.

Here is one of those contrived examples that do nothing except demonstrate the difference between call by value and call by reference.

```
#include <iostream>
#include <stdlib.h>

void value(int v)
{   v = 99;   }

void reference(int& r)
```

```
{  r = 88;  }

int main()
{
  int m = 0;
  cout << "m initially = " << m << endl;
  value(m);
  cout << "m after call of value = " << m << endl;
  reference(m);
  cout << "m after call of reference = " << m << endl;
  return EXIT_SUCCESS;
}
```

The output is

```
m initially = 0
m after call of value = 0
m after call of reference = 88
```

Why would you use call by reference? Isn't it safer, cleaner and altogether better to pass arguments in by value and have results returned explicitly, than to have a function alter its arguments? Yes it is, but call by value requires the creation of a copy of the actual argument, and an explicit return requires the creation of a copy of the returned value. If the values involved are large data structures the overhead of this copying may be unacceptable. For most aggregate datatypes, call by reference is often preferable. (C++ compilers aren't able, for reasons that lie outwith the scope of this guide, to perform the sort of optimizations that functional language compilers use to deal with this problem.)

Another common reason for using call by reference is to simulate functions that return more than one result. Suppose you wanted to compute the sum and product of all the numbers between a and b. Since both computations require you to iterate over all the numbers, keeping a running result, you might choose to carry out both computations in parallel in a single loop. That's easy, but if you then want to make an abstraction out of that computation, you need a function that returns both results, and there is no mechanism in C++ for doing this. You can simulate the effect, though, by passing the variables you want the two results assigned to by reference, and doing the assignment inside the function instead of executing a return statement, like this:

```
void sum_and_product(int lower, int upper,
                     int& sum, int& product)
{
  int partialsum = 0, partialproduct = 1;
  for (int x = lower; x <= upper; ++x)
  {
    partialsum += x;
    partialproduct *= x;
  }
  sum = partialsum;
  product = partialproduct;
}
```

A call `sum_and_product(1, 10, s, p)`, where s and p are variables declared in the calling function, will then set s equal to 55 and p to 3628800, for example.

The distasteful aspect of call by reference is that it allows a function to modify variables from outside itself. Sometimes, as we've just seen, this is exactly what you need to do, but very commonly call by reference is used simply to optimize the passing of large data structures when you don't want to change the values of the actual arguments. Such changes can be prevented by adding the qualifier `const` in front of an argument in the function header. As with declarations, this has the effect of making any assignments to that argument into compiler-detected errors, so a `const` reference argument is an efficient and safe way of passing a data structure into a function. For example, copying a string may be expensive, so I usually pass strings by reference, but qualify the argument with `const` if I do not want it modified, like this:

```
void out_string_twice(const string& s)
{
  cout << s << endl;
  cout << s << endl;
}
```

We will see many less artificial examples of this technique.

It may not be obvious that, if an argument is passed by reference, but the formal argument is not declared `const`, you cannot pass a constant as the actual value. For example,

```
void f(int& i)
{
    body of f
}

const int n = 0;
f(n);
```

Since f does not carry the assertion that its reference argument will never be updated within the function body, the C++ compiler has to assume that it might be—it doesn't, in general, have enough information available at the right time to find out for sure. That being so, the assertion that n is constant would be in doubt if the call was allowed, so it isn't. If you know that a function you are writing will never update its reference argument, you should declare the argument `const`—whether or not you care about the extra safety that the compiler's checking will give you. The reason is that, if you don't, nobody can ever call your function with a constant argument. You never attempt to update the argument, so what justification can there be for preventing such calls?

You will notice, though, that I never bother using `const` with arguments passed by value. This is because it is of little use in making my programs more robust—the formal argument is initialized with a copy of the actual, so no changes can propagate out of the function. It's hard to see how you could do much damage by updating the argument, so adding `const` does little more than make your function header harder to read. Some programmers may prefer to use it as documentation, though.

What if you stipulate call by reference and the actual argument is an expression, not just a simple variable? If the formal argument is not `const`, this is an error, otherwise, a variable will be supplied! Notionally anyway, C++ creates a temporary variable and initializes it with the actual's value for you and then passes it by reference.

Using Functions

Many aspects of function definitions and calls are illustrated in the following two complete programs.

Counting vowels. This program will perform some input and output using the iostream library and it makes use of strings, so the first thing it must do is include the declarations for these libraries.

```
#include <iostream>
#include <string>
```

It is also going to use a standard function for manipulating characters. This is declared in another header, which is also included here.

```
#include <ctype.h>
```

Since I like to use EXIT_SUCCESS, I need to include `stdlib.h` too.

```
#include <stdlib.h>
```

The `is_vowel` function shown earlier is used to determine whether a character should be counted.

```
bool is_vowel(char c)
{
  return c == 'a' || c == 'e' || c == 'i'
    || c == 'o' || c == 'u';
}
```

Rather than check upper and lower case vowels separately, all the upper case letters in a string will be replaced by their lower case equivalents before counting takes place. This is done by the following function, which modifies its string argument, passed by reference, in place, to avoid having to copy it. The library function `tolower` (declared in `ctype.h`) takes a character as its argument and, if the character is an upper case letter, returns its lower case equivalent, otherwise it returns it unchanged. Use of `tolower` is preferable to the idiom

```
if ('A' <= s[i] && s[i] <= 'Z')
  s[i] = s[i] -'A' + 'a';
```

which may be familiar to you, because `tolower` is independent of the character set employed and is implemented in a highly efficient manner. Despite appearances, it is probably faster than the character arithmetic. The termination condition in the while loop relies on the fact that every string in a C++ program has a null character, which is equivalent to zero and thus to `false`, on the end.

```
void convert_to_lower_case(string& s)
{
  int i = 0;
  while (s[i])
  {
    s[i] = tolower(s[i]);
    ++i;
  }
}
```

▷ C and C++ are known for their succinctness. Some programmers find this very attractive and try to make their programs as short as possible. This can tempt you to foolishness, such as trying to combine the increment of i with the conversion:

!

```
        s[i] = tolower(s[i++]);
```

It's really much, much better to write so that it's obvious what you mean. That's easy to say, but opinions differ as to what is obvious. Is this a better formulation of the loop?

```
    for (int i = 0; s[i]; ++i)
        s[i] = tolower(s[i]);
```

◁ You decide.

The next function does the actual counting, using a similar control structure, to look at each character in its argument in turn.

```
int number_of_vowels(const string& s)
{
  int nv = 0;
  int i = 0;
  while(s[i])
  {
    if (is_vowel(s[i]))
      ++nv;
    ++i;
  }
  return nv;
}
```

The function prompt_for is used to obtain a string to count from the standard input. It returns it by overwriting its reference argument.

```
void prompt_for(string& f)
{
  cout << "?  ";
  cin >> f;
}
```

Finally, the main function is a loop that keeps prompting for strings, counting their vowels and reporting the result, until a silly string causes it to stop. Note the use of the conditional expression (nv==1? "": "s"), to prevent the computer barbarism 1 vowels appearing in the output.

```
int main()
{
  cout << "Enter a word at the prompt" << endl
    << "If it is nuff, the program will terminate" << endl
    << "otherwise it will tell you"
    << " how many vowels it contains." << endl;
  string s;
  prompt_for(s);
  while (s != "nuff")
  {
    convert_to_lower_case(s);
    int nv = number_of_vowels(s);
    cout << "The string \"" << s << "\" contains "
      << nv << " vowel" << (nv==1? "": "s") << endl;
    prompt_for(s);
  }
  cout << "Finished" << endl;
  return EXIT_SUCCESS;
}
```

A typical run goes like this:

```
Enter a word at the prompt
If it is nuff, the program will terminate
otherwise it will tell you how many vowels it contains.
?   OWSATSIROWASITEHOUT!
The string "owsatsirowasitehout!" contains 9 vowels
?   drat!!
The string "drat!!" contains 1 vowel
?   nuff
Finished
```

Square roots   This example will be an old friend to some readers. Others might prefer to skip it, since it is a bit mathematical.

The program computes square roots using Newton's method. The essence of this is easy to convey: you take a guess at the square root, see if it's good enough and if it is, return it as the answer, otherwise improve it and test again. We thus have to answer three questions: What guess should we take? When is a guess good enough? How do we improve a guess? This is no place to go into the theory, so the answers can pretty much come out of a hat.

It turns out that it doesn't hugely matter what first guess you take, so I shall always guess that $\sqrt{a} = 1$ for any value a whose square root I'm looking for. The question of what makes a good enough guess is more problematical, and its answer really depends on what you're using the square root function for. I shall take a simple-minded view that x is a good enough approximation to *What if* $\sqrt{a}$ if $|x^2 - a| \leq \epsilon$ for some suitably small value ϵ; in this example, I will take *$a < \epsilon$?* $\epsilon = 0.001$, giving three decimal places of accuracy. Finally, how do we improve the guess? Well, that's what Newton figured out: he observed that if x is an approximation to $\sqrt{a}$, then $\frac{1}{2}(x + a/x)$ is a better one; if you know any calculus you can fairly easily see where this formula comes from.

Once you know all that, the program is easy to write. We begin by including some files containing library definitions, first the familiar ones for using iostreams and the symbolic constant denoting successful completion.

```
#include <iostream>
#include <stdlib.h>
```

Next, some we haven't seen before, both of which are actually from the standard C library—remember, it's easy to mix C and C++ code and libraries. The first of these allows me to include assertions in the program, which will be checked at runtime; the second defines some useful mathematical functions. (Yes, there is a square root function in the maths library, but we won't use it—we're trying to learn something here.)

```
#include <assert.h>
#include <math.h>
```

Next, define the value ϵ used in determining whether a guess is good enough. We use a `const` to make the program more readable and easy to change.

```
const float epsilon = 0.001;
```

Next a very simple function to compute $|x|$. You've seen this code before.

```
float magnitude(const float x)
{   return x < 0 ? -x : x;   }
```

Now for the function that actually does the work. It takes the number whose square root we want as its argument, and then finds the root by a totally straightforward implementation of the algorithm just outlined. There is just one point to note: since we are not dealing with complex numbers $\sqrt{a}$ is meaningless if $a < 0$. This algorithm will go into an infinite loop if given a negative argument. To prevent this, I've included an assertion that the argument is non-negative. If the assertion fails at runtime, an error will occur and a helpful message will be produced. However, this should never happen: an assertion should be treated as a form of documentation, backed up by a runtime check, and the user of the function should ensure that the assertion is satisfied whenever the function is called. Assertions are not acceptable forms of error handling.

```
float square_root(float a)
{
  assert (a >= 0.0);
  float guess = 1.0;
  while (magnitude(guess*guess - a) >= epsilon)
    guess = (guess + a/guess)/2.0;
  return guess;
}
```

(There might be some point in including tests for the special cases when you know the answers, $a = 0$ or $a = 1$, in particular.)

The rest of the program is a framework for testing the square root function. First, a function to prompt (tersely) for a number:

```
float prompt_for_a_float()
{
  float f;
  cout << "?  ";
  cin >> f;
  return f;
}
```

And lastly the main program, which is simply a loop that repeatedly prompts for a test value and then computes its square root. Notice that a negative number is used to terminate the loop; it is thus impossible for `square_root` ever to be called with a negative argument.

```
int main()
{
  cout << "Enter a number at the prompt."
     << "  If non-negative, its square root" << endl
     << "will be computed, otherwise the program"
     << " will terminate" << endl;
  float n = prompt_for_a_float();
  while (n >= 0.0)
  {
    cout << "The square root of "  << n
      << " is " << square_root(n)
      << " (to within " << epsilon << ")" << endl;
    n = prompt_for_a_float();
  }
  cout << "Finished" << endl;
  return EXIT_SUCCESS;
}
```

Scope

With the introduction of functions, new questions concerning scope arise. We have already seen that the scope of variables is limited by the } of the block they are declared in. It follows that, outside a function, any variables declared *inside* the function body are out of scope and cannot be referred to by name. We call them the function's *local variables.* The formal arguments to a function behave as if they were local variables declared in the outermost block of the function, as far as scope is concerned.

What about functions themselves and any variables declared outside of functions? (Nobody ever said you couldn't do that.) To understand the full story of this, we need to know about two things: first, function declarations and, second, separate compilation.

I've been careful so far to refer to function *definitions*, although, implicitly, I've taken it that a function definition introduces the function's name into a program, so it is also a function *declaration*. But you can declare a function separately from its definition. A function declaration is just like the header of a function definition except that you can leave out the argument names, but not their types, if you like (or not, if you don't) and you need a semicolon at the end of the declaration, whereas you mustn't have one at the end of a definition header.

Here are declarations of the functions used in the vowel counting example.

```
bool is_vowel(const char c);
void convert_to_lower_case(string&);
int number_of_vowels(const string&);
void promptfor(string& p);
int main();
```

The presence or absence of argument names in these declarations is entirely arbitrary. Notice that, if you provide a name, it doesn't even have to match the name used in the definition. On the whole, argument names should only be included in function declarations that are separate from definitions if they provide or assist with documentation of the function, otherwise, they are just noise. It is a good idea, if you are working as part of a group, to agree on some conventions about whether and when to name the arguments in function declarations. You may well find, if you are working in industry, that your employer has already agreed on them for you.

It might be helpful to think of a function definition as being a declaration with an initializer, which takes the form of the code of the function body.

Like any other declaration, a function declaration introduces a name into the program. The function name is in scope from the end of the declaration until ...where? Hang on, and this question will be answered. Notice, though, that since the header of a function definition is also a declaration, a function's name is in scope inside its own body: you can call it recursively without having to resort to any subterfuge.

Functions cannot be declared within the body of a function. This is a cue for pointless arguments about whether C++ is "truly" block-structured. What matters is that it rules out a certain style of programming and information hiding dating from Algol60. This isn't the loss that some of its fans claim, because classes provide C++ with a more effective and flexible method of information hiding.

All well and good, but why do I want to declare a function separately from its definition?

I can think of three reasons. The first is simple convenience. The tyranny of single-pass compilers has forced programmers to get used to the idea that we have to define functions "in the right order", so that each is defined before it is used. By putting declarations for all functions at the head of the program, we are at liberty to put the definitions in some other order, if that suits us. For example, we might prefer an order which better serves the exposition of the algorithms being employed, or simple alphabetical order, to make it easier to look up the definitions. (You might be forgiven for thinking that a computer program would be quite good at re-ordering the definitions or generating the necessary declarations for the compiler's benefit. Some programs, for example literate programming systems, do, indeed, do this, or something equivalent.)

If that reason seems frivolous, how about mutual recursion? If a function tomsk calls a function orinoco, which in turn calls tomsk, then there is no way of ordering the definitions of tomsk and orinoco so that each is in scope in the body of the other (because tomsk's definition would have to precede orinoco's which would have to precede tomsk's, which ...). By putting, let us say, a declaration of tomsk first, then the definition of orinoco followed by the definition of tomsk, we ensure that both names are in scope when they are needed. Any language that insists that functions be declared before they are used must have some mechanism for coping with mutual recursion—because it really does happen. In C++ this is one of the uses of function declarations which are separate from function definitions—arguably, a more elegant expedient than some *ad hoc* "forward declaration" for use in the special case only.

The third use is the most compelling, and brings in the matter of separate compilation, which in turn introduces the idea of source files. Although files are essentially an operating system concept, the fact that the source text of a C++ program is commonly stored in a file is recognized as being the case, and is used to provide a level of program structure. That is, a C++ program is assumed to consist of a collection of files. Each file consists of a collection of declarations and definitions.

▷   In most contemporary environments, the "file" that is a component of the C++ program is going to be identical to the "file" stored on disk. If we want to be picky, though, the two concepts are distinct; the one belonging to the language, the other to an operating system. It seems more than likely that, in the near future, C++ development environments will use persistent data structures other than text files to hold the source of a program. A more neutral term, such as "program source unit" would be preferable, but "file" is much less cumbersome, and, at the moment, the
◁   distinction is academic.

A file is itself a unit of scope—almost as if it were enclosed in curly brackets—so any variables declared in a file but outside any function body are in scope in any functions defined later on in that file. They are said to be *global variables* (even though they aren't necessarily global to the whole program). The scope of functions declared in a file is also terminated by the end of the file. The question therefore arises: How can functions and variables be used in files outside the one they are defined in?

For this, we need to achieve two things. First, ensure that all necessary names are in scope in all the files they are used in, and second, link up all these declarations to the appropriate definition.

The first is easy: in principle, you just copy the declarations into every file where the names they declare are used. Actually copying declarations all over the place is tedious and error-prone, so it is usual to make use of a C++ facility that automatically inserts the contents of one file into another at compile time. (If you want to be really fastidious, it's actually done by a pre-processor, just before real compilation.) This is what this #include stuff you've seen in some of the examples is about. If you put

```
#include "filename"
```

in your C++ source file, then the contents of the file called *filename* will be read by the compiler at that point, before it goes on with the rest of your file. So, if you need to refer to the same names in separately compiled files, you put declarations of all these names in a file, called a *header file*, and #include it in all program files that use these names. Conventions about naming header files (and, indeed, source files) vary between compilers. I will always use names ending in .hpp for my header files. Other commonly used extensions include .h, .H, .hp and .hxx.

The tolerably observant reader will have noticed that in the program examples using iostreams, it doesn't say #include "iostream", it says #include <iostream>. This demonstrates a useful feature: if the filename in a #include is enclosed in angle brackets, then the system will look for the header file in some central system directory. This way, declarations for all the standard system libraries can be kept in one place and the programmer doesn't need to know where that is, or to specify long path names. Which directories are searched for header files enclosed in "s is system dependent and may be controllable by compiler options. It's a pretty safe bet that the directory where the source file containing the #include is kept will be searched first, wherever that concept makes sense.

As I remarked before, the conventions for naming the standard header files are in a state of flux. I follow those employed by the compiler I used while writing this book: standard C++ headers have no extension, while headers shared with the standard C library end in .h.

This arrangement of header files and source files takes care of declaring all names where they are needed. Linking declarations to the appropriate definitions is a task carried out by a separate system program called a linker or linking loader. The linker takes the compiled form of all the files making up a program, together with any libraries that are used, and combines them into a single executable binary. The compiler's output contains enough information to enable the linker to match up the use and definition of names in separate files, or to produce an error message if this is not possible (because a definition is missing or duplicated, for example).

▷ With C++, nothing is entirely simple, so some extra details may be helpful.

Names can be divided into two categories, those with *internal linkage* and those with *external linkage*. In mechanical terms, names with external linkage are known to the linker, those with internal linkage are not. A name with internal linkage is not known outside one file; the same name can thus be defined in another file without confusion. On the other hand, all uses of a name with external linkage refer to the same object or function, which can therefore only have one definition among all the files making up a program.

The notions of scope and linkage are *not* the same, but they are not independent, because the scope of a name determines its linkage in the absence of any explicit specification. By default, names declared at the file level have external linkage, those within a function or other block have internal linkage. A name with default external linkage can be made internal by putting the reserved word static in front of its declaration; a name with default internal linkage can be made external by putting the reserved word extern in front. In the case of a variable, extern does not cause space to be reserved—it is a declaration only, not a definition, unlike the variable declarations we have seen so far, hence the "unless..." on page 36. The truth is, any name can be declared as often as you like, but it must be defined exactly once ◁ (unless you never use it, in which case you need never define it).

The use of file scopes and header files provides C++ with a module facility, even though it's a rather ramshackle affair. A module is implemented by a collection of definitions in a file. Declarations for those objects and functions exported by the module are then placed in a header file. Any program wishing to use the services provided by the module can do so by including the header file.

▷ A major problem with separate compilation in C++ is its reliance on system linkers. Once you've designed a linker, any compiler will have to produce output which is compatible with the linker's input format. This implies that, if the linker is redesigned, all compilers that rely on it must be changed. This is rarely practicable or acceptable, so linker designs tend to be frozen—even when a new operating system version is released. For many widely used operating systems, this freezing took place a long time ago. In truth, many linkers are still best suited to linking separately compiled Fortran programs, but since C++ is supposed to be portable to any platform, it has to cope with their deficiencies. The worst of these is that most linkers are not capable of type checking at link time. Thus, if in one file I define a function

```
void womble(int x, char c)
```

and elsewhere I declare and call

```
int womble(float)
```

the program would still link, since all the linker sees is the name, were it not for a trick employed by the C++ compilers.

This trick, known as "name mangling" is either a masterstroke of ingenuity or a terrible hack, I'm not sure which. Name mangling simply encodes the number and type of a function's arguments into a new version of its name, which is handed to the linker. For example, the function defined above might be passed to the linker as something like wombleFic (F indicating that the name denotes a function, i and c showing the argument types). This technique ensures that declarations and defi- ◁ nitions will only be linked together if they are consistent.

Namespaces, a recent addition to C++ described on page 341, offer an improved module facility, but they are not widely available yet. In the meantime, if modules are the extent of your idea of large-scale program structure, you would be better off using a language with an inherent module structure, such as Modula-2 or Ada, if you have the choice. In C++, classes provide a much better modularization technique.

CLASSES

A class is a user-defined type. This simple statement appears several times in the ARM (so it must be true). Although most programmers probably feel they know more or less what it means, providing a proper answer to the question it raises: What exactly is a type?, is very hard to do without getting involved in a lot of semantic theory and formalism that would be totally out of place here. The discussion of abstract datatypes in chapter 1 provides a partial answer, but begs several important questions. Probably, more confused and confusing words have been written about types than about any other aspect of programming languages. Instead of adding to them, it will be more constructive to skirt round the issue by looking at how types are used.

Thinking about the types we have seen so far, we can identify two aspects to their use. First, they allow us to create objects whose properties are determined by their type. Second, they allow us to impose constraints on variables, by associating a type with the variable's name when it is declared. The type declared for a variable restricts the values that may be stored in it, and the operations that may be applied to it. If we are going to define our own types, we must be able to provide a description of them that is adequate for the C++ compiler to use for these two purposes.

The ARM also tells us that an object is a region of storage. As a minimum, then, the definition of a type must tell the compiler how big objects of that type are. We want to go further than that, though: in a high level language we don't simply manipulate regions of storage as undifferentiated lumps of bytes, we provide some structure for them. This is done by dividing the region up into fields, each of which can hold an object of some type, either a built-in type or some other user-defined type. (We do this in assembly language, too, by defining symbolic offsets into blocks of storage.) So an object is considered to be composite: it is a collection of values taken together.

Carrying out an operation on an object will involve accessing and possibly changing the values of its fields. It should not be forgotten that we want to define types for a purpose; a type should model a "sort of thing", with objects of that type being the things of that sort. As I discussed in chapter 1, sorts of things are characterized by the operations you can carry out on them, so, when you define a type, you don't want to allow arbitrary changes to be made to the fields, you want to specify exactly which ones are allowed. A compiler can then check that we only use objects of a particular type in the way we said they would be used.

So, in order to define a type T, you need to provide a description of the fields making up objects of type T and a set of operations that can access those fields. This is pretty pointless unless you also provide a means of creating and initializing objects of type T, a way of declaring variables of type T, a way for T operations to access the fields of a T object and a way of invoking T operations.

Class Declarations

You introduce a new type into a C++ program by declaring a class. A class declaration names the class and provides the necessary description of its fields and operations. In C++, fields and operations are both referred to, in an unfortunate choice of terminology, as class *members*. (So, although one tends to say an object belongs to a class, it isn't a member of the class.) The fields are data members, the functions are member functions, which isn't very consistent, but you'll find it sounds natural. A class's declaration provides names for all its members and specifies their types.

It has been argued by critics of C++ that treating both data and functions as members and requiring them to be declared together is a serious mistake in the language's design. It can certainly be misleading, since it may seem to suggest that each object contains a set of data members and a set of member functions. This isn't so: each object has its own data members, but there is only one set of member functions for the whole class. Declaring them as part of the class only affects how they can be used. A more practical problem with declaring all your members together is that it fails to distinguish between those members that are part of the implementation and those that provide operations which may be applied to objects. Typically, we will want to use classes to implement abstract datatypes. In that case, the implementation is supposed to be hidden.

Because C++ classes are intended to be flexible and not just to be used for one particular style of programming, no rigid rule such as "all data members are always inaccessible" is applied. Instead, the members of a class are separated into two kinds: public and private. (This is a lie: there are *three* kinds, but you'll have to wait to until chapter 9 to find out about the third.) The precise distinction between public and private members will be explained shortly. For now, suffice it to say that, if we choose to use classes to implement abstract datatypes then the operations of the class should be public, and will be available to users of the type, and any representation details should be private, which will make them inaccessible to everything but the operations on the type.

Before we can go any further, it is necessary to introduce some syntax and examples to make the description concrete.

The simplest form of a class declaration is

```
class name { member-list };
```

It is introduced by the reserved word `class`, which is followed by the name given to the class. This name can subsequently be used as a type name in declarations. A hint for anyone who has never written in C: Watch out for the semicolon at the end of the declaration. It is very easy to forget. The resulting syntax error message often seems to be about something else, as the missing semicolon throws most C++ compilers thoroughly off track. A hint for everyone: It is a good idea to use one of the super-charged editors like Gnu-emacs or Alpha that can be cajoled into inserting the syntactic details for you.

The *member-list* is just a list of variable and function declarations, like the ones we've seen already, except that two *access specifiers* may appear. An access specifier is

```
public: | private:
```

These can actually appear anywhere between member declarations, but I shall follow the convention that `public:` appears right at the beginning and there is only one subsequent appearance of `private:`, so my member list will usually have the form

```
public:  public members
private: private members
```

It must be emphasized that only the simplest form of class declaration is being described in this section. There are significant embellishments, which will be explored in later chapters.

To illustrate what we have learned so far, I will develop some classes that might form part of a computerized system providing centralized control of domestic appliances in that House of the Future we keep being threatened with. The sort of thing I have in mind is a central console that would allow a Modern Person to program the timers in their video recorder, central heating controller, radio alarm, oven, exercise bicycle and any other gadget that has taken their fancy. Judging from recent interface design trends (like the on-screen calculator with buttons to press with the mouse), the interface to such a system will resemble the interfaces used to program the timers on individual machines at present. When you want to set a time for something to happen, you indicate the fact and the timer displays a time, which you adjust by pressing up and down buttons until it is set to what you require.

To keep the quantity of code you have to read reasonable, I shall confine myself to time settings within a twenty-four hour period and not worry about days of the week—the extension is simple and adds nothing of substance. My fundamental "sort of thing" is therefore a time, which I will take to comprise a number of hours and a number of minutes. A twenty-four hour clock will be used. Usually, you can adjust hours and minutes separately up and down in single increments, so the operations I need to be able to perform on a time are to display it and to increase or decrease the hours and minutes. I will also provide an operation to set an initial value, so that random values, that may be nonsensical (like 35:97), cannot occur.

You may be concerned that relying on a member function to set the initial value still leaves the possibility of random values occurring if a user of the class fails to call the initialization function—there is nothing to stop you calling the other member functions before it. This is really no worse than having to remember to initialize all your variables, but it's no better, either. In C++, every class may be declared to have a special member function called a *constructor*, which is automatically invoked whenever an object of that class is created. Constructors turn out to be rather subtle, and appreciating their subtleties calls for more knowledge of C++, so I have deferred their description until chapter 6, where a full account can be given. In the meantime, if you are worried about some of the examples being unsafe because of the possibility of forgetting to initialize objects, remember constructors—and peek ahead to chapter 6, if you like.

At this stage, I will adopt the "hack it and see" method of design. I will start by defining a class `TimeSetting` with member functions that provide the operations just described. The class declaration looks like this:

```
class TimeSetting {
public:
  void init(int, int);
  void hrs_up();
  void hrs_down();
  void mins_up();
  void mins_down();
```

```
    void display();
private:
    private members of the class
};
```

To fill in the rest of the class declaration and provide definitions for the member functions it is necessary to decide how to represent times. How about doing the most obvious thing and storing the hours and minutes in two separate data members? These can be integers. I will rely on the operations to ensure that their values are always in range. The stored values are an implementation detail, so the data members are made private.

```
class TimeSetting {
public:
    void init(int, int);
    void hrs_up();
    void hrs_down();
    void mins_up();
    void mins_down();
    void display();
private:
    int hours;
    int mins;
};
```

The declaration of the class is now complete, but more work remains to be done: the member functions have been declared but not defined. Before considering their definitions, we can look at the way in which the class declaration can be used.

Using Classes

As with functions, it is usual to place the declaration of a class into a header file which is included in any source file where the class is used, so assume that the class TimeSetting is declared in TimeSetting.hpp. Remember, the #include directive causes a textual inclusion that is exactly equivalent to repeating the declaration wherever it is needed. The class declaration follows the same scope rules as any other, and is in effect from its appearance to the end of the scope unit (block or file) enclosing it; almost always, the #include appears at the top of a file and the declaration remains in scope until the end of the file. Within that scope, the class name is, in effect, a reserved word, and can be used to declare variables or arguments, just as int and char can. For example

```
    TimeSetting heating_on;
```

This, as ever, introduces a new variable name into the program and causes space to be reserved for an object of type TimeSetting, consisting of two integers. As you would expect, it is possible to initialize objects of user-defined classes, but it requires the use of those constructors I mentioned, which will not be described until chapter 6. We can manage without, for now.

Having declared a variable, I can use the member functions of its class. This is done with a special notation. If *var* is a variable of some class and *memf* is a member function of that class, then

```
var.memf ( [args] )
```

is a call of that function, with arguments if necessary. We say that the member function *memf* is called *through* the object denoted by *var*. For example, the two statements

```
heating_on.init(0, 0);
heating_on.hrs_up();
```

first initialize `heating_on` to midnight by setting both components to zero and then add one to its `hours` component. The syntax here may seem curious compared with the functions we have already seen. Why isn't the `hrs_up` function applied to a reference argument, with the call being written as `hrs_up(heating_on)`, as usual?

The short answer is that member functions are special in several ways, so it is reasonable to use a special syntax when they are invoked. A more detailed answer must take into account the special role of the object through which the member function is being called. The `hrs_up` function is part of the class `TimeSetting` to which the object stored in the variable `heating_on` belongs. This means that `hrs_up` has privileged access to the data members of the `TimeSetting` object, in a way which other functions that might be applied to it do not. Conversely, it doesn't have any special relationship to objects of any other type. It is reasonable, therefore, to adopt a special notation, rather than some arbitrary convention about the first argument to a member function. The particular notation used has the advantage that it offers a uniform way of referring to data and function members. If *var* is a variable of some class and *dmem* is a data member of that class, then

```
var.dmem
```

is an expression denoting the corresponding data member of the object held in *var*. For example

```
heating_on.hours
```

is the `hours` member of `heating_on`. Expressions of this form are used like variables, as part of expressions or on the left hand side of assignments, but are subject to some extra restrictions that will be described soon.

An alternative explanation of the notation used for calls of member functions is available if you adopt what I called in chapter 1 the romantic view of object-oriented programming. According to this view, incrementing its hours is one of the things a `TimeSetting` object knows how to do. We can send the object a message requesting it to do so. On this view of things, the expression

```
heating_on.hrs_up()
```

could be paraphrased: "Hey, `heating_on`! Add one to your hours!" (Object-oriented programming enthusiasts like to talk of objects "politely requesting" services from each other, but I can see nothing in the syntax corresponding to "please".) Although this is just a question of presentation, adopting this view draws attention to the role of the receiver in interpreting the message. There might be other classes with a member function called `hrs_up`—one recording uptime of machines on a network, for example. The effect of the member function `hrs_up` depends on the class of the object it is being applied to. Or, we might say, the object interprets the message `hrs_up` in its own way, according to the sort of object it is. We'll see more of this sort of thing, later.

Now that we know how to call member functions (or pass messages to objects) we are in a position to write a program that uses `TimeSetting` objects, even though we haven't defined the member functions yet. All we need to use the class is the interface described in the public part of its declaration—I could have written the program below before even deciding on the representation of times. This illustrates the separation of concerns that is such a helpful feature of object-oriented programming in general and C++ in particular, when it comes to developing large programs or working in groups.

Figure 3.1 on the next page shows a little program that uses streams input and output to simulate the setting of a timer. Instead of dedicated up, down and done buttons, the +, – and x keys are used to increase and decrease the components and to finish a setting operation. You should be able to appreciate (if not now, then later) that a properly designed interface abstraction would make it easy to perform the same interaction through dedicated hardware or a graphical interface. The form of the interaction may well be familiar to you. First the hours are set, then the minutes. You would probably expect the up and down operations to wrap round so that, for example, subtracting one from zero in the hours component would give twenty three. This desired behaviour will have to be borne in mind when defining the member functions.

The `TimeSetting` class is a perfectly good type. As well as defining `Time-Setting` variables, you can pass `TimeSetting`s to functions and, most interestingly, you can define other classes with `TimeSetting` objects as members. Usually, timer settings come in pairs, an on and an off time. Such pairs are referred to, by VCR manufacturers at least, as events. It is quite simple to define a `TimerEvent` class to hold pairs of `TimeSetting`s. In a way that is typical of hack it and see development, doing so suggests modifications to the `TimeSetting` class and its interface.

▷ Preventing re-design on the fly is a major reason for the existence of object-oriented design methods and the gurus who propound them. For large-scale projects, systematic designs are necessary, but consideration of them goes beyond the scope of this book. Incremental development—a posh name for hacking it—has a place though. Typically, a class is implemented and goes through several versions before a satisfactory interface is arrived at. After that, the class is metaphorically closed and only changes that do not affect the interface and users of the class are permitted. (That, of course, is what I'm doing here and not just bashing out the first thing I think of.) Later, we'll see a way of adding operations to closed classes without
◁ destabilizing them.

First, on reflection, it seems that the operation of setting a time performed by the test program in figure 3.1 should really be considered as part of the

```
#include "TimeSetting.hpp"        Including the TimeSetting declarations is
#include <iostream>               fundamental. We also need iostreams and
#include <stdlib.h>               stdlib in the usual way.
char prompt_for_a_char()         You have seen things like this before.
{
  char c;
  cout << ">>";
  cin >> c;
  return c;
}
int main()              Declare a TimeSetting variable, initialize it to
{                       midnight and start the interaction by displaying it.
  TimeSetting t;
  t.init(0, 0);
  t.display();
  char c = prompt_for_a_char();        This variable will hold the
                                       characters as they are input.
  while (c != 'x')                      Loop to set the hours. Any input
  {                                     other than +, − or x is rejected.
    if (c == '+')                       The time is displayed after each
      t.hrs_up();                       adjustment.
    else
      if (c == '-')
        t.hrs_down();
      else cout << "?" << endl;
    t.display();
    c = prompt_for_a_char();
  }
  t.display();                          Now do the same for minutes.
  c = prompt_for_a_char();
  while (c != 'x')
  {
    if (c == '+')
      t.mins_up();
    else
      if (c == '-')
        t.mins_down();
      else cout << "?" << endl;
    t.display();
    c = prompt_for_a_char();
  }
  cout << "set to ";          Confirm the final value.
  t.display();
  cout << endl;
  return EXIT_SUCCESS;
}
```

Figure 3.1   Setting a Time

interface to the `TimeSetting` class. Even though it can be composed out of other member functions, so it is not necessary for a minimal interface, it seems likely to be an operation required in different contexts that is most conveniently provided as a member function. Second, if you think about what constitutes a valid pair of times for the on and off components of an event, you will realize that the off time must be later than the on time. I will need to think carefully about what that means in a twenty-four hour timer, but it clearly depends on the values stored in the two `TimeSetting` objects. I could provide a member function to carry out the comparison, but I can see that being able to enquire what time a `TimeSetting` has been set to might be a more generally useful operation. Shrewdly guessing that I may need to perform arithmetic on times, and not wishing to prejudice my design in favour of any implementation, I will provide a member function `secs_after_midnight`, which returns the stored time as a number of seconds after midnight.

Finally, this is a good point to introduce a further refinement of C++ classes. There is an important distinction between member functions like `secs_after_midnight` and `display`, which don't change the value of any data member, and those such as `init` and `hrs_up`, which do. We can distinguish the former by adding the keyword `const` after their declaration, as in

```
void display() const;
```

The C++ compiler will issue a message if any member function declared `const` like this—a constant member function—does update any data member.

Constant member functions can help to enforce constraints on the constancy of objects belonging to user-defined classes. Calling a constant member function through an object will not alter that object, whereas calling a member function that is not constant might. For that reason, if you declare a variable of a user-defined type with `const`, the compiler will only allow you to call constant member functions through that variable. At the moment, this is totally useless with variable declarations, since we would have no way of initializing such a variable. That problem will be sorted out in chapter 6. Meanwhile, we do have constant reference arguments, and the same restriction applies to them. If I tried to define a function to add a specific number of hours to a `TimeSetting`, passing the argument as a constant reference would not be permitted.

```
void add_hours(const TimeSetting& t, int n)
{
  for (int i = 0; i <=n-1; ++i)
    t.hrs_up();
}
```

Since we do often want to pass objects by constant reference, it is necessary to declare member functions that do not alter data members—the functions it is sensible to call through constant objects—as `const`.

After these reflections, I enlarged the definition of `TimeSetting`.

```
class TimeSetting {
public:
  void init(int, int);
  void set();
  void hrs_up();
```

```
      void hrs_down();
      void mins_up();
      void mins_down();
      void display() const;
      int secs_after_midnight() const;
    private:
      int hours;
      int mins;
    };
```

A TimerEvent will store an on and an off time; these can be data members of type TimeSetting. We need to supply operations to initialize a TimerEvent so its on and off times are in a sensible state, to set it interactively and to display it as confirmation. I will also supply a function to verify that the off time is greater than the on time. Since this function is only intended to be used internally to ensure that TimerEvent objects are only set to legitimate values, I will make it private—member functions can be private as well as data members. The class definition is very simple.

```
    #include "TimeSetting.hpp"

    class TimerEvent {
    public:
      void init();
      void set();
      void confirm() const;
    private:
      bool valid() const;
      TimeSetting time_on, time_off;
    };
```

Using TimerEvent objects is very easy. The following program initializes a TimerEvent variable, then sets it and confirms its value until the user is satisfied.

```
    #include "TimerEvent.hpp"
    #include <iostream>
    #include <stdlib.h>
    char prompt_for_a_char();

    int main()
    {
      TimerEvent e;
      e.init();
      char c = prompt_for_a_char();
      while (c != 'x')
      {
        if (c == 'c')
          e.confirm();
        else
          if (c == 's')
```

```
        e.set();
      else cout << "??\n";
    c = prompt_for_a_char();
  }
  return EXIT_SUCCESS;
}
```

Defining Member Functions

To make all this work, we need to supply definitions of the member functions that so far we've just declared and used. Doing so will bring out some more aspects of classes.

▷ Defining the member functions is the only means we have in C++ of saying what they do. There is no concept of a datatype specification, in the form of equations or pre- and post-conditions, within the language itself. ◁

First of all, we need to consider the question of access to data members. I have described member functions as having a "privileged" access to the data members. What does this mean?

This privilege has two parts to it. First, there is scope: a class declaration, together with the definitions of the class's member functions, makes up a unit of scope. This is a new sort of scope unit, distinct from block, function and file scope; it may be physically distributed over the program. Within this region, the names of the class's members can be used on their own as identifiers. Outside it, they can only be used with the name of an object belonging to the class and the dot operator described earlier. So, within the class scope, which object's members are being referred to when the member names are used directly as identifiers? After all, only objects have members, so it must be *some* object. The answer is obvious when you think about that. Since only objects have members, only objects have member functions, and the only way in which a member function can be invoked is through an object. Within the function, it is *that* object (the message receiver, if you like) to which member names refer. For example, when I invoke `hrs_up` by writing `heating_on.hrs_up()`, the name `hours` is bound, within `hrs_up`, to the data member of the `heating_on` object, whereas if I invoked it with, say, `heating_off.hrs_up()`, it would be bound to that of the object stored in `heating_off`. It's rather as though the member names were invisible formal arguments to the member function (although they are not listed in the function's declaration), which are bound, when the function is called, to the members of the object used to invoke it.

▷ Member functions can be implemented as ordinary functions which take an extra argument, the object the member function is called through, so this is actually quite close to what really happens. ◁

In a similar way, member functions may call other member functions without using an object—implicitly, they are called through the same object. If you prefer to think of objects receiving and responding to messages, you would say that, when an object receives a message, it responds by executing the appropriate member function, with unqualified member names referring to its own members.

The second aspect of member functions' privileges relates to the access specifiers `public` and `private`, which I introduced a while ago and never referred to again. Access specifiers are the key to information hiding in C++. Quite simply, members (both data and functions) declared as private may only be referred to in member functions. This includes reference via an object and a dot, as well as the direct reference to an object's own members just described. So, only within the member functions of the class `TimeSetting` is it possible to access the data members of any `TimeSetting` object, since I declared both data members private. This is entirely in accordance with the idea of information hiding in abstract datatypes, as you will readily appreciate. If you want to be pernickety, the information isn't really hidden—anyone can see it from the class declaration—but access to it is forbidden. The idea behind public and private access is actually closer to that of access privileges in operating systems than it is to classical linguistic ideas of data hiding based on scope.

If these concepts are unfamiliar, the preceding few paragraphs may well be somewhat indigestible. Things should be made easier on the stomach by looking at how the `TimeSetting` and `TimerEvent` classes can be completed.

The usual way of arranging matters is to place the definitions of the member functions of each class in a separate file, which uses `#include` to incorporate the header file containing the class declaration. Any file that uses the class must also include this header, and must be linked with the compiled form of the definitions. Exactly how you do this depends on your system.

We'll start with the lower level class `TimeSetting`. Its member functions' definitions are just like any other function definitions, except that they are identified as members of the `TimeSetting` class, by preceding their names by the class name and two colons, as in `TimeSetting::hrs_up`, which may be considered as the full name of the function. (So if I did have a SystemStats class, which also had an `hrs_up` member, its full name would be `SystemStats::hrs_up`, which is different.)

There is nothing particularly exciting about the code. We begin by including some necessary standard definitions.

```
#include <iostream>
#include <assert.h>
```

and then the class declaration, stored in `TimeSetting.hpp`.

```
#include "TimeSetting.hpp"
```

The member function for setting the value of an object merely assigns its arguments to the appropriate data members. I have included an assertion to make sure that the arguments are in range. Notice how the data member names are used on their own to refer to the members of *this* object (as it were).

```
void TimeSetting::init(int h, int m)
{
  assert (0 <= h && h < 24 &&
```

```
              0 <= m && m < 60);
   hours = h;
   mins = m;
}
```

The up and down functions for the components could not be much simpler. They use a conditional expression to handle the necessary wrapping of values.

```
void TimeSetting::hrs_up()
{
   hours = hours==23 ? 0 : hours+1;
}

void TimeSetting::hrs_down()
{
   hours = hours==0 ? 23 : hours-1;
}

void TimeSetting::mins_up()
{
   mins = mins==59 ? 0 : mins+1;
}

void TimeSetting::mins_down()
{
   mins = mins==0 ? 59 : mins-1;
}
```

Displaying a time just means writing its components, separated by a colon in the conventional way. (Ensuring that we get times like 04:01 instead of 4:1 would require some magic that will not be explained until chapter 8, but it can be done.) Note that a `const` is required in the definition to match the one in the declaration.

```
void TimeSetting::display() const
{
   cout << hours << ":" << mins;
}
```

Computing the number of seconds after midnight is not difficult.

```
int TimeSetting::secs_after_midnight() const
{
   return 60 * (60*hours + mins);
}
```

The member function to set a time interactively is almost the same as the test program in figure 3.1, but again, notice that the names of data members and member functions are used unadorned because they always refer to the object the function is being called through.

```
void TimeSetting::set()
{
```

```
      display();
      char c = prompt_for_a_char();
      while (c != 'x')
      {
        if (c == '+')
          hrs_up();
        else
          if (c == '-')
            hrs_down();
          else cout << "?\n";
        display();
        c = prompt_for_a_char();
      }
      display();
      c = prompt_for_a_char();
      while (c != 'x')
      {
        if (c == '+')
          mins_up();
        else
          if (c == '-')
            mins_down();
          else cout << "?\n";
        display();
        c = prompt_for_a_char();
      }
    }
```

The function `prompt_for_a_char` would have to be defined in some file that was linked with this one, and declared appropriately.

That completes the member function definitions for the class `TimeSetting`. `TimerEvent`'s member functions are simpler—`TimeSetting` does most of the work for them. Here we see how abstractions can be built in layers, with a lower layer providing powerful primitives for a higher one.

```
    #include "TimerEvent.hpp"
    #include <iostream>

    void TimerEvent::init()
    {
      time_on.init(0, 0);  time_off.init(0, 0);
    }
```

Before we can write the member function to set a `TimerEvent`, we have to decide when one time is later than another, so we can ensure that the off time is greater than the on time. I assume we all agree that an event can span midnight, so subtracting two times and seeing whether the result is negative is not correct. In the absence of any other restriction, any time could be greater or less than any other, so I shall assert that times can be no more than twelve hours apart. I can use `secs_after_midnight` to access the values of `time_off` and time_on, subtract, convert the difference to minutes, and check the necessary cases. (I'm sure that if I was better at arithmetic I could combine these into a single expression with remainders, but why try to be smart?)

```
bool TimerEvent::valid() const
{
  const int diff = (time_off.secs_after_midnight()
                      - time_on.secs_after_midnight())/60;
  return (0 < diff && diff <= 12*60)
           || (-24*60 < diff && diff <= -12*60);
}
```

The set member function prompts for an on and an off time and checks them until a valid pair of times has been entered.

```
void TimerEvent::set()
{
  bool ok = false;
  while (!ok)
  {
    cout << "set the on time" << endl;
    time_on.set();
    cout << "set the off time" << endl;
    time_off.set();
    ok =valid();
    if (!ok)
      cout << "OFF time must be greater than ON time" << endl;
  }
}
```

Finally, confirm displays the two times, calling on TimeSetting::display to do so.

```
void TimerEvent::confirm() const
{
  cout << "ON at ";
  time_on.display();
  cout << "\nOFF at ";
  time_off.display();
  cout << endl;
}
```

All very good, but now suppose that these classes are part of a software system that controls actual physical devices and that within these devices times are stored in registers as a count in units of hardware clock ticks. We could transform from our present representation into that of the devices at the point where times are transferred into the device's register (by a machine-dependent member function not included in the example) or we could use the number of clock ticks as the representation in the TimeSetting class. The change is easily accomplished. In the header file, all that needs altering is the private part of the class declaration.

```
private:
  int ticks;
```

This does mean that every program which includes this header must be recompiled, but they need not be changed in any other way. The public part of the class declaration is its interface, and that is still the same, so the class can be used in the same way, for example, by my `TimerEvent` class. The definitions of most of the member functions of `TimeSetting` must be rewritten, becoming rather more complicated in the process.

First I must define a constant for the number of clock ticks in a second.

```
const int ticks_per_sec = 50;
```

It will be convenient to use similar constants for the number of ticks in a minute and an hour, too. I think it is safe to assume that the number of seconds in a minute and the number of minutes in an hour is not going to change, so I don't mind using the actual numbers in the code, instead of defining more constants for these.

```
const int ticks_per_min = 60 * ticks_per_sec;
const int ticks_per_hour = 60 * ticks_per_min;
```

Armed with these constants, we can write the definitions of all the member functions. The conversions back and forth between ticks and hours and minutes are dull but not demanding.

```
void TimeSetting::init(int h, int m)
{
  assert (0 <= h && h < 24 &&
          0 <= m && m < 60);
  ticks = (h*60 + m)*ticks_per_min;
}
void TimeSetting::hrs_up()
{
  int hours = ticks/ticks_per_hour;
  int remainder = ticks%ticks_per_hour;
  hours = hours==23 ? 0 : hours+1;
  ticks = hours*ticks_per_hour + remainder;
}

void TimeSetting::hrs_down()
{
  int hours = ticks/ticks_per_hour;
  int remainder = ticks%ticks_per_hour;
  hours = hours==0 ? 23 : hours-1;
  ticks = hours*ticks_per_hour + remainder;
}

void TimeSetting::mins_up()
{
  int hours = ticks/ticks_per_hour;
  int mins = (ticks%ticks_per_hour)/ticks_per_min;
```

```
    mins = mins==59 ? 0 : mins+1;
    ticks = hours * ticks_per_hour + mins * ticks_per_min;
}

void TimeSetting::mins_down()
{
    int hours = ticks/ticks_per_hour;
    int mins = (ticks%ticks_per_hour)/ticks_per_min;
    mins = mins==0 ? 59 : mins-1;
    ticks = hours * ticks_per_hour + mins * ticks_per_min;
}

void TimeSetting::display() const
{
    int hours = ticks/ticks_per_hour;
    int mins = (ticks%ticks_per_hour)/ticks_per_min;
    cout << hours << ":" << mins;
}

int TimeSetting::secs_after_midnight() const
{
    return ticks/ticks_per_sec ;
}
```

The member function `set` is unchanged, since it is defined in terms of other
member functions. The class `TimerEvent`, and any other class or program that
uses `TimeSetting` will behave as before without being altered, except for possible changes to their performance. If you were developing a real system you
could swap between the two implementations to see which was more effective.

Summary

It is no exaggeration to say that classes are the most important part of C++—they
make the language what it is and put the ++ in C++. The full range of language
features associated with classes is quite extensive, but it all depends on the
basic ideas presented in this section, which are therefore worth summarizing.
    A class is a user-defined type. It consists of a collection of data members and
member functions. A class declaration introduces a new class, giving it a name
and declaring its members. Within the scope of the declaration, objects of the
class can be created and variables can be declared to hold them. Data members
can be accessed using the dot operator, which takes an expression (often a
single variable) denoting an object as its left operand and a member name
as its right operand. Member functions are called using the same notation,
with the arguments to the function, if any, given in brackets after the member
function's name.
    Members of a class can be either public or private; this is determined by
access specifiers which form part of the class declaration. If they are public,
they are in scope wherever the class is and can be accessed as just described.

If they are private, they may only be accessed within the class scope, which consists of the class declaration together with the definitions of member functions. (Member functions are defined separately from the class declaration.) Within the class scope, members may be accessed without using an object; implicitly, such unqualified use of the member name refers to the members of the object used to invoke the member function. Member functions and private data members provide an adequate means of implementing abstract datatypes, as illustrated in the example developed in the preceding section. This showed how information hiding can make the use of a type independent of its representation, so that its implementation can be changed without affecting any programs that use it (except, perhaps, for some change in their performance).

Extending classes as we have learnt about them with inheritance and dynamic binding would produce an object-oriented programming language. If we also provided some basic concrete data structures, that would be a useful programming tool. There is, though, an awkwardness and irregularity in the notations that it provides. Whereas I can write

```
int x = 0;
cout << "Old x = " << x << endl;
cout << "Enter a new one ";
cin >> x;
cout << "After incrementing, the value of x is "
     << ++x  << endl;
```

if I want to do something similar with time settings, I have to write

```
TimeSetting t;
t.init(0, 0);
cout << "Old t = ";
t.display();
cout << endl;
cout << "Enter a new one ";
t.set();
t.hrs_up();
cout << "After incrementing the hours, the value of t is ";
t.display();
cout << endl;
```

We can take two views of this. One is the austere view: the facilities are adequate for the job, what they lack in surface appearance is made up for by their simplicity. Notations are not that important—think of ==, or look at Lisp. The alternative view is more radical: notational convenience does matter, and user-defined types should be just as convenient to work with as built-in types. There is no room for second class types.

C++ is based on this radical view and plunges right in to elevate user-defined classes to the status of first class citizens of the type world. The ripples from this plunge will spread far, and the cost in language complexity of this decision will turn out to be considerable and to surface in unexpected places.

Pointers and Arrays

4

The class is the focus of data structuring in C++ but, in order to build the full range of data structures necessary for advanced programming, some further language facilities are required. A class only allows you to put together a collection of data values and treat them as a single object, using the member functions of the class. This is fine for some jobs, but doesn't allow you to do two important things that are often required in programs: First, it doesn't permit dynamic data structures—ones which can grow and shrink unpredictably as a program runs. Second, it doesn't support indexing—the selection of one out of a collection of objects by a numerical index value, computed dynamically. In a class, the only way to access a member is by using its name, which is a compile time constant. There is no way to select, say, the seventh data element, or the nth where n is the current value of a variable.

Most high level languages do support these two sorts of data structure, the first usually using some kind of pointer values, the second in the form of arrays, or vectors. There is considerable scope for variation in the precise language support for both these concepts. C++, in keeping with its aim of being, amongst other things, a systems programming language, offers support at a very low level indeed, using constructs that reflect the way these data structures are represented inside a machine. The pointer concept is much the same as that of a machine address, and arrays are just contiguous chunks of memory; indexing maps closely on to the use of index registers, and the equivalence of pointers and the addresses of array elements is explicit. All this is inherited directly from C.

The logically distinct concepts of pointer, array and object become gloriously confounded in C++. The result, though efficient and useful for low-level data representation and manipulation, is a potentially dangerous muddle. However, it is here that the data abstraction facilities of C++ begin to come into their own, as classes provide a way of wrapping up the primitive C data structures in more civilized and robust data types.

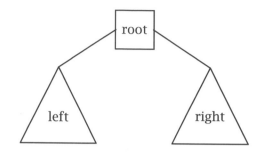

Figure 4.1 A binary tree consists of a root and two sub-trees

POINTERS

Many well-known useful data structures are most naturally defined recursively. For example, the usual definition of a binary tree is: A binary tree is either empty, or it consists of a node called its root and two binary trees, the left sub-tree and the right sub-tree (see figure 4.1). If you wanted trees with nodes holding strings, this definition might lead you to try and define a binary tree class with three data members, like this:

```
class Tree {
public:
  member functions providing the interface to this class
private:
  string TN_value;
  Tree left, right;
};
```

This won't work in C++, though, and the compiler would reject this class definition. You can find a rule forbidding it in the ARM. This is no arbitrary whim on the part of the language designer. The rule is the result of an underlying problem: the compiler can have no idea how much space to allocate for a `Tree` object. We know from the definition of a binary tree that there is a tree with no nodes, and that, for any tree with n nodes, there are trees with $n + 1$ and $n + 2$ nodes, but that is all we know. Putting it another way, every tree that isn't empty contains two trees, each of which, unless it is empty, contains two trees, and so on, with no *a priori* limit. Trees can be absolutely any size, but the poor compiler has to do its space allocation on the basis of the information in the program text alone, and here it cannot do so. The ARM rule amounts to saying that a class's name can only be used within its own definition where its size is not required to be known, so it effectively forbids such recursive class definitions.

What can be done? There's an old computer science folk saying that every problem can be solved by adding an extra level of indirection. This means that instead of storing an object at some location x, we store the object somewhere else and put its address at x. To access the object, instead of taking the contents of x and using them directly, we take the contents of x and then take the contents of the location whose address we found there. An address used in this way is called a pointer, and the indirect access just described is referred to as "following the pointer" or sometimes "dereferencing" it. Adding a level of indirection in this way means we use storage to hold the pointer and we have to use an extra memory cycle to dereference it, but in return we get the ability to use unbounded data structures. Pointers will certainly solve our present problem. We cannot know the size of a tree object, but we know the size of its address, so we can store that instead. A tree object is then represented as the node value and two pointers to the subtrees, so the compiler knows exactly how much space it occupies.

Where the pointers point is another story.

▷ It is quite possible to design a language where recursive data structures are permitted, but it cannot be implemented without some overhead. The easiest way to do it is to represent every value by a pointer and never store objects themselves. This is feasible for objects of user-defined classes, because that is what you often do anyway, but it causes a problem with built-in types. These are usually objects that can be efficiently stored in machine words and operated on by machine instructions, so insisting on always accessing them through pointers is going to incur a substantial overhead in both time and space. But trying to treat built-in types as a special case either leads to irregularities in the language's semantics, or to convoluted implementation techniques for distinguishing pointers from other values. At best, this will require the use of marker bits, at worst, some implementation-dependent strategy based on memory segmentation boundaries. With present-day architectures, there seems to be no alternative to using pointers whenever efficiency is considered important. (Which is not to say that pointers can't be included in a language ◁ in other ways than they are in C++.)

Creating Pointers

For every C++ type, whether user-defined or built-in, there is a corresponding pointer type. If T is a type, then the type of pointers to objects of type T is written as T*. For example, if we did define a class called Tree, then Tree* would be the type of pointers to Tree objects. Tree itself could then legally be defined as

```
class Tree {
public:
    member functions providing the interface to this class
private:
    string TN_value;
    Tree* left;
    Tree * right;
};
```

Although the name `Tree` is used within the class definition, it is only used to declare pointers, whose size is known, hence this definition, unlike the previous one, is not excluded by the rules forbidding recursive data structures.

The definition of pointer types can be applied recursively. That is, you can have pointers to pointers, such as `Tree**`. We will meet such things again later, as well as pointers to the built-in types, but, for now, we will concentrate on pointers to objects of user-defined classes.

Since a pointer type is a type, we can declare pointer variables and classes with pointer members, and functions taking pointer arguments or returning pointer results. There is a slight subtlety to the syntax here, explanation of which requires a slight digression.

If you have managed to declare a pointer variable, p, say, and store a pointer to some object in it, then you can follow the pointer using the prefix operator `*`. That is, `*p` is an expression whose value is the object which p points to. In C++, this is not a very useful or intelligent operation, but it was more so in C, and gave rise to the syntax used to declare pointer variables in C and C++. This is based on the principle that the declaration of a variable should mimic its usage. Now, if p is a pointer to objects of type T, then `*p` is of type T. The declaration of p is designed to look like a declaration of something (`*p`) of type T, thus:

```
T *p;
```

What, apart from the position of a space, is the difference between this and something that looks like a declaration of an object p of type T*? Nothing much, but it does explain the T* notation for pointer types, and the little difference there is provides a potential trap for the unwary. Suppose you like combining multiple declarations into a single one, like

```
int i, j;
```

You'd probably like to do the same for pointers. By analogy with integers, you might try to declare a couple of pointers to `Tree`s like this:

!
```
Tree* p, q;
```

Surprise! This declares one variable p of type `Tree*`, but the other, q, is of type `Tree`. The declaration is parsed so that the `*` is only applied to p. To the compiler, this looks like a declaration of two `Tree` variables, `*p` and q, if you like to think of it that way. So, to declare a pair of pointers to `Tree`s, you need stars before both names in the declaration:

```
Tree *p, *q;
```

Many C++ programmers prefer not to do this, because of the way the type information gets distributed through the declaration, and so they confine themselves to single declarations, as I did in my `Tree` class on the preceding page.

Declaring a pointer doesn't make it point to anything. Pointers that haven't been made to point to anything in fact can point to absolutely anything at all. Using such an undefined pointer is almost guaranteed to lead to disaster so it is a good idea to initialize a pointer variable when you declare it, to make sure that it points somewhere sensible. There are several ways to make it do so, some of them safer than others. We'll start with the safest and easiest. For any type T, the expression new T creates an object of type T and returns a pointer to it. So, if I had declared a TimeSetting class as in the previous chapter, I could create a TimeSetting object and obtain a pointer to it with the expression new TimeSetting. I might use this pointer to initialize a pointer variable:

```
TimerEvent *te_p = new TimerEvent;
```

The pointer variable te_p now points to an anonymous TimeSetting object that has been created. The expression *te_p denotes this object, so it makes sense to call the member functions of the TimeSetting class through it, for example (*te_p).confirm()—the brackets are needed because of operator precedence. In fact, the only sensible thing you can do with a pointer to an object is access the members (function and data) of that object. Because this is so common, the pointer following and member selection can be combined using a single infix operator, written ->. If *e* is an expression denoting a pointer to some object, and *mf* is a member function of that object's class, *e*->*mf* () is exactly equivalent to (*e*).*mf* (); similarly, if *d* is a data member, *e*->*d* is equivalent to (*e*).*d*. Thus, one would normally write, for example, te_p->confirm().

You can use const when you declare a pointer variable, but pointers require two different types of constancy, leading to two different usages. Suppose you have declared te_p as above to point to a TimerEvent object. Then you can change what te_p points to in two quite different ways. Either you can change the data members of the object pointed to, by calling a non-constant member function:

```
te_p->set()
```

or you can assign a different pointer to te_p:

```
te_p = a_nother_te_p ;
```

If you want to prevent all updates of the first sort—changes to the object pointed to—you must insert const before the type name in the declaration:

```
const TimerEvent *te_p = new TimerEvent;
```

(With our present knowledge, this would be pointless, since we could never initialize the object pointed to, but shortly we will see some pointers that it makes a lot of sense to declare in this way.) To prevent assignments which make the pointer point to a different object, const goes between the pointer type and the variable's name:

```
TimerEvent* const te_p = new TimerEvent;
```

To prevent both sorts of update, you use const in both positions:

```
const TimerEvent* const te_p = new TimerEvent;
```

It is possible that when new T is executed there will not be enough memory available for a T object. In that case, by default, your program will terminate more or less gracefully. On modern machines,[1] such a failure often indicates

---

[1] Provided they aren't running certain well-known alleged operating systems.

an error in program logic rather than genuine memory exhaustion, although requests for many large objects will eventually use up the biggest memory. We will discover in chapter 12 that you can alter the behaviour of a program when memory exhaustion does occur. I must warn you that old implementations of new may return the value zero to indicate failure. If you have such a version and you don't check, it is likely that your program will terminate rather less gracefully. We will also see in chapter 12 how to make old versions of new behave the way the standard says they are supposed to.

Sometimes, you want a pointer to point to nothing. By this I mean you want it to have a definite "null value", for example, to indicate an empty sub-tree or the end of a linked list—a quite different situation from an uninitialized pointer having a random unknown value. Defining a null pointer is a bit tricky, because a variable of type T* can only hold pointers to T objects; if we also want to allow it to hold a null pointer, what type is the null pointer? You only want to have one null pointer so you can compare any pointer to null. So it isn't going to work to say that there is a null pointer for each pointer type: one of type T1*, another of type T2*, yet another of type T1**...What you want to say is that the null pointer is of every pointer type, but this sounds a little strange, to say the least. Nevertheless, it is what most languages do, in effect.

C++ adds its own little twist to this: the null pointer is zero. That's zero, the integer. Or, to be strictly accurate, any constant expression that evaluates to zero is converted to the null pointer, and there's no other way of writing down a null pointer. The question of what the null pointer actually is (or are) is thus sidestepped. Furthermore, pointers can be used in conditions where a null pointer, being zero, is converted to false and any other pointer to true, so, if p is a variable of some pointer type,

```
if (p)
  cout << "p is not null";
else
  cout << "p is null";
```

is a code fragment that tells the truth. This is quite a neat idiom, even though it involves a sort of programming linguistic pun on the different meanings given to zero.

▷ Despite all this, null pointers need not be represented by the same bit patterns as zero, or even by a unique pattern of bits. The implicit conversions carried out by the compiler mean it behaves as though it was.

The ability of zero to be turned into a null pointer has some strange consequences. If p is a pointer variable, then

```
p = 2 + 2;
```

is a type error—trying to assign an int to a pointer—but

```
p = 2 - 2;
```

isn't, since 2 − 2 is a constant expression equal to zero, which can be converted to
◁ a null pointer and legitimately assigned. Madness, madness...

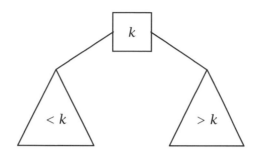

Figure 4.2   A binary search tree

Although C++ has no null pointer as such, many programmers like to behave as though it did. The library header `stddef.h` provides an implementation-dependent definition of a constant NULL, which will behave as if it was a null pointer.

Using Pointers

Now we'll look at pointers being used, by developing an implementation of a class of binary search trees. This also further demonstrates the definition and use of classes.

A binary search tree is a binary tree whose nodes contain values called keys, and every node satisfies the condition that, if the node's key is k, then all the keys in the left subtree are less than k and all those in the right are greater than k, according to some appropriate ordering of keys (see figure 4.2). This data structure permits simple and efficient lookup of stored keys. I will use a slightly different approach from the obvious one of defining a tree class with a key and two pointers to sub-trees. Although the basic data structure will be the same, I'll actually use two classes.

The first class is called `Tree`, and it has public member functions providing the operations to insert a key, which I'll take to be a string, and to determine whether a given string is present in the tree; it also has an operation to initialize a new `Tree` and one to print the entire tree structure, in increasing key order. (Since this isn't a book on data structures, I'll leave out the tricky operation of deleting a key.) It has only one data member, a pointer to an object of my other class, which I call `TreeNode`. The `Tree` class allows me to wrap this pointer up in an object with member functions, which simplifies, in particular, the handling of empty trees.

The class `TreeNode` is where the data are really stored, and where most of the work is done. A `TreeNode` comprises a key and two `Trees`, which are really just pointers to `TreeNodes`. The member functions of `TreeNode` are the same

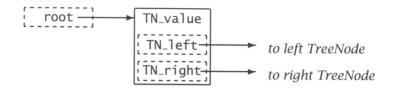

Figure 4.3   Data structure for binary search trees

as those of `Tree`; its initialization function must take a string as its argument and store it in the node. The jobs of inserting and looking up a string are distributed between the two classes. The data structure is illustrated in figure 4.3, where dashed boxes are `Tree` objects, and the solid box is a `TreeNode` object containing two `Trees`, each containing a pointer to a `TreeNode`.

   Notice that a `Tree` contains a pointer to a `TreeNode` and a `TreeNode` contains two `Trees`. The two classes are mutually recursive, which presents the same problem as mutually recursive functions: how can their definitions be ordered correctly? Again, they can't, and again, we have to adopt the expedient of putting a declaration of one of them before the definitions. A declaration of a class name consists of the reserved word `class` followed by the class name and a semicolon. However, with mutually recursive classes, things aren't quite as rosy as they were with mutually recursive functions. If you declare a class name, all you are telling the compiler is that there is a class of that name. You are telling it nothing about how big objects of that class are. (Here we go again!) Consequently, if you declare a class without defining it, you can only declare pointers to objects of that class. Since `TreeNodes` contain `Trees`, not pointers to them, I can't put the definition of the class `TreeNode` before that of `Tree`. Fortunately, since `Trees` only contain a pointer to a `TreeNode`, I can get away with doing it the other way round.

   Figure 4.4 on the next page shows a header file that defines the two classes. The code for the member functions of both classes is very short. First, the usual *pourparlers*. We'll be using iostreams, NULL, and, of course, the declarations for the tree classes.

```
#include <iostream>
#include <stddef.h>
#include "tree.hpp"
```

The member functions of the `Tree` class come first. Initializing a `Tree` object consists in setting its root pointer to NULL—you shouldn't ever rely on the system doing this for you, because it won't.

```
void Tree::init()
```

```
#include <string>

class TreeNode;

class Tree  {
public:
  void init();
  void insert(const string& s);
  bool find(const string& s) const;
  void print() const;
private:
  TreeNode* root;
};

class TreeNode  {
public:
  void init(const string& s);
  void insert(const string& s);
  bool find(const string& s) const;
  void print() const;
private:
  string TN_value;
  Tree TN_left;
  Tree TN_right;
};
```

Figure 4.4 Header file for tree classes

```
{
  root = NULL;
}
```

There are two cases to consider for each of the other operations: either the root pointer is NULL or it points to a TreeNode. In the case of insertion, if the root is NULL, then we must get a pointer to a new TreeNode object and store the string in that, using its init function. If the root was already pointing to a TreeNode, we just pass the string on to its insert function to do the actual work.

```
void Tree::insert(const string& s)
{
  if (root == NULL)
  {
    root = new TreeNode;
    root->init(s);
  }
  else root->insert(s);
}
```

The `find` operation fails if the root is NULL—the key can't possibly be there in an empty tree; if the root isn't NULL, we call the `find` member of the `TreeNode` it is pointing to. Here I use the equivalence between NULL and `false`, as well as the lazy behaviour of `&&`.

Is this slick, or just obscure?

```
bool Tree::find(const string& s) const
{
    return root && root->find(s);
}
```

The case of an empty root is especially simple for the `print` member function. If the root is empty, there is nothing to print; otherwise, hand over to the `TreeNode`, as usual.

```
void Tree::print() const
{
    if (root) root->print();
}
```

That is all that the `Tree` class needs to do. Now for the `TreeNode` class. Initializing a `TreeNode` means setting its left and right sub-trees to NULL, and its value to the key passed as an argument to the function. We know how to set the left and right sub-trees, that's what the `init` member of a `Tree` does, and the storing of the key can be done by a simple assignment.

```
void TreeNode::init(const string& s)
{
    TN_left.init();
    TN_right.init();
    TN_value = s;
}
```

Because the binary tree is a recursive data structure, the easiest way to write the operations on it is recursively. Here the recursion is indirect, as the `insert` member function of `TreeNode` calls that of `Tree`, which may then call that of `TreeNode` again, and so on. All this function needs to do is find out which of its sub-trees to insert the key into. This means comparing it with the key in this particular node. Rather than use the usual comparison operators on strings, I shall use a member function called `compare`. This returns a number less than, equal to, or greater than zero, depending on whether the string it is called through is less than, equal to, or greater than its argument (in dictionary order). By using `compare` and remembering the result, I avoid potential duplication of the expensive comparison operation on strings. We are only interested in the less than and greater than possibilities—if the two are equal, we do nothing at all, since a binary search tree should not contain duplicate keys. The result of the comparison is used to select a sub-tree to insert the key into. The recursion will continue, until eventually an empty tree is found, when the key will actually get inserted, by `Tree::insert`, as we just saw.

```
void TreeNode::insert(const string& s)
{
    int cf = s.compare(TN_value);
```

```
    if (cf < 0)
      TN_left.insert(s);
    else if (cf > 0)
        TN_right.insert(s);
}
```

The find operation works by a similar indirect recursion through Tree::find. Here, of course, the possibility that the argument is equal to the stored value *is* interesting. Again, use is made of laziness, in this case of ||, to permit a compact formulation.

```
bool TreeNode::find(const string& s) const
{
  int cf = s.compare(TN_value);
  return cf==0 || (cf < 0?
    TN_left.find(s): TN_right.find(s));
}
```

You should be able to write print for yourself by now. The pattern is the same one of indirect recursion. Tree::print handles the end case, making sure the recursion unwinds. The ordering of keys ensures that, by recursing to the left before printing the value of the current node and to the right after, all the keys come out in the required order.

```
void TreeNode::print() const
{
  TN_left.print();
  cout << TN_value << endl;
  TN_right.print();
}
```

You might find this way of organizing the classes too elaborate, or just too cute. It's worthwhile rewriting this example without using the intermediary class Tree to hide the pointers. You have to be careful with the null pointers.

You may also be worried about efficiency. As far as space efficiency goes, there is no cause for concern. A Tree object occupies only the space needed for its single data member, so a TreeNode as defined here is exactly the same size as one with two TreeNode* data members. There may be some additional time overhead incurred by the extra calls of Tree member functions. We will see later what we can do to prevent this, although it should be said that an optimizing compiler might well eliminate these calls entirely anyway. The main source of inefficiency is in the recursive formulation of the insert and find functions, but that is independent of the class organization employed.

Addresses and Pointers

The operator new creates an anonymous object and returns its address. Provided you keep a calm head and draw lots of diagrams made up of boxes and arrows, working with data structures built out of pointers created in this way is fairly easy. There are two other ways of creating pointers; one will be described in the next section, the other is nasty and dangerous. I will describe it mainly in order to tell you why you shouldn't use it.

The prefix operator & enables you to create a pointer to an existing object. If v is a variable, the expression &v denotes its address; that is, &v is a pointer to whatever is held in v, so if v is of type T, &v is of type T*. For example:

!

```
TimeSetting video_on;
video_on.init(0, 0);
video_on.set();
TimeSetting *v_on_pntr = &video_on;
```

v_on_pntr is now a pointer to the TimeSetting object held in video_on whose value has just been set. Why the ! in the margin? Because this means that the value held in video_on can be changed without any mention of the variable's name, for example

```
v_on_pntr->hrs_up();
```

And you've missed Babylon5

You have just advanced the time at which your VCR comes on by one hour, but no operation appears to have been applied to the variable video_on. Nevertheless, the member function call video_on.display() will show the later time. I could have passed this pointer into a function and performed the update far away in the code from any mention of video_on. The & operator creates a second way of accessing the value of a variable, which always holds the potential for obscure manipulations and tricky code that is hard to understand. (Of course, *you* understand it, but spare a thought for the graduate entrant trainee programmer whose first job is to upgrade your program after you've left to become a senior software engineer with MegaProg Corporation.) One best-selling text on C++ contains the statement that "A pointer variable... contains an address, usually the address of another variable". Let us all hope that this is not true.

▷ In C, there was a legitimate reason for using &. Because C does not support argument passing by reference, if you want to return a value from a function through its argument, the only thing you can do is pass an address as the argument and use it as a pointer. For example, the sum and product function from page 41 could have been declared with pointer arguments instead of reference ones:

```
void sum_and_product(int lower, int upper,
                     int* sum, int* product)
```

Then, the assignments to the arguments which finally return the values would have had to use indirection on these pointers:

```
*sum = partialsum;
*product = partialproduct;
```

and the function would have had to be called with the addresses of the variables that were to receive the computed values, for example,

```
sum_and_product(1, 10, &s, &p);
```

In C++, reference arguments provide a more convenient mechanism for achieving the same effect. Nevertheless, a reference is a synonym, so, even in the restricted context of argument passing, references that are not constant should be used with ◁ care.

One other hazard of taking addresses will be described in the next section.

Pointers to variables do occur in C++ in another, possibly unexpected, guise. Whenever a member function is called through an object, a pointer to that object is created. It can be accessed inside the member function via the name `this`, which is a reserved word, but behaves like a `const` variable. For example, if `aTree` is a variable of type `Tree` and I call `aTree.insert("orinoco")`, then, during this call, within `Tree::insert`, `*this` is equal to `aTree` (i.e., `this==&aTree`). Uses of member names such as `root` are abbreviations for indirections through this pointer, such as `this->root`. (This may help assure some readers, who have been burned by pointer manipulations in other languages, that `Tree::insert` really does update the right location when it creates its new `TreeNode`.) The implicit access of members through `this` means that it is rarely necessary to use the pointer's name explicitly. It is needed, though, to write member functions to insert elements into linked list structures.

Lifetime

There is a school of thought which holds that programmers who use a high level programming language should not be concerned with how it is implemented on a machine. This is understandable, since high level languages are supposed to let us get away from the details of computer operation. The alternative view is that you shouldn't use powerful tools like C++ without knowing something about what's going on, otherwise you might get hurt. Certainly, there are some aspects of the behaviour of C++ programs that can be easily understood with the help of a little knowledge about the language's implementation, but are somewhat hard to grasp without it. The lifetime of values is one such aspect.

What you need to know to understand lifetime is how variables in a C++ program are related to memory locations when the program runs. If there was no recursion, this would be trivial. In C++, the size of the objects that can be stored in a variable is known at compile time, so it is possible for the compiler to calculate the total amount of storage required for all the variables declared in a function and to allot a suitably sized area of memory to that function. Arguments are treated in the same way as local variables and a separate area is used for globals. Every use of a variable name in the program can be mapped to a memory access at a unique location.

But there is recursion, so that won't work. Consider this:

```
void rec()
{
  char c;
  cin >> c;
  if (c != '!') rec();
```

```
        cout << c;
    }
```

Amuse
yourself
for hours
When `rec` is first called, it reads characters from the standard input up to a ! and then echoes them in reverse order, the local variable `c` being used to remember each character while the following ones are read and then echoed as the recursion unwinds. If `c` was associated with a unique storage location this wouldn't work; the location would be overwritten with each new character as it was read and so the effect would be that, as the recursion unwound, the terminating ! would be written out over and over again. It is necessary for a new location to be allocated to `c` each time `rec` is called recursively, but we can't know in advance how many times it will be called, so the compiler can't know how many locations to reserve for `c`. The space will have to be allocated at runtime. What is required is a new region of store to hold the locals and arguments of a function every time it is called. Such a region is called an activation record. The compiler knows how big an activation record must be for each function, it just doesn't know how many of them are needed.

It is almost self-evident that if a function, p, calls another, q, the execution of q is wholly contained in that of p. That is, p is executing before the call of q and when q returns, control returns to p, which then carries on until it returns in turn. Similarly for recursive functions, if p calls itself, the execution of p resulting from this new call is wholly contained in the execution of p that made the call. And so on for recursive calls inside the recursive call: function calls and returns are properly nested. Putting it another way, the last call made is the first to return. Last-in, first-out? It follows that activation records can be allocated on a runtime stack. When a function is called, a new activation record is pushed on the stack; the locations within it corresponding to arguments are suitably initialized and control passes to the called function. If this calls itself recursively, a new activation record will be created for the new call. When the function returns, the current activation record is popped off the stack; the activation record thus exposed will be the one corresponding to the caller, which is about to resume execution. A current activation record pointer (probably held in a register) points to the base of the current activation record, and locals and arguments can be accessed using fixed offsets from this pointer. The compiler has enough information to compute these offsets and generate code accordingly.

Figure 4.5 shows how the runtime stack grows and then shrinks as the function `rec` is called with the input C++!. Each diagram shows the input, stack and output at successive stages in the computation. The arrow points to the base of the current activation record, the shaded area at the base of each activation record indicates locations used by the C++ system to hold administrative information, such as the return address for the call. Above this is the location in the activation record corresponding to the local variable `c`, showing the value stored for each recursive call.

The stack-based allocation of activation records is necessary for recursion and sufficient for all other function calls. It is the method of runtime space allocation invariably used by C++ implementations. Some of its consequences affect the way you can use pointers.

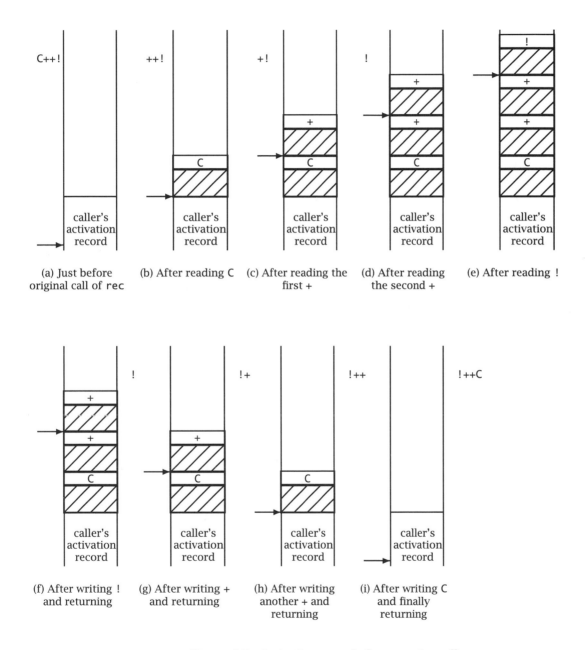

Figure 4.5   Activation records for recursive calls

Consider this attempt to allocate and initialize the nodes in a tree without using new.

```
TreeNode* new_TreeNode(const string& s)
{
  TreeNode TN;
  TN.init(s);
  return &TN;
}
```

which might be used inside Tree::insert.

```
void Tree::insert(const string& s)
{
  if (root == NULL)
    root = new_TreeNode(s);
  else root->insert(s);
}
```

I have actually seen programmers try to write code like this. Their programs failed to live long and prosper. The problem is that the space for the TreeNode object is reserved inside the current activation record for newTreeNode when it is called. You can think of the object as occupying three memory locations within that activation record on top of the runtime stack. The value of &TN is the address of the first of these, so after newTreeNode returns, root is updated to point there. But because newTreeNode has returned, the pointer isn't pointing into an activation record any more. It is simply pointing to a region of store which is almost certainly going to be re-used for a new activation record when some function is called later.

A pointer like this is said to be "dangling", because it points into memory that, conceptually, isn't there anymore. The fact that it is still really there, but might get re-used at any time means that dangling pointers can lead to very strange behaviour. One of two things might happen when a new activation record gets built in the space the dangling pointer is pointing to. Either the space occupied by the data members of the object originally pointed to might get over-written with new values, so that stored data might suddenly change, or linked data structures become broken; or, member functions called through the pointer might assign to data members and overwrite data in the activation record for some function, whose local variables would change value unexpectedly. It is also possible that such operations could overwrite the system house-keeping information kept in activation records, and corrupt the entire runtime environment of the program.

The ultimate effects of dangling pointer bugs can vary. If you're very lucky, they will cause your program to crash more or less immediately. However, if the call to the function returning the dangling pointer is deep in a call chain, it may be some time before anything goes wrong. It is even possible that nothing will go wrong before the program terminates, and you get away with it... until one day you add a new function and suddenly the program crashes or starts producing wrong answers. This is when you frantically start trying to find something wrong with the code you've just added, when the real bug is somewhere else in a part of the program you believe to have been working for ages.

The moral is simple and clear: Never, ever, write a C++ function that returns a pointer to one of its local variables. If you want an object to be used beyond the end of a function call, allocate it using new.

You need to know roughly what new does. It finds enough space to hold the object being created, if it can, in a separate area of memory, away from the stack, called the heap. A heap can be organized in a variety of clever ways (consult a good data structures book),[2] but all of them have the effect of partitioning it into a used and a free area. When you call new, space is allocated from the free area and moved to the used area, and a pointer to it is returned. The storage this points to is entirely unaffected by any activation records being popped off or pushed on the runtime stack, so the pointer can safely be returned from inside a function or stored in a data structure.

But one of the nice things about using a stack of activation records is that the space they occupy is automatically recovered when it is no longer needed. It is often the case that objects from the heap are only required for a limited time, even though they must persist beyond a single function call. Unless some way is provided of recovering these objects, the heap might get used up.

In C++, it is the programmer's responsibility to return objects to the heap when they are no longer required. If p is a pointer that was originally allocated with new, then the statement

```
delete p;
```

has the effect of returning the object p points at to the free area of the heap. This sounds simple, but it is still possible to get it wrong.

If the pointer was created some other way than with new, the effect of delete p is officially undefined, but almost bound to be disastrous. If you try and use p's pointer after it has been deleted, the effect is officially undefined, but it, too, is almost bound to be disastrous. So is the effect of trying to delete p twice. Deleting the null pointer is always safe, though, and does nothing.

More subtle problems can arise in connection with delete, as a result of failing to delete things you should have deleted. It isn't always easy to be sure that an object isn't needed any more, so you might fail to insert a call of delete somewhere, or just not bother. Failure to do so leads to an insidious sort of bug, graphically termed a "memory leak": memory that could be recovered is not. If this goes on long enough, the heap will eventually become exhausted. This could take a long time and perhaps only show up on big runs or after many hours of runtime (remember, some programs are designed never to terminate). An easy way of causing memory leaks for beginners lies in failing to delete pointers within an object. If, for example, I wanted to clean up my binary trees, it would be inadequate to add the following member function:

---

[2]If you don't have any good data structures books, there are some suggestions on page 347.

```
       void Tree::cleanup()
!      {
         delete root;
       }
```

All this does is delete the `TreeNode` pointed to by `root`; it doesn't delete its subtrees, or their subtrees, and so on. What is needed is a recursive cleanup that traverses the whole tree from the bottom up.

```
       void Tree::cleanup()
       {
         if (root)
         {
           root->cleanup();
           delete root;
         }
       }

       void TreeNode::cleanup()
       {
         TN_left.cleanup();
         TN_right.cleanup();
       }
```

▷ Many languages that need a heap relieve the programmer of the responsibility for recovering heap objects by using an "automatic garbage collector". This is a part of the runtime system which identifies unreachable objects on the heap and deletes them for you. The garbage collector is usually a function that gets called when the heap becomes used up. The trouble with garbage collection is that it imposes an overhead which may be unacceptable in many applications for which C++ is used: if garbage collection is done naïvely, everything suddenly stops while the collector does its work. Avoiding this behaviour by running garbage collection in parallel with computation requires some very tricky algorithms. Garbage collection may also impose a space overhead on all objects. Stroustrup maintains that it is possible for those who want to do so to plug optional garbage collection into C++. I don't believe it, since good garbage collectors have to be designed into the system from the start, otherwise the job of identifying pointers at runtime may be impossible. It is possible to garbage collect objects of selected classes if they are only used in restricted ways, but for most C++ programmers, memory management is something that needs to be done by hand. There are software tools available that can help by
◁ monitoring `new` and `delete` and diagnosing memory leaks.

ARRAYS

You can solve any data structuring problem by using pointers to construct trees, lists and all the usual linked data structures that will be familiar to any experienced programmer. Doing so provides you with flexible, dynamic, data structures, but it may not enable you to take full advantage of your machine's efficient addressing operations. In particular, if your data can be represented as an ordered sequence of elements, they can usefully be stored in consecutive memory elements. Accessing an element anywhere in the sequence can be done efficiently, usually through an index register, in a single memory access; if the same sequence is held in a linked list, it is necessary to follow a chain of pointers, so that accessing the ith element requires i memory accesses (except, perhaps, for the last element). In order to support efficient consecutive sequential storage, C++ provides an additional form of data aggregate, called the array.

An array is an aggregate that can store a fixed number of objects, all of the same type, in an ordered fashion. It permits the operation of subscripting, also called indexing, to access a specific object given an integer index corresponding to its position in the sequence. An array will be stored in a contiguous chunk of memory, so that this operation will be efficiently implemented. Indexed arrays can be used in expressions, when the stored value of an element is required, and on the left hand side of an assignment, to update its value.

Indexing and Declaration of Arrays

Since all the elements of an array must be of the same type, and the array is of a fixed size, there is an infinite number of array types, each of the form `array of T of size` N, where T is a built-in or user-defined type, and N is an integer greater than zero. If a is an array of some type, of size n and *exp* is an integer expression, whose value i lies between 0 and $n - 1$ inclusive, then a[*exp*] denotes the $(i-1)^{th}$ element of a. This is the first practical joke arrays can play on you: if the size of the array is N, the subscripts range from 0 to N-1, so a[0] is the first element, a[1] the second, and so on, until a[N-1] (*not* a[N]) is the last. You will get this wrong at least once. And later, after you've got used to it, you'll get it wrong again. Everyone does, from time to time, even though there's a good case for maintaining that this is the "right" way to count.

The following loop will print out each element of an array of size N.

```
for (int i = 0; i <= N-1; ++i)
    cout << a[i];
```

This shows what the header of any loop that traverses an array doing something to each element must look like. (The test can, of course, be replaced by i < N, if you prefer, to reflect the form of the array's declaration. Or even i != N if you feel very confident.)

The second practical joke is that, although a[i] is only defined if 0 ≤ i < N, neither the C++ compiler nor the runtime system is able to check whether any expression you use as an array subscript is within range. If you use an index outside the defined range, you will access some other memory location and be rewarded with wrong answers, corrupt data or a program crash.

As with pointers, the syntax for declaring an array mimics its use, in this case, subscripting. The syntax is

```
type [size];
```

where *size*, the number of elements, is a constant expression. For example,

```
int a[100];      declare an array of 100 integers...
Tree copse[50];      ...and one of 50 trees.
```

Extending the notation again, you can refer to the type of these two arrays as `int[100]` and `Tree[50]`, respectively.

Some care is needed when you mix pointers and arrays. Is

```
TreeNode *a[10];
```

a declaration of an array of ten pointers to `TreeNode`s, or a pointer to an array of ten `TreeNode`s? Under the rule that declaration mimics use, either is plausible. In fact, it is taken to be an array of pointers, which is probably what you want. If you do want to declare a pointer to an array, you must use brackets to force the right interpretation, as in

```
TreeNode (*p)[10];
```

Array declarations can be global, with file scope, or local, with function scope. Arrays can also be members of classes. In all these cases, it is necessary for the compiler to be able to compute the size of the array so it can allocate space for it. This is why the size in an array declaration must be a constant expression; the array is said to have "static bounds".

▷ Some compilers, notably GNU C++, do allow you to declare arrays whose size is not a constant expression, but is computed at runtime. Code that relies on this extension is not portable to other compilers. It is always foolish to rely on features ◁ not included in the standard.

Arrays are normally used inside classes when the natural representation of an abstract datatype is an ordered sequence and the type's operations require access to arbitrary elements of the sequence. Because of arrays' fixed size, it is always necessary to ensure that an array does not fill up, and array representations are only appropriate if this is unlikely to occur.

As an example of a class containing an array, here is another staple data structure: the queue, or first-in, first-out sequence. This can be efficiently stored in what is called a circular array, which is just an ordinary array, accessed in a particular way.

A queue is like a line of well-behaved customers waiting to be served in a bank: people join it at the end and leave it (to be served) from the front, without changing places in the order, dropping out or pushing in. Translated into programming terms, this means we want an abstract datatype with operations to add an item to the end (`enqueue`, as they say) and remove an item from the front (`dequeue`, why not?). It turns out that it is most useful to have a separate operation, let's call it `front`, that returns the item at the front of the queue while leaving it there, instead of having `dequeue` return this item. It is also useful to have an operation `length`, which tells us how many items are presently in the queue, and a Boolean function `empty`, which is true if and only if there are no items in the queue. We will also need an `init` operation to set up a new queue.

```
#include <string>

const int queue_size = 500;

class StringQueue {
public:
  void init();
  void enqueue(const string&);
  void dequeue();
  string front() const;
  int length() const;
  bool empty() const;
  bool full() const;
private:
  string the_queue[queue_size];
  int the_front, the_back;
};
```

Figure 4.6   Definition of a Queue class, implemented as a circular array

The implementation strategy is this: queue items will be stored in consecutive elements of an array, the_queue. Two integer members will remember the indices of the front and back of the queue; when an item is inserted, it is put in the_queue[the_back] and the_back is incremented; when an item is removed from the front, the_front is incremented, so at any time, provided the_back and the_front start out with the same value, the items in the queue occupy the_queue[the_front] to the_queue[the_back 1], and this occupied region moves up the array as a series of enqueue and dequeue operations occurs. Eventually, the_back will exceed the size of the array. At this point, it is reset to zero (as if the elements of the array were arranged in a circle) and the locations at the bottom of the array are re-used. Obviously, if there is a long run of enqueue operations with no dequeuing, it is possible for the_back to catch up with the_front—the queue is full. It is convenient to supply an operation full, which returns true when this condition occurs. A whimsical twist to this is that, if there are no free locations, the_back is equal to the_front—exactly the situation that prevails when the queue is empty. It is customary, therefore, to say that the queue is full when there is only one free location in the array.

Once you've got the idea, implementing a queue as a circular array is easy. Figure 4.6 shows a suitable header file for a queue of strings. The constant queue_size has an arbitrary value; for a real application, it would have to be chosen on the basis of analysis or measurement to be large enough to hold the longest anticipated queue. Later, we will see ways of parameterizing the class definition in this size, or using a computed value at runtime.

The definitions of the member functions are all extremely short. Partly this is because of the cavalier attitude I have adopted towards error handling. It should be evident that the enqueue operation is undefined if the queue is full, and `dequeue` is undefined if it is empty. Since the class provides operations to test these two conditions, I have assumed that the user of the class will take responsibility for doing suitable checks before attempting any operation that might fail. Assertions in the code make sure that a bad operation will cause a relatively graceful crash. Additionally, I have dealt with the wrapping round of indices by using modular arithmetic, that is, instead of doing something like

```
the_back += 1;
if (the_back == queue_size)
  the_back = 0;
```

I have simply added one to `the_back` and taken the remainder after division by `queue_size`. It probably doesn't make much difference to efficiency either way, it's just...a certain style. Apart from these points, the code doesn't seem to need further commentary; it is shown in its entirety in Figure 4.7.

Arrays let you store linear sequences of objects. Sometimes, your information is most naturally represented as a table of objects. Many languages generalize the idea of arrays to multi-dimensional arrays—tabular, or matrix-like storage structures, indexed by more than one subscript. For example, to represent the distances between each of a set of towns, I could assign a number to each town and store the distances in a two-dimensional table d, such that the entry in column j of row i of that table, d_{ij}, was the distance between the ith and j^{th} towns.

C++ provides multi-dimensional arrays in the form of arrays of arrays. This falls out quite cleanly from the existing notation. Sort of. If, for example, d is an array of arrays of integers, `d[i]` must be an array of integers, so `d[i][j]` will be an integer, and so d can be treated as a two-dimensional table, as required, even if the notation is a bit clumsy. (Don't try writing `d[i,j]`—you'll get quite a surprise.) But how do I declare such a thing?

Here is a suitable declaration of d

```
int d[50][50];
```

whose meaning is pretty obvious, since again it mimics the usage for indexing d. If you like, you can think of declaring `d[50]` to be of type `int[50]`. The sizes of each array dimension need not all be the same, of course. The first size declared is the range of the first subscript, and so on, so if M is declared by

```
int M[N1][N2][N3];
```

then, in a subscripted expression `M[i1][i2][i3]`, i1 must lie between 0 and N1-1, i2 between 0 and N2-1 and i3 between 0 and N3-1. Expressions such as `M[i]` are legal and meaningful, provided i is in range.

It is possible to initialize the elements of an array when you declare it. An initialized array declaration has the syntax

```
type name[ size ] = { value { , value } };
```

For example

```
int smallprimes[9] = {2, 3, 5, 7, 11, 13, 17, 19, 23};
```

```
#include <iostream>
#include <assert.h>
#include "queue.hpp"

void StringQueue::init()
{
  the_front = the_back = 0;
}

void StringQueue::enqueue(const string& a_string)
{
  assert(!full());
  the_queue[the_back] = a_string;
  the_back = (the_back + 1)%queue_size;
}

void StringQueue::dequeue()
{
  assert(!empty());
  the_front = (the_front + 1)%queue_size;
}

string StringQueue::front() const
{
  assert (!empty());
  return the_queue[the_front];
}

int StringQueue::length() const
{
  return (queue_size + the_back - the_front)%queue_size;
}

bool StringQueue::empty() const
{
  return the_front == the_back;
}

bool StringQueue::full() const
{
  return length() == queue_size - 1;
}
```

Figure 4.7   Definitions of the queue member functions

Since the compiler can count, it can deduce the size of the array from the number of values in the initializer, so you can, if you wish, omit the *size*. It's hard to see what you gain by doing so, generally. On the other hand, you gain a little extra safety and control over the initialization by including it, because if the number of initializing values exceeds the declared bounds of the array, an error is reported; if there are fewer values than array elements, the trailing elements corresponding to the missing values are set to zero (converted to the appropriate type). For multi-dimensional arrays, nested initializers can be used:

```
int d[2][3] = {{0,1}, {1,0}, {1,1}};
```

You can omit the inner braces, but it just makes life complicated, especially when you consider missing values in the initializers.

Arrays and Pointers

Arrays and pointers embody two different approaches to low-level data representation. The array is sequential and efficient, but fixed in size; the pointer allows you to build flexible dynamic data structures at a price in efficiency. It is as well to have this distinction clear, because in C++ an array is a pointer. To be precise, if a[N] has been declared as an array of some type T, then a can be used as a pointer of type T* to its first element, that is, a is identical to &a[0].

Heavy handed irony

Why? Because in practice, this is how an array will be represented at run-time: a location corresponding to it is initialized to point to the area where the elements are stored, so these can be accessed using indirection and indexing on the pointer. You may argue with the wisdom of making this implementation detail visible in the language, but the equivalence of arrays and pointers is the basis of several well established C programming idioms, which continue in C++. The ability to write *a instead of a[0] is not going to get you very far on its own. However, when a pointer points to an array element you can do arithmetic on it, too.

Suppose you have declared an array A of size N and type T. Any pointer of type T* whose value lies between &A[0] and &A[N] is said to point into A. Now, if p is a pointer into A, let's say with value &A[i], and j is an integer, then p+j is a pointer into A with value &A[i+j], provided i+j is not greater than N. That is, if you have a pointer into an array and add *j* to it, you get a pointer to the object *j* elements further along in the array. The number added to the numerical value of the pointer (the number of bytes, if pointers are byte addresses) depends on the size of the elements of the array, which in turn depends on their type.

Subtraction of integers from pointers works the same way, and you can use the shorthand assigning operators +=, -=, ++ and -- on pointers. Finally, if p1 and p2 are both pointers into the same array, p1-p2 gives the number of elements between them (again, not necessarily the number of bytes). The arithmetic operations on pointers imply an ordering of pointer values, and it is possible to use the comparison operators on pointers into the same array, with the expected results. That is, p1 < p2 if p1 == &A[i], p2 == &A[j] and i < j, and so on.

You can't do any other sort of arithmetic on pointers, and it's dubious whether you should even do this much, because it is not possible for the compiler to check that your pointer operations are in range, and the runtime system won't do it for you. If they are not, the usual tiresome consequences may result.

I have an old copy of an early tutorial on C, which makes the strange claim that the most common use of pointers is to step through arrays. What this unlikely statement means is that you can access the elements of an array in turn by incrementing a pointer, like this:

```
const int N = 10;
int a[N] =  { 0, 1, 2, 3, 4, 5, 6, 7, 8, 9 };
int *p = a, *end = &a[N];
while (p < end)
   cout << *p++ << " ";
```

instead of

```
int i = 0;
while (i < N)
   cout << a[i++] << " ";
```

(If you were puzzled as to why &a[N] is allowed to be a pointer into a, even though a[N] isn't an element of a, you know now.) Stepping through arrays with pointers is usually done in the belief that it is more efficient, a belief that may well not be justified in the context of modern optimizing compilers and high performance processor architectures.

Pointer arithmetic is helpful in explaining what is going on with subscripting. By definition, a[e] means *(a+e). You notice that this is equal to *(e+a) and, yes, you really can write e[a] to mean the same thing. This does look a lot like the notation used in many assemblers for indexing off a register, but writing things like 2[a] in C++ is unusual, at best playful, more likely precious.

▷ A multi-dimensional array is an array of arrays, and no less of an array for that, so it too can be used as a pointer to its first element, and subscripting is defined in the same way. Let's look at an example to see this working. Suppose I have declared

```
int a[3][4];
```

an array of integers, with three rows and four columns. What is a[2]? It is *(a+2), where a is treated as a pointer to the array's first element; this element is the first of three arrays of four integers. The addition is done by adding twice the size of each element that a points to, since this is pointer arithmetic, so a+2 is a pointer to the third of these arrays of four integers, *(a+2) is therefore a pointer to the first element of this third array, meaning that a[2] is, as you would hope, an array of type int[4], so that expressions like a[2][3] make sense and identify an individual entry in the 3 × 4 matrix.

If you think about what this must mean in terms of the layout of multidimensional arrays in memory, you'll see that the elements of each row of a two-dimensional array are laid out one after the other and access to individual elements is done by computing an offset from the base of the whole array. To do this computation, the compiler must know the second (and subsequent) dimension of the array. So, despite what you may have thought, even though an array is a pointer, an array of arrays is not an array of pointers. However, you *can* have such a thing, ◁ and may often be better off with it.

Even if you eschew pointer arithmetic, you cannot get away from the fact that an array is a pointer to its first element, unless you avoid passing arrays as arguments to functions, because when you do so, it is the pointer which is used to initialize the formal argument. Any updates to an array argument will affect the storage that the formal argument points to—that is, the elements of the actual argument array—even though the argument is passed by value. For example

```
void swap(int A[10], int i, int j)
{
  int t = A[i];
  A[i] = A[j];
  A[j] = t;
}
```

when called with `swap(an_array, 2, 7)` really will swap the third and eighth elements of `an_array`. There is no way to pass an array to a function "by array value", as it were, creating a separate array to initialize the formal, so that updates are not propagated back to the actual argument in the caller. In effect, arrays are always passed by reference. This is often what you want, since arrays can be large objects which you might prefer not to copy all over the place. Still, it would be nice to have the choice, as you have with all other objects.[3]

The pointer is the only thing which gets passed as an array argument. No information about the size of the array goes with it. Not only that, the compiler does not check that the size declared for an array formal argument matches the size of the array used as an actual argument. To be fair, this is not possible, in general, and is often more of a nuisance than a help, as experienced Pascal programmers will testify, but it can come as a surprise to learn that, with `swap` declared as above, the following will compile without so much as a warning, despite the errors staring you in the face.

```
int a1[10];
int a2[20];
int a3[5];
swap(a1, 2, 7);      a1 is the right size
swap(a2, 2, 7);      a2 is too big
swap(a3, 2, 7);      a3 is too small—there is no a3[7]
```

The size in the declaration of an array argument is just window-dressing and may be omitted. Many—probably most—C++ programmers prefer to come clean and declare array arguments as being of the appropriate pointer type. Either of the following is a possible declaration of `swap`:

```
void swap(int[], int, int);
void swap(int*, int, int);
```

---

[3]You can hack it, by declaring a class with an array as a public member, wrapping up your array in an object of that class and passing the object, but there are better things to do with classes with array members.

If you want to do range checking on array accesses, or anything else that depends on the size, inside a function then you must pass the size explicitly as a separate argument.

▷ Things get worse when we come to pass multi-dimensional arrays to functions. If, extrapolating from the single dimension case, you try to declare a function to swap a pair of elements of a two-dimensional array like this

```
void swap2D(int m[][], int i1, int j1, int i2, int j2,
            int nrows, int ncols);
```

you will get an error message complaining of an "incomplete type" for the matrix m. This is because, in order to compute m[i1][j1], the compiler needs to know ncols, otherwise it doesn't know how to compute *(m+i1). Nor will declaring the argument m as int** work—that's an array of pointers, which is different from an array of arrays, as I mentioned before. You can get away with omitting the first size, since this isn't needed to compute the offset. It's all a terrible mess, really, that makes most sense when you remember it's been designed for the compiler's sake, not the users'. The best thing is to stick to one-dimensional arrays and do the mapping by hand, or build arrays of pointers, until you have read to the end of this ◁ chapter.

The treatment of arrays as pointers applies to returning them out of functions as well as passing them in: when you return an array as the result of a function what gets returned is the pointer to its first element. So, if the array was local to the function, the pointer will be left dangling. The following function is, therefore, an example of that which you should never, ever, do (page 85):

```
int* dangly()
{
  int some_ints[100];
  return some_ints;
}
```

(You can't define a function with an array return type, which is a little inconsistent, but does help make it obvious that you might be in danger of returning a dangling pointer.)

It is perfectly reasonable to want to create arrays with a lifetime greater than a function call, just as it was to create pointers. The way you manage this is the same: you can create arrays on the heap. You do this with an extended version of the new operator for creating heap objects. An expression of the form

```
new type [ size ]
```

returns a pointer to the first element of an array of *type* with *size* elements. For example, new int[100] returns a value of type int*, pointing to the first element of an array of one hundred integers. If, as is usual, the returned value is to be used to initialize a variable, the variable must be declared with the correct pointer type, for example

```
int *some_ints = new int [100];
```

An array type, even if the size is omitted, will not do. If you think about this for long enough from the compiler's point of view, it makes sense. Users just have to say "Aw, shucks", or the appropriate idiomatic equivalent, and shrug it off as one of those inconsistencies that makes C++ so endearing.

Arrays on the heap not only have an extended lifetime, they can also have their size computed at runtime. Whereas `int a[N]` requires N to be a compile-time constant, `new int [N]` doesn't, so heap arrays have "dynamic bounds".

The advantages of putting data on the heap don't come for nothing. Allocating objects and arrays from the free store involves some computation, which can actually dominate the runtime of some programs, and heap objects usually require some extra, secret, space for internal book-keeping information. You shouldn't rush out, therefore, and use `new[]` to create all your arrays, unless you really need the advantages of the heap. Furthermore, you need to return arrays created by `new[]` just as you do pointers created with `new`. If `heap_a` is a pointer to an array on the heap, you delete it with the statement

```
delete [] heap_a;
```

It's quite easy to remember that if the call of `new` that created a pointer had square brackets, you must use square brackets to delete it, too. If you don't, the effect is undefined. Always assume that undefined effects will be unpleasant ones.

Arrays of Characters

So far, in program examples that use character strings, I have invariably employed the library class `string`, which provides a convenient way of dealing with this sort of data. Traditionally, though, character strings have been stored more directly as arrays of `char` and it is as well to know about this. A `char` is usually an 8-bit byte (although it needn't be), so ASCII characters can be packed efficiently in `chars`; the array structure is a natural choice, since a string is a sequence, if anything ever was. To distinguish between strings that are arrays of `char` and those that are objects of the library class `string`, I will refer to the former as C-strings, unless it's obvious from the context which I'm talking about.

Most operations on a C-string require you to know how long it is—think about comparing, copying or printing. An array carries no information about its size, so an array containing just the characters is not much use. C++ tackles this problem by adopting a convention: when an array of `char` is used to hold a character string, the actual characters are followed by a null character (zero, written '\0' as a character constant) which indicates the end of the C-string data (not necessarily the last element of the array). So, a string of n characters can only be stored in an array of `char` of size at least $n + 1$. Bear in mind that this way of storing C-strings is only a convention, but string constants in a C++ program will be stored this way by the compiler and the library functions for manipulating C-strings all rely on it. (A good case here for data abstraction, you would think, but here, of course, I'm describing C things, which live on in C++.)

The question of how strings interact with C-strings—you will have noticed that strings are initialized with C-string constants—will have to remain unanswered until chapter 8.

The fact that C-strings are terminated by '\0', which may be treated as an integer and converted to bool, when it will cause the test in a while-loop to fail, leads to some highly characteristic programming idioms, usually playing at the same time on the equivalence of pointers and arrays. For example, here is one way to define a function to copy its first C-string argument to its second.

```
void too_obvious(const char *from, char *to)
{
  int i = 0;
  while (from[i] != '\0')
  {
    to[i] = from[i];
    ++i;
  }
  to[i] = '\0';
}
```

But it would much more often be seen written like this:

```
void perspicuous(const char *from, char *to)
{
  while (*to++ = *from++);
}
```

The majority of experienced C and C++ programmers would fail to see any irony in this function's name and would recognize this code immediately and know what it does—the whole thing is recognized as a single chunk that copies strings. However, if you take that chunk apart, what have you got?

The function body consists of a while-loop with an empty body, which does all its work by means of a side effect in the loop test. The test includes further side-effects in the form of the post-increments to the pointer variables from and to, and is critically dependent on evaluation order. The whole effect relies on the equivalence between arrays and pointers to their first element, and the successful termination of the loop depends on the *convention* that C-strings are terminated by a null character, which is zero, which is false. Don't forget that the function only has a lasting effect on the arrays its actual arguments point to, but doesn't corrupt the pointers themselves, because of the unique way arrays are passed to functions.

This is what passes as stylish in some circles

▷ I was disappointed to find that, with the compiler I use, the generated code for perspicuous really is more efficient than that for too_obvious, which supports the usual justification for writing the more obscure function. There is no real reason why a compiler shouldn't generate almost identical code for the two.
◁

Both formulations of the C-string copy function are unsafe: if from doesn't point to a null-terminated array or if to doesn't point to a large enough array to hold all the characters being copied, either function will misbehave.

Several commonly required operations on C-strings can be found in the form of functions in the standard C library, declared in the header `string.h` (not the same as `string`—but bear in mind my earlier warnings about possible differences in names of headers used by different compilers). C-strings will be printed out as character strings by the `<<` operation from the iostreams library. You can often get away with working on C-strings exclusively through these library functions. This situation suffers from the drawbacks of a procedural approach to libraries outlined in the introduction. Arrays of `char` can be manipulated in ways inconsistent with the view of them as null-terminated character strings; the C-string functions can be passed arguments that are not null-terminated, and no checks will prevent the resulting disaster. It is far safer (and more convenient for you) to use the string class, unless efficiency is really important. Even then, be aware that things might be going on behind the scenes to make some operations on strings more efficient than the equivalent operations on C-strings. If you really dislike the string class, write your own to isolate use of the lower-level representation.

▷ Using nulls to terminate a string of characters isn't the only way to indicate where it ends. In BCPL, the zeroth byte was used to hold a count of the number of characters. This, however, imposes a length limit of 255 on all strings, which may be unacceptable, forcing the programmer to use a second, hand-crafted, representation for longer strings. Using something larger than a `char` to hold the length count means that a string is no longer a simple array. The use of a null terminator imposes no limit on length and avoids the introduction of a new concept for handling strings. It is only efficient if most of the operations on a C-string require you to scan it right down to the end (i.e., if what you need to know is where the C-string ends, not how many characters it has). If this is so, use of the null in conjunction with pointers, as in the `perspicuous` example, does provide a very smooth, albeit perilous, way of dealing with string data. The function to compute the length of a C-string, `strlen` is inefficient, though, since it must count all the characters, so any idioms based on counting, like

```
for (int i = 0; i <= strlen(from); ++i)
    to[i] = from[i];
```

should be avoided.

Using null as a terminator means you can't have null characters embedded in a C-string and still pass it to a function expecting the null character to be a terminator. Embedded nulls are sometimes needed in control strings for peripheral devices or in certain file formats. You can't have everything. ◁

The use of `const` is especially compelling in conjunction with `char*` variables initialized with C-string literals. The C++ standard explicitly allows implementors to share memory locations between string literals. This works well if one is a suffix of another. For example, suppose we had the following:

```
char* greeting = "hello";
char* moor = "Othello";
```

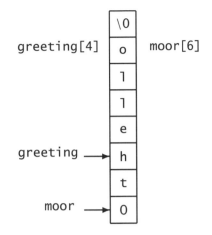

Figure 4.8   String literals sharing memory

A suitably smart compiler could save space by using the same locations for both, as shown in figure 4.8. If you were to turn your greeting into a curse:

```
greeting[4] = '!';
```

you would throw Shakespeare's character into confusion, turning him into Oth-ell!. For this reason you should always use const pointers to point to C string literals. (The only reason they aren't themselves considered to be of constant type is for compatibility with C.)

```
const char* greeting = "hello";
const char* moor = "Othello";
```

Not every compiler employs this memory sharing strategy, but if you want your program to be portable you should never rely on compiler features. No such problem occurs with string objects, since each makes its own private copy of the data.

Better Behaved Arrays

On page 212 of the ARM you can find the verdict that "...the C array concept is weak and beyond repair". Indeed, arrays as C++ has inherited them from C are very low level affairs, and it is easy to come up with a list of features which would be desirable but which they lack. First on this list for many people would be range checking—making sure that any value used as an array subscript is less than the size of the array and not negative—since range errors are responsible for many nasty bugs. A second useful feature is a facility to find out the size of an array at runtime, to remove the need to pass an extra argument with this information to functions with array arguments. Both of these features imply that arrays should carry around information about their size at runtime.

Many programmers like to specify the lower and upper bounds of an array, instead of having all arrays with lower bound zero, for applications where the array is used to store a lookup table or mapping whose domain runs from N to M for some arbitrary N and M. This idea can be taken further, to arrays whose indices are arbitrary values, not necessarily integers; this gives you general tables, or associative arrays, as they are sometimes called, similar to those built in to the Awk and Perl languages, for example. Flexible arrays are also valuable; these go beyond dynamic heap arrays in dynamism as their size can vary (or appear to), with the array expanding or shrinking subsequent to its creation. True multi-dimensional arrays would be preferable to the present half-hearted arrays of arrays or pointers.

There are two reasons why none of these array features is included in C++. First, the negative reason: each feature carries a performance and space over-head. C and C++ arrays are an almost perfect match to the memory and address-ing capabilities of mainstream contemporary computers. They can therefore be used very efficiently and they can be turned to a variety of purposes quite adequately. The C++ design philosophy says that programmers who are happy with these arrays should not have to pay a performance price for the sake of those who aren't. Second, the positive reason: classes enable you to define your own array types with the extra features. You may well be able to find suitable classes in a library. We have already seen that the standard C++ library includes the string class as a substitute for arrays of char. It also includes dynamic arrays.

It is easy enough to construct a rough-hewn array class that is better be-haved than the built-in arrays. I'll take as my target a class of arrays with arbitrary upper and lower bounds, operations to find out what these are, and access and update operations with range checking against these bounds. If this exercise was being carried out in earnest, the most difficult question would be: What should be done when an error occurs? In this version, I take the view that all possible errors should be trapped and an informative message produced, but no attempt at recovery will be made. Bearing in mind that the alternative is a bus or segmentation error, or some such, and a core dump (maybe), this isn't too bad.

If range checking is to be performed, then the array must include a record of its lower and upper bounds. This makes providing query operations to dis-cover the values of the bounds trivial. Since we don't know the size of arrays in advance, it will be necessary to allocate the actual array space on the heap. These considerations tell us that the class must have private data members to hold the lower and upper bounds and a pointer to the allocated array. The interface will be simple, consisting of a function to initialize an array, by setting its bounds and, while we're at it, initializing all its elements to a specified value, and one to clear up when it is no longer required; functions to interrogate the bounds, a function to get the value of the element at index i and one to assign it a new value. These will be called `alpha`, `omega`, `lwb` (lower bound), `upb` (upper bound), `get` and `put`, respectively. Several private member functions will be used to detect and deal with errors. The function `check_index` takes an integer and sees whether it is in range or not; if it is not it will call `range_error` to issue the message and terminate execution. Other error functions deal with

```
class MyIntArray  {
public:
  void alpha(int, int, int);
  void omega();
  int lwb() const;
  int upb() const;
  int get(int) const;
  void put(int, int);
private:
  int lower_bound, upper_bound;
  int *the_array;
  void check_index(int) const;
  void bounds_error() const;
  void deleted_error() const;
  void range_error(int) const;
};
```

Figure 4.9 Class definition for range-checked arrays

illegal bounds, where the specified lower bound is greater than the upper, and an attempt to use an array after it has been deleted by omega. Sadly, it is not possible, with the amount of C++ that has been described so far, to protect against attempts to use an array before it has been initialized. But it will be possible once we know about constructors.

A suitable class declaration for an array like this which holds integers is shown in Figure 4.9.

This is not the place to go fully into the design of interfaces to classes, but a useful guideline is that the interface should be complete and minimal, meaning that you should provide enough public member functions to do the job, but no more. So, for example, I have not included a print member function, because this can be written as an ordinary function using the operations that have been provided. Here is one possibility.

```
void print_my_array(const MyIntArray& mia)
{
  for (int i = mia.lwb(); i <= mia.upb(); ++i)
  {
    cout << "[" << i << "] = " << mia.get(i);
    cout <<  (i%5 == 0? '\n' : ' ');
  }
  cout << endl;
}
```

This is not brilliant, but because it is not part of the class, you can always replace it with something better of your own.

The code for the member functions contains no tricks, but care is needed to make sure that all the necessary checks are made—otherwise the entire exercise is pretty pointless. The initialization function `alpha` must check that the bounds are sensible and allocate the array. The function `bounds_error` is called if the check fails—it doesn't need any arguments because it is a member function and so can access `lower_bound` and `upper_bound`. If all goes well, the newly allocated array is initialized to the value specified as `alpha`'s third argument.

```cpp
void MyIntArray::alpha(int lower, int upper, int initial)
{
  lower_bound = lower;
  upper_bound = upper;
  if (lower > upper)
    bounds_error();
  else
  {
    int size = upper - lower + 1;
    the_array = new int[size];
    for (int i = 0; i <= size-1; ++i)
      the_array[i] = initial;
  }
}
```

The `omega` function only has to delete the array that `alpha` allocated, but while it's at it, sets `the_array` to the null pointer, so that subsequent attempts to access it can be detected.

```cpp
void MyIntArray::omega()
{
  delete [] the_array;
  the_array = NULL;
}
```

The interrogation functions for upper and lower bounds are trivial; they just return the value of the appropriate member. (Note, in case it's not obvious, that it would not be sensible just to make the data members public, because that would allow users of the class to update them and destroy the integrity of the data structure.)

```cpp
int MyIntArray::lwb() const
{
  return lower_bound;
}

int MyIntArray::upb() const
{
  return upper_bound;
}
```

The `get` and `put` functions must each do two things: check the index is in range, which they do by calling `check_index`; and map the index given to an offset from the base of `the_array`, which, being a real C++ array, has indices starting at zero. This is not a terrifically intellectually demanding calculation.

```
int MyIntArray::get(int i) const
{
  check_index(i);
  return the_array[i - lower_bound];
}

void MyIntArray::put(int i, int x)
{
  check_index(i);
  the_array[i - lower_bound] = x;
}
```

The important work is done by check_index, which verifies that the_array is not null and that its argument, the index, is in range.

```
void MyIntArray::check_index(int i) const
{
  if (the_array == NULL)
    deleted_error();
  if (i < lower_bound || i > upper_bound)
    range_error(i);
}
```

Finally, the error handling functions each produce an informative message and then abandon execution. The message is not sent to the standard output stream, which might be a file, but to the error output stream, identified by cerr—an object declared in the header <iostream>. This understands the stream output operations just as cout does, but will send its output to the terminal or a log file, irrespective of where the standard output is going.

```
void MyIntArray::bounds_error() const
{
  cerr << "!! Lower bound of " << lower_bound
      << " exceeds upper bound of "
      << upper_bound << endl;
  abort();
}

void MyIntArray::deleted_error() const
{
  cerr << "!! Attempt to access an element"
      << " of a deleted array" << endl;
  abort();
}

void MyIntArray::range_error(int i) const
{
  cerr << "!! Attempt to access array element"
      << " outside specified bounds" << endl;
  cerr << i << " not in " << "(" << lower_bound
      << "..." << upper_bound << ")" << endl;
```

```
    abort();
}
```

This class will get the job done, but, compared with the built-in arrays, it is inconvenient to use. Compare

```
MyIntArray m;
m.alpha(1, 15, 0);
m.put(5, 99);
cout << m.get(12);
```

with

```
int a[15];
a[5] = 99;
cout << a[12];
```

Furthermore, you can omit to call `alpha`, and all the range-checking in the world will be of no use to you.

I have obviously still got something up my sleeve, since the string class is user-defined, but string objects can be used almost like built-in arrays of `char`, with initialization and subscripting not requiring member function calls. Indeed, there are facilities in C++ that enable you to present a user-defined type so that it can be used as conveniently as (occasionally, more conveniently than) a built-in type. The supporting language technology required to do this is extensive—surprisingly so—and forms the subject matter of the bulk of the middle part of the book.

Inheritance

5

There is one thing on which all writers on object-oriented programming, object-oriented design and object-oriented everything else agree. With a cheerful disrespect for the English language, they unite behind the slogan: Inheritance means *is-a*. This is not only ungrammatical, it is also potentially misleading. It is intended to express the fact that the use of inheritance in a program captures a relationship between sorts of things, which is expressed in sentences such as "A waiter is a person", "A compiler is a program" or "A C++ compiler is a compiler". The usage here is imprecise, though, since inheritance should definitely not be used to capture the relationship between individual things and the class they belong to, expressed for example by the sentences "Jean-Jacques is a waiter" or "MegaProg C++ is a C++ compiler". Here, in each sentence, we are stating that a particular thing (Jean-Jacques, MegaProg C++) is an instance of a sort of thing (waiter, C++ compiler). Paradoxically in view of the form of the sentences, these are not what is meant, in object-oriented circles, by an *is-a* relationship. Nor is the relationship expressed in a sentence such as "The stack used by this compiler is a linked list". What is meant this time is that the stack *is implemented as* a linked list. You might take the view that the stack is a linked list behaving in a particular way. However, the majority of thinkers hold that we can only model a relationship between two sorts of things, *A* and *B*, by inheritance where everything that is true of a *B* is also true of an *A*, and that everything you can do to a *B* can also be done to an *A* (although not necessarily vice versa). Anyone who knows anything about linked lists and stacks can see that not everything that is true of a linked list is true of a stack: you can't add things to the end of a stack, for example. In the case of Jean-Jacques the waiter, it makes no sense to say "Everything that is true of *a* Jean-Jacques...", since Jean-Jacques is a single unique individual. An improved slogan for object-oriented designers would be: Inheritance means *is-a-kind-of*. Not so snappy, perhaps, but less likely to lead you astray, even though, in real systems, you are always going to find marginal cases that call for nice judgement.

With that cleared up, we can all probably appreciate the sort of relationships that inheritance can be used for. You can still be forgiven for wondering why inheritance is worth making a fuss about. Sure, sorts of things are sometimes related in this way, but looking around you or thinking about entity-set relationship modelling and database design, if you've ever done any of that, you can see that sorts of things can be related to each other in lots of different ways. Why build a programming method around inheritance?

If you do find yourself wondering this, it's probably because it is easiest to think of inheritance as an *analytical* tool for modelling relationships that exist (in whatever sense you like) in a real-world situation. This view of inheritance is fostered by the way it is usually introduced by analogies. Whereas inheritance does have its analytical uses, in practice it is equally useful as a *synthetic* tool, which can be used to express and exploit commonality among datatypes. For example, if two datatypes A and B have some operations and data in common, rather than implementing A and B separately and duplicating the common code, we could implement a type AB that implemented only the common parts of A and B, and then construct A and B as types that inherited these parts from AB. Each of them would only have to implement its own unique behaviour. Similarly, when a new type Z is being developed, if an old type Y can be found that already does some of the things that Z must, Z can inherit these from Y. Once you've done that, you'll be able to look at the resulting classes and observe that a Z is a kind of Y or that A and B are each kinds of AB.

Inheritance provides a way of sharing and re-using code. This is usually sold as a way of increasing productivity, but if you want to feel less like an industrial machine, you can think of it as a way of avoiding repeating some boring old stuff you've done before, so that you can get on with something new. (How many hash tables do you want to implement?)

FUNDAMENTALS OF INHERITANCE IN C++

Many commentators will not consider a language to be object-oriented unless it provides linguistic support for inheritance. (You can always simulate it using the right sort of pointers, but the best you can hope to be then is "object-based".) By this criterion, C++ is certainly object-oriented. Its support for inheritance is elaborate, but it starts out simple.

Derived Classes and Base Classes

In a class declaration, the name of the class being declared may be followed by a colon, the reserved word `public` (doing some extra work) and the name of another class, which must already have been declared:

```
class name₁ : public name₂ { member-declarations };
```

The class being declared, $name_1$, is called a *derived class*. The meaning of the declaration is that an object of type $name_1$ will have all the same members as an object of type $name_2$ as well as any additional ones specified in the *member-declarations*. That is, the derived class $name_1$ inherits all the members of class $name_2$, which is referred to as its *base class*. A derived class is an extension of its base class.

The use of the keyword `public` here indicates that the public members of the base class will also be public members of the derived class, so the interface to the new class is truly an extension to that of the old one: anything you can do to an object of the base class you can also do to one of the derived class. What about the private members of the base class? Probably, most newcomers to C++ expect that these will become private members of the derived class, but this is not what happens. If it were, then any member function of the derived class would have access to the private members of the base class, so, in order to get round the access protection of a class's members, all you would have to do would be define a new class derived from it. The whole protection mechanism would be rendered totally impotent. Instead, although every instance of the derived class has members corresponding to the private members of the base class, they are not accessible to the member functions of the derived class, they can only be accessed by the member functions of the base class—which may well be called from inside member functions of the derived class. Within such functions, any member, including inherited public members of the base class, may be referred to by its name, using the usual abbreviation of `mem` for `this->mem`.

The preceding paragraph is summarized in Table 5.1 for the following declarations. (You may like to reflect that a waiter can speak just as any person can, but is wise not to mix up his own cash with the money he handles in his work.)

```
class Person {
public:
  void speak();
private:
  float cash;
  void count_cash();
};

class Waiter: public Person {
public:
  void serve();
private:
  float tips;
  void count_tips();
};
```

In most respects, a derived class is just like any other class. All its member functions that are not inherited must be defined somewhere. Whenever its definition is in scope, objects belonging to it can be declared, defined or created by the use of `new`. As this implies, pointers to objects can also be created and used. New classes can be derived in turn from a derived class, so that hierarchies of classes can be built up.

An object of a derived class has an important special property: it can be used wherever an object of its base class is required. The compatibility between base and derived classes is most useful when objects are manipulated through

	members	public	member function...	...can access
Person	speak() cash count_cash()	speak()	speak()	speak() cash count_cash()
Waiter	speak() cash count_cash() serve() tips count_tips()	speak() serve()	serve()	speak() serve() tips count_tips()

Table 5.1   Public inheritance

pointers or passed as arguments by reference. For example, if a function is declared as follows:

```
void greet(const Person& p);
```

and a couple of variables are also declared

```
Person Rousseau;
Waiter Jean_Jacques;
```

either of the following calls is legal

```
greet(Rousseau);
greet(Jean_Jacques);
```

although inside greet, only the public members of Person can be accessed through p, even when it refers to an object of type Waiter.

In a similar way, when objects are manipulated through pointers, a pointer to an object of a derived class can be used wherever a pointer to an object of the base class is expected. For example, you can assign a pointer to a waiter to a variable of type pointer to a person:

```
Waiter* Jean_Jacques_p = new Waiter;
Person* p_p = Jean_Jacques_p;
```

In other contexts, mixing objects of base and derived classes is not advisable. Consider

```
Person Rousseau;
Waiter Jean_Jacques;
```

Assume these two objects are suitably initialized. The assignment

```
Rousseau = Jean_Jacques;
```

is legal, but it only assigns the part of Jean_Jacques consisting of members of the class Person; that is, it slices off part of the object—notably the tips. (It has to, because there's nowhere in Rousseau to put them.) The same thing would happen if `Jean_Jacques` was passed by value to a function expecting an argument of type `Person`. This is unlikely to be what anyone concerned would want to happen. Object slicing does not occur with reference arguments because a reference argument is just a synonym for the original object passed to the function.

The compatibility between base and derived classes extends transitively through class hierarchies: if class `WineWaiter` is derived from `Waiter`, which is derived from class `Person`, an object of type `WineWaiter` can be passed by reference to a function with an actual reference argument of type `Waiter` or `Person`. And so on.

That should be enough about inheritance in C++ for you to understand a small example demonstrating its use. Despite the remarks about inheritance as a synthetic tool, this particular example is based on inheritance relationships we can observe between different sorts of files in a computer installation. The intention is to construct a tool to help ease the burdens of a system administrator's job.

Imagine, if you can, a computer installation whose users have not unanimously succumbed to the charms of C++. In fact, these people like to use lots of different languages, so the system administrator has to provide lots of compilers. Imagine further that most of these compilers have been pinched off the Internet in the form of source files which must themselves be compiled before they can be used. Finally, imagine that, since the demand for languages among this user community is unpredictable, the system administrator prefers not to compile any compiler until it is needed. The problem here is that, since a compiler is itself written in some programming language, it is necessary to find a compiler to compile the compiler, which in turn may require finding a compiler to compile the compiler to compile the compiler, which, it is not inconceivable, may require...Need I go on? It is quite possible that this sequence may be a cycle. It is not uncommon for the compiler for language $\mathcal{L}$ to be written in $\mathcal{L}$. If you don't have anything to bootstrap with, your user is stuck.

A slightly far-fetched story, perhaps, but it contains the seeds of a useful system utility.

Our tale is about compilers and programs, both of them in executable (binary) and source form. The most general concept involved is that of a file, which encompasses both sources and executables, and, in particular, sources and executables of compilers. In this case, then, a class hierarchy does drop out rather naturally.

Files can be represented as objects of a class `File`, whose only data member is a string giving its name in the file system. In practice, more information, for example the size, creation date, modification date and owner, could reasonably be included in `File` objects, but for present purposes, such gratuitous realism is best avoided as it only gets in the way. Following a pattern that is becoming familiar, we will need a member function to set up a new file by recording its name. It will also be useful to have a member function that returns the filename. Assuming the string class header is suitably included, the class declaration can look like this:

```
class File  {
public:
```

```
  void newfile(const string&);
  string filename() const;
private:
  string the_file_name;
};
```

and the declarations of the member functions are trivial.

```
void File::newfile(const string& fn)
{
  the_file_name = fn;
}


string File::filename() const
{
  return the_file_name;
}
```

▷ There's something a bit weird, perhaps, about carefully making the_file_name private, and then providing one member function that assigns to it and another that returns its value. This might look like making a fetish out of avoiding public data, to no particular effect. Accessing data through member functions is always more flexible—I could change my mind about what newfile does without necessarily affecting programs that use the class. In this particular case, though, the peculiarity ◁ can be avoided by using a constructor, as you will see in chapter 6.

Program source files are a kind of file, so a derived class ProgSource will be defined to represent them. An additional piece of information is needed for a ProgSource object, the implementation language in which the program is written. Again, an initialization member function sets this, and an extra query function returns the value.

```
class ProgSource: public File  {
public:
  void newprogsource(const string&, const string&);
  string language() const;
private:
  string implementation_language;
};


void ProgSource::newprogsource(const string& fn, const string& il)
{
  newfile(fn);
  implementation_language = il;
}


string ProgSource::language() const
{
  return implementation_language;
}
```

See how `newprogsource` calls `newfile` to initialize the data member of a `File` object; the member function is called without using the name of an object, so the call `newfile(fn)` is an abbreviation for `this->newfile(fn)`. The pointer `this` is pointing to a `ProgSource` object, and `ProgSource` is derived from `File`, so `*this` has a `newfile` member.

An executable binary is also a kind of file, so another class, `Executable`, is derived from `File`. There is no inheritance relationship between `Executable` and `ProgSource`—although a `ProgSource` object can be compiled into an `Executable` object, there is no sense in which a `ProgSource` is a kind of `Executable`, or vice versa. On the contrary, try editing an executable file or running a source file and see how far you get.

For the present exercise, there is no extra information to record about an executable beyond its filename, so there are no new data members, and initialization can be done by `newfile`. What is distinctive about executables is that you can run them, so a member function `run` is provided to model doing so. Here, all it does is write a message indicating that the program is being run; possibly, in practice, it could start up a process to actually do it.

```
class Executable: public File  {
public:
  void run() const;
};

void Executable::run() const
{
  cout << "Run " << filename() << endl;
}
```

Finally, we come to the classes representing compilers. A compiler source is a special kind of source program (I make the totally infeasible assumption that it is a single file); it needs as additional information the source language which it can compile (e.g., C++ for a C++ compiler). Its initialization member function must set this, as well as its filename and the implementation language it is itself written in. (We can fairly safely assume we don't need to record the target language, since our system administrator is only going to be interested in compilers that produce programs that can run on the available machine.) We also need a member function to return the source language, so we can check whether a particular compiler is appropriate for compiling a program in a particular language.

Compiler binaries are more interesting. Like compiler sources they must record the language they compile; in addition, they have member functions to model carrying out a compilation. The member function `compile` takes a pointer to a program source object and returns a pointer to the executable object resulting from its compilation. A second member function `compile-compiler` is needed to compile a compiler source, in order to get the types right—this function must take a compiler source and return a compiler binary, which has extra information lacking in an ordinary executable. The two compiler classes are defined like this:

```
class CompilerSource: public ProgSource  {
public:
  void newcompilersource(const string&, const string&,
                                        const string&);
  string compiles() const;
private:
  string the_source_language;
};

class CompilerBinary: public Executable  {
public:
  void newcompilerbinary(const string&, const string&);
  Executable* compile(ProgSource*) const;
  CompilerBinary* compilecompiler(CompilerSource*) const;
private:
  string the_source_language;
};
```

The member functions for `CompilerSource` are trivially defined.

```
void CompilerSource::newcompilersource(const string& fn,
                  const string& il, const string& sl)
{
  newprogsource(fn, il);
  the_source_language = sl;
}

string CompilerSource::compiles() const
{
  return the_source_language;
}
```

Initializing a `CompilerBinary` object is simple and similar.

```
void CompilerBinary::newcompilerbinary(const string& fn,
                                        const string& sl)
{
  newfile(fn);
  the_source_language = sl;
}
```

`CompilerBinary::compile` must first check that it can handle the language its argument program is written in, then run the compiler; it produces a message saying what it is doing and then constructs an executable to return as its result. The name of the executable is formed by putting .Xq on the end of the source filename—doing realistic things with filename extensions is easy, using some of the member functions of class `string` that I haven't mentioned, but fussy.

```
Executable* CompilerBinary::compile(ProgSource *the_prog) const
{
  if (the_prog->language() == the_source_language)
```

```
    {
      run();
      cout << the_prog->filename() << ": "
          << the_source_language << "->Xq" << endl;
      Executable* the_executable = new Executable;
      the_executable->newfile(the_prog->filename() + ".Xq");
      return the_executable;
    }
    else return NULL;
  }
```

The `compilecompiler` member function is similar, but it must return a `CompilerBinary` object.

```
  CompilerBinary*
  CompilerBinary::compilecompiler(CompilerSource* the_c_source) const
  {
    if (the_c_source->language() == the_source_language)
    {
      run();
      cout << the_c_source->filename() << ": "
       << the_source_language << "->Xq" << endl;
      CompilerBinary* the_binary = new CompilerBinary;
      the_binary->newcompilerbinary(the_c_source->filename()+".Xq",
            the_c_source->compiles());
      return the_binary;
    }
    else return NULL;
  }
```

These classes allow me to create and use objects corresponding to the sort of files in my supposed computer installation. To carry out the required job of determining which compilers need to be compiled, they must be set in motion within a conventionally constructed program.

The approach I adopt is to keep two arrays of pointers, one to objects representing all the executable compilers already installed, the other to ones representing all the compiler sources available. I also need a pair of counters to remember how many of each there are. Since we are using arrays, a maximum will have to be imposed; an arbitrary figure has been used. These arrays and counters have been made global. If you find this offensive, you can easily add them to the argument list of each function, passing by reference where necessary, but since they must be accessed inside every function, there does seem to be a good argument for making them global. The keyword `static` is used to keep them local to one file, at least.

```
  static const int max_files = 50;
  static CompilerBinary* CBs[max_files];
  static CompilerSource* CSs[max_files];
  static int nCBs, nCSs;
```

The way the program works is as follows. When given a program to try and compile, an attempt is first made to compile it with each executable compiler.

If all of them fail (in this system, the only reason for failure is inability to handle the program's implementation language), a search is made for the source of a compiler for the right language. If one is found, an attempt is made to compile it, using the same two-stage strategy. The whole process is driven by a small function:

```
void attempt(ProgSource *p)
{
  Executable* x = compileprog(p);
  if (x)
    cout << "successful" << endl ;
  else
    cout << "failed" << endl ;
  delete x ;
}
```

The function `compileprog` called here looks for the executable—it just uses a linear search in the CBs array. If this succeeds, it returns the compiler's output, otherwise, it calls `findcompiler` to look for and compile a suitable compiler source. If this succeeds, it uses the result to do the compilation, otherwise it returns NULL to indicate failure.

```
Executable* compileprog(ProgSource *prog)
{
  int i = 0;
  while (i < nCBs)
  {
    Executable *x = CBs[i]->compile(prog);
    if (x) return x;
    else ++i;
  }
  CompilerBinary* c = findcompiler(prog);
  if (c)
    return c->compile(prog);
  else return NULL;
}
```

A little care is required in the `findcompiler` function: it may be called to compile a compiler, and it is possible that a compiler C for some language $\mathcal{L}$ is written in $\mathcal{L}$ itself. There is a risk of an infinite recursion happening if `findcompiler` tries to compile C in order to obtain a suitable compiler to compile C. Thus, we must make sure that the compiler we choose isn't the same as the program we are trying to compile. Apart from this, the code is simple: if a compiler that can handle the right language is found, a function cc is called to try and compile it. If cc succeeds, the compiler binary it returns is installed in the CBs array and returned by `findcompiler` to be used by `compileprog`. This version of `findcompiler` produces messages to trace what it is doing.

```
CompilerBinary* findcompiler(ProgSource *prog)
{
  string pl = prog->language();
```

```
cout << "Seeking a " << pl << " compiler to compile" << endl;
int i = 0;
while (i < nCSs)
{
  if (CSs[i]->filename() != prog->filename()
      && CSs[i]->compiles() == pl)
  {
    CompilerBinary * xc = cc(CSs[i]);
    if (xc)
    {
      if (nCBs == max_files)
      {
        cerr << "sorry, too many compiler binaries" << endl;
        abort();
      }
      CBs[nCBs++] = xc;
      return xc;
    }
  }
  ++i;
}
cout << "Given up" << endl;
return NULL;
}
```

(In reality, one might hope to do better than give up if the capacity of the CBs array was exceeded.)

Finally, cc is much like compileprog, except for the types. It looks for a suitable executable, and, if that fails, calls findcompiler, which may, therefore, call cc recursively, if necessary.

```
CompilerBinary* cc(CompilerSource* comp)
{
  string pl = comp->language();
  cout << "Seeking executable compiler for " << pl << endl;
  int i = 0;
  while (i < nCBs)
  {
    CompilerBinary *x = CBs[i]->compilecompiler(comp);
    if (x) return x;
    else ++i;
  }
  CompilerBinary* c = findcompiler(comp);
  if (c)
    return c->compilecompiler(comp);
  else return NULL;
}
```

With suitable #include directives and a forward declaration to cope with the mutual recursion, these functions can be used to perform the required job. No doubt, a real system administrator's program would have a splendid interactive interface and use a persistent database to remember the state of the CBs and CSs arrays. Just as a demonstration, though, here is a main program that exercises the functions.

```
int main()
{
    ProgSource *x_cpp = new ProgSource;
    x_cpp->newprogsource("x.cpp", "C++");
    ProgSource *x_c = new ProgSource;
    x_c->newprogsource("x.c", "C");
    ProgSource *x_m = new ProgSource;
    x_m->newprogsource("x.m", "Modula2");
    CompilerSource *MPCpp = new CompilerSource;
    MPCpp->newcompilersource("MPC++", "C", "C++");
    CompilerSource *MPM2 = new CompilerSource;
    MPM2->newcompilersource("MPM2", "Modula2", "Modula2");
    CompilerBinary *MPC = new CompilerBinary;
    MPC->newcompilerbinary("MPC.Xq", "C");
    CompilerSource *GNUM2 = new CompilerSource;
    GNUM2->newcompilersource("MPM2", "C++", "Modula2");

    CBs[0] = MPC;   nCBs = 1;
    CSs[0] = MPCpp; nCSs = 1;
    CSs[1] = MPM2; ++nCSs;
    CSs[2] = GNUM2; ++nCSs;

    attempt(x_c);
    attempt(x_cpp);
    attempt(x_m);

    return EXIT_SUCCESS;
}
```

And here is the output it produces:

```
Run MPC.Xq
x.c: C->Xq
successful
Seeking a C++ compiler to compile
Seeking executable compiler for C
Run MPC.Xq
MPC++: C->Xq
Run MPC++.Xq
x.cpp: C++->Xq
successful
Seeking a Modula2 compiler to compile
Seeking executable compiler for Modula2
Seeking a Modula2 compiler to compile
Given up
Seeking executable compiler for C++
```

```
Run MPC++.Xq
MPM2: C++->Xq
Run MPM2.Xq
x.m: Modula2->Xq
successful
```

Re-defining Member Functions

It is by no means uncommon for a derived class to extend the functionality of some of the operations it inherits, as well as adding new ones of its own. A commonly encountered and easily understood example of this is provided by a member function that simply prints the values of all the data members of an object. In the software administrator's simulation, a member function to print the data of a File object would only have to print the filename suitably formatted, whereas that for a ProgSource would also have to print its implementation language, and that for a CompilerSource would print the source language in addition. One way to achieve this would be to add separate member functions to each class, defined as follows:

```
void File::print_file() const
{
  cout << "Filename is " << the_file_name;
}

void ProgSource::print_prog_source() const
{
  print_file();
  cout << " written in " << implementation_language;
}

void CompilerSource::print_compiler_source() const
{
  print_prog_source();
  cout << " compiles " << source_language;
}
```

This works, but it doesn't feel quite right. If the intention is to have a member function that prints all the data of an object, should this operation have a different name for each class in the hierarchy? And where do the member functions print_prog_source and print_file fit into the CompilerSource class? How much sense does printing part of the data make? The answer depends on the application, of course, but generally it makes sense to have each class present a uniform interface with a function that prints all its data members.

You can do exactly this. If a derived class has a member function with the same name as a member function of its base class, then you can provide a separate definition for the member of the derived class and this will be used for objects of that class, instead of the base class's definition.

But now there's a new problem: the member function of the derived class cannot access the private members of the base class, so it will have to invoke a base class member function to print them. Unfortunately, the appropriate member function is precisely the one being redefined. To get round this, you are allowed to refer to a member function using its full name, for example `File::print` to invoke a member function that has been hidden by a redefinition in a derived class. I could add a `print` member function to each of the classes in the `File` hierarchy, with definitions like these:

```
void File::print() const
{
  cout << "Filename is " << the_file_name;
}

void ProgSource::print() const
{
  File::print();
  cout << " written in " << implementation_language;
}

void CompilerSource::print() const
{
  ProgSource::print();
  cout << " compiles " << the_source_language;
}

void CompilerBinary::print() const
{
  File::print();
  cout << " compiles " the_source_language;
}
```

No special declaration or definition is needed for `Executable::print`, since `File::print` already does the right thing.

▷ You can use the fully qualified name of a member function in any context. For example, if I wanted just to print the filename of the compiler source object MPM2, I could write

```
MPM2->File::print();
```

This sort of code is generally considered rather shoddy, and it is held to lead to maintenance problems. On the whole, it is best to restrict your use of fully qualified member functions to accessing hidden base class members from within the member ◁ functions of a derived class.

VIRTUAL FUNCTIONS

Assuming I have added print member functions in the way I just described, I could define a function like this:

```
void print_file_details(File *fp)
{
  fp->print();
  cout << endl;
}
```

and legitimately call it like this:

```
print_file_details(MPM2);
print_file_details(x_cpp);
```

since a pointer to an object of either of the derived classes `ProgSource` and `CompilerSource` can be passed as an argument to any function expecting a pointer to an object of their base class `File`. What output would you expect? Would you expect this?

```
Filename is MPM2
Filename is x.cpp
```

Expected or not, it's what you would get, but it might not be what you want. Very likely, you would want `print_file_details` to print out all the details of whatever object it was handed a pointer to, giving:

```
Filename is MPM2 written in Modula2 compiles Modula2
Filename is x.cpp written in C++
```

When `print_file_details(MPM2)` is called, you know and I know that the formal argument `fp` will be initialized to point to a `CompilerSource` object, but the compiler, which translates each function in isolation, can only believe what it has been told in the function header, that is, that `fp` is a pointer to a `File` object. Hence, it will always call `File::print`. The jargon for this is that `print` is *statically bound*—the definition chosen is determined by the static, or compile-time, type of the pointer `fp` and not by the dynamic, or run-time, type of the object it is actually pointing to when `print_file_details` is called.

Virtual Function Declarations

Does this mean I have to write an entire collection of separate functions `print_source_prog_details`, `print_compiler_source_details` and all the whole crew? I probably wouldn't have brought the question up unless the answer was "No". To achieve the effect of *dynamic binding*, where the definition chosen is determined by the type of object the pointer is actually pointing to when the function is called, all you have to do is precede the declaration of the member function with the reserved word `virtual`. Dynamically bound member functions are called *virtual functions*. Member functions are the only sort of function that can be virtual, so "virtual member function" would be a tautology. To distinguish between redefining a virtual function and a statically bound member function, it is customary to speak of *overriding* the virtual function.

Thus, in order to have `print_file_details` produce full details of whatever object its argument points to, each class should declare its `print` member function as

```
virtual void print() const;
```

(except for the class `Executable`, which doesn't need to declare it at all, since it really should use `File::print`). The same definitions can be used as before; the `virtual` keyword is not repeated in the function definitions. (More "Yes, but in fact...": Yes, but in fact, you only need `virtual` in the base class at the root of the hierarchy; it may be repeated in the derived classes, where it serves as useful documentation, but many programmers don't bother.) It is important to note that a virtual function must have the same type of arguments in every class it is declared in. If you specify different argument types, you will be defining a new function—the compiler will warn you, but you may not immediately understand the message. Specifying a different return type is an error according to the ARM, but the draft standard will allow you to override a virtual function returning a pointer to an object of some derived class by one returning a pointer to an object of a base class from which it is derived. If that would give you pleasure.

Virtual functions are bound dynamically when they are called through reference arguments as well as when they are called through pointers. I could have defined `print_file_details` like this:

```
void print_file_details(const File& fp)
{
  fp.print();
  cout << endl;
}
```

and call it like this:

```
print_file_details(*MPM2);
print_file_details(*x_cpp);
```

The full details of both files would be printed. However, if I was unwise enough to pass the argument by value:

```
void print_file_details(const File fp)
{
  fp.print();
  cout << endl;
}
```

then the function `File::print` would always be called. The formal argument is initialized with a sliced down copy of any actual argument; it is unambiguously a `File` object and there is no question of dynamic binding.

To illustrate virtual functions, we will revisit an example I sketched in chapter 1: simulating the collection of local taxes from buildings of several kinds.

For this example, I'll assume there are four kinds of building in a town: a town hall, from which local taxes are never collected; monasteries, which pay nothing (a subtle difference); commercial premises, whose tax is computed by multiplying their rateable value (a figure magically arrived at by the council) by the current business rate; and dwellings, which pay a tax computed by multiplying the number of inhabitants by a per capita rate and adding a second component computed by multiplying the assumed market value by a domestic rate. (Sounds strange, but the real system in this country is even stranger, and you don't even want to think about the rebates and exemptions.)

Here is a clear case for inheritance, since town halls, monasteries, dwellings and commercial premises are each a kind of building. Here is also a case for virtual functions, since it is possible to compute the tax due from any kind of building, but the computation is done differently for each kind.

The nasty bit here is not the computation of taxes—virtual functions make that beautifully easy—but maintaining a data structure to hold a collection of all the buildings in a town. The way this is done is not ideal, and I again have to hide behind the excuse that we are still missing some knowledge of C++ that would allow it to be done better.

Here's the plan. Every building, no matter what kind, has an address, so that it can get letters and parcels, so each building object should include an identifying string holding its address. It will also include two pointers to buildings, `next` and `previous`, so that all the buildings can be joined up into a two-way linked list. A well-known trick that avoids special cases when using two-way linked lists is to insert a dummy node at the head of the list. Since every town must have a town hall, this can be used as the dummy list head. A member function will be provided to construct a building; as well as an address, this will need a pointer to the head of the list as an argument, so that it can link the new building in. Another function will demolish a building by removing it from the list, an easy operation with two-way links, requiring no extraneous arguments. The member function to compute the local tax is virtual, as just explained. It must take three arguments, the domestic, per capita and business rates, since, although no type of building requires all three to do the computation, each requires something different, but the type of the virtual function's arguments must be the same in all derived classes.

Finally, the really grotty bit: a function is required to traverse a list of buildings and calculate the total tax revenue, by adding together the tax liability of all the buildings. To do this, the function needs access to the `next` pointers of all the buildings. Since these are private data members—making them public would open the way to data structure corruption—the function must be a member of the `Building` class (so far as we know, at present) although it will only ever be invoked from the town hall at the head of the list. It, too, needs the three tax rates as arguments, so it can pass them on to the individual tax computing functions.

All this leads to the following declaration of the class `Building`.

```
class Building  {
public:
  void construct(const string&, Building*);
  void demolish();
```

```
float collect_taxes(float, float, float) const;
virtual float compute_tax(float, float, float) const;
private:
  string the_address;
  Building *previous, *next;
};
```

Now the definitions. The definition of `construct` is a bit devious. After recording the building's address, it must insert the object into the two-way linked list pointed to by its argument `head`, which it does by making the pointer adjustments you can find described in any decent book on data structures. However, this only works if the empty list is set up correctly by setting both the `next` and `previous` pointers of the dummy object at the head to point to that object itself. If the `next` pointer is set to `this` at the start of the operation, the pointer assignments for doing a general insertion achieve this effect. By always doing the assignment of `this` to `next`, we don't have to treat constructing the town hall as a special case. This simplification is achieved at a cost of a couple of machine instructions per building. Notice that I couldn't easily have overridden `construct` in the `TownHall` class so as to deal with the special case only where it arises, because the `next` and `previous` pointers are private members of the base class `Building` and therefore not accessible in any derived class.

```
void Building::construct(const string& addr, Building *head)
{
  the_address = addr;
  next = this;
  previous = head;
  next = head->next;
  next->previous = head->next = this;
}
```

Demolition involves removing a building from the list—again, see any reputable data structures book.

```
void Building::demolish()
{
  previous->next = next;
  next->previous = previous;
}
```

The `collect_taxes` function (the grotty one) chains along the list until it gets back to where it started, accumulating the results of invoking the virtual function `compute_tax` through every building it encounters. We know that you can't tax the town hall, so it correctly fails to compute the tax of the building pointed to by `this`.

```
float Building::collect_taxes(float domestic, float per_capita,
                              float business) const
{
  float tax = 0.0;
  Building *p = this->next;
  while (p != this)
```

```
     {
        tax += p->compute_tax(domestic, per_capita, business);
        p = p-> next;
     }
     return tax;
  }
```

Trying to collect taxes from a general building makes no sense, so `Building`'s `compute_tax` does no more than generate an error message, but returns 0 to keep the types right.

```
  float Building::compute_tax(float domestic, float per_capita,
                              float business) const
  {
     cerr << "Error: attempt to tax a building of unknown kind"
          << endl;
     return 0.0;
  }
```

Each kind of building is represented by a class derived from `Building`. Each of these classes overrides the virtual `compute_tax` function, as well as adding extra data members to store information specific to each kind of building, and member functions to set and return the values of data, where appropriate. The definitions of these trivial member functions have been omitted.

```
  class Dwelling: public Building  {
  public:
     void inhabit(int);
     void set_valuation(int);
     float compute_tax(float, float, float) const;
  private:
     int no_of_inhabitants;
     int the_valuation;
  };
```

(The function `inhabit` changes the number of inhabitants, to simulate people moving in or out of the dwelling.)

```
  class TownHall: public Building  {
  public:
     float compute_tax(float, float, float) const;
  };
```

We can't do anything to the town hall except, perhaps, erroneously attempt to collect tax from it.

```
  class Commerce: public Building  {
  public:
     void set_rateable_value(int);
     float compute_tax(float, float, float) const;
  private:
     int the_rateable_value;
  };
```

```
class Monastery: public Building  {
public:
   float compute_tax(float, float, float) const;
};
```

The important thing here is that the various tax computations are done in separate functions. There is no question of having to determine the type of a building, by some means such as keeping a tag field in every building object, and using a switch statement to select the right computation. All that is done for us by the virtual function mechanism. We can add a new kind of building with its own tax computation by adding a new class derived from `Building`, without interfering with any existing code.

The individual functions to compute the taxes are trivial.

```
float Dwelling::compute_tax(float domestic, float per_capita,
                              float business) const
{
   if (no_of_inhabitants == 0)
   {
     cout << endl << "You can't collect taxes from " << where()
         << " --- nobody lives there" << endl;
     return 0.0;
   }
   return no_of_inhabitants*per_capita
       + domestic * the_valuation;
}

float TownHall::compute_tax(float domestic, float per_capita,
                              float business) const
{
   cout << "You'll never tax the town hall" << endl;
   return 0.0;
}

float Commerce::compute_tax(float domestic, float per_capita,
                              float business) const
{
   return the_rateable_value * business;
}

float Monastery::compute_tax(float domestic, float per_capita,
                              float business) const
{
   return 0.0;
}
```

We can set everything in motion by defining a class Town, which has a pointer to a town hall (and thus, in time, a list of buildings) as a data member, and a member function to found a town, by building its town hall (and thus correctly initializing the list of buildings). It will also need some member function to interact with the town planner, or whoever is using this program, allowing her to set tax rates for the year (which will be remembered in further data members), and collect taxes at the end of the year. In between, another member function performs an interaction with the user, and causes simulated people to move into dwellings, start businesses, have children, get divorced and move out, die, and do all those soap opera things that simulated people do—to the extent that it affects their tax liability. For these purposes, Town can be declared as follows:

```
class Town  {
public:
  void found();
  void set_rates();
  void compute_revenue();
  void run();
private:
  TownHall *the_town_hall;
  float domestic_rate, per_capita_rate, business_rate;
   other private members
};
```

The definitions of Town's members need not concern us—doing things realistically would require a proper graphical interaction that is way beyond the scope of this book, and doing it any other way is trivial and dull. The whole simulation could be driven by a loop, something like

```
Town T;
T.found();
while (true)
{
  T.set_rates();
  T.run();
  T.compute_revenue();
}
```

There is a small time and space overhead incurred by using virtual functions—the ARM goes into some detail describing their implementation to show just how small—and their use interferes with some compiler optimizations. This is why member functions are not virtual by default. Classes are not always destined to be used as base classes; derived classes sometimes extend their bases without doing any overriding. In both these cases, the overhead of virtual function calls would be incurred, even though no dynamic binding was going on. (A very smart compiler might figure this out, but compilers *that* smart are not common.) It is a cornerstone of the C++ philosophy that you shouldn't pay for features you don't use. Hence, you only get virtual functions if you explicitly specify them.

Pure Virtual Functions and Abstract Classes

In the local tax example, the `collect_taxes` member of `Building` is defined to produce an error message, on the grounds that it makes no sense to try and collect taxes from an object that is just a building, only from one that is a specific sort of building. But things ought to be stronger than that. Within this simulation, it makes no sense even to *be* just a building, the simulation only works on specific building types. Creating an object of class `Building` at all is an error in program logic. Having this result in a runtime error is not very satisfactory; it would be much better to have such an error picked up by the compiler, so that the erroneous program was never run. Why should users see your mistakes?

C++ provides compile-time protection against such errors, by allowing you to declare a member function to be not just virtual, but *pure* virtual.[1] If a class has at least one member that is a pure virtual function, it is called an *abstract class*, and any attempt to create an object of that class is an error, detected by the compiler. Abstract classes can only be used as base classes; pure virtual functions can be overridden in derived classes, so that objects of such derived classes can be created. If a derived class doesn't override an inherited pure virtual function, then it, too, is an abstract class and can only be used as a base for further derived classes.

Nice idea, strange syntax. A virtual function is made pure by adding = 0 after its declaration. To make `Building` into an abstract class, it should be declared like this:

```
class Building  {
public:
    void construct(string, Building*);
    void demolish();
    float collect_taxes(float, float, float) const;
    virtual float compute_tax(float, float, float) const = 0;
private:
    string the_address;
    Building *previous, *next;
};
```

No definition of a pure virtual function is required; you may supply one, but it can only ever be called using its fully qualified name from a member function of a derived class.

▷ The excuse for the = 0 syntax is that the addition of a new reserved word to C++ is always controversial—presumably, too many C++ programmers have bad memories of Cobol and PL/I—and pure virtual functions were a late addition to Release 2.0 of C++. Stroustrup felt that there wasn't time to argue for a new keyword, so he extended the meaning of zero as some sort of null value even further. If you think of a function definition as initializing the variable declared as the function's name,

---

[1] I am convinced that this ought to be "purely virtual"—is it a virtual function that is pure, or a function that is not only virtual, but *purely* so?—but we'd better follow the standard terminology or nobody else will understand what we're on about.

then a pure virtual function is a function initialized to the "null function". Which does make sense, even though no other sort of function is initialized using = in C++.

◁

C++ Into the Night

All I've sold you during the happy hour is a conventional imperative language, with a slightly peculiar syntax and machine-oriented semantics (C with a few spots of fresh paint daubed over the shabbier bits) augmented with a class construct suitable for implementing abstract datatypes and a simple inheritance mechanism. It isn't C++. This is.

Construction and Destruction

6

One of the messiest aspects of the C++ programs you have seen so far in this book is the means by which objects belonging to user-defined classes are established in their initial states. There has been a small multitude of member functions called `init` or `setup` or some such, whose job is to set the data members of a newly created object to suitable values. You have to remember to call these member functions each time an object is created, or risk the consequences of uninitialized members, consequences that can be particularly unpleasant when the members are pointers. A secondary nuisance is that an anonymous object can be created and initialized only in an extremely awkward way at best. The situation is no worse than you would find in many programming languages, and probably doesn't surprise you, but wouldn't it be nice if you could define a special member function that was automatically invoked whenever an object was created, and automatically performed whatever initialization was necessary at that time? As I've hinted in previous chapters, you can: such a member function is called a *constructor*.

For the reasons just outlined, constructors seem to be a very helpful innovation, but, as you may have heard, the road to hell is paved with good intentions, and Mr Shakespeare, who knew a thing or two, noticed how lilies that fester smell far worse then weeds. Constructors turn out to be more complicated than is altogether comfortable and, in conjunction with certain other features of C++, they present some novel traps for the unwary programmer. Once mastered and treated with care, they do provide an essential aid to making user-defined types as convenient to use as built-in ones.

At the far end of an object's lifetime we find that there are often actions that must be performed in order to dispose of it tidily. In particular, heap storage pointed to by data members must be deleted. Hence, you also see plenty of member functions, with names like `cleanup`, that must be called at the end of an object's lifetime. Failure to define and call these correctly can lead to memory leaks. More dangerously, on larger projects, a failure to make clear where the responsibility for deleting heap storage lies can lead to storage being deleted while it is still in use, or being deleted twice. Neither of these possibilities is healthy.

131

To help cope with the orderly destruction of objects, member functions called *destructors* may be defined; they are called automatically at the end of an object's lifetime. Although they are not a panacea for problems associated with the deletion of storage—only garbage collectors can be that—destructors do provide an orderly framework for the organization of deletions, making it easier to reason about what is going on—or going wrong, as the case may be.

CONSTRUCTORS

Dijkstra[1] remarks somewhere that once one has understood the assignment statement, one has, as it were, understood programming. He might have added: once one has understood constructors, one has understood C++. That is to say, in both cases, a seemingly innocuous language feature which one takes for granted really embodies the semantic basis of the language. In the case of assignment and imperative languages, the whole business of the update-able store, side-effects and statement sequencing is implicit in the meaning of an assignment. To really understand assignment, you must understand these things. In C++, constructors hold the key to understanding what an object is, and how it is created. Or, you could as well say, to understand constructors, you must understand these things.

We'll start with easy matters. A constructor is a member function with the same name as the class being defined. It has the peculiarity of not having any return type, not even `void`. The reasoning behind this is, roughly, that a constructor is doing something different from any other sort of function, namely turning a region of storage into an object. If a constructor was treated as a function returning an object, then logically, a constructor would have to be called to construct the object being returned. And so on. This would hardly do, so constructors don't return anything, they just ... construct.

Constructors and Declarations

Let's rework some old examples, replacing explicitly called initialization member functions with constructors.

The simplest constructors place every object of a class into the same initial state when it is constructed. An example where this is the right thing to do is the `StringQueue` class, seen in chapter 4. The member function `StringQueue::init` must always be called straight after a `StringQueue` object has been declared or created by `new`, to set the indices `the_front` and `the_back` to zero, lest the newly created queue appears to have some strings in. A constructor is just the ticket here, so the class should be defined as follows:

```
class StringQueue  {
public:
  StringQueue();
```

---

[1] A notorious computer scientist.

```
    All other members except init are as they were before
};
```

The constructor's declaration is recognizable by the name and the absence of any return type. The definition is trivial:

```
StringQueue::StringQueue()
{
  the_front = the_back = 0;
}
```

With this revised class definition, a declaration of a variable

```
StringQueue a_queue;
```

has the effect of initializing a_queue with a StringQueue object whose indices have already been correctly set up; a_queue can be safely used to enqueue strings immediately. Similarly,

```
StringQueue* a_queue_p = new StringQueue;
```

causes a_queue_p to be initialized with a pointer to a StringQueue object on the heap, whose pointers are zeroed.

More commonly, you want to specify the initial state of an object when you create it, usually by supplying some initial values for its data members. A constructor is a function, albeit a special one, so it can take arguments. The only question is: Since the constructor isn't explicitly called, how can you pass arguments to it? Where are you going to write the actual arguments?

If a class has a constructor taking arguments, then, when a variable of that class is declared, actual argument values may be written, enclosed in brackets, after the variable name. For example, if a class Womble has its constructor declared as

```
Womble(string name, int age);
```

then to create a Womble called Orinoco aged 4, we would declare

```
Womble silly_womble("Orinoco", 4);
```

The Womble constructor is called to create a Womble object, using "Orinoco" and 4 as the actual values for its name and age arguments; the object constructed is used to initialize the variable silly_womble.

We might alternatively need to create a Womble on the heap and initialize a pointer variable to point to it. In this case, the constructor's arguments are written after the class name in the call to new, like this:

```
Womble *wom_p = new Womble("Orinoco", 4);
```

A typical example of a simple constructor with arguments is provided by the TimeSetting class, for which we previously had to use the init operation to initialize objects. The class definition could be rewritten:

```
class TimeSetting {
public:
  TimeSetting(int, int);
    all other members except init as they were before
}
```

with the constructor defined to do what init did previously:

```
TimeSetting::TimeSetting(int h, int m)
{
   assert (0 <= h && h < 24 &&
           0 <= m && m < 60);
   hours = h;
   mins = m;
}
```

The presence of the constructor could make `init` redundant, thereby increasing data protection.

Consider now the `TimerEvent` class, which includes `TimeSetting` objects as data members. Should not this class's constructor initialize `time_on` and `time_off` to some well-defined value? The best way of doing so is by using the `TimeSetting` constructor. Conceptually, when an object is created, its data members are created first, so it is natural for their constructors to be called. When we create a `TimerEvent`, the `TimeSetting` constructor is called twice, once to construct the `time_on` object, once for the `time_off` object. We can make sure these two objects are constructed in a well-defined state in one of two ways.

The first way is to define what is called a *default constructor*, which is a constructor that can be called with no arguments. `StringQueue::StringQueue` is a default constructor. The default constructor is called whenever an object is created but no constructor arguments are supplied; in those cases, as we saw with `StringQueue`, the brackets are also omitted, so the declaration or the call of `new` looks as though no initialization was being performed.

▷ Even if you think that the brackets ought to be there, so you can see that a constructor is involved, there are syntactical difficulties.

```
StringQueue a_queue();
```

looks like the declaration of a function taking no arguments and returning a
◁ `StringQueue`.

Assuming we wanted to set `time_on` and `time_off` to midnight when a `TimerEvent` is first created, we could define a default constructor for `Time-Setting` in the following way.

```
class TimeSetting {
public:
   TimeSetting(int, int);
   TimeSetting();
    all other members as they were before
}

TimeSetting::TimeSetting()
{
   hours = mins = 0;
}
```

As this example shows, it is permissible to provide a class with more than one constructor. In fact, it is unusual not to do so. This is a special case of a more general facility, called function overloading, which will be described at length in chapter 7. With `TimeSetting`'s default constructor available, the constructor for `TimerEvent` can be particularly simple.

```
TimerEvent::TimerEvent() {}
```

All it does is silently invoke the default constructor for `TimeSetting` to initialize its two data members,

Perhaps this solution to initializing the data members of a `TimerEvent` is not acceptable. It may be felt inappropriate to provide default initializations for all `TimeSettings`, or perhaps whoever wrote the `TimeSetting` class failed to provide a default constructor. This leaves you having to initialize the data members using the `TimeSetting` constructor that takes arguments. Where are you going to write *their* values?

When you define a constructor for a class K, you may follow the formal argument declarations by a *member initialization list*. This has the form

```
: member-name( expression ) { , member-name( expression ) }
```

where the *member-name*s are the names of data members of K. The effect is to pass the *expression*s as arguments to the members' constructors when a K object is constructed. Hence, a different way of setting `time_on` and `time_off` when creating a `TimerEvent` would be by defining `TimerEvent`'s constructor with a member initialization list.

```
TimerEvent::TimerEvent():time_on(0, 0), time_off(0, 0) {}
```

Constructors with a member initialization list and an empty body are very common. They simply pass arguments, via the initialization list, to their data members' constructors.

The order in which the members are named in a member initialization list is irrelevant. Constructors for data members are always called in the order in which the members are declared in the class definition. It is unwise to rely on this order unless you really must: code that depends on the order of declarations is obscure and unstable—it can be upset by a simple piece of editing.

"But", you point out smugly, "built-in types don't have constructors." Well, they do actually. I just didn't mention it. Of course, they don't really, but you are allowed to behave as if they did. For example, you may initialize an `int` variable like this:

```
int i(19);
```

And why not? Hence, the default constructor for `TimeSetting` could have been defined like this:

```
TimeSetting::TimeSetting():hours(0), mins(0) {}
```

Although a constructor does not return a value, as such, you can still make an explicit call to a constructor to obtain an anonymous object. This is explained by saying that a "temporary variable" is created and then initialized by the constructor. Whether that makes sense or not, you can use explicit constructor calls to get close to writing down constants of user-defined types. For example,

```
TimeSetting(12,0)
```

is an expression which can be used as if it were a literal of type `TimeSetting`, with value midday. You could use it like this:

```
cout << "Wake up, it is " ;
TimeSetting(12, 0).display();
cout << endl ;
```

Constructors provide a means of initializing constant objects. If a variable of a user-defined type is declared with `const`, its constancy begins when its constructor has finished its work, just as the constancy of a variable of a built-in type begins after its initialization. Thus, you could have defined a named constant to represent midday as follows:

```
const TimeSetting midday(12, 0);
```

Only constant member functions of the class `TimeSetting` could be called through `midday`. These, as you will recall, cannot change the value of any data members, so the variable `midday` will forever hold the value 12:00.

Constructors' member initialization lists allow you to initialize constant members, which you specify by putting `const` in front of their declaration. Such data members can be used when a member should be given a value once and for all at the time an object is created. For example, the base class `File` used in the compiler simulation of chapter 5 would have had a constructor if we had known about them then. Had it done so, the member `the_file_name` could have been constant, preventing its being changed.

```
class File  {
public:
   File(const string&);
   string filename() const;
   virtual void print() const;
private:
   const string the_file_name;
};
```

The constructor would be defined simply to initialize the data member.

```
File::File(const string& fn): the_file_name(fn) {}
```

The member initialization list must be used for this purpose, since an assignment to a constant data member is forbidden, even in the constructor for the class it is part of—the data member is initialized by its constructor before the body is executed.

Constructors and Resource Allocation

We have seen two common patterns of constructor: ones with an empty body that use a member initialization list to pass on their arguments to constructors for their data members, and ones that do some checking on their actual arguments' values before assigning them to data members. A third common and important pattern comprises constructors that allocate some resources to be used by the object being constructed. By far the most common resource that must be allocated in a constructor is heap memory; you find this being required when a class has pointer members that must be dynamically initialized.

Most of the time in my examples, I've made life easy for myself by using the `string` class out of the standard library to hold character strings. Sometimes, when you aren't going to do anything very exciting or difficult with your strings, it may not be worthwhile incurring the overhead of the library class, but if you use C-style strings (arrays of `char`) you will have to allocate space for them yourself. When the C-strings in question are data members of some class, the allocation typically happens inside constructors.

As an example, consider a class to be used inside some program that provides an interface to network resources on the Internet. Increasingly, most resources are identified by Uniform Resource Locators, or URLs, those extended filenames that you see everywhere the Internet is mentioned. A typical example, identifying a World-Wide Web page is

```
http://www.w3.org/hypertext/WWW/Addressing/URL/Overview.html
```

URLs possess an internal structure. The full story is quite complicated, but a simplified version provides enough material for a non-trivial class. The first part of the URL is called a *scheme* and identifies the type of object. Here, the scheme is `http` (which stands for Hypertext Transfer Protocol), showing that this URL identifies a World-Wide Web page. Separating the scheme from the rest comes the magic sequence `://`. The remainder of the string concatenates a machine name (strictly speaking, an Internet domain name) with a pathname. The machine name goes up to but does not include another `/`; everything from this `/` on is the pathname, typically consisting of a sequence of components separated by `/`s. (The components probably are directory names, with the last one a filename.) So, in this example, we have the pathname `/hypertext/WWW/Addressing/URL/Overview.html` on the machine `www.w3.org`.

To use a URL inside some client program, it may be necessary to take it to pieces and separate the components. For the moment, considering only World-Wide Web pages, we will define a class that stores the machine name and pathname as separate C-strings. The constructor for this class will have to take apart the URL string and, if it is syntactically well-formed, allocate space on the heap to hold the two parts. The class declaration could look like this:

```
class WebPage  {
public:
    WebPage(const char*);
    void connect();
private:
    char* the_machine;
    char* the_path;
};
```

The member `connect` will do whatever is necessary to access the page through cyberspace; it will be as well for us not to enquire into its definition. It is the constructor that interests us; it could be defined like this:

```
const int prefix_len = 7;

WebPage::WebPage(const char* u_string)
{
  int n = strlen(u_string);
  if(strncmp(u_string, "http://", prefix_len) != 0)
  {
    cerr << "malformed URL string \""<< u_string <<
        "\" did not begin http://" << endl;
    abort();
  }
  const  char* suffix = u_string + prefix_len;
  int i = 0;
  while (suffix[i] != '\0' && suffix[i] != '/')
    ++i;

  the_machine = new char[i + 1];
  strncpy(the_machine, suffix, i);
  the_machine[i] = '\0';
  int p_len = n - (i + prefix_len);
  the_path = new char[p_len];
  strcpy(the_path, suffix+i);
}
```

The code makes use of C-string manipulation functions from the standard C library, as well as a bit of unscrupulous pointer arithmetic.[2] The constant `prefix_len` is equal to the length of the prefix `http://`; the function call `strncmp(u_string, "http://", prefix_len)` compares the first seven characters of `u_string` with `http://`, returning zero if they match; `strncpy(the_machine, suffix, i)` copies the first i characters of `suffix` into the area pointed to by `the_machine`; `strcpy(the_path, suffix+i)` copies all of the string beginning at the address `suffix+i` into `the_path`.

Although heap space is the resource most commonly allocated in constructors, it is not the only one. A constructor might be the appropriate place to obtain a lock on some shared device, or to open and read a disk file containing a persistent representation of the object's data. In general, a constructor's job is to create an environment in which the other member functions will be able to perform as specified. In other words, a constructor establishes an object as one of its class.

It follows that, as well as convenience, constructors provide you with a degree of safety, by making it impossible to create uninitialized objects. You will recall that my class of range-checked arrays suffered from the major weakness that it was necessary to call the initialization function `alpha` after an object was created, before any other operation could safely be applied to it. If we replace `alpha` by a constructor:

---

[2]Whereas the main purpose of this example is to show how constructors provide a helpful means of encapsulating the allocation of heap memory, it also shows why it is generally a better idea to use strings than C-strings.

```
MyIntArray::MyIntArray(int lower, int upper, int initial)
{
    body the same as the original alpha function
}
```

then the following becomes illegal, since there is no default constructor.

```
MyIntArray not_initialized;
not_initialized.put(12, 34);
```

Instead, `MyIntArray` objects can (and must) be initialized when they are created.

```
MyIntArray correctly_initialized(1, 100, 0);
```

Constructors and Inheritance

Inheritance is the only major lacuna remaining in the story of initializing objects using constructors. If you are constructing an object of a class derived from some base class, how can the private data members belonging to the base be initialized? They are inaccessible to the constructor in the derived class just as much as they are to any other member function in the derived class.

This problem and its solution can be illustrated by an attempt to generalize the `WebPage` class to handle other sorts of network objects. Talk of "sorts of" objects immediately suggests public inheritance. Assume (with apologies to Internet experts) that every sort of thing that a URL can identify has a pathname on some machine, but that each sort of object might have other attributes. Assume also that the idea of connecting to an object always makes sense, but that the way you connect depends on the sort of object. In other words, the `connect` operation is a pure virtual function. This analysis suggests that the classes for specific sorts of net resources should be derived from an abstract base class, which I'll call `NetResource`.

```
class NetResource  {
public:
  NetResource(const char*);
  virtual void connect() = 0;
  const char* machine() const
  {  return the_machine;  }
  const char* path() const
  {  return the_path;  }
private:
  char* the_machine;
  char* the_path;
};
```

Public functions to access the values of the data members have been provided on the assumption that member functions of derived classes, particularly their versions of `connect`, will need to use them. (In chapter 9 we will see a slightly nicer way of providing this access.)

We will consider two classes derived from `NetResource`, one for representing World-Wide Web pages, another for files accessible by the file transfer protocol `ftp`. The former needs no extra data, as we saw previously; it need only supply a definition of `connect`—but we're still not going to go into that—and a constructor.

```
class WWW: public NetResource {
public:
  WWW(const char*);
  void connect();
};
```

For files that can be transferred by ftp, we also need to record a login name and password to be used to connect to the remote machine. These will be passed as additional arguments to the constructor.

```
class FTP: public NetResource {
public:
  FTP(const char*, const char*, const char*);
  void connect();
private:
  char* the_username;
  char* the_password;
};
```

Now for the definitions of the constructors. I will assume the entire URL is passed to `NetResource::NetResource`. The scheme is of no interest at that point, it can just be stripped off.[3] Otherwise, the constructor behaves just like the earlier example.

```
NetResource::NetResource(const char* u_string)
{
  int n = strlen(u_string);
  const char* seppix = strstr(u_string, "://");
  if (seppix == 0)
  {
    cerr << "malformed URL string \"" << u_string
        << "\" doesn't contain ://" << endl;
    abort();
  }

  const char* suffix = seppix + 3;
  int i = 0;
  while (suffix[i] != '\0' && suffix[i] != '/')
    i += 1;

  the_machine = new char[i + 1];
  strncpy(the_machine, suffix, i);
  the_machine[i] = '\0';
```

---

[3]I know that not every sort of URL has `://` in it, but adding still more grubby C-string manipulations to deal properly with all schemes adds little to the example.

```
    int p_len = n - (i + prefix_len);
    the_path = new char[p_len];
    strcpy(the_path, suffix+i);
}
```

We can never create `NetResource` objects, only FTP and WWW ones, so consider next the constructor for the class WWW. It will take a URL as its argument and should check that it has the prefix `http`, for this is the scheme for World-Wide Web pages. The constructor must also arrange for the URL string to be dissected and for the data members `the_machine` and `the_path` to be initialized with the corresponding substrings, but how?

Constructors are not inherited, so the class WWW does not have a member `NetResource` that could be used for this purpose. This turns out to be just as well, as some strange behaviour would result if constructors were inherited—see the ARM for details. Constructors can't be virtual either, in case you think that would help. (Would it? A virtual constructor might be a very weird sort of function.) An explicit call to the `NetResource` constructor from within the WWW constructor, perhaps? Perhaps not. As I previously explained, an explicit call of a constructor causes a temporary variable to be created and initialized. A call of `NetResource::NetResource` from within `WWW::WWW` will have no effect on the WWW object under construction; it will merely create, initialize and throw away a temporary `NetResource` object. It is necessary to invoke the base class's constructor in some other way. The member initialization list notation is used to achieve the desired effect. The names appearing in such a list may include, in addition to data members, the name of an immediate base class. (An immediate base class is one that is explicitly named in a class's declaration.) The constructor for WWW can pass the argument it doesn't know what to do with to the constructor for `NetResource`, which will take it apart and initialize the appropriate data members. Thus, we get the constructor:

```
const int w_prefix_len = 7;

WWW::WWW(const char* u_string):NetResource(u_string)
{
  if (strncmp(u_string, "http://", w_prefix_len) != 0)
  {
    cerr << "Alleged WWW URL" << u_string
     << " doesn't begin \"http://\""
     << endl;
    abort();
  }
}
```

The constructor for FTPs is hardly more complicated.

```
const int f_prefix_len = 6;

FTP::FTP(const char* u_string, const char* username,
                              const char* password)
        :NetResource(u_string)
{
```

```
if (strncmp(u_string, "ftp://", f_prefix_len)!=0)
{
  cerr << "Alleged ftp URL" << u_string
    << " doesn't begin \"ftp://\""
    << endl;
  abort();
}
the_username = new char[strlen(username)+1];
strcpy(the_username, username);
the_password = new char[strlen(password)+1];
strcpy(the_password, password);
}
```

The constructor calls implied by a member initialization list are made before the body, if any, of the constructor is called. Base classes are initialized before data members. This means that objects are constructed from the base upwards. For example, when an FTP object is created, the data members of its `NetResource` part are initialized first, then, since no data members are named in the member initialization list, the body of the constructor is executed. This may seem a bit backwards, with the scheme being checked after the `NetResource` has already been set up, but the ordering doesn't seem terribly serious. If you like, there is nothing to stop you using explicitly called `init` member functions, in whatever order you prefer, if the order in which constructors are executed isn't right for your application. Constructors can be convenient, but you don't have to use them if you don't want to.

▷ You can call member functions from inside constructors. You can even call virtual functions from inside constructors, but they perforce behave somewhat differently in this context. During construction, an object of class K isn't yet a proper object. In implementation terms, this is literally true: in particular, the data structure used for virtual function calling isn't set up while the constructors for base classes are being executed. If your class K is derived from some base class B, then, if a virtual function v is called from inside a constructor for B, then the function called will be B::v, no matter if the B constructor has been invoked while constructing a K. Even though you might reason that the pointer `this` is pointing to a K object, it isn't: it's ◁ pointing to something in the process of becoming a K object.

Copy Constructors

One form of initialization requires special treatment: initialization of a variable with the value of an existing object. Just as one can write:

```
int i = j;
```

or, if you prefer

```
int i(j);
```

where j is an integer variable that already exists, so you might want to write

```
TimeSetting s = t;
```

or

```
TimeSetting s(t);
```

where t is a TimeSetting variable that already exists. The second form shows clearly that, in order to do this, we need a constructor for TimeSetting objects that takes a TimeSetting object as its argument, and makes a copy of it. Such a constructor is called a *copy constructor.*

Here's a trick question: What should be the type of the formal argument to a copy constructor? It's a trick question because I've encouraged you to believe that constructors are called when a variable is initialized in a declaration or when an object is created by new. True, constructors are called under those circumstances, but they are called at other times, too. A constructor is called whenever an object is created. The sensitive reader will catch a faint whiff of festering lilies at this point: if you don't know exactly when objects are created, you won't know exactly when C++ calls a constructor. Constructors are different from familiar sorts of function in that they may be called implicitly without your knowing about it, and if you're not prepared there may be surprises in store. As we shall see.

The most important case that has been overlooked so far is that, when a function is called, constructors are invoked to initialize each formal argument passed by value with the actual argument values supplied. (Argument passing is semantically the same as variable initialization.) Similarly, when a function returns an object by value, a constructor will be called to copy the returned value back to the caller.

Returning to my question, you should now be able to see why the copy constructor for a class K cannot be declared in the obvious way as K::K(K). If it were, then the object being copied would be passed to the copy constructor by value, so a copy of it would have to be constructed using the copy constructor. The object being copied to be passed to the copy constructor to be copied would have to be passed to the copy constructor by value, so a copy of it would have to be constructed using the copy constructor. I could go on like this for a long time, but let us just say: and so on. Infinite regressions are not welcome on finite computers, hence a copy constructor *must* take its argument by reference. Most likely, a copy constructor will not alter its argument, so it is usual to define K::K(const K&); this has the helpful effect of making it possible to copy constant objects.

Copy constructors are often quite trivial. For example,

```
TimeSetting::TimeSetting(const TimeSetting& t)
            :hours(t.hours), mins(t.mins) {}
```

Even when a constructor would normally have to do range checking of its arguments, a copy constructor can be more relaxed, because its argument is an object that has already been successfully constructed.

We have seen two different syntactic forms for initializing a variable of a built-in type when it is declared,

```
int i(9);
```

```
int j = 9;
```

but only the equivalent of the former for variables of a user-defined class. Both can actually be used. Here are some examples.

```
TimeSetting t(18, 15);
TimeSetting s = t ;
TimeSetting v = TimeSetting(17, 58);
```

The first calls the constructor `TimeSetting::TimeSetting(int, int)`; the second uses the copy constructor. The third form of initializing declaration first calls `TimeSetting::TimeSetting(int, int)` to create a temporary object which is then used to initialize the variable v using the copy constructor. (The ARM says that this copying can be optimized away. The draft standard appears to say that it can only be optimized away if there are no side-effects that you could detect.)

Copy constructors for classes with data members which are pointers must be written with care; if you just copy the pointer you end up with two objects sharing heap memory, so that updates to one affect the other. This may or may not be what you want. More likely, it may not. Here is a copy constructor for `WebPages` that avoids the problem by allocating new memory for its data members.

```
WebPage::WebPage(const WebPage& u)
{
    the_machine = new char[strlen(u.the_machine)+1];
    the_path = new char[strlen(u.the_path)+1];
    strcpy(the_machine, u.the_machine);
    strcpy(the_path, u.the_path);
}
```

If inheritance is involved, the usual complications ensue. For example, the copy constructor for the class FTP must copy the strings being pointed to by the members `the_username` and `the_password`, but it must also ensure that the strings pointed to by its argument's `the_machine` and `the_path` members are copied too. The copy constructor of the `NetResource` class will do this, but not without being asked to. As with other constructors, a copy constructor may have a member initialization list, which can include base classes, so, to copy all of an FTP object, the following constructor is required:

```
FTP::FTP(const FTP& f):NetResource(f)
{
    the_username = new char[strlen(f.the_username)+1];
    the_password = new char[strlen(f.the_password)+1];
    strcpy(the_username, f.the_username);
    strcpy(the_password, f.the_password);
}
```

The argument passed to the `NetResource` constructor via the member initialization list is of type FTP, but inside the `NetResource` constructor it will be treated as a `NetResource` object—an object of a derived class can always be used where an object of its base class is expected.

DESTRUCTORS

A constructor constructs, so a destructor... destroys. More precisely, and less violently, a destructor undoes the work of a constructor, by releasing any resources that the constructor allocated, dismantling the environment that allowed member functions to work correctly on an object. After a destructor has done its work, you no longer have an object, just some bytes. So, the destructor had better not do its work until you no longer need an object.

Almost always, destructors are called automatically, at the end of an object's lifetime, without any explicit call. The end of a local object's lifetime is when control reaches the end of the block it is declared in; for a global object, it is usually just after the execution of `main` finishes; for a heap object it is when `delete` is called on a pointer pointing to it.

▷ Treat with suspicion anyone who tells you that a destructor is called for a local object "when the object goes out of scope", even though that is what the ARM says. A scope is a region of program text, and only names have scope. It only makes sense to talk about "*where* a *name* goes out of scope" and that is only indirectly ◁ relevant to destructors.

If a program terminates by a call to `abort`, no destructors are called. Beware of this behaviour if your destructors are supposed to release device locks or some similar system resource.

Defining and Using Destructors

A destructor for a class is declared as a member function taking no arguments and, like a constructor, having no return type. Its name is unlike the name of any other entity in a C++ program: it consists of the class's name with a tilde (~) in front of it. That is, the destructor for a class `Womble` is declared as `~Womble()`. The benefit of this unusual form of name is that it is hard not to read the ~ as "not", which emphasizes that a destructor like ~Womble negates the effect of a constructor like `Womble`.

Because a destructor's mission is to undo the work of a constructor, to decide what the destructor for a class must do, you can usefully start by looking at what the constructors for that class will have done. Very often, consideration of the constructors leads you to conclude that the destructor need do nothing. For example, `TimeSetting` constructors set `hours` and `mins` to specific values. After a `TimeSetting` object is destroyed, the values of its members should be undefined. The values they happen to have at the point of destruction are no worse or better than any others, so the destructor does not need to do anything.

There are some marginal uses of destructors that do not conform to the pattern of dismantling the environment set up by a constructor. A destructor that simply announces it has been called can provide useful tracing information for debugging and profiling. Another useful debugging aid based on destructors is that of setting members to some "impossible" value—a negative time of day, for example. This can't always be done—all available values may be meaningful—but when it can, it helps you find bugs caused by continuing to use memory after it has been deleted. This sort of mistake, which just about everyone makes sooner or later when using complicated data structures with pointers to shared memory, leads to unpredictable bugs, with behaviour that is hard to reproduce consistently. By deliberately corrupting the data members of deleted objects, you make sure that the bug surfaces in a consistent and identifiable form.

The real job of a destructor is to delete space, decrement reference counts, release locks, close files, and so on. Each of these actions is the negation of an operation that will usually have been performed by a constructor—allocating space, incrementing reference counts, obtaining locks, opening files—although the constructor may only have done some preliminary work—setting a pointer member to NULL or zeroing a reference count—to allow a member function to perform the operation. The MyIntArray class is a perfect example: the constructor calls new [] to allocate the array, so the destructor should call delete [] to free it.

```
MyArray::~MyArray()
{
    delete [] the_array ;
    the_array = NULL ;
}
```

Here, I've set the pointer to NULL, so that check_index will detect any attempts to use an array after it has been destroyed. The task of disposing of an array, which previously had to be done by explicitly calling the member function omega, will now be done automatically at the end of the object's lifetime, so such errors should be rare. They can still occur, though, if there are several pointers pointing to the same object, for example.

If an object of type K has members which are themselves objects, the destructors for those members will be called after the body of ~K has finished execution. Recall the classes TreeNode and Tree from chapter 4. TreeNode has the following data members:

```
string TN_value;
Tree TN_left;
Tree TN_right;
```

The member function init as originally presented would most naturally be made a constructor.

```
TreeNode::TreeNode(const string& s) :TN_value(s) {}
```

A default constructor for Tree will correctly initialize TN_left and TN_right:

```
Tree::Tree():root(NULL) {}
```

Since a TreeNode includes no dynamically allocated space or other resources, the destructor for TreeNode need do nothing explicitly.

```
TreeNode::~TreeNode() {}
```

After this destructor has finished doing nothing, the destructors for the data members will be called, in reverse order of declaration. We know that, as strings are inserted into a tree, its root will be updated to point to a `TreeNode` on the heap, so we can see that the destructor should delete `root`.

```
Tree::~Tree()
{   delete root; }
```

Whereas, when `Tree` objects were deleted by an explicitly called cleanup function, it was necessary to walk the tree recursively, deleting its nodes, when a destructor is used, nothing more than the deletion of the root is required. This deletion causes the destructor for the `TreeNode` that `root` points to to be called, which in turn will call the destructors for the left and right sub-nodes, which will then be deleted, causing the destructor calls and deletions to spread right down the tree.

Destructors are automatically called for local variables, when a function returns, and for global variables on normal termination of the program. Any pointer to a heap object must always be deleted explicitly, to cause the destructor to be called for the object that was pointed to.

There remains the question of the string member `TN_value`. As you probably suspect, a string object usually contains a dynamically allocated array of `char` inside it. (The library standard doesn't actually stipulate this implementation, but it is certainly the easiest and most obvious way of providing the behaviour it does specify.) You might even have wondered how this array gets deleted, since you would hardly expect a library class to carry a built-in memory leak. If you're bright enough to wonder about that, by now you will know the answer. The string class has a destructor and the destructor deletes any heap space used storing the characters of the string. In the case of a `TreeNode` the string destructor will be called to free the space used by `TN_value` after the subtrees `TN_left` and `TN_right` have been destroyed.

Destructors and Inheritance

It should come as no surprise that, when an object belongs to a derived class, the destructor for its base class is called after the destructors for its data members. The object is destroyed in the opposite order to that in which it was constructed. If the destructor in each class takes care of deallocating its own resources, everything will work fine.

Destructors are not inherited, but unlike constructors, destructors can be virtual. Indeed, the destructor in a base class better had be virtual. A reasonably feasible function for decoding URLs illustrates this. Suppose I have written a function that takes a URL string as its argument, looks at the scheme, constructs an object of an appropriate class, derived from `NetResource`, on the heap, and returns a pointer to it.

```
NetResource* decode_URL(const char* a_URL)
{
  if (strncmp(a_URL, "ftp://", f_prefix_len) == 0)
    return new FTP(a_URL);
  else if (strncmp(a_URL, "http://", w_prefix_len) == 0)
    return new WWW(a_URL);
```

```
    else return NULL;
}
```

I can initialize a variable using this function and then use it.

```
NetResource *uu  =
  decode_URL("ftp://research.att.com/dist/c++std/WP/body.pdf");
if (uu)
  uu->connect();
```

The fact that `connect` is virtual means the right protocol will be used to access whatever the URL denotes. Once I've finished with the connection, I will have finished with the object holding the components of the URL, and, being a tidy programmer, I will return it to the free store.

```
delete uu;
```

Feasible definitions of the destructors for the relevant classes would be:

```
NetResource::~NetResource()
{
  delete [] the_machine ;
  delete [] the_path ;
}

FTP::~FTP()
{
  delete [] the_username ;
  delete [] the_password ;
}
```

The type of `uu` is `NetResource*`, so, if the destructors are statically bound, the object pointed to will be destroyed by `NetResource::~NetResource`. Since the object in question is really an FTP, there is no possible way for its `username` and `password` members to be deleted. There will be a memory leak.

There are more serious things in programming than memory leaks. Extrapolate this example to destructors that should release locks on shared devices and you can see that failure to make a destructor virtual can seriously mess up a computing environment. So make destructors virtual in base classes.

This doesn't mean that every destructor should be virtual. As ever, the use of the virtual mechanism imposes a time and space overhead, which you will want to avoid if you can, so a class that is not intended for use as a base class—ever—need not have a virtual destructor.

▷ It might seem unlikely, but a pure virtual destructor can be useful. A class is an abstract base class if it contains at least one pure virtual function. It is possible to find yourself in the position of defining a class that you want to be abstract—you don't want to be able to create objects of this class, only ones of classes derived from it—but all of its member functions should be inherited, not virtual, because any derived class is a proper extension of the base. Since the base class's destructor ought to be virtual, why not make it pure virtual, so that you have an abstract base class? You still have to provide a definition of the destructor, because, despite being pure, it will be called when objects of classes derived from your abstract base class are destroyed.

The use of this technique does require you to come to terms with the idea that no object belonging to an abstract base class can be created, but such objects can be destroyed.

THE TROUBLE WITH CONSTRUCTORS

Something ought to be bothering you. How have we managed without constructors and destructors until chapter 6? Simple: if you don't define these functions yourself, the C++ system will do it for you. Don't throw up your hands, asking "Why didn't you say so in the first place, instead of going on about defining constructors and all that?". The whole trouble with constructors is that the C++ system is defining and calling functions you didn't explicitly instruct it to, and sometimes *they don't do what you require.* You must understand how to define your own constructors and destructors so that you can see what effect the ones generated by the system will have, and so you can take over when necessary.

Automatically Generated Member Functions

If you define a class without declaring a destructor or any constructors, these member functions will be generated for you. You might be concerned that automatically generated functions will increase the size of your code when you've carefully tried to keep it down (perhaps by deliberately omitting exactly these member functions, who knows?). It's all right—the missing functions are always declared, but definitions are only generated if they are used. So no definition of a copy constructor will be generated, for example, unless you pass an object to a function by value, or initialize a variable by copying another object. If, on the other hand, your concern is with execution speed, then you can expect the generated functions to be simple, and their calls to be optimized.

The simplest generated function is the default constructor—a constructor that takes no arguments. It is only generated if the programmer has declared no constructors at all. If you declare a constructor taking some arguments, no default constructor will be generated and you will have to supply values for the arguments whenever you create an object—not a bad idea, perhaps. If you declare no constructors, a default constructor that does nothing will be generated; it is a convenient fiction allowing you to create objects of your class with the usual semantics. Default constructors for the members of your class and its base class, if it has one, will still be called; if the members are also of a class with no constructors, a default constructor will be generated for them in turn.

The next simplest generated function is the destructor. A destructor is only generated for a class K that doesn't declare one if K is derived (directly or indirectly, because the automatic generation is done recursively) from a class that does have a destructor, or if K has at least one data member belonging to a class with a destructor. Once again, the generated function does nothing itself, but its presence causes the destructors for data members and base classes to be called. The empty destructor `TreeNode::~TreeNode` which I explicitly defined in the previous section performs exactly the same way. Since `Tree` and `string` have destructors, I could safely have omitted the definition.

So far, so good. That leaves the copy constructor.

If a class `K` does not declare a copy constructor, one will be automatically generated. It will copy all the data members. For each data member `X` of type `T`, if `T` is a pointer type or a built-in numerical type, a copy of the bits of `X` will be made; if `T` is a class with a copy constructor, that constructor will be used to make the copy; if `T` is a class without a copy constructor, one will be generated for `T` in the same way, applying the generation algorithm recursively as deeply as necessary, and used to make the copy. The unlovely jargon for the resulting copying operation is "memberwise copying".

Thus, my copy constructor for `TimeSetting` objects was strictly redundant; exactly the same effect would have been achieved by letting the system generate a memberwise copying operation for me.

In chapter 7 we will see that one other mischievous function may also be generated automatically, to deal with assignment of objects.

▷ You can apply the "address of" operator & to any object. You may like to think this is because an `operator&` member is automatically generated for every class that does not define its own, or you may prefer to think that taking the address of an object if a fundamental operation in the execution model of C++ (store and sequencing and all that), which can't help but be defined for all types of object. ◁

The generated functions provide sensible and useful default behaviour, so what is the excuse for all these dire warnings about constructors? What harm did a constructor ever do to anybody? Just this: a constructor copied a pointer, but not the object it pointed to.

Objects pointed to by pointers are never copied by default in C++. When you assign a pointer or pass it to a function by value, it is only the pointer that is copied. There is considerable justification for this interpretation of pointer semantics. To do otherwise would be grossly inefficient, both in time and space; it would be difficult to do correctly for arbitrary structures; it would prevent some of the characteristic ways of using pointers; it would be so incompatible with C and just about every other imperative language of any importance that mixing code in different languages would be impossible. So automatically generated copy constructors perform a shallow copy: only pointers and objects actually stored inside the object are copied, anything pointed to is not.

Anyone used to writing programs in a language that provides pointers will be familiar with the phenomenon of shallow copying, and will know when it is harmless and how to do deep copying when necessary. The trouble with copying in C++ is that the shallow copying may be going on in a function you didn't write and didn't explicitly call. It's easy not to realize, or to forget, or not to understand what is happening in code you've never seen. If you lapse in this way, you could be in for a rough ride.

A Short Catalogue of Disasters

My excuse? Sheer ignorance. My only plea in mitigation, a lengthy period writing programs in languages with a pure value semantics. Nevertheless, I should have known better. What really happened was marginally more obscure than the tale I'll tell, but not much.

The starting point was a simple lookup table, nothing fancy, just a set of pairs of strings consisting of a key and a value, with operations to insert a new pair and to find the value corresponding to a given key. In those days (this was a while ago) proper C++ libraries were not available, so string objects could not be used, these strings were going to have to be arrays of char.

The first attempt fell foul of shallow copying.

```
#include <iostream>
#include <string.h>
#include <stdlib.h>

const int table_size = 25;
```

A table entry is a key and value pair.

```
class Entry  {
public:
  Entry(char*, char*);
  char* key() const;
  char* value() const;
private:
  char *the_key;
  char *the_val;
} ;

Entry::Entry(char *k, char *v): the_key(k), the_val(v) {}

char* Entry::key() const {  return the_key;  }

char* Entry::value() const {  return the_val;  }
```

Let's pretend that the table was just an array of pointers to Entry objects, searched linearly.

```
class Table  {
public:
  Table();
  void insert(char*, char*);
  char* lookup(char* );
  void print() const;
private:
  Entry* the_table[TABLE_SIZE + 1];
  int n;
} ;

Table::Table()  {  n = 0;  }
```

```
void Table::insert(char* k, char* v)
{
  if (n == table_size)
  {
    cerr << "table overflow"  << endl;
    abort();
  }
  Entry *e = new Entry(k, v);
  the_table[n++] = e;
}
```

A well recommended way of carrying out a linear search is to put the thing you are searching for at the end of the table to begin with, so you are guaranteed to find it and don't have to test for the end of the table every time round the search loop. (This means the lookup member function can't be declared const, though.)

```
char* Table::lookup(char *k)
{
  Entry* dummy = new Entry(k, "");
  the_table[n] = dummy;
  int i = 0;
  while (strcmp(the_table[i]->key(), k) != 0)
    ++i;
  delete dummy;
  return i == n ? NULL: the_table[i]->value();
}
```

A simple test harness is enough to reveal something sadly awry.

```
int main()
{
  char buff1[255];
  char buff2[255];
  Table t;
  char c = 'y';
  cout << "Strings please" << endl;
  while (c=='y')
  {
    cout << "?   ";
    cin >> buff1;
    cout << "& ";
    cin >> buff2;
    t.insert(buff1, buff2);
    cout << "more?   ";
    cin >>c;
  }

  c = 'y';
  while (c == 'y')
```

```
    {
        cout << "Look up... " << flush;
        cin >> buff1;
        char *lk = t.lookup(buff1);
        cout << (lk == NULL? "not there": lk) << endl;
        cout << "Another?  ";
        cin >> c;
    }
    cout << "Bye...it was real" << endl;
    return EXIT_SUCCESS;
}
```

A typical run displays undesirable behaviour—although, of course, the program does exactly what the code says it will.

```
Strings please
?  marx
& engels
more?  y
?  marks
& spencer
more?  y
?  spenser
& marlowe
more?  n
Look up... marx
marlowe
Another?  y
Look up... marks
marlowe
Another?  y
Look up... spenser
marlowe
Another?  n
Bye...it was real
```

Adding a diagnostic print of the table after the entries have been inserted reveals all.

```
spenser & marlowe
spenser & marlowe
spenser & marlowe
3 entries
```

Every `Entry` object points to `buff1` and `buff2`, because the generated copy constructor used to initialize the data members of `Entry` only copies the pointers; every time the buffers' contents are changed, the entries in the table change. Every lookup succeeds because `buff1` is always being compared with itself.

That was certainly stupid, wasn't it? Never mind, it's easily fixed. The member `insert` should dynamically allocate space to hold copies of the buffered strings. Some people just have to try and do things in a classier way, though. In this instance, a class of dynamically allocated strings seems to offer an elegant solution. Perhaps one does, but this class is not that class.

```
class DynamicString {
public:
  DynamicString(char*);
  char* string() const
private:
  char* the_string;
};
```

The member functions are defined as follows:

```
DynamicString::DynamicString(char* s)
{
  the_string = new char[strlen(s)+1];
  strcpy(the_string, s);
}


char* DynamicString::string() const
{  return the_string; }
```

Returning a pointer to internal data, as I did in DynamicString::string, is not generally a good idea, but this class is only intended as a front for char* so it doesn't matter. Really. Perhaps. However, DynamicString does look more like a bug fix than a well thought out class. Changing the type of the arguments to Table::insert and the Entry constructor from char* to DynamicString and adding an extra call of the member function string to each of Entry::key and Entry::value minimizes the changes to the rest of the program.

```
class Entry  {
public:
  Entry(DynamicString k, DynamicString v);
  char* key();
  char* value();
private:
  DynamicString the_key;
  DynamicString the_val;
};

Entry::Entry(DynamicString k, DynamicString v)
       :the_key(k), the_val(v) {}

char* Entry::key() const {  return the_key.string();  }

char* Entry::value() const {  return the_val.string();  }

class Table  {
public:
  Table();
  void insert(DynamicString k, DynamicString v);
  char* lookup(char* k);
```

```
    void print() const;
  private:
    Entry* the_table[table_size + 1];
    int n;
};
```

The calls to `insert` in the test program now have to construct `DynamicString` objects for their arguments, but that doesn't seem too painful. In return, the calls of `new` and `strcpy` have been isolated in the `DynamicString` constructor.

And it works. But hang on a minute—there's a massive memory leak. This looks like a case for a destructor.

```
DynamicString::~DynamicString()
{
  delete the_string;
}
```

Oops! A bad move. The destructor I defined will be called whenever a `DynamicString` object reaches the end of its lifetime. Look carefully at the revised version of `Table::insert`.

```
void Table::insert(DynamicString k, DynamicString v)
{
  if (n == table_size)
  {
    cerr << "table overflow"  << endl;
    abort();
  }
  Entry *e = new Entry(k, v);
  the_table[n++] = e;
}
```

The arguments are `DynamicString` objects, whose lifetime extends to the point when control returns from the function. At that point, the `DynamicString` destructor is called to delete the C-string member. These two arguments were initialized with the actual arguments used to call `insert`—in the test program, two temporary objects constructed out of the character buffers. Argument passing is equivalent to initialization, so k and v will be initialized as if by the declarations

```
DynamicString k = DynamicString(buff1);
DynamicString v = DynamicString(buff2);
```

and that initialization is performed by...the copy constructor. No such member was declared for `DynamicString`, so the automatically generated one will be used, and it will copy the string *pointers* only from one `DynamicString` to another. The same thing will happen when the arguments to `insert` are passed on to the constructor for `Entry`. In total, three pairs of `DynamicString` objects are constructed and destroyed. Each destruction, however, deletes the same two arrays of `char`. The effect of deleting something three times is undefined. On the machine I was using when I first tried this program, heap memory was apparently reallocated immediately after a deletion, with the immensely amusing result that the program reverted to its original misbehaviour. On my current machine, it just crashes after a while, which is better, really.

Adding a copy constructor to `DynamicString` will fix this problem, but thinking about why the version without it fails makes you aware of how much space allocation, copying and de-allocation is going on, so it's more likely that you would change to passing all your dynamic strings by reference, which will also fix the program. A better idea would be to redesign the classes. Since the example has hopefully made its point, we can do better still and abandon it.

You might well think that this story is not so much a catalogue of disasters as a catalogue of incompetence—the design was flawed from the beginning, the muddle with constructors isn't the only thing wrong with the code, and the attempt to patch it up was ill-considered. Alternatively, instead of blaming constructors, you might blame C-strings and the aliasing that results from using pointers. Whichever way you look at it, these things can and do happen.

Two general strategies can be adopted to prevent such debacles. The first is to be prepared for anything, the second is to prevent the things you are not prepared for. Each might be appropriate in different contexts.

To be prepared for everything, write all your own constructors and a destructor. For this strategy to be a successful one, the members ought to do something sensible. In the case of memory allocation, it is not necessary to religiously implement deep copying of all objects; other, more sophisticated tactics can be adopted, but the constructors and destructor must cooperate to ensure that no memory is deleted more than once and that memory is only shared when such sharing is harmless.

"Fie on that!", you may say, "I shall always pass my objects by reference, only ever copy them explicitly and manage my own deletions." Sure you will, but how can you be sure anyone else who uses your classes will do the same? You do want your code to be reusable, don't you? You can try documenting it, but not everyone reads documentation, and not everyone who reads it understands it.

If you choose not to implement the copy constructor and so on, you must not simply ignore it—if your software is good enough to be re-used, even by you, you can be pretty sure that, sooner or later, somebody will pass an object by value. You can prevent this: declare the copy constructor but make it a private member of your class. Almost any attempt to use private member functions, even implicitly, will generate a compiler error. The reason for the "almost" is, of course, that member functions of your class are legally able to use private members. If, however, you omit to provide any definitions of these functions— which will presumably suit you, since it's a bit silly to define functions you want to prevent being called—the linker will complain about any attempt to use them that gets past the compiler.

If I thought that copying a `MyIntArray` object was excessively expensive, and I wanted to prevent it, I would add the declaration

```
MyIntArray::MyIntArray(const MyIntArray&) ;
```

to the class's private members, and never define the copy constructor.

Declaring private members is preferable to the, perhaps more immediately obvious, alternative:

```
MyIntArray::MyIntArray(const MyIntArray&) ;
{
  cerr << "You can't copy a MyIntArray!!" << endl;
}
```

What happens next? No doubt the end user of your program will find this message particularly enlightening, and may well draw strength from it as the program subsequently crashes, misbehaves or limps along. If the attempted copy had resulted in a compiler message, seen by the programmer, the error could have been corrected before anyone tried to use the program.

Don't think you have some sort of moral obligation to implement copying operations, or that forbidding them instead is a weedy option or a neglect of duty. Copying large objects or pointer-based data structures that may involve cycles can be expensive and complicated. Such data structures should not be copied except when necessary. Allowing them to be casually passed by value or used to initialize variables may be doing a disservice to anyone using your classes. Then again, you may want to forbid copying for the sake of semantic consistency. You are not able to pass built-in arrays by value, should you be able to do so with an enhanced array type that you have devised? You may even come across cases where it is only meaningful to have one object of some class, so you should not be permitted to make copies of it.

There are no easy decisions. Programming, life…it's all the same.

More About Functions

Classes provide structure to a program, but (member) functions still do all the work. Classes can be made more convenient to work with by providing some alternative syntax for function calls. This has been done in C++ in such a way that member functions of user-defined classes can be used as if they were built-in operators. In mathematics, when you write an expression like $a + b$ you are just using a convenient notation for applying a function that performs addition to two arguments. We know how to use this infix operator notation with built-in types in C++; the language has facilities that allow you to apply functions to user-defined types using the same operator notation. This means that built-in types are not privileged over user-defined ones; both can be manipulated in a uniform way. This uniformity cannot be achieved by a syntactical extension alone; it is also necessary to extend the power of functions before they can be used like operators, because of the peculiar nature of some of the C++ operators that have to be imitated.

Functions in themselves provide some structure to a program. In fact, for many years they have been used as the only structuring mechanism. Recent developments in data abstraction have tended to overshadow functions, to the extent that some of their potential is often overlooked. After considering extensions to the simple functions we already know about, I will describe some ways of using functions that take you beyond the obvious.

Syntactic and semantic enhancements to function calls would be enough to make them suitable components with which to build convenient new types, and functions may provide interesting possibilities for program structuring, but many programmers would refrain from using them extensively if doing so would make their programs less efficient. Before looking at any other new aspects of C++ functions, we will see how, in many cases, the overhead traditionally associated with function calls can be eliminated.

INLINE FUNCTIONS

We have become used to thinking of functions as an abstraction technique, but you shouldn't forget that they are also a way of saving space in the generated code—the code for the function body is generated only once; the function is called with a short instruction sequence many times. Because there is an execution time overhead in calling a function, and because most compiler optimizations only work on blocks of straight line code, from a performance point of view, using functions allows you to trade off code space against execution speed. All modern program structuring methods encourage the extensive use of functions; using object-oriented programming tends especially to lead to many small member functions being defined, for example, forwarding functions, which do nothing but call another function, or inspection functions, which simply return the value of a private data member. This desire to use functions as a structuring technique means that the space/time tradeoff always gets resolved in favour of space, even though that may not be what you would choose to do on performance grounds alone.

Inlining is a wonderful idea for restoring the choice between space and time optimization. By preceding the declaration of a function with the keyword `inline`, you specify to the compiler that, instead of generating code for this function and its calls in the usual way, it should generate a copy of the code for the function body wherever it is called. So you have something that looks like a function, provides the structuring and argument type checking required of a function, but executes and can be optimized like in-line code. For example, the function used to check whether its argument is a vowel in my vowel counting example could be made inline:

```
inline bool is_vowel(char c)
{
  return c == 'a' || c == 'e' || c == 'i'
              || c == 'o' || c == 'u';
}
```

Now, code will be generated for the test

```
if (is_vowel(s[i]))
```

as if it had been written

```
if (s[i] == 'a' || s[i] == 'e' || s[i] == 'i'
              || s[i] == 'o' || s[i] == 'u')
```

(with the possibility of optimizing by only computing `s[i]` once), without any function call overhead.

That's the story, anyway, and the reality is only slightly less rosy. The `inline` specification is usually described as a "hint" to the compiler that the function being declared is a good candidate for inlining. It isn't an order. This means that a compiler is free to ignore inline hints, and most will sometimes do so. In particular, if a function is recursive, most compilers won't try to inline it. Although it is possible to analyse certain recursive function definitions at compile time and discover how deep the recursion will go, in general this cannot be done. You can see this without having to go into exotic recursion theory: the depth of recursion might depend on user input at runtime. (Chances are, that in cases where you can discover the depth of recursion at compile time, you can pre-evaluate any call of it and never have to generate code at all.) Most compilers will take the easy way out and just refuse to inline any recursive functions. All but the very cleverest compilers will also fail to inline calls to virtual functions—these can be chosen at runtime and so, in general, cannot be efficiently replaced by inline code.

Other compilers will go further and not inline functions that are too complex for it to be worthwhile—where it is usually the compiler writer who judges what constitutes "too complex". Typical criteria used here might be the number of statements in the function body, or whether it includes any loops. The reasoning behind this is that inlining is only worthwhile if the overhead of calling the function is significant compared with the execution time of the function body. If it isn't, you might as well save the space.

Inlining sounds like such a neat idea that it's very tempting, when you think execution speed matters, to inline everything in sight. If a function is called from many places, or, more subtly, if its body contains calls to other functions which are themselves inlined, the size of the generated code can expand dramatically if you do so. This expansion can interact with virtual memory and cache systems to actually slow down execution. So choose carefully the functions you want to inline. Ones consisting of a single return statement are almost bound to benefit; forwarding functions might, although a good compiler will optimize them out of existence anyway. But don't just guess: use a profiler to find out where the time is going and to check the effectiveness of any inlining.

If you think about what is required to generate inline code for a function, instead of an ordinary call, you should be able to see that inlining can only be done, by a conventional compiler, if the definition of the function is available when the call is compiled. Since C++ programs consist of separately compiled files, this means that the definition must appear in the same file as each call. Usually, therefore, you will put the definitions (not just declarations) of inline functions in header files, and use `#include` to make them available wherever the functions are used. So that this arrangement doesn't cause problems with multiple definitions, inline functions by default have internal linkage.

And here you find a small thorn on the rose of inlining. There is a definition of each function you have declared inline in every file wherein it is used. You have no guarantee that the function really will be inlined, and, if it isn't, a copy of the code for the function body will be generated for each source file, together with conventional calls to it. So, that way, you end up with multiple copies of the code, but no compensating increase in speed; you would have been better off leaving out the `inline` directives. If your compiler offers to warn you whenever it fails to inline a function you've asked it to, take it up on the offer and then you will be able to prevent this problem.

In case it isn't obvious from what has gone before, member functions can be inline, as well as global functions. In fact, they are often the ones that benefit most. You can inline a member function by adding `inline` to its definition, just like any other function. If you do that, you had better put the definition in the header file that declares the class. Strictly speaking, you don't have to do that, but you will need a definition for the inline member wherever it is used. The language definition ties itself into a knot about this: inline member functions have to have internal linkage so that they can be defined in more than one place, but if you are allowed to give different definitions in different places, the idea that a class is an abstract datatype falls apart. So the rule is that whenever a member function is defined more than once, all the definitions must be the same. Of course, this is impossible to check. If you include the definitions in the header file and use these in the conventional way, though, everything works as required and expected.

Which being so, the alternative way of making a member function inline can be handy. If you replace the *declaration* of a member function in the class definition with its *definition*, the member is implicitly specified as inline. The Queue class from chapter 4 is an ideal candidate for inlining, since the definitions of all its member functions are minute. It could be defined like figure 7.1 on the next page (cf. figure 4.7).

This is convenient, it's compact and avoids repeating the function definitions. Opinions differ as to whether it is neater or clutters up the class definition. Most C++ programmers seem to prefer to declare member functions inline this way. It is important to remember that that is what you are doing. Don't get into the habit of always putting member function definitions in the class definition just to keep everything in one place, because it may not always be appropriate to inline them. Worse, it may not be possible, and then you'll end up with multiple copies of the function body.

▷ Should programmers have to think about inlining functions? There are two schools of thought on this. One says, "No. Optimizing compilers should do it automatically." The technology for this exists. The other school says, "Yes. Programmers will always know better than a compiler." Since highly optimizing C++ compilers are more written about than written for production, this may be true at the moment, but the balance may shift as optimizers become more widely available. Consider the example of the register directive. This was introduced in C, and is still available in C++. Like inline, register is a keyword that may precede a declaration, in this case of a variable, and offers a hint to the compiler that the variable may usefully be held in a register instead of on the stack. Nowadays, most compilers simply ignore register, because sophisticated optimization algorithms, such as register colouring, enable the compiler to allocate registers to variables more effectively than most programmers can do by hand. It seems almost inevitable that a similar fate awaits ◁ inline, but not yet.

ARGUMENTS AND RESULTS

In mathematics, a function takes some arguments and maps them to a result. In programming, things are messier: a function will take some arguments, do some computation on them, and return a result, but the computation may have side-effects on global variables, on arguments passed by reference, on the environment, or, in the case of member functions, on the data members of

```
class StringQueue {
public:
  StringQueue()
  {
    the_front = the_back = 0;
  }

  void enqueue(const string& a_string)
  {
    assert(!full());
    the_queue[the_back] = a_string;
    the_back = (the_back + 1)%queue_size;
  }

  void dequeue()
  {
    assert(!empty());
    the_front = (the_front + 1)%queue_size;
  }

  string front() const
  {
    assert (!empty());
    return the_queue[the_front];
  }

  int length() const
  {
    return (queue_size + the_back - the_front)%queue_size;
  }

  bool empty() const
  {
    return the_front == the_back;
  }

  bool full() const
  {
    return length() == queue_size - 1;
  }
private:
  string the_queue[queue_size];
  int the_front, the_back;
};
```

Figure 7.1   The Queue class with inline member functions

the object through which the function is called. Still, arguments and results are the primary means by which a function communicates values to its caller. A couple of minor twists on the mechanisms so far described provide some new ways to use functions.

Default Arguments

One of the choices you make when designing programs is between convenience and generality. One of the places this manifests itself is in the argument lists of your functions. Consider the constructor `MyIntArray::MyIntArray` from chapter 4. Its task is to set up a new range-checked integer array. I defined the constructor to take three `int` arguments: the lower and upper bounds, and an initializing value to which each element should be set. The caller is thus provided with complete control over these three attributes of the array that is created. Putting it another way, the caller always has to provide values for all of them. If it turns out you always want to initialize your arrays with zeroes, this may seem a nuisance, but if I had decided always to initialize arrays with zeroes and dispensed with the final argument, it would have been more of a nuisance for someone who wanted to initialize an array with ones, since they would have to do so explicitly, after the constructor had initialized it once already to zeroes.

The idea of using default values to resolve the conflict between convenience and generality is an old one; it is particularly common in operating systems' command line interpreters. For example, a user who wishes to specify a particular directory to be searched for header files may do so by including an appropriate switch on the command line used to invoke the C++ compiler; if none is specified, then the system uses a default value, some central location where the standard headers are kept.

This idea has been imported into C++ in the form of default initial values for function arguments. You specify a default for a formal argument by following its name with

    = expression

in a function declaration. (There are rules about what you may do when you have more then one declaration of the same function, which ensure you don't provide conflicting defaults. If you follow the usual practice of declaring your functions once in a header file, then you can just put the default there and everything will work out right.)

Consider first a simple example of the use of default arguments. In simulation programs, you often need to generate random numbers in the range 0 to N, for some N. The C standard library provides a function `rand()` (declared in `stdlib.h`), which returns a random integer in the range 0 to `MAX_RAND`, an implementation-dependent (large) integer. So, to generate random numbers in the range 0 to N, you could write a function such as this:

```
int random_int(int n)
{
  return rand()%(n+1);
}
```

If it happened that, most of the time, you were only concerned with simulating events with one of two outcomes, you would have to keep calling random_int(1) to get random binary digits. By declaring the function with a default argument:

```
int random_int(int n=1);
```

you could call it with no arguments for the common case, as random_int() and need only provide arguments for the less frequent ranges.

▷ Even though you can call random_int(), random_int is still a function with one
◁ int argument, returning an int.

The added convenience of using a default here is marginal. Default arguments can be used to good effect in constructors, though. Returning to MyIntArray, if I usually wished the elements of MyIntArray objects to be initialized to zeroes, the constructor's declaration could be

```
MyIntArray::MyIntArray(int lower, int upper, int initial = 0)
```

and a user wishing to use the default could do so by omitting the final actual argument when creating objects.

```
MyIntArray five_hundred_zeroes(0, 500);
```

If this scheme looks like a good idea to you, it probably also seems like a good idea to default the lower bound to zero as well, but you can't just do this:

!
```
MyIntArray::MyIntArray(int lower = 0, int upper, int initial = 0)
```

You would have to invoke such a constructor with something like

!
```
MyIntArray five_hundred_zeroes(, 500);
```

If you don't understand that sentence, don't worry, just be profoundly grateful.

which is not only ugly, it's error-prone too. C++ has absorbed many influences, but OS/360 JCL is not among them. You can default as many arguments as you like, but the defaulted ones must come together at the end of the argument list, and only trailing arguments can be omitted from calls.

Since there is no sensible default to apply to the upper bounds of an array, the best thing to do here is to exchange the order of the first two arguments.

```
MyIntArray::MyIntArray(int upper, int lower = 0, int initial = 0)
```

Objects can now be initialized with one, two or three arguments. All of the following declarations are equivalent.

```
MyIntArray five_hundred_zeroes(500, 0, 0);
MyIntArray five_hundred_zeroes(500, 0);
MyIntArray five_hundred_zeroes(500);
```

If you want an initial value other than the default, you are forced to provide an explicit lower bound too, though, to avoid gaps in the actual argument list:

```
MyIntArray five_hundred_zeroes(500, 0, -1);
```

A constructor with a single argument, for which a default is provided, can be invoked with no arguments. It is thus a default constructor. For example, possibly the best way to provide a default constructor for the `TimeSetting` class of chapter 3 is by supplying defaults for the two arguments of the general constructor.

```
class TimeSetting {
public:
  TimeSetting(int = 0, int = 0);
    the constructor with an empty argument list is not needed
}
```

▷ The value specified for a default can be any expression, it needn't be a constant. Note, though, that any variables involved are statically bound, so be careful when using default argument values with virtual functions. Also, the order of evaluation of the default values is implementation-dependent, so it is highly inadvisable to ◁ make them dependent on each other.

Returning References

The truth about argument passing is that arguments are *always* passed by value: the process of associating formal arguments with actuals is semantically identical to that of initializing variables. When you "pass an argument of type *T* by reference", what you are actually doing is initializing a formal argument of type *reference to T* with the actual argument value. So far, I have kept quiet about the existence of reference types. However, to understand all the possibilities offered by functions, you need to know about references.

For almost every type *T* there is a type *reference to T*, the major exception being that there are no references to references. If you declare a variable of a reference type (which I hope you never do) it must be initialized with something that could appear on the left of an assignment. Thereafter, the reference variable is another name for whatever it was initialized with. Operations on the reference affect the object referred to; you cannot change the value of the reference itself to make it refer to something else. Reference variables are a bad idea, they do nothing but create synonyms, so I will not include any example of their use. Reference data members can be useful, sometimes, but are not without problems. Reference arguments, though, are a good idea, as we have seen. You should be able to see how the account of initializing a reference is consistent with the way in which arguments are passed by reference. It is best to think of reference types as being a neat way of explaining the argument passing mechanism, and a similar trick with return values, and to forget all about the possibility of reference variables, whose existence seems to be a case of misguided orthogonality.

It probably isn't immediately obvious that returning references isn't just as misguided as declaring reference variables. However, when you remember that when an object is returned by value a copy is made, just as it is when an argument is passed by value, you can see that returning references can be a useful optimization for functions returning large objects. As well as this, returning references allows you to perform a nifty trick, that of putting function calls on the left of an assignment. Take an example that is a cliché of this, another altered version of the range-checked array.

```
class MyIntArray  {
public:
  MyIntArray(int lower, int upper, int initial = 0);
  ~MyIntArray();
  int lwb() const;
  int upb() const;
  int& element(int i) const;
private:
    private members as before
};
```

Compare this with the version on page 101; all I have done is replace the `get` and `put` operations with a single member `element`, which returns a reference to the ith array element, if its argument i is in range. The function body is identical to the old `get`.

```
int& MyIntArray::element(int i) const
{
  check_index(i);
  return the_array[i - lower_bound];
}
```

However, `element` returns a *reference* to `the_array[i-lower_bound]`. A reference is another name for this array element. I can assign to a reference, and the effect is to update the object referred to. This is why I no longer need the `put` operation; I can obtain exactly the same effect by calling `element` on the left hand side of an assignment. If `m` is a suitably initialized `MyIntArray` object, and `i` and `x` are integers, I could write:

```
m.element(i) = x;
```

The assignment updates `m.the_array[i-lower_bound]`, the array element for which the reference returned by `m.element(i)` is a synonym. Now, if only I could write `m[i] = x`...

All in good time. Meanwhile, a health warning is in order. A reference is a new name for an object; as long as the reference is available, the object had better exist. Objects that are local to a function only exist during a call of that function. If you pass a reference to an object like that out of a function, you can create a "dangling reference", just as you can create a dangling pointer by performing the same trick with pointers. It doesn't take all that much insight to see that references are probably implemented as pointers behind the scenes, so this is really nothing new.

Returning a reference to a data member gives you a way of updating that data member from outside the class. In the case of `MyIntArray::element`, this is exactly what you want to do, but if you are merely returning a reference in order to avoid an expensive copying operation, it may open a hole in your access protection that you didn't mean to. To prevent this, the return type can be qualified with `const`. For example, if I needed a class of "read-only" arrays, for some reason, I could declare the appropriate member function as:

```
const int& element(int i) const;
```

Pointers returned from a function can also be usefully made constant, if they would otherwise provide a means of altering private data.

You might think that you don't need references, because you can achieve the same effects by passing pointers into functions and explicitly dereferencing them. This is true, but is not very kind to users of your code, because it means that the caller of a function has to distinguish between the different argument passing mechanisms, whereas this is really a concern of the function itself. When you use reference arguments, the caller does not need to worry about how arguments are passed, the call always looks the same.

OVERLOADING

The use of algebraic operators as an alternative notation for writing down function applications is something we've all grown up with. It is a very convenient notation, which makes it easy to build up complex expressions from simple ones; the conventions of operator precedence help keep down the need for brackets. Compare

$$a \times (b + c)/(2a + b)$$

with

```
times(a, divide(plus(b, c), add(times(2, a), b)))
```

In many programming languages, you are forced to write something like the functional expression as soon as you start to operate on user-defined types, even though you are allowed to use conventional notation for built-in arithmetic types. Not so in C++, where user-defined types can be manipulated as conveniently as built-in ones. To see how this is achieved, we must start with a related matter.

Function Overloading

In most established programming languages, you can only have one function with a particular name in scope at once. If you define a function called `orinoco`, and later define any other function also called `orinoco`, then either your new definition will hide the first or you will get an error message. We have seen already that in C++ you are allowed to have member functions with the same name in different classes. This can be explained mechanically by appealing to the fact that member functions have a fully qualified name so that two member functions called `orinoco` in different classes have different names:

`Womble::orinoco` and `River::orinoco`, for example. Fine, but we don't usually need to use these full names; the compiler can determine which member function to call by looking at the type of the object used to call it.

The idea of using the types of a function's arguments to choose between different functions with the same name is taken further in C++. In general, you can define as many functions as you like with the same name in the same scope; provided the different functions differ in the type or number of their arguments, they will be considered as different functions. When you call a function with more than one definition—a so-called *overloaded* function—the compiler inspects the types of the actual arguments and calls the functions whose formal argument types match.

Here's a silly example.

```
void song(char c)
{
  cout << "Hey! ";
}

void song(const char* s)
{
  cout << "Mr Tambourine Man," << endl;
}

void song(int n)
{
  cout << "Play a song for me..." << endl;
}
```

Given these definitions, the sequence of calls

```
song('B');
song("Dylan");
song(1965);
```

produces the familiar invitation

```
Hey! Mr Tambourine Man,
Play a song for me...
```

Function overloading works equally well with arguments of user-defined types. Notice that the values of the arguments are irrelevant—it is their type that is used to select the right version of the function to call.

Just used like this, overloading is probably no more than a new way of causing confusion. In the next section, we'll see how it can become genuinely useful.

▷ You may think it logical that it be possible to overload functions on the basis of their return type. That is,

```
    int song(int);
```

and

Operator Symbol	Built-in Operand Types[a]	Default Meaning
->	pointer, member name	dereferencing and member selection
[]	pointer (array), integer	indexing
()	function, argument types	function call

Table 7.1 Operators with special syntax

---

[a]The types given in these tables do not take account of any type conversions that may occur

```
char song(int)
```

should be different. This is not possible in C++, though, for nasty technical reasons.

◁

▷ Here's a treat for the detractors of C++. What output results from this call?

```
song(NULL);
```

Answer:

```
Play a song for me...
```

But, of course, NULL is just zero, which is an int. But zero is always converted to the null pointer, so why isn't the call ambiguous, with NULL being treated as the null pointer of type const char*? Why, indeed? A sort of answer is on page 204.

◁

Operator Overloading

So that you can write expressions involving objects belonging to classes you have defined, C++ allows you to overload some functions with peculiar names, such as operator+, operator* and operator[]. These functions have a unique property: they may be called with an alternative notation. For example, instead of writing operator+(a, 2), you may write a + 2. These operator functions, as they are called, may also be members of some class. In that case, a + 2 is an alternative to a.operator+(2).

Before going any further with this, we need to know what operators there are, and, since the interpretation of expressions like a+b*c/d, built up using the infix notation for operator functions, depends on the precedences of the operators, we also need to take a look at these. Tables 7.1–7.4, starting on this page, summarize the relevant details.

We have seen most of these operators being used with their default meanings on built-in types; a few remain to be described in later sections. One or two are so esoteric that you will have to consult the ARM to find out about them, if you really want to know.

The horizontal lines within Table 7.3 separate operators at the same level of precedence, with the highest level at the top; all the operators in any one of the

Operator Symbol	Built-in Operand Type	Default Meaning
++	scalar[a]	pre- or post-increment
--	scalar	pre- or post-decrement
~	integer[b]	"bitwise" complement
!	bool	logical negation
-	numeric	negation
+	scalar	no effect
&	any	address of
*	pointer	dereference
new	type name	create a pointer to a heap object
new []	type name	create an array of objects
delete	pointer	destroy object pointed to
delete []	array	destroy array of objects

Table 7.2 Unary operators

---

[a]scalar denotes a pointer or numeric type. Operations involving pointers are subject to restrictions, as described in chapter 4.

[b]integer types include all varieties of `int`, `char` and `bool`

tables are of higher precedence than all those in succeeding tables. You will notice immediately that there are a lot of levels. Operators have been assigned precedences so that, as far as possible, expressions behave as you would expect. For example, `x > 0 && 1/x < y` means `(x > 0)&&((1/x) < y)`; you don't need to add brackets round the two sub-conditions, the way you would in a Pascal-derived language. There is still room for surprises for the naïve, so it is a good idea to put in brackets where you are uncertain.

Unary operators and assignment operators are right associative, so `-*ip` means `-(*ip)`, `*ip++` means `*(ip++)` and `x = y += z` means `x = (y += z)`; all other operators are left associative. It is the mixture of postfix and prefix operators together with these associativity rules that means `*v[10]` is interpreted as `*(v[10])`—dereferencing an array element—and explicit brackets must be used to force the other feasible interpretation `(*v)[10]`—indexing a dereferenced pointer. The need for brackets in unusual places in declarations that mix pointers and arrays follows from this and the way declaration syntax mimics that for use.

The operators in these tables are the ones you can overload. The intention behind operator overloading is usually expressed by saying that the notation is "extensible but not mutable". You can't change the precedence or associativity of any operator. You can't change the number of operands an operator takes. You can't define your own operator symbols. You can't change the meaning of operators when they are applied to objects of the built-in types. You can't overload the `.` operator because it already has a meaning for operands of any class. What you can do, and what you usually will want to do, is overload operators so that you can write expressions involving objects belonging to classes

Operator Symbol	Built-in Operand Types	Default Meaning
->*	pointer, pointer to member	dereferencing and indirect member selection
*	numeric	multiplication
/	numeric	division
%	numeric	remainder
+	numeric	addition
−	scalar	subtraction
<<	integer	shift left
>>	integer	shift right
<	scalar	less than
<=	scalar	less than or equal
>	scalar	greater than
>=	scalar	greater than or equal
==	scalar	equal
!=	scalar	not equal
&	integer	"bitwise" and
∧	integer	"bitwise" exclusive-or
		integer	"bitwise" or
&&	bool	logical and (conjunction)
||	bool	logical or (disjunction)

Table 7.3 Binary operators

you have defined, so that the notation you use in your programs will resemble some notation you find it natural to use on paper when dealing with the sorts of things your class models.

In looking at the details, there are three sets of operators to consider: unary operators, "ordinary" binary operators, and "special" binary operators.

I regret having to report that there are two ways of overloading a unary operator, but you can see that there must be. A unary operator function can be defined either as a global function taking a single argument, or as a member function taking no arguments. Similarly, a binary operator function can be defined either as a global function taking two arguments, or as a member function taking one argument.

Given that the intention of operator overloading is to help make programs more readable, one of the hardest aspects can sometimes be choosing the right operator symbols for each operation. There is nothing the C++ compiler can do to ensure that my use of operators is in any sense semantically consistent with the built-in ones, or even self-consistent. This also applies to algebraic properties, such as commutativity, that you might expect, and to the relation-

Operator Symbol	Built-in Operand Types[a]	Default Meaning
=	any	assign
*=	numeric	multiply and assign
/=	numeric	divide and assign
%=	numeric	take remainder and assign
+=	numeric	add and assign
-=	numeric	subtract and assign
<<=	numeric	shift left and assign
>>=	numeric	shift right and assign
&=	numeric	"bitwise" and and assign
|=	numeric	"bitwise" or and assign
^=	numeric	"bitwise" exclusive-or and assign

Table 7.4   Assigning operators

[a]For assigning operators, the left hand operand must evaluate to an object with an address: a variable, an array element, a data member etc.

ships that usually hold between operators and assigning operators, such as ++x ≡ x += 1 ≡ x = x + 1. Indeed, if I wanted to, I could define a class of matrices and overload – as a matrix addition operator and define ++ and *= so that, with I an identity matrix, ++p ≡ p *= I ≡ p = p – I. I don't think I really want to do that, but the question of which symbols to use in any given situation remains.

As a rudimentary example of how operators may usefully be overloaded, let's see how far we can get trying to extend C++ to include a class that mimics the behaviour of the vectors provided in the METAFONT language for font design.[1]

A vector in METAFONT is a pair of numbers. In a sort of mathematical pun, such pairs are used both to specify points, as pairs of coordinates relative to an origin, and as displacements, or, if you like, movements along the x and y axes. (You can think of a point as being given by its displacement from the origin, to unify matters.) If we start at a point (x_1, y_1) and move x_2 units in the x-direction and y_2 units in the y-direction, we end up at (x_1+x_2, y_1+y_2). It is natural to think of this movement as an addition of vectors, so, by definition, if $z_1 = (x_1, y_1)$ and $z_2 = (x_2, y_2)$ are vectors, their sum is $z_1 + z_2 = (x_1 + x_2, y_1 + y_2)$. Similarly, $z_1 - z_2 = (x_1 - x_2, y_1 - y_2)$. It also makes sense to talk about "moving c times as far as" a vector z. This sounds and behaves like a multiplication, and so, for $z = (x, y)$, $cz = (cx, cy)$.

We can easily define a class MFVec of METAFONT vectors, and overload operator+ and operator- for this class, so they behave as defined. There is no intrinsic multiplication (without an explicit operator symbol) in C++, though, so the METAFONT product notation cannot be used. The obvious thing to do

[1]Vectors are a fairly minor feature of the METAFONT language, which has many more interesting capabilities—see D. E. Knuth, *The METAFONTbook*, Addison-Wesley, 1986.

is to overload `operator*`, since this is the operator used instead of intrinsic multiplication on arithmetic quantities. The assigning form of these operators will also be provided. By convention, $-z$ is used to mean $(-1)z$, so we will overload the unary minus operator as well.

A question immediately arises: Should operator functions be defined globally, or as members of the `MFVec` class? It may seem extraordinary, given how far through this book we are, but there are still some more things you need to know about C++ before you can have a full answer to that question. You can already see, though, that some operators shouldn't be members. It is most common to write, for example, `1.5*z` where `z` is an `MFVec` object, not `z*1.5`. But if `operator*` is a member of `MFVec` we can only use the second form. This would be equivalent to `z.operator*(1.5)`, but what would `1.5*z` be, then? `1.5.operator*(z)`? That is nonsense, whereas if `operator*` is global, `1.5*z` is `operator*(1.5, z)` and `z*1.5` (which ought to mean the same) is `operator*(z, 1.5)`, so if both `operator*(MFVec, float)` and `operator*(float, MFVec)` are defined, both forms are permitted. The same sort of reasoning should convince you that making assigning operators global isn't such a good idea: they are fundamentally asymmetrical in the same way as member functions. There's no compelling reason to make the unary minus operator either global or a member, so we'll make it a member, on the grounds that it is part of the abstract datatype.

Choosing the obvious representation for the `MFVec` objects, and adding a trivial constructor, we have the following class definition.

```
class MFVec  {
public:
  MFVec(float x, float y);
  MFVec& operator+=(const MFVec& z);
  MFVec& operator-=(const MFVec& z);
  MFVec& operator*=(const float c);
  MFVec operator-() const;
private:
  float xcoord, ycoord;
};
```

The automatically generated copy constructor does the right thing, so I don't need to provide one of my own. The member functions' definitions are trivial, and ideal candidates for inlining.

```
inline MFVec::MFVec(float x, float y)
{
  xcoord = x;  ycoord = y;
}
```

The assigning operators all return a reference to `*this`, so that they can be used within expressions, to be consistent with their normal usage. Even if you don't like that usage, there's no excuse for being wilfully inconsistent and confusing potential users of your class.

```
inline  MFVec& MFVec::operator+=(const MFVec& z)
{
```

```
    xcoord += z.xcoord;
    ycoord += z.ycoord;
    return *this;
}


inline  MFVec& MFVec::operator-=(const MFVec& z)
{
  xcoord -= z.xcoord;
  ycoord -= z.ycoord;
  return *this;
}

inline  MFVec& MFVec::operator*=(const float c)
{
  xcoord *= c;
  ycoord *= c;
  return *this;
}
```

Unary minus is a member, too. It has to return its result by value, to avoid creating a dangling reference.

```
inline MFVec MFVec::operator-() const
{
  return MFVec(-xcoord, -ycoord);
}
```

The binary operators are global. By using the assigning operators in their definition, we neatly avoid embarrassments caused by the fact that global functions cannot access private data.

```
inline MFVec operator+(const MFVec& z1, const MFVec& z2)
{
  MFVec res = z1;
  res += z2;
  return res;
}

inline MFVec operator-(const MFVec& z1, const MFVec& z2)
{
  MFVec res = z1;
  res -= z2;
  return res;
}
```

For multiplication by a constant, two overloadings are supplied, to allow the operands to appear in either order. Rather than repeat the code, the second version just flips its operands and calls the first; the argument types ensure that this works as required instead of causing an infinite recursion.

```
inline MFVec operator*(const MFVec& z, float c)
```

```
{
  MFVec res = z;
  res *= c;
  return res;
}

inline MFVec operator*(float c, const MFVec& z)
{
  return z*c;
}
```

Once we have overloaded operators, explicit calls to constructors to provide anonymous objects become more useful. For example, suppose I create an MFVec object

```
MFVec m_v(0, 0);
```

Subsequently, I can move m_v through the vector $(7, 7)$, by writing

```
m_v += MFVec(7, 7);
```

which is almost as convenient as METAFONT's $z + := (7, 7)$.

Nothing in this notation will be new to anyone with any mathematical training. METAFONT extends the conventional vector notations somewhat. If z_1 and z_2 are vectors, and t is a real number, then $t[z_1, z_2]$ is the point t times the distance between z_1 and z_2; t is often less than one, and you use this notation for writing down "the point half way between z_1 and z_2" and so on—quite a useful facility when you are specifying lines and curves for font shapes. Now, $z_1 + (z_2 - z_1) = z_2$, so $z_2 - z_1$ is the vector that corresponds to moving from z_1 to z_2, and therefore, $t[z_1, z_2] = z_1 + t(z_2 - z_1)$.

Here is a case where C++ does not provide the notational freedom a mathematician enjoys. Subscripting, operator[], is a binary operator that has its second argument in a funny place—between the brackets—and you can't overload it, either to take the necessary extra argument or to have an integer as its first argument. We therefore have to express this operation in a different way. One possibility is to define a class MFVecPair of pairs of MFVec objects, and overload operator* again, to express this operation.

```
class MFVecPair  {
public:
  MFVecPair(const MFVec& z1, const MFVec& z2)
  {
    first = z1;  second = z2;
  }
  MFVec operator*(float t) const
  {
    return MFVec(first + t*(second - first));
  }
private:
  MFVec first, second;
};
```

```
MFVec operator*(float t, const MFVecPair& zz)
{
  return zz*t;
}
```

The example shows how "ordinary" operators behave; there are six "special" ones, which need slightly different treatment. They are `operator[]`, `operator->`, `operator()`, `operator=`, `operator new` and `operator delete`. A description of overloading the assignment operator deserves the next section to itself, and overloading the last two will have to wait right until chapter 12. The first three can be described here. They are special in that they may only be overloaded as member functions, and the alternative syntax for applying them is not the standard infix notation.

Overloading `operator[]` is most often used to provide subscripting for any class that can be used to store sequences of items. By overloading `operator[]` to return a reference, such a class can be made to look like an array, with items selected by an index being written on either side of an assignment to provide retrieval and update. If you were really defining a range-checked array as in the previous section, you wouldn't define an `element` function, but you would overload `operator[]` to provide the same functionality.

```
int& MyIntArray::operator[](int i) const
{
  check_index(i);
  return the_array[i - lower_bound];
}
```

Now you can write, for example, `m[i] = m[j]`, which is an improvement on our original `m.put(i, m.get(j))`.

There is still a problem, though. As I mentioned before, returning a reference allows you to update data members from outside the class. It also undermines constancy. For example, you can declare a constant `MyIntArray` object.

```
const MyIntArray m(1, 10, 100);
```

And then you can update one of its elements, even though `operator[]` is `const`.

    `m[2] = 99;`   *Legal, and does what it appears to.*

Some constant! Declaring constant member functions only prevents updates of data members inside those member functions. It doesn't prevent the updating of locations data members might point to, nor updates through references. To be precise, the effect of appending `const` to the declaration of a member function of a class T is to make the compiler behave as if the pointer through which member functions access the members of the object (`this`) was declared as

    `const T * const this;`

In any member function that is not constant, it is treated as if it had been declared as

```
T * const this;
```

so you can never assign to `this` itself, but in member functions not declared `const` you can assign to anything it points to, that is, to data members of `*this`. But it is only these assignments which are prevented if the member function is declared `const`.

The case of `MyIntArray::operator[]` is quite subtle. The update of the supposedly constant object occurs through the reference returned by the operator. The update could be prevented by making `operator[]` return a constant reference, but then it would be impossible to update *any* `MyIntArray` object by assigning to an element obtained by subscripting. All is not lost, though. You can overload a member function merely on the basis of constancy. That is, if you provide a class with two members, say

```
void mf();
void mf() const;
```

then when you call `x.mf()`, the first version will be called unless `x` is a constant object, and the second only if it is. To prevent updates of constant `MyIntArray` objects I would declare two subscription operators.

```
const int& operator[](const int i) const;
int& operator[](const int i);
```

The body of both functions is identical:

```
{
  check_index(i);
  return the_array[i - lower_bound];
}
```

The reference returned from the member function called for constant `MyIntArray` objects is a constant, so that it cannot be updated by assigning to it. For objects that are not constant the other version of the operator function is called, returning a reference that can be updated, just as required.

You can overload `operator[]` so that it takes a second operand of any type, not just an integer. This allows you to define table classes that behave like arrays—so-called "associative arrays"—indexed by, for example, strings.

The most rational reason for overloading `operator->` is the desire to add extra functionality to the pointer dereferencing operation. C++ pointers are very crude abstractions of machine addresses, and the pointer-following operations do nothing more than follow a pointer, wherever it may lead. You might well wish to do some checking to make sure that the pointer is pointing somewhere sensible before following it, just as you might have liked to perform range-checking when indexing an array. A good place to carry out such checks is in the code for an overloaded `operator->`. Other feasible ways in which you might usefully overload `operator->` include updating reference counts in the object pointed at, to ensure that it is deleted when it is safe to do so, and not before, and implementing persistent data that looks as if it is stored in main memory but is actually held on disk until it is referenced, at which point it is loaded into memory. A class with an overloaded `operator->` can pretend to be a pointer to a persistent object, and do the necessary loading when it is used to access the object.

Objects that look like pointers but, thanks to overloading, do more than the primitive pointers do are sometimes called "smart pointers". Applications using them tend to be quite sophisticated; we will have to be content with looking at a simplified scenario that illustrates how they work.

It is not totally far-fetched to suppose that you might want to profile the performance of a data structure, such as the binary search tree of chapter 4, by counting the number of accesses of any sort made through each pointer in the structure. You can do this by replacing all the pointers by objects containing both a pointer and a counter variable, and arranging that each time the pointer is used, the counter is incremented. Naturally, you can do this anyway, without overloading, but if you use overloading to make these counting pointers look, syntactically, like ordinary pointers, the disruption to the rest of the code is minimized.

The intention when using smart pointers is that an expression p->m(), where p is a smart pointer to an object of some class C, should call the member function m of the C object p points to (in a smart way), just as if p were a stupid pointer. This can only work if, contrary to expectations, -> is not a binary operator, with operands p and m, but is a unary one, with p as its only operand, returning a pointer to a C object, which is then dereferenced to call m. This unique behaviour of operator-> can be summarized by saying that p->m() is equivalent to (p.operator->())->m(), where the second -> is the built-in one.[2]

To help make sense of that, here is an attempt at a definition of a class of counting pointers that point to the TreeNode objects of chapter 4 and count all accesses made through them. The private data need only consist of an integer to hold the access count and a pointer to a TreeNode. The member function operator->() returns this pointer, pausing only to increment the count to record the access being made. Naturally, this operation is made inline: imposing a function call overhead for such an operation is intolerable.

```
class TreeNode;

class CountingTreeP {
public:
  CountingTreeP()   {
    access_count = 0;
    the_pointer = NULL;
  }
  TreeNode* operator->()   {
    ++access_count;
    return the_pointer;
  }
private:
  int access_count;
  TreeNode* the_pointer;
};
```

[2] If you have trouble seeing why -> is not a binary operator, consider why there is no assigning operator ->=.

Now, if `tp` is a `CountingTreeP` object pointing to a `TreeNode`, then whenever you call `tp->insert(s)`, the `access_count` of `tp` will be incremented.

If the intention is simply to replace the `TreeNode*` member `root` of the `Tree` class with a `CountingTreeP`, then this is hopelessly inadequate: the member functions of the class `Tree` assign to `root` and carry out comparisons on it. However, by adding additional member functions to overload assignment (see the next section) and equality suitably, very few changes are required. However, as a general rule, deciding what to do when you copy any kind of smart pointer is problematical. If you want to use smart pointers to automate allocation and deallocation of heap memory, or to maintain reference counts, a great deal of thought is required. Although `operator->` is a nice piece of syntax, truly smart pointers are a topic which really belongs more in an advanced C++ programming book than in an introduction like this.

The main peculiarity of `operator()` is that, in an outrageous piece of fudgery, it is considered to be a binary operator, whose second operand is a list of expressions—which may be empty! That is,

```
f(a, b, c) ≡ f.operator()(a, b, c)
```

Some useful idioms based on the overloading of `operator()` are becoming common; they are widely used in the standard library. We will see some examples later.

To finish off this first look at operator overloading we must return to unary operators. Both `++` and `--` can be overloaded, but, on arithmetic types and pointers, they can be used in either prefix or postfix form, with slightly different semantics: `p++` is not quite the same as `++p`. How can both these notations be supplied when the corresponding operator functions are overloaded?

All other unary operators are prefix only, so the rule is that simply overloading `operator++` or `operator--` as a global function taking one argument or a member function taking none, overloads *prefix* `++` or `--`. To overload the postfix version, a slightly desperate expedient is employed: overload the function as if it were a binary operator taking an extra `int` argument, which is never used. Well, it works. Let us add prefix and postfix increment operators to the `MFVec` class, to add the unit vector $(1, 1)$ to their operands. They will behave like their built-in counterparts, in that the prefix form will return the updated `MFVec` object, while the postfix version will increment it, but return the original value.

```
inline MFVec& MFVec::operator++()
{
  ++xcoord;  ++ycoord;
  return *this;
}

inline MFVec MFVec::operator++(int)
{
  MFVec old_this = *this;
  ++(*this);
  return old_this ;
}
```

Defining postfix increment in terms of prefix is always a good idea, since it makes it easy for you to preserve the expected relationship between the two operators. Whereas the prefix version can safely return a reference like other assigning operators, the postfix version must return an MFVec object, despite the overhead that copying it on return entails. If a reference to old_this was returned it would be dangling; if old_this was allocated on the heap to prevent this happening, how would it ever get deleted?

Operator overloading all seems quite simple, doesn't it? The full truth can wait.

Assignment

If I can write, as I did in chapter 6,

```
MFVec m = n;
```

to initialize one MFVec variable with the value stored in another, I ought to be able to write

```
m = n;
```

where m and n are MFVec variables, to update the value of m to that stored in n. The two operations are subtly different: in the first, the value of n is being used to set up a newly created object, in the second, it is being used to replace an existing one's value. Depending on the internal structure of the objects concerned, the necessary actions may be different.

Since no new object is being created in the second case, there is no reason to suppose that a copy constructor will be invoked. Syntactically, assignment is considered an operator, so m = n is equivalent to m.operator=(n). If you want to specify the effect of assignment on objects of classes you have defined, you need to provide an overloaded operator= as a member function of each class.

If you think of an object as a region of storage, then, just as assigning to a variable of a built-in type means updating the value stored in the corresponding memory locations, so assigning to a variable of a user-defined type should mean updating the contents of that area of storage, that is, assigning to all the data members. So operator= is almost certainly going to have to update data members, which means that it is most natural to make it a member function. So much so that C++ requires operator= to be a member, never a global function, unlike most other operators.

A naïve attempt at writing an assignment operator for MFVecs might result in this code:

```
void MFVec::operator=(MFVec m)
{
  xcoord = m.xcoord;
  ycoord = m.ycoord;
}
```

It will work most of the time, but there are two things wrong with this definition.

First, the type of the argument m. Yes, we do want to take an MFVec object as the argument, but passing it by value is daft: the copy constructor will be invoked to initialize m with a copy of the actual argument, when all we want to do is copy its xcoord and ycoord values. The argument should be passed by reference, to avoid doing the copying twice, and, what is more, it should be passed by const reference, since we're not going to change it.

The second thing wrong with this definition of assignment is its return type. To those of us raised on languages that maintain a strict distinction between statements and expressions, it seems proper that assignment should be a statement and hence not return a value, so operator= should be a void function. C++ does not respect this distinction, though—not consistently, anyway—and regards an assignment as an expression that returns a value. Hence a multiple assignment p = q = r is treated as p = (q = r), with the value assigned to p being the value of the expression q = r. If you don't like this attitude to assignment, then, by all means, define a void member function becomes and write m.becomes(n), but, if you want to use the assignment notation, you'd best be consistent with the rest of C++ to avoid confusing everybody. Hence, operator= should return a reference to the object that has just been assigned to, which can then be used in a chain of assignments.

A better definition of an assignment operator for the MFVec class is this:

```
MFVec& MFVec::operator=(const MFVec& m)
{
  xcoord = m.xcoord;
  ycoord = m.ycoord;
  return *this;
}
```

Assignment of objects with only numeric data members presents no further problems, and usually you don't even need to do anything about it, as we shall see. Introduce pointers into your classes and things get more exciting.

Back to the net resources of chapter 6. If I want to be able to assign the value of a WebPage variable v to another u, by writing u = v, what should WebPage::operator= do? Like the copy constructor, it shouldn't simply copy the pointers inside v, it should allocate some new space and copy the string pointed to (unless you really want the two variables to share their strings, perhaps because you are using reference counts, but in that case, you probably know what you're doing).

It is in the nature of assignment that the object being assigned to (the destination) may already have a value. In the case of a WebPage object, that means that the_machine and the_path may already point to arrays of char on the heap. Since there is no guarantee that the sizes of the strings in the object being assigned (the source) are the same as the corresponding strings in the destination, these arrays cannot be used to hold the new values. It is the responsibility of operator= to dispose of the old strings in the destination, that is, to call delete to return them to the free store.

▷ OK, if you think it's worth it, you could check whether the source's and the destination's strings are the same size and, if so, overwrite the originals. Most of the time this won't be the case; operator= still has the responsibility of managing the ◁ space.

There is an easily overlooked banana skin here. What if the source and destination are the same? Suppose I have defined my assignment like this:

```
WebPage& WebPage::operator=(const WebPage& u)
{
    delete [] the_machine;
    delete [] the_path;
    the_machine = new char[strlen(u.the_machine)+1];
    the_path = new char[strlen(u.the_path)+1];
    strcpy(the_machine, u.the_machine);
    strcpy(the_path, u.the_path);
    return *this;
}
```

If u and *this are the same object, the first thing that will happen is that its strings will be deleted. Shortly, an attempt will be made to copy them into the newly allocated strings. The effect is anybody's guess—accessing deleted objects is undefined. To avoid this embarrassment—and some unnecessary work—an assignment operator should always check that an object is not being assigned to itself. The quick way to do so is by comparing this (the pointer) with the address of the argument.

```
WebPage& WebPage::operator=(const WebPage& u)
{
    if (this != &u)
    {
     delete and copy as before
    }
    return *this;
}
```

▷ You might think that anyone who writes a = a wants their head examined and deserves anything they get. Such an attitude ill becomes a professional programmer and any mathematician will always tell you you should never neglect the degenerate cases. More persuasively, you should reflect that references and pointers, even array subscripting, provide plenty of opportunities for creating aliases so that an assignment of an object to itself may not be evident from the appearance of the
◁ code.

The assignment operator and the copy constructor (on page 144) for the WebPage class should be compared. Notice that neither of them has to do any extensive checking, because their argument is known to be a valid WebPage object. Notice also that the copy constructor doesn't have to worry about deleting any space, because it is initializing a brand new object, whereas the assignment operator must not only delete the space being used in the destination object, it must also check for the pathological case of assignment of an object to itself, which also cannot occur when a new object is being constructed.

The similarities between copying and assignment go further: if you do not overload assignment for some class, then an operator= member is automatically generated. It performs "memberwise assignment", that is, it assigns each member using the assignment operator for its type. The default ("bitwise", if you must) meaning of assignment is used for built-in numeric and pointer types; any overloaded assignment operator applicable to a class type will be used, otherwise a memberwise assignment will be recursively generated. Thus, in particular, the automatically generated assignment operator does shallow copying, which could be as undesirable in assignments as it is in copy constructors, so you may need to define your own `operator=`. A slightly simplistic rule for when to do so is: If a class allocates resources, such as heap space, it should define a copy constructor, an `operator=` member function, and a destructor. An alternative formulation of the rule is: If a class has one of those three members, it ought to have all of them. For this strategy to be a successful one, the members ought to do something sensible. In the case of memory allocation, it is not necessary to religiously implement deep copying of all objects; other, more sophisticated tactics can be adopted, but the constructors, assignment and destructor must cooperate to ensure that no memory is deleted more than once and that memory is only shared when such sharing is harmless.

Just because an assignment (`operator=`) is generated, there is no reason to suppose any other assigning operator (such as `operator+=` or `operator/=`) will be generated. None is. As with copy constructors, you can prevent assignment of objects of your class by declaring `operator=` as a private member function.

In many classes, including `WebPage`, the code for the copy constructor is a subset of that for assignment, but it would be wrong to call the copy constructor from within the assignment. As ever, doing so would merely create and initialize a temporary object, without affecting the destination of the assignment. The way to share the code is to put it in a private member function called by both the copy constructor and `operator=`.

Inheritance presents the same problem to assignment as it did to constructors: when you assign to an object of a derived class, you must update its base class data members, but if they are private they are inaccessible to the derived class's member functions.

This time, a call to the base class's assignment operator is the right thing. Since `operator=` is being overwritten in the derived class, you can only get at the base class's `operator=` by using its fully qualified name. Doing that, you cannot use infix notation, you must call it as a function, which results in some odd-looking, but effective, code. For example:

```
WWW& WWW::operator=(const WWW& w)
{
  if (this != &w)
    NetResource::operator=(w);
  return *this;
}
```

Elegant, no?

Leaving out the call to the base class's assignment operator will lead to some extraordinary behaviour, with objects retaining part of their old value when assigned to. The result may be a perplexed programmer or, much worse, a perplexed user. Don't let it happen.

If you don't write your own assignment operator for a derived class, the automatically generated one will recursively assign to the members of the base class, as you would probably expect.

POINTERS TO FUNCTIONS

Ask yourself "Why would I want a pointer to a function?" Why would you want a pointer to anything? A pointer gives you a handle, of a fixed known size, to an object of arbitrary or unknown size. You can pass this handle as an argument to a function or store it in a data structure, when you couldn't do the same thing with the object itself. So, if you can get a pointer to a function, you can, in effect, pass functions to other functions, return them as results, or store them in data structures. This rather begs the question "Why would I want to do that?" Because it opens the way to some fun.

Higher Order Functions

A higher order function is one that takes functions as arguments or returns a function as its result. They have been used for many years in the functional programming world to provide powerful control structures that allow you to combine functions in a very general way. The same sort of effects can be achieved in C++ using pointers to functions, although the comparatively restricted nature of C++ functions does not permit the full range of techniques available to funky programmers.

Functions taking other functions as arguments have been provided by programming languages for a long time—even Fortran allows you to do this. The reason is that many numerical algorithms come naturally parameterized in a function. For example, there are several techniques for evaluating a definite integral $\int_a^b f(x)dx$. The technique employed—evaluating $f(x)$ at discrete intervals across the range from a to b, multiplying by the interval to obtain an area and then summing these areas, for example—is independent of any specific f, just as the algorithm given for computing $\sqrt{a}$ in chapter 3 is independent of the value of a. In both cases, we can abstract; provided there is adequate language support available, we can make f an argument to the integration function, just as we made a an argument to the square root function.

▷ Newton's method can itself be generalized into one of the classic examples of a higher order function. It was presented earlier as a way of finding $\sqrt{a}$. The problem can be rephrased as that of finding a solution to the equation $x^2 - a = 0$, that is, $f(x) = 0$ where the function $f(x)$ is $x^2 - a$. The algorithm of guessing, checking whether the guess is good enough, improving the guess using $f'(x)$, and iterating, works to find solutions to other equations of the form $f(x) = 0$, with square roots falling out as a special case. (OK, it's not that simple, you need to worry about convergence.) The general Newton-Raphson method for finding roots of equations can be programmed in a natural way as a function performing the guess-check-
◁ improve routine, with the function f being passed as an argument.

These numerical algorithms are considered rather specialized nowadays, but higher-order functions can be useful in more mundane applications. Perhaps the best examples are functions for combining the elements of aggregate objects. To be specific, if trivial, consider a linked list of floating point numbers. You might want to compute the sum of all the elements, or their product, or apply some other numerical function to the whole collection; you might want to count the number of elements in the list, or print them all out. Rather than providing individual member functions for each of these operations, a higher-order function can be used to provide a framework out of which these operations, and any other similar combination as yet unforeseen, can be constructed.

For most of us, the easiest way of discovering a general pattern is to look at some specific examples. A `FloatList` class directly supporting sum and product operations on all its elements might be defined using an auxiliary class `ListNode`, as follows:

```
class ListNode  {
public:
   float the_val;
   ListNode *next;
};
```

It doesn't much matter having the data members public, because you can never get at a `ListNode` object directly, but we'll see ways of avoiding it later.

```
class FloatList   {
public:
   FloatList(): the_head(NULL) {}
   ~FloatList();
   void hdinsert(float);
   void hdremove();
   float head() const;
   float sum() const;
   float product() const;
private:
   ListNode *the_head;
};
```

Probably more member functions would be available. Consider now the definitions of the pair of member functions `sum` and `product`.

Overflow? What's that?

```
float FloatList:: sum() const
{
    float result = 0;
    ListNode *p = the_head;
    while(p)
    {
        result = result + p->the_val;
        p = p->next;
    }
    return result;
}
```

```
float FloatList:: product() const
{
    float result = 1;
    ListNode *p = the_head;
    while(p)
    {
        result = result * p->the_val;
        p = p->next;
    }
    return result;
}
```

There are only two differences between the bodies of these two functions: the initial value of `result` and the operation used to combine the running result with each value in the list. (Mathematicians might like to insert some observations using the word "monoid" here.) The operation is just a function taking a pair of floats and returning a float, so, to generalize the pattern, we need to parameterize in the initial value and this function.

Once you've got this far, the trickiest bit is writing down the type of the function argument. This isn't a function, it's a pointer to a function. Using the principle that declaration mimics use, we could declare an object of type pointer to a function taking two floats and returning a float like this:

```
float (*fp)(float, float);
```

Think of declaring *fp as a function; the brackets round *fp are necessary to distinguish a pointer to a function returning a float from a function returning a pointer to a float. (This is the same confusion as that between an array of pointers and a pointer to an array.) You can take the address of a function using the prefix & operator, and dereference a pointer to a function using * to obtain a function you can call, but, as if to make up for the awkwardness of declaring pointers to functions, the C++ compiler performs some automatic conversions for you. If a function's name is used in any other way than to call it or take its address, it is treated as a pointer; you may call a function through a pointer without explicitly dereferencing it.

We can now define and use a member function to combine the elements of a list. One of the drawbacks of operator overloading is that it can encourage the whimsical programmer's whimsicality, which might lead to overloading `operator()` for this purpose.

```
float FloatList:: operator()(float (*f)(float, float),
                             float a) const
{
  float result = a;
  ListNode *p = the_head;
  while(p)
  {
    result = f(result, p->the_val);
    p = p->next;
  }
  return result;
}
```

Adding up or multiplying together all the elements of a `FloatList` object can be easily achieved by short global functions, no additional members are needed, just a couple of trivial auxiliary functions to wrap up the operators in a suitable way.

```
float add(float a, float f)
{
   return f + a;
}

float mul(float a, float f)
{
   return f * a;
}
```

These functions are just passed to `FloatList::operator()` together with the identity for the operation (0 for +, 1 for *).

```
float sum(const FloatList& fl)
{
   return fl(add, 0);
}

float product(const FloatList& fl)
{
   return fl(mul, 1);
}
```

With a bit of coaxing, this combining operator can be made to do some other jobs for us. For example, although it's not really cool to use floating point numbers for counting, it does work, so, a function to find the length of a list can easily be constructed.

```
float lgth(float a, float f)
{
   return a + 1;
}

float length(const FloatList& fl)
{
   return fl(lgth, 0);
}
```

And if you don't mind calling functions purely for their side-effects, ignoring their result, you can use it to print the contents of a list, too.

```
float pr(float a, float f)
{
   cout << f << endl;
   return 0.0;
}
```

```
void print(const FloatList& fl)
{
  fl(pr, 0);
}
```

This one is arguably a little off-colour, and probably shouldn't be shown to impressionable young persons or staid software engineers—another overloaded `operator()` would be more suitable.

Arrays of pointers to functions provide another useful tool for some sorts of programming. Suppose you wish to display a menu so that someone using your program can select one of a number of actions. Suppose also that you have access to a library function that takes an array of n strings, displays a menu with these strings as the entries, and returns an integer between 0 and $n-1$, indicating which of them has been selected. You can select an appropriate action by using this returned value to index an array of pointers to functions.

Function Objects

More sophisticated tricks can be played with pointers to functions by embedding them in objects. In particular, by defining classes with a data member of some pointer to function type and an overloaded `operator()` member that applies it, you can construct objects that look like functions, but are capable of richer behaviour. As a slightly playful example, consider Schönfinkel's device.

It is a widely known secret that, in a world with higher-order functions, you don't need functions that take more than one argument, since any function taking, for example, two arguments can be replaced by a function that takes one argument and returns a function that takes one argument. So, instead of applying a function f to two arguments a and b, we apply an equivalent function f' to a, obtaining a new function, $f'(a)$ that can be applied to b, so the effect of $f(a,b)$ is achieved by $f'(a)(b)$. This fact has been discovered independently several times; amongst its discoverers are the Schönfinkel just alluded to and also the logician H. B. Curry, whence functions like f' are sometimes piquantly referred to as "curried functions".

One of the reasons curried functions are of more than academic interest is that the expression $f'(a)$ on its own can be a useful function. If f' represents some general computation, $f'(a)$ will be a specialized version, with one of the parameters of the general computation frozen. To take a trivial example, suppose that σ is a curried addition function, so that $\sigma(a)(b) = a + b$. Then $\sigma(1)$ is the successor function, which adds one to things. Curried functions which take other functions as arguments provide a means of describing families of computational structures.

C++ does not directly support curried functions, but it is quite easy to construct function objects that behave in the same way.

Just to keep everything down to manageable size, we'll only look at binary functions with integer arguments and results. In the abstract, such a function, after currying, can be applied to an integer object to obtain a function taking a single integer argument and returning an integer result. We will define a class of `CurriedBinaryFunction` objects with an `operator()` member, such that when it is applied to an integer we get something that looks like a function taking a single integer argument and returning an integer result, but isn't. Instead, it will be an object, in this case a member of a class I'll call `PartiallyAppliedFunction`. It's easier to start with the definition of this latter class.

The function that has been partially applied will be stored in a data member, `the_fn`, of the correct pointer to function type, with the argument it has been partially applied to kept in another data member, `first_arg`. The class will need a constructor to create a new object from a pointer to a function and an integer. The automatically generated copy constructor and assignment operator do the right thing, so the only other required member function is the overloaded `operator()`, which applies its function member to the value stored in `first_arg` and the second argument passed to `operator()`. Everything can be inlined.

```
class PartiallyAppliedFunction  {
public:
  PartiallyAppliedFunction(int (*f)(int, int),
                             int a):the_fn (f), first_arg(a)
  {}
  int operator()(int b) const
  {
    return the_fn(first_arg, b);
  }
private:
  int (*the_fn)(int, int);
  int first_arg;
};
```

`CurriedBinaryFunction` is now easy. It uses a data member to hold the uncurried version of the function we start with; this is set by a constructor. Again, `operator()` is overloaded, so that `CurriedBinaryFunction` objects can apparently be applied; the effect is to create a `PartiallyAppliedFunction` with the argument bound in to its `first_arg` member, so it will behave as required if it is subsequently applied to a second argument.

```
class CurriedBinaryFunction  {
public:
  CurriedBinaryFunction(int (*f)(int, int)):the_fn(f)
  {}
  PartiallyAppliedFunction operator()(int a) const
  {
    PartiallyAppliedFunction paf(the_fn, a);
    return paf;
  }
private:
  int (*the_fn)(int, int);
};
```

Here is how such an object can be used to create a successor function as just described. First we need to wrap up the ordinary integer addition operator into a function.

```
int plus(int a, int b)
{
   return a+b;
}
```

Now we can use this to initialize a CurriedBinaryFunction, and use the resulting object to build a successor function.

```
CurriedBinaryFunction sum(plus);
PartiallyAppliedFunction successor = sum(1);
```

The variable sum is initialized with a curried addition function; this is partially applied to 1, and the result is used to initialize successor, which becomes, to all intents and purposes, a successor function. It can be used just like one: successor(9) returns 10. Alternatively, I could have created a predecessor function:

```
PartiallyAppliedFunction predecessor = sum(-1);
```

predecessor(10) returns 9.

This is a fun game, but it's more than that. Function objects are widely used in the C++ standard library, particularly in the Standard Templates component, where they offer a convenient and hospitable interface to many of the algorithms provided. To get the full benefit of function objects, you will need to know about templates, which are described in chapter 10.

Pointers to Member Functions

If playing with pointers to functions appeals to you, you will probably want to try similar games with member functions. A member functions is not quite the same sort of thing as a function—it can be called through an object and it may be virtual. A pointer to a member function cannot, therefore, be quite the same sort of thing as a pointer to a function—dereferencing it must give you something that can be called through an object and that may be virtual. Hence, pointers to member functions are syntactically distinguished from pointers to other functions.

As with pointers to functions, the really hard part is declaring pointers to member functions. The syntax is taken from the header of a member function's definition. Consider, for example,

```
void TimeSetting::hrs_up()
```

Considered as a declaration (which it isn't), this makes hrs_up the name of a member function of TimeSetting taking no arguments and returning void. By analogy, the declaration

```
void (TimeSetting::*pmf)()
```

declares pmf to be a pointer to a member function of TimeSetting taking no arguments and returning void. As with declarations of pointers to functions, brackets are required to disambiguate the declaration—observe where the opening bracket goes.

A pointer to a member function can be called through an object or a pointer to one. Two new operators, .* and ->* are used for this purpose. Each is a single operator, but it may help to think of the * as dereferencing the pointer to member before . or -> is applied with its usual effect. No shorthands are allowed: if you want to create a pointer to a member you must take its address explicitly and use its fully qualified name; if you want to apply it through the pointer this you must say so.

This may be obsessive

Pointers to member functions can be used to clean up a slightly unsatisfactory piece of code from chapter 3. The definition of the member function set on page 63 consists of two virtually identical while-loops. The only difference between them is that, in the first, hrs_up and hrs_down are used to adjust the hours component, whereas in the second mins_up and mins_down are used to do the same to the minutes. I hate writing code like that. I want to abstract, and make the two member functions into arguments of a function that captures the common pattern of the two loops. That is not hard; the function in question should be a private member of TimeSetting.

```
void TimeSetting::set_component(void (TimeSetting::*up)(),
                                void (TimeSetting::*down)())
{
  display();
  char c = prompt_for_a_char();
  while (c != 'x')
  {
    if (c == '+')
      (this->*up)();
    else
      if (c == '-')
        (this->*down)();
      else cout << "?\n";
    display();
    c = prompt_for_a_char();
  }
}
```

The two loops in set are replaced by two calls to set_component, one to set the hours with hrs_up and hrs_down, the other to set the minutes with mins_up and mins_down.

```
void TimeSetting::set()
{
  set_component(&TimeSetting::hrs_up, &TimeSetting::hrs_down);
  set_component(&TimeSetting::mins_up, &TimeSetting::mins_down);
}
```

That's more like it.

More About Types

8

C++ is a strongly typed language, in which types and type checking play a major role in helping programmers write correct programs. It is important, therefore, to have a good understanding of the types provided in the language, the means for defining new types, and the relationships between types. We met most of the built-in C++ types and the most important methods of defining new types in the first part of the book, but a few remain to be described. The relationships between types have hardly been addressed yet. Important questions here include: How do you write down the name of a type? When, if ever, are two types the same? How, and under what circumstances, can an object of one type be converted into an object of another type? Exactly how are types used to resolve overloading?

PROPERTIES OF TYPES

If you would have power over something you must first know its name. We shall begin our look at types, therefore, by finding out how to write down the name of any type. For simple types this is easy, but for compound types that mix up arrays and pointers and functions, it becomes much more difficult. Once you have mastered type names, determining whether two types are the same becomes possible. It also becomes possible to use a type's name as the argument to a special sort of function, to discover some property of that type. In chapter 10 we will see that being able to write down the name of a type is vital if we wish to program with parameterized abstract datatypes and take advantage of the more advanced parts of the C++ standard library.

Type Names and Typedefs

There is a deceptively simple rule for constructing type names: Write down a declaration of a variable of the required type; strike out the variable name. What is left is the type name. For elementary types this really is simple. Declare an integer variable:

```
int i;
```

Remove the variable name. (Yes, and the semicolon. Obviously.) The type name is `int`. We knew that already. Likewise, a pointer to an integer would be declared

```
int *ip;
```

so the type name is `int*`. An array of ten `int`s:

```
int p[10];
```

The type of `p` is `int[10]`. Constants need an initializer when they are declared; this is not part of the type.

```
const float pi = 3.14159;
```

The type of `pi` is `const float`.

This rule works with user-defined types, too.

```
TreeNode tn;
```

declares a `TreeNode`, the type of which is `TreeNode`. That is, a class declaration introduces a new type name at the same time as defining the named type. Just as well.

So, what's deceptive about this simplicity? For complicated types, involving pointers and arrays or functions, writing down the declaration is itself non-trivial. Recall from chapter 4

```
TreeNode *a[10];        The type TreeNode *[10] is an array of ten pointers to
                        TreeNodes

TreeNode (*p)[10];      while TreeNode (*)[10] is a pointer to an array of
                        ten TreeNodes.
```

The brackets are important, even though some of the resulting type names look peculiar with them.

As we saw in chapter 7, a pointer to a function has quite an awkward declaration. For example

```
void (*h)();
```

is how you declare a variable `h` that is a pointer to a void function taking no arguments—its type is `void(*)()`. At the next level of complexity there are useful functions that take a pointer to a void function taking no arguments as *their* argument and return another such pointer as their result. At this level of complexity the "declaration mimics use" syntax becomes, frankly, confusing. The necessary declaration is not, as I confess to having expected,

!
```
(void(*)())(*f)(void(*)())
```

but

```
void (*f(void(*)()))()
```

which parses something like: *f applied to a void(*)() is a void function with no arguments. The type of f is void(*(void(*)()))().

I daresay there are people who would have no trouble writing down the type of an array of pointers to an array of such pointers to functions. If you are not of their number, and find complex type names just a tiny bit awkward, C++ allows you to define synonyms for type names. You define a type synonym by writing down a variable declaration preceded by the keyword typedef. The name in the declaration is then taken, not as a variable, but as a synonym for the name of the type it would have had if the typedef had not been there—the type name you would get by crossing out typedef and the name. Type synonyms defined in this way can subsequently be used like the names of built-in simple types and classes in declarations. For example

```
typedef int I;
```

makes I into another name for int. More usefully,

```
typedef TreeNode (*TNP)[10];
```

makes TNP into another name for TreeNode(*)[10]. The use of capitals for such typename synonyms is a widely used convention. You can use the synonym to declare variables.

```
TNP p;
```

is an easier to read version of

```
TreeNode (*p) [10];
```

You can also use typedef to build up complicated types.

```
typedef void (*PF)();
```

makes PF a name for the type of pointers to void functions with no arguments. Although when you declare such a pointer directly the names comes in the middle with brackets all over the place, once you have a simple name for the type, variable declarations look just like the simplest.

```
PF f;
```

Furthermore, PF can be used to define the type of functions taking a PF and returning a PF in a much more obvious way than the notation we saw previously.

```
typedef PF (*PFF)(PF);
```

And so the type consisting of arrays of ten such pointers to functions can be given a name by

```
typedef PFF APFF[10];
```

and an array of twelve pointers to such arrays could be of type AAPFF if the following definition was provided

```
typedef APFF *AAPFF[12];
```

and such an array could be declared simply.

```
AAPFF menu_of_menus;
```

(Consider the name and the menu selection scheme outlined on page 188 if
you think this example the twisted product of a mind that used to set exams.)
Although most types are much simpler than this, type synonyms are widely
used by C++ programmers to improve the readability of declarations.

Type Equivalence

When are two variables or expressions of the same type? When their types have
the same name. And that's the end of the story, really. Typedefs don't really
define new type names (they give the name a new name, but not the type, you
could say) so after

```
typedef TreeNode *TNP;
typedef TreeNode *UOQ;
TNP p1;
UOQ p2;
```

the variables p1 and p2 both have the same type: TreeNode*.

What needs to be emphasized here is that C++ has no truck with structural
equivalence. Just because objects of two different types have identical layouts
in memory, and the same operations, even the same member names, they are
only of the same type if their type names match (modulo the scope of declarations).

For example, whereas I have defined a class MFVec to model METAFONT vectors, if you were writing a program concerned with motion in two dimensions,
you might define a class TwoDVec of two-dimensional vectors representing locations in a plane. You might well declare it like this:

```
class TwoDVec  {
public:
  TwoDVec(float x, float y);
  TwoDVec& operator+=(const TwoDVec& z);
  TwoDVec& operator-=(const TwoDVec& z);
  TwoDVec& operator*=(float c);
  TwoDVec operator-() const;
  TwoDVec& operator++();
  TwoDVec operator++(int);
private:
  float xcoord, ycoord;
};
```

The memory layout of this class, and the operations on it, are identical to those
of MFVec (hardly surprisingly). Nevertheless

```
MFVec v1(0, 0);
TwoDVec v2(0, 0);
```

declares variables of different types, and assignment of either of them to the
other is illegal. You can argue for years about whether name equivalence or

structural equivalence is "right", but in C++ you have name equivalence. And that is that.

The `sizeof` Operator

Sometimes—not often, in fact hardly ever, but sometimes—you need to know how much space an object occupies. The `sizeof` operator is provided for just those times. It can be used in two different ways, either

```
sizeof(typename)
```

or

```
sizeof expression
```

The first form is used to find out how much space any object of a particular type—identified by the `typename`—occupies; the second is used to find out how much space a particular object—the value of the *expression*—occupies. The value returned is of type `size_t`, which is defined to be some unsigned integer type, large enough to hold the largest value `sizeof` might return. The `sizeof` operator returns the size in units called *bytes*, but these are not necessarily the bytes equal to eight bits that most of us know about. A byte in this context is defined as being the unit of storage such that `sizeof(char)` equals one byte. Although you and I may never be too concerned with the fact, there do exist strange high performance machines that cannot manipulate anything as small as eight bits efficiently, on which a `char` is stored in a whole word. Portability demands that we do not assume that all machines use eight bit bytes.

The value returned by `sizeof` can hold some surprises. On many machines, it is efficient to pad out objects with unused bytes in order to facilitate extraction of individual members, so it is quite possible that, for some class C, `sizeof(C)` is greater than the sum of the sizes of the individual members of a C object. Furthermore, objects of classes with virtual functions will have some housekeeping information stored in them, and the value returned will reflect the presence of this information.

In C++, you only really need to know about the space occupied by objects if you are intent on writing your own space allocation routines to replace `new`—a legitimate and popular occupation (or so the writers of C++ books would have us believe), described in chapter 12. You will also find that some of the finer points of the language definition are neatly expressed in terms of `sizeof`, so it does help to know what it means even if you never use it in one of your programs.

You can't overload `sizeof`—be reasonable!

TYPE CONVERSIONS

Strong typing is a topic that is difficult to write about without sounding dogmatic, authoritarian, patronizing, and everything else that this book is supposed not to be. (Unless you're against it, which I'm not any more.) Strong typing has a bad reputation among some of the more creative programmers, and deservedly so, with the types provided by older programming languages such as Pascal and C. A primitive type system strongly enforced is a tiresome limitation, forcing you to do things awkwardly just to keep the compiler happy, when you could do them elegantly if you were given the extra freedom that comes from relaxing or removing type constraints.

With a powerful and extendible type system, things are different. The types you define and the way you use them express a great deal about the intended logical structure of your program. The compiler's type checking then provides a consistency check that helps ensure your program is correct.

All this is by way of providing a context for the subject of type conversion. It follows from what I just said that type conversions shouldn't be necessary. Given a rich enough type system or a narrow enough problem domain, perhaps they aren't. However, C++ has a type system that is designed to be easily and efficiently implementable, and the language is intended to be convenient for a wide range of programming tasks, including low-level systems programming. Somewhere between these two, we find the need for occasional type conversions.

We can categorize type conversions in two different ways: implicit or explicit, applied to built-in or user-defined types, giving four separate cases to consider. If *implicit* conversion from a type T_1 to another type T_2 is allowed, then merely using a value of type T_1 where one of type T_2 is required will cause the conversion to take place. An *explicit* conversion only occurs if you use some notation to make it happen. Although no type conversions are truly safe, the notation required to effect an explicit conversion makes it clear from the program text what the programmer's intention was. Even if it turns out you didn't know what you were doing, someone reading your program can see what you did. A wider range of conversions is therefore allowed explicitly than implicitly.

There is a third way of classifying type conversions, whose relationship to the other two is convoluted. Some conversions imply the generation of code to change the stored representation of a value at runtime. The commonest example is the conversion of a number from integer to floating point form, which usually involves a radical change of bit pattern. Other conversions don't change any bits at all; they are conceptual operations whereby the same bit pattern is interpreted in a different way. Typically, the type conversion affects the way the compiler treats an expression. For example, where a pointer to an object of some class is changed into a pointer to an object of its base class, the same bit pattern is used, but type checking is carried out as if on a pointer to an object belonging to the base class. Similarly, if a numerical value is converted from a signed to an unsigned type, the bits almost certainly stay the same, but the machine instructions generated for any subsequent operations on the value may be different from what would be generated without the type conversion.

Implicit Conversions Between Built-in Types

The rules for conversions between the built-in types of C++ have been variously described as "subtle", "rather messy" and "chaotic". The most complex conversions involve numerical types; if you skipped the detail about the plethora of arithmetic types on page 21, now is a good time to go back and read it. The whole mess originates with C, and a laudable ambition to provide the C programmer with a set of arithmetical operations that provide the same choices among sizes of numbers and numerical accuracy offered by the hardware, so that the most efficient use can be made of machine resources. Putting it another way, the intention was to expose the C programmer to the diversity, vagaries and complexities of number representations and arithmetic on real machines. To add the convenience of mixed mode arithmetic (just about *de rigeur* when you've got that many arithmetic types) requires an equally complex set of conversions.

There are very few safe conversions between numerical types—safe, that is, in the sense that no information is lost. The actual details of what might go wrong with an arithmetical conversion depend on how numbers are represented on your particular machine, and how the C++ numerical types are mapped onto machine representations by your compiler. The language definitions offer few certainties. The only universally applicable advice on arithmetical conversions seems to be: be wary and know your machine.

If you want to be wary about implicit conversions, you'll need to know when they are performed. There are several, related, cases. The binary operators listed in Table 7.3 as accepting arguments of `numeric` or `scalar` types will cause type conversions to be applied, if necessary, until both operands are of the same type. For the details, consult the most recent language definition you can find—they have a history of changing. The basic pattern is that narrower values are converted to wider ones (e.g., `int` to `long int`), signed to unsigned, integer to floating point, and narrower floating point types to progressively wider ones. For example, if you add an `int` to a `float`, the `int` will be converted to `float` before the addition is done. The obvious risk is that some integer values will not be represented exactly in floating point, so accuracy may be lost in the course of a computation. A more subtle risk is that converting from signed to unsigned representations may have unexpected consequences, depending on how negative numbers are stored and how sign bits are treated during the conversion.

Assigning operators are slightly different: the right hand operand is converted to the type of the left, when that is possible using the implicit conversions. As well as the conversions applied within expressions, you may assign a floating point number to an integer variable—the value is truncated. The same type conversions may be applied when variables are initialized. The semantics of argument passing is, by definition, equivalent to initialization, so implicit conversions may also be applied to actual arguments. The following example program illustrates some initializations that cause conversions.

```
#include <iostream>
#include <limits.h>
#include <stdlib.h>

int main()
{
    int n = -7;
    unsigned int u = n;        Implicit conversion from signed to unsigned
```

```
int m = INT_MAX;       The biggest possible int value
float fm = m;          Implicit conversion from integer to floating point
int pi = 3.142;        Implicit truncation of floating point to int
cout << "n = " << n << " u = " << u << endl
     << "m = " << m << " fm = " << fm << endl
     << "pi = " << pi << endl;
return EXIT_SUCCESS;
}
```

The output of this program may not be what everyone expects.

```
n = -7 u = 4294967289
m = 2147483647 fm = 2.14748e+09
pi = 3
```

(The output may be different on your machine, but this is what mine does.)

Besides these messy conversions between numerical types, some other conversions are carried out implicitly—we have already seen such conversions. A constant expression yielding zero is converted to the null pointer; any pointer may be converted to a void*; any pointer or integer value may be converted to bool by using it in a condition (bool is already an integral type, so it can be involved in arithmetic conversions such as we have just seen). And, of course, a pointer to a derived class can always be converted into a pointer to a base class, and a reference to a derived class can always be converted into a reference to a base class. Initializing objects with the values of other objects is done by a copy constructor, and copy constructors take reference arguments, so it follows that an object of a derived class may be converted into an object of its base class during initialization, and similarly during assignment if operator= takes a reference argument. (If you understand that, you've probably understood copy constructors and assignment.)

Explicit Conversions Between Built-in Types

In C++ terminology, an explicit type conversion is called a *cast*, although there are unreconstructed Algol68 experts hanging around C++ who still talk about "coercions".

It isn't true—really it isn't—that in C++ you can convert a value of any type into one of any other type, although after I'd successfully turned a pointer into a float and taken its square root I began to wonder. In fact, besides the conversions you can do implicitly, the only additional ones you can do explicitly are: from a pointer to any integer type, and vice versa; from a pointer to one class to a pointer to another, including the special cases of converting a pointer to a base class into a pointer to a derived class (subject to a few technical restrictions) and even from a pointer to a function to any other sort of pointer, and vice versa.

All of these pointer conversions are inherently unsafe; most of them are crazy. It may be necessary to resort to them in some low level systems work. Casts may also be needed if you find yourself mixing C++ with code written in other languages that place a different interpretation on the same memory layout. The fact that these legitimate (if you will) uses of casts belong among a sort of virtuoso programming lends them a certain glamour. Can you call yourself a real programmer until you've cast a `char*` into a pointer to a function? This sort of feeling hasn't any place in the clean and logical world of software engineering, but programmers are human. Maybe you'd better choose something nobody else is going to use or maintain for your rites of passage, though.

What does a cast look like? At the time of writing there are three competing notations, the result of an ongoing attempt to improve on the cast notation inherited from C, while retaining compatibility with old code. You can see how it happened, but the resulting situation is not a happy one. Despite its syntactic incongruity, and other less obvious drawbacks, the original notation probably remains the most popular, so we'll stick with it, though I'll mention the others, later.

A cast expression has the form

(*typename*) *expression*

The *expression* may itself involve a cast, so, for example, the (entirely pointless) trick of taking the square root of a pointer can be done, assuming the presence of a `sqrt` function taking a `float` argument, like this:

!   `sqrt((float)(int)the_pointer)`

(Although the `int` to `float` conversion could be done implicitly instead.)

The type name in a cast doesn't need to be a simple name; although typedefs are often used to make casts more readable, you often see such expressions as `(char*)p`.

Pretending casts don't exist would be patronizing, and so is lecturing you on their evils, but...If you find yourself trying to use a cast, think carefully about whether there isn't a better way, before losing the advantage of static type checking—a virtual function or a template (see chapter 10) often does the trick.

Conversions of User-Defined Types

It only takes a twist of mind, a shift of perspective, to find out how much you already know about user-defined type conversions. Take this initialization of a `WebPage` variable:

`WebPage tex = WebPage("http://www.loria.fr/tex");`

In goes a `char*`, out comes a `WebPage`. *Voilà!* A type conversion before your very eyes. Constructors that take a single argument *are* type conversion functions (unless they are copy constructors). Any time you want to explicitly convert a value of type T into one of type C, you only have to call the constructor `C::C(T)`, if it exists.

▷   Because all types, whether built-in or user-defined, are held to have constructors, the functional notation for type conversion can be used as an alternative to a cast, provided the type being converted to has a simple name. For example, `int(3.14)` means the same as `(int)3.14`, and is arguably more readable. However, you can't ◁ say `char*(p)` instead of `(char*)p`.

When you are defining a class, constructors give you a way of converting values of other types into objects of your class. I sometimes think of this sort of conversion as "casting in". If you want to have a complete range of type conversions, you also need to be able to "cast out"—to convert an object belonging to your class into a value of some other type. A separate mechanism for casting out of a class is necessary, because you may want to convert to a built-in type or to a class whose definition you cannot modify; in either case, the possibility of casting in is not available to you.

A casting out operation is defined as another special member function, with neither argument nor result type, whose name is of the form

```
operator typename
```

For example, if I wanted to provide a facility for turning `WebPage` objects back into C-strings, I could include

```
operator const char*() const;
```

among the member declarations of the `WebPage` class, and define the conversion function suitably so that it puts the components of the net resource's URL back together again. I could subsequently use a cast to obtain a C-string from a `WebPage`:

```
(const char*)the_WebPage
```

In the absence of the conversion operator, this cast would not be allowed. Note that the type name in an operator function of this sort need not be simple—I have used `const` here to prevent the converted string it returns being changed by its caller.

Why are there special functions for carrying out type conversions? Why not just declare a member function with any old name and call it in the usual way? No reason at all, as far as explicit conversions are concerned, but if you use constructors and conversion operators then your type conversions can also be applied *implicitly*.

User-defined conversions are applied implicitly during assignment and during initialization, which includes passing arguments to functions and returning results from them. Since overloaded operators are functions, implicit conversions may be applied when objects are used within expressions. The major difference between user-defined and built-in conversions is that only one user-defined conversion will ever be applied implicitly, whereas a whole sequence of built-in ones may be.

A common idiom resulting from implicit user-defined conversions is the initialization of a variable of some class with a constant value of some built-in type, whenever a suitable constructor exists. For example,

```
WebPage tex = "http://www.loria.fr/tex";
```

The constructor `WebPage::WebPage(const char*)` will be used implicitly to construct a `WebPage` object, which will then be used to initialize the variable.

At last, an outstanding mystery is cleared up. In previous chapters, I have used objects of the library class `string`, which I have initialized with C++ string constants, which are of type `char*`. This is fine, because the class `string` has a constructor `string::string(const char*)`, which is used implicitly to convert C-string constants into strings.

Having your type conversions applied implicitly can be very handy, but it isn't always entirely appropriate. Think about the following. In programs using binary trees, some programmers prefer not to create empty trees, but wait until the first value is available and create a singleton tree, consisting of a root and two empty sub-trees. Such a programmer would define a constructor `Tree::Tree(const string&)` to create these singleton trees. With such a constructor declared, conversions from strings to trees could be carried out implicitly; in particular, any function requiring an argument of type `Tree` could be called with an argument of type `string`, which would be converted by embedding it in a newly constructed tree. Would you want that? Whereas you might argue that a `WebPage` object and a string recording the characters of a URL hold the same information in different forms, so that implicit conversion between them is reasonable, could you say the same about a string and a tree containing it? A tree is a very different thing from a string.

To make a more extreme example, suppose you defined a function to flatten a tree, let us say by visiting it in infix order and concatenating the strings at all its nodes. You might reason that this operation is converting a tree into a string while preserving the information and ordering structure, so that the flattening operation should be declared as a type conversion operator. (Well, you *might*.) A consequence of this decision would be that any function requiring a string argument could be passed a tree, and the (potentially expensive) flattening would be carried out implicitly. Would you want *that*?

Deciding when a function that takes a value of one type and returns a value of another type should be considered a type conversion and be performed implicitly calls for some nicety of judgement. Asking yourself whether the two values are different representations of the same abstract information is some help, but the question isn't often an easy one to answer. Experience, intelligence and intuition will have to be applied. Or you could choose to avoid implicit conversions altogether.

For casting out, this is easily done—don't give your member functions the fancy `operator` *typename* names and they won't be applied implicitly. For casting in, you have the same option—define a member function that isn't a constructor—but this may be inconvenient if you need the constructor to do ordinary constructing. If your C++ compiler is up to date with the draft standard you can precede the declaration of the constructor with the new keyword `explicit` to prevent its implicit use for type conversion.

Type conversion functions should not be defined casually. Apart from the general principle that type conversion in a strongly typed language is not cool, they may produce ambiguities. For example, suppose I was working on the compiler management system from chapter 5. Realizing that nobody can afford to ignore the Internet at the moment, I might reason that all my `File` objects should be accessible by ftp. Having heard about the `NetResource` classes in chapter 6, I could define a conversion function `File::operator FTP()`

to build FTP objects out of Files. Meanwhile, a colleague working on the FTP class might have the same thought, and provide it with constructor FTP::FTP(const File&). Now any implicit conversion of a File into an FTP will be ambiguous—either their constructor or my operator could do it.

More subtly, suppose I decide to extend the class File so that it could record some extra information about an open file on some operating system where integers are used to identify file descriptors after opening. A File will now record a filename and a descriptor. Different functions could need one or other of these different pieces of information. Feeling clever, I could define operators to convert a File into either a string, giving its filename component or an int, giving the file descriptor. The class definition might look like this:

```
class File {
public:
  File(const string&);
  File(const string&, int);
  operator string() {  return the_file_name; }
  operator int() {  return the_fd; }
private:
  int the_number;
  string the_name;
};
```

(plus a few members that do something useful, presumably). Now, suppose you have declared an overloaded function

```
void f(string s);
void f(int n);
```

Which function will be called here?

```
File w("orinoco", 7);
f(w);
```

In fact, neither... the program will not compile because of an ambiguous reference to an overloaded function. Without one or other of the type conversion operators, there would be no problem. If either of them was added as an afterthought, by adding it, you would have made code that previously compiled fail. To fix it, a cast would have to be added to calls of the function f.

When you add operator overloading to implicit conversions, the effect is much the same as that obtained by adding too much oil at once when you are making mayonnaise. Let's go back to the Dylan song in chapter 7. Recall that I declared

A curdled mess, in case you never tried it

```
void song(char);
void song(const char*);
void song(int);
```

By passing arguments of each of the types char, const char* and int, I was able to call each of these functions in turn, thereby writing the opening of the song. Consider now the fact that I am allowed to initialize an int variable with a floating point value, for example

```
int one = 1.25;
```

It follows that I can pass a floating point value as an argument to a function expecting an integer, since argument passing is the same as initialization. Therefore, you would expect song(1.25) to be a call of song(int). Perhaps you would, but you would be disappointed. Not because there isn't an exact match on the argument types—implicit conversions are allowed when you call overloaded functions—but, on the contrary because too many matches are possible when conversions are taken into account. You can initialize a char with a floating point value, too, so the call is ambiguous.

This is beginning to look confusing: you can also initialize a char with an int and vice versa, so why are the calls song('B') and song(1965) not ambiguous? Or try this:

```
short int s = 5;
song(s);
```

You'll find that the compiler calls song(int) with no complaint, inserting the conversion from short int to int, as you would probably expect. Why is there no ambiguity here?

The answer is roughly as follows. An object of some type T_a is said to match a formal argument of type T_f if it would be possible to pass it as the corresponding actual argument. It may match because T_a is the same as T_f, or because a value of type T_a can be implicitly converted into one of type T_f, using a sequence of built-in conversions and at most one user-defined conversion. Argument type matching in C++ isn't democratic; some matches are better than others. Exact matches are the best, the royalty of type matches. Matches using only integral promotions (short int to int, int to long int, and so on) are the dukes and belted earls, with other standard conversions (the ones you can use implicitly during initialization and assignment) forming the lesser aristocracy. User-defined conversions are little more than the *haute bourgeoisie.*

When choosing between overloaded functions, the C++ compiler is a pure snob: it will choose the one that gives the best match for the type of the actual argument. If more than one possibility gives an equally good match, the call is ambiguous. In my original song example, unambiguous exact matches were possible for all the arguments I provided; in the call of song(1.25) no exact match or match using integral promotions exists, but two possibilities use standard conversions. The fact that you probably don't expect to be able to convert a floating point number into a character is irrelevant; C and C++ let you do so, so the call cannot be resolved. The complexity and untidiness of the standard conversions means that surprises are always possible when they get tangled up in your overloaded functions and operators. When you are in doubt, there is an easy, if tedious, way out: provide exact matches for the whole lot.

If you read the ARM you will find that the full story about the interaction between implicit conversions and overloading is more complicated—I have deliberately kept quiet about how you determine which match is best when you have more than one argument. Most of the time, though, the questions shouldn't bother you, because if the type structure of your program is sensible, conversions will be rare. It's just those built-in conversions you have to be careful with, really.

▷ Incidentally, and I suppose I should have mentioned this before, the type of a floating point constant like 1.25 is double, not float. If you provide a version of song(float), the call song(1.25) will still be ambiguous. The standard conversion from double to float has no bluer blood than any other standard conversion, so float is no better a match for a double than int or char. If you want your floating point literals to be of type float, you must append an F, as in 1.25F.

▷ I have described two notations for casts: old-style, with type names in brackets, and function style, where suitable constructors or conversion functions exist. The third notation is another relatively new language feature. It distinguishes between three different uses of casts. *Static casts* are either explicit applications of casts that can be performed implicitly or they are casts that perform the inverse of an implicitly allowed conversion. For example, the conversion from a pointer to an object of a base class into a pointer to an object of a derived class is a static cast, because the conversion on the opposite direction is always allowed implicitly. A *re-interpreting cast* is one that converts a value, usually a pointer, to another unrelated type. Finally, a *const cast* (sic) is one that allows you to remove the const attribute from a variable or member. These three types of cast are performed by three different operators, though all have the same form: a keyword with the type being converted to enclosed in angle brackets.

```
static_cast<typename>
reinterpret_cast<typename>
const_cast<typename>
```

For example, if I want to explicitly truncate a float by converting to an integer within an expression, I can do it with a static cast, since float to int conversions are allowed explicitly:

```
zi_covariance = static_cast<int>(zeta * 1.5) + 0.989;
```

I know what I'm doing here (since I just invented the formula for *zi-covariance*), so the cast is safe. Other static casts, such as the conversion from a pointer to a base class into a pointer to a derived class, are less safe in general, but can work in a suitable context—when you know that the pointer really is pointing to an object of the derived class, despite what its declaration says.

On the other hand, converting pointers into integers is inherently unsafe and so a reinterpreting cast is required in

!

```
sqrt(static_cast<float>(reinterpret_cast<int>(the_pntr)))
```

The new notation makes it clearer what is going on. The frankly unattractive form of these operators was deliberately chosen, to make casts stick out and to make programmers think twice before using them. This strategy seems likely to be too successful: the old notations are still allowed (they are not even "deprecated"—standards-speak for "don't use them because we want to take them out if we get a chance to revise this standard") so it is hard to see the new ones catching on, even ◁ though everyone agrees you *ought* to use them.

Casting Away `const`

Part of the C++ philosophy is that compilers' checks are there to help prevent you making accidental errors, not to stop you doing things deliberately. This applies to constancy checks: the compiler will tell you if you inadvertently attempt to update a constant object, but if you really want to do so you can, as long as you explicitly state what you are doing by "casting away `const`". A cast can be used to convert a value of type `const` T into one of type T so that it is no longer constant.

▷ With the new-style notations, a `const` cast is distinguished from any other sort of type conversions. Static casts and re-interpreting casts cannot be used to alter the
◁ constancy attribute of a value.

One possible legitimate excuse for casting away `const` is to rectify the oversights of other programmers. If you are using a library, it is possible that whoever wrote it was not sufficiently careful about specifying `const` with formal arguments and member functions. If you know for certain that a function does not modify a reference argument, despite the declaration, then using a cast to pass a constant to it is harmless and justified. For example, suppose that, beguiled by promises of improved performance, you adopt a proprietary library for manipulating C-strings, instead of using the standard library functions. It is sadly conceivable that you might find a declaration like the following of a function for computing the length of a string:

```
extern int stringlen(char*);
```

You will then find that an attempt to use `stringlen` to find the length of a constant C-string causes the compiler to complain about an illegal implicit conversion of a `const`.

!
```
const char* const s = "I am a fish";
int slen = stringlen(s);
```

So, make the conversion explicit:

```
int slen = stringlen((char*)s);
```

▷ Better still, if you have access to a compiler supporting the new style of cast notation, make the conversion stick out like a sore thumb:

```
int slen = stringlen(const_cast<char*>(s));
```
◁

Leaving aside the rights and wrongs of deliberately violating program assertions—the presence of an explicit cast shows you know you are doing it—a drawback of casting away `const` is that it might not work if you are actually trying to update the constant object, not just get round an incorrect interface specification. A compiler is at liberty to place constants into read-only memory, in which case an attempt to write to one would either fail or cause a runtime error. A cast of this sort is only a compile time operation that alters what your compiler considers an error; it does nothing at runtime to magically make a constant writable.

▷ Many applications of casting away `const` that one might consider legitimate are aimed at allowing you to update some members of a constant object. Legitimate? Yes, because an object can still appear to be constant in all its observable behaviour while some of its internal state is changed invisibly. Suppose an object contains a reference count, for example. You might still want to declare a particular object constant, but you don't mean that the invisible reference count should be immutable; you presumably want to go on counting references in your usual way so that the object can be deleted when it becomes unreachable. Nevertheless, you want this object to appear to be constant, and to forbid any operations that affect the values of any of its other members. In former times, you would use a cast to relax the constancy constraint to update the reference count. Now, you can instead qualify the declaration of a data member with the keyword `mutable`, meaning "this data member can be updated even in constant objects". It is up to you to ensure that the updates to your mutable data members preserve what is referred to as "conceptual constancy".

*"Concep-
tual".
Good
grief!*
◁

SOME NEW TYPES

In this short section, we will look briefly at some types that have not, so far, been examined. Some esoteric low level types will be omitted, because they are only of interest if you are doing very low level systems programming, and if you are doing that sort of work you will have to read the ARM. (And anyway, all the types I am leaving out are leftovers from C, and most systems programmers probably know more about C than I do.)

void and void*

The type `void` is really one of those convenient notational fictions that make life neater without actually doing anything. It is the hero of a French existentialist novel: the Type With No Values. You can't create objects of type `void`, there aren't any. All you can do with it is use it as the return type of a function that doesn't return a value. That way, all functions have a return type and there is no need to create a new entity such as a procedure.

The type `void*` is not the type of pointers that can't point to anything. It's much more of a Zen concept: the type consisting of pointers that can point to *anything*. A value of any pointer type whatsoever may be assigned to a `void*` variable or data member, or passed as an actual argument to a function where the corresponding formal argument is declared as `void*`.

Opponents of strong typing may rub their hands with glee at this information: Untyped pointers! It's true that `void*` (another legacy from C) is hard to reconcile with strong typing, but in C++ you can't actually do anything with a `void*` value without explicitly converting it to some other pointer type. How could you? Only particular classes have members, so a pointer must point to an object of some particular type, known to the compiler, before you can use it to access data members or call member functions. So, in order to use void* to blow up the type structure of your program you must use explicit casts, so everyone can at least see what you've done.

For about twenty years, the consensus among people who think about programming has been that strong typing is a good thing, and subverting type checking a bad one. (Except at MIT.) The tasks which appear to call for untyped pointers can almost always be done better using other means, such as inheritance and templates, in C++. So what is void* for?

Like most of the C++ features purists might like to throw out, void*'s presence can be justified on the grounds of efficiency and the requirements of low-level systems programming. We will see in chapter 10 how prudent use of void* pointers can sometimes prevent unnecessarily large code being generated. In some systems programs, it can be the case that a low level function must be able to manipulate undifferentiated bytes of memory. The epitome of such a function is the lowest level of dynamic space allocator, which has to be able to reserve space for objects of any type, before they are properly constructed (see chapter 12). As a simpler example, think of a diagnostic function to print the contents of memory locations as a hexadecimal dump. Pointers of type void* provide a suitable intermediary, allowing pointers to objects of any class to be passed into such a function, where they can be converted to char* pointers so that individual bytes can be examined.

Although void* has its legitimate uses, most of the time it is best avoided; before using it, think carefully whether inheritance or templates could be used to do your job better. If you decide not, then the use of void* should be localized as much as possible, and well documented. If you find you really, really can't work within the C++ type system, and you are using void* extensively to simulate untyped pointers, you are never going to be a happy C++ programmer, and should perhaps look at other languages.[1] On the other hand, if you're just not convinced by the intellectual arguments in favour of strong typing, try treating it as a game, or a challenge to your programming ability, to work within the strong typing discipline. You might get to like it after all.

There is no void& type.

Wide Characters

Not everyone in the world speaks English. It has taken the computing industry a long time to come to terms with this fact, but increasing attention is being given to the problems of computing in a multi-lingual world. One of the major problems is that of character codes. This area has become a minefield of international standards, national variants of international standards, manufacturers' proprietary coding schemes and unofficial standards supported by manufacturers' consortia. The salient fact is simply that many non-European languages are written using scripts consisting of more than the two hundred

---

[1] Are you ready for the BCPL revival? See http://www.cl.cam.ac.uk/users/mr/BCPL.html.

and fifty six distinct characters that can be encoded in a single eight-bit byte, the most common machine representation of the type char.

To accommodate multi-byte characters, C++ includes a wide character datatype, called wchar_t. The size of a wchar_t value is implementation dependent. Wide character constants may be written as sequences of characters enclosed in single quotes and preceded by a letter L. The interpretation of these sequences depends on the character encoding being used. For example, using a sixteen-bit subset of the ISO standard character set ISO-10646, the two-byte constant L'&m' would correspond to the code for a musical flat sign, ♭.

You can have arrays of wide characters, and there is a library class wstring, corresponding to string. Versions of the input and output stream classes are defined to work on wide characters. Don't get too excited, though. The compiler I have been using while writing this book defines wchar_t as a synonym for char—which it is perfectly entitled to do.

▷ Wide characters provide a means of manipulating extended character sets, they do not address the problem of allowing programmers to use their own language's script to write C++ programs. This is already something of a problem, even for users of Latin alphabets, because the characters [,], {, }, | and \, which have special meanings in C++, occupy positions in the seven-bit ASCII encoding—the one most often used by C++ compilers—which are occupied by "national characters" according to ISO's character set encodings. The corresponding codes are used by locally configured hardware to hold accented letters and other alphabetic characters not used in English. As a result, programmers from some European countries find themselves writing some very bizarre looking C++ programs. To help compensate for this, there are some extra keywords and character combinations that can be used as alternatives for the standard C++ notations employing these characters, for example or for ||, <% and %> for { and }, <: and :> for [and]. When we all have eight bit keyboards (and email relays don't mess up eight bit characters) these will become unnecessary for European languages, but the problem of using other scripts for writing C++—or any other programming language—is one that still remains to ◁ be properly addressed.

Streams

The data types concerned with stream input and output are not part of the C++ language, but they are so pervasive that they might as well be. They are defined in the standard library, and it is something of a tribute to the power of the facilities that *are* part of C++ that it is possible to define such powerful types without going outside the language.

Many of you will find stream input and output quaint, preferring to use graphical user interfaces. Please yourself...this is not the place to debate the relative merits of command line and graphical interfaces. Nor is it the place to go into the specifics of interface programming for any particular system. One of the virtues of stream input and output is that you can rely on their being available wherever C++ is. In any case, not all input and output is performed at the user interface. When you need to perform input from and output to files, the stream provides an eminently suitable abstraction. It is even quite easy to see how a portable abstraction of graphical interfaces could be built out of similar components to those used by streams. Even if you never intend to do input and output with files, it is instructive to see how this well understood form of input and output has been abstracted, in the hope that the less well understood newer forms may be susceptible to a similar process. It has taken a very long time for programming language designers to come up with a way of doing input and output that is not a dreadful mess; we can all learn something from streams.

The Stream Classes

The iostreams library has evolved, like C++ itself, into something large and complex. Its description occupies seventy two pages of the draft standard, and at least one entire book has been written about an earlier, simpler, version. To make matters worse, the official definition of the iostream library has undergone a quite radical shake-up during the standardization process and a stable definition is unlikely to emerge before the final version of the standard. Fortunately, a simplified account is sufficient to enable you to do the most common input and output tasks. What follows is not necessarily an entirely accurate description of what the standard says the iostreams library should provide, but it is intended to cover the features most people will need, at least to begin with, and which you can expect to be provided by most implementations now and in the future.

We have so far used three stream objects `cin`, `cout` and `cerr`. Like all objects, they belong to a class. The standard input stream `cin` belongs to the class `istream`, the output streams belong to the class `ostream`. All streams belong to classes derived from one or other of these classes of stream. The names `cin`, `cout` and `cerr` are declared in the header `iostream` and initialized for you by the system.

Most operating systems provide you with some means of associating the standard streams with files when you start up your program, so that they can be used for input from and output to files. The simple pattern of taking your input from a standard input stream and sending (most of) your output to a standard output stream is only adequate for a limited class of programs (what the UNIX people call "filters"). More often, you want to be able to read from and write to several files, selected dynamically as execution proceeds. The classes `ifstream` and `ofstream`, derived from `istream` and `ostream` respectively, allow you to do this. They are defined in the header `fstream`.

Because the file stream classes are derived from the stream classes, you can use a pointer or reference to a file stream object wherever you could use a pointer or reference to a stream. So, if you write a function with a formal argument of type `ostream&` it will work equally well with an actual argument of type `ofstream` or with `cout` or `cerr` as its argument. Usually you do not need to worry about what kind of `ostream` you are writing to—another triumph for inheritance.

The difference does matter when you create a stream that you want associated with a file. For mundane purposes, using a suitable constructor for a file stream class, taking a filename as its argument, is sufficient to create a stream object associated with the named file, which is made ready for input or output. Here is a main program that uses the functions defined in our old vowel counting program from chapter 3 to read a series of strings from one file and write them, preceded by their vowel counts, to another.

```
int main()
{
  ifstream in("input.dat");
  if (!in.is_open())
  {
    cerr << "couldn't open input file" << endl;
    return EXIT_FAILURE;
  }
  ofstream out("output.dat");
  if (!out.is_open())
  {
    cerr << "couldn't open output file" << endl;
    return EXIT_FAILURE;
  }
  while (in && out)
  {
    string s;
    in >> s;
    convert_to_lower_case(s);
    int nv = number_of_vowels(s);
    out <<  nv << ":" << s << endl;
  }
  cout << "Finished" << endl;
  return EXIT_SUCCESS;
}
```

The member function `is_open` can be called through any stream and returns `true` or `false` according as the file is open. The idiom `while (in && out)` is used to loop until the stream is finished or a read or write error occurs.

The classes `istream` and `ostream` are both derived from a common base class called `ios`, which implements the operations and stores the data common to all kinds of stream. An `ios` object is a front for a more primitive abstraction of buffered input and output called a `streambuf`. To a large extent, the differences between the different sort of stream lie in the different sorts of `streambuf` that you associate with a stream. For example, the file streams have a file buffer of type `filebuf`. One of the ways you can extend the stream library is by defining different types of stream buffers.

Most of the time, though, you will not need to think about buffers. The constructors for file stream objects will automatically create a buffer as part of the stream, connect it to a file, and open it for reading or writing as appropriate. There are, however, two particular instances where you may need to get at the buffer directly. To do this, you can use the member function `rdbuf()`, which returns a pointer to the buffer associated with the stream it is called through.

Being a member of the base class, it can be applied to any stream object.

The first common use for explicit buffers is slightly startling. The operator << is overloaded to take an operand of type `streambuf*` and to send the entire contents of that buffer to an output stream. Conceptually, buffers are infinite, so that means that it will send the entire contents of the file that is connected to the buffer. Hence, the smart way of copying one file to another is this:

```
#include <fstream>
#include <stdlib.h>

int main()
{
  ifstream in("input.dat");
  ofstream out("output.dat");
  out << in.rdbuf();
  return EXIT_SUCCESS;
}
```

The second occasion for accessing buffers is for opening the same file for reading and writing. Once upon a time, a separate class of streams was required to accomplish this, but the structure of the streams classes has been simplified (in this respect) by making all buffers, whether for reading or writing, of the same type. All the stream operations do is put characters in or take them out of a buffer. Depending on how the buffer was created, it can empty itself into a file or refill itself from one as necessary to achieve output and input. If you want to read from and write to the same file using streams, you must explicitly open a buffer connected to the file for both reading and writing and then associate it with both an `istream` and an `ostream`. The necessary code is best treated as a ceremonial incantation, without bothering yourself about what it all means at this stage.

```
ifstream istr(filename, ios::in|ios::out);
ofstream ostr;
ostr.rdbuf(istr.rdbuf());
```

Another useful sort of stream is the string stream, which does neither input nor output, but allows you to treat a string in memory as if it was a string. The classes `istringstream` and `ostringstream`, are declared in the header `<sstream>`. The default constructors for `ostringstream` creates a string object to use as a buffer. Subsequently, you can use << to insert the character representations of objects into the string. For example,

```
ostringstream oss;
oss << 3.142 << "i am a fish";
```

has the effect of inserting the string of characters `3.142i am a fish` into the string associated with `oss`. This string can be accessed using the member function `str`, so

```
cout << oss.str() << endl;
```

prints

```
3.142i am a fish
```

on the standard output. An `istringstream` is most usefully constructed using a constructor that takes a string argument. The string is copied to the buffer, and then elements of it can be extracted using >> as if it were an input file. For example, continuing from the previous example,

```
istringstream iss(oss.str());
float f;
char c, d;
iss >> f >> c >> d;
```

sets f to 3.142, c to 'i' and d to 'a'. Notice that white space is skipped, just as it is when reading from `cin`.

String streams are useful in allowing you to write functions that translate between objects and their character representations without having to distinguish between operations that also perform input or output from or to some external device and those that merely read from or write to memory. As well as string streams, there are "strstreams", which are like string streams, but use C-strings—arrays of `char`—as their buffers. We will see an example of strstreams in action in chapter 10.

Stream Operations

We have seen the operators >> and << being used to read and write objects belonging to built-in types. One of the nicest aspects of stream input and output is that these operators can be overloaded, like any other, to allow you to read and write objects of user-defined classes. Consider output: `operator<<` can be overloaded as a global function taking two arguments, a reference to the `ostream` to write to and the object to be written. It returns a reference to its `ostream` argument so that output operations can be strung together in expressions, as we have seen. One way of arranging for the output of user-defined classes is to provide them with a member function, taking a reference to an `ostream` as an argument, to perform the output, and overloading `operator<<` as a forwarding function. For example, I could write a print operation for `MFVec` objects.

```
ostream& MFVec::print(ostream& os)
{
  os << "(" << xcoord << ", " << ycoord << ")";
  return os;
}
```

and then overload `operator<<` to make this operation look like other output operations.

```
ostream& operator<<(ostream&os, MFVec& mv)
{  return mv.print(os);  }
```

Similar effects can be achieved, *mutatis mutandis*, for input operations. We will see in chapter 9 how an `operator<<` function can be given access to the private members of an object in a more economical way, without the need for the largely superfluous print member function.

For output, operator<< usually does what you want, but for input, it is often necessary to control operations more tightly than you can using operator>>, in order to deal appropriately with corrupt or unexpected input. In the end, for anything but mundane situations, it is usually best to do everything yourself by reading input one character at a time. This is not what happens if you use >> to read into a char variable: by default, white space is stripped out of the input stream. The istream member function get(char&) will read the next character into its reference argument, no matter what it is, returning a reference to the input stream it is called through. Although it is superfluous, a corresponding member function put(char) is provided for symmetry. A more obvious, but probably less efficient, program to copy one file to another is as follows:

```
#include <fstream>
#include <stdlib.h>

int main()
{
  ifstream in("input.dat");
  ofstream out("output.dat");
  char c;
  while (in.get(c))
    out.put(c);
  return EXIT_SUCCESS;
}
```

Input of strings presents a special problem: how do you decide where the end of a string is? By default, white space is used as a delimiter, so if you read a string from the input, what you get is everything up to, but not including, the next space, tab or newline. (You may have noticed how I fudged this question in earlier examples.) To read strings with arbitrary delimiters you can use a different overloaded version of istream's member function get. Unfortunately, this reads characters into a C-string, which you must supply as the first argument. The second argument is an integer specifying the maximum number of characters to read (so it will usually be the capacity of the array of char) and the third argument is a delimiter character, which defaults to '\n' is you omit it. The function will read characters into its first argument until it finds the delimiter or reaches the limit or the end of the file. My faithful vowel counting program could be adapted to count the number of vowels in each line of input by first declaring an array of char of a suitable size in main.

```
char inbuf[max_line_length];
```

and then replacing the declaration of s and the input statement cin >> s inside the while-loop with:

```
in.get(inbuf, max_line_length);
string s = inbuf;
```

The member function gcount() will return the number of characters read by the previous get operation.

A function related to `get` is `istream::ignore`, which will read and discard characters. It, too, takes a count and a delimiter character as arguments and discards characters until it reaches the count, encounters the delimiter or reaches the end of the input stream. For really fiddly input operations it is sometimes useful to use `istream::peek()`, which returns the next character from the input stream, but leaves it in the buffer for subsequent input operations, `istream::putback(char)`, which puts its argument back at the front of the input buffer, and `istream::ungetc()` which undoes the effect of `get` so that the next character to be read will be the same as the one most recently read.

The final aspect of iostreams input and output I will briefly describe is format control. You know this can never be pretty. The library provides rather too many ways of controlling such aspects of the appearance of your output as the base of numbers, width of fields, format of floating point numbers and suppression of decimal points. The most convenient way uses a version of `operator<<` overloaded as a higher order function, and special functions that it can apparently send to an output stream to achieve the desired effects.

Suppose, for example, you are... you know, one of *those* programmers, and so you want to output an integer in hexadecimal. There is a global function that you can call which will cause the next integer output operation to print the value in hex. It is declared as

No it isn't, but you'll probably never know the difference

```
ios& hex(ios&);
```

You could write code like this

```
cout << "the hex value of n is ";
hex(cout);
cout << n << endl;
```

but that's a bit crummy. A little inspiration coupled with what you know about higher order functions from chapter 7 could lead you to overload `operator<<` to take such a function as an argument and apply it:

```
ostream& operator<<(ostream& os, ios&(*f)(ios&))
{  return f(os);  }
```

Now you can use the function `hex` as an argument to `operator<<`.

```
cout << "the hex value of n is " << hex
     << n << endl;
```

You don't actually need that inspiration, because a suitably overloaded version of `operator<<` is provided in the standard streams headers. Functions that can be sent to an output stream are called output *manipulators*. Table 8.1 shows the principal output manipulators that should be available. Note that some of these manipulators take arguments. To use them you must include the header `<iomanip>` in your program.

There are also a few input manipulators, as indicated in the last column of Table 8.1. In addition, the object `endl`, which we have been using so long is implemented as a manipulator function, as is a related object `flush`, which causes the output stream buffer to be flushed.

Manipulator	Effect	Input/Output
boolalpha	read strings true and false as bool values	IO
noboolalpha	don't	IO
showbase	print an indication of number base before integers	O
noshowbase	don't	O
showpoint	always print the decimal point when printing floats	O
noshowpoint	don't print the decimal point if a float is an exact integer	O
showpos	print + sign before positive numbers	O
noshowpos	don't	O
skipws	skip leading white space before reading values	I
noskipws	don't	I
uppercase	replace lower case letters with upper case equivalents	O
nouppercase	don't	O
internal	add fill characters within the printed value	O
left	left justify values in specified field width	O
right	right justify values in specified field width	O
dec	integers to base ten	IO
hex	integers to base sixteen	IO
oct	integers to base eight	IO
fixed	print floating point output in fixed point notation	O
scientific	print floating point output in mantissa plus exponent notation	O
setbase(int n)	set base for operations to n	IO
setfill(char c)	set the character used to pad fields to c	O
setprecision(int p)	set the number of digits to print after a decimal point to p	O
setw(int w)	set the field width to w	O

Table 8.1 Manipulators

Enumerations

It is fairly common to find that a variable can only ever meaningfully take on values from a particular finite, and usually small, set. For example, in a low-level communications application, you might need to test a return code set by a modem. For any type of modem, there is only a limited number of possible return codes, corresponding to the possible outcomes of an attempt to make a connection: busy, error, connect at 1200 baud, connect at 2400 baud, and so on. Your variable should only ever be able to take on one of these values. You could make it an `int`, or one of the other integer types, but then the type of the variable would allow it to take on values which do not correspond to any of the return codes. In keeping with the philosophy of strong typing, it ought to be possible to associate a type with this variable that only allows it to take on values from the set of legitimate codes.

Enumeration types are provided for this purpose. An enumeration declaration allows you to define a new type as a set of named constants. Subsequently, variables, class members, and function arguments and results of that type may be declared and assigned values from the set of names. The syntax for defining an enumeration is

```
enum name { name [ = const ] { ,name [ = const ] } };
```

where none of the *name*s is already in scope; the *const*s must be constant integer expressions; `enum` is a reserved word. The effect is that the name following `enum` becomes a new type, whose values are denoted by the set of names in the brackets. Where constants are specified they are the values corresponding to the names; following names without constants are given values increasing by one; if no constants at all are specified, the values are assigned starting at zero. Often, you don't care what the values actually are, as long as they are distinct from each other and can be referred to by a name.

A suitable type for return codes could be defined as

```
enum ReturnCodes   {
    no_carrier = 3, error = 4, connect_1200 = 5,
    busy = 7, connect_2400 = 10, connect_9600 = 13,
    connect_4800 = 18, connect_7200 = 20, connect_12000 = 21,
    connect_14400 = 25, connect_28800 = 107
};
```

Assume it is possible to define a function `get_rc`, which attempts to make a connection via the modem; its result is the return code set after the attempt. We can then determine whether it succeeded and return the connection speed to the calling program, as follows:

```
ReturnCodes get_rc();

int connect(int max_retries)
{
    int speed = 0;
    int tries = 0;
    while (speed == 0 && tries <= max_retries)
```

```
    {
      ReturnCodes the_return_code = get_rc();
      tries += 1;
      switch (the_return_code)  {
      case connect_1200:  speed = 1200; break;
      case connect_2400:  speed = 2400; break;
      case connect_9600:  speed = 9600; break;
      case connect_4800:  speed = 4800; break;
      case connect_7200:  speed = 7200; break;
      case connect_14400:  speed = 14400; break;
      case connect_28800:  speed = 28800; break;
      case no_carrier:  cerr << "no carrier" << endl;
                           abort();
      case error: cerr << "error in connecting, trying again"
                       << endl;
              break;
      case busy:  cerr << "busy, trying again" << endl;
              break;
      default:    cerr << "unrecognized response " << endl;
              break;
      }
    }
    return speed;
  }
```

Not exactly production quality stuff, and, in reality, you would probably want to wrap this code up in a Modem class, but it demonstrates a realistic pattern of usage. Enumerations and switch statements might have been made for each other, and you will recall my saying (in chapter 2) that the use of switch statements is less common in C++ than in 1970s languages, because virtual functions provide a better way of doing some of the things switches were traditionally used for. A similar remark applies to enumerations: a common use of them was to provide a set of tag names to distinguish between different sub-types of a type. For example, ten years ago I would probably have tackled the local tax simulation from chapter 5 by defining an enumeration for all the possible types of building.

```
    enum building_types { town_hall, dwelling, commerce, monastery };
```

I would then have included a tag field of this type in my building structure to show what sort of building was being represented, so I could use a switch on that field to choose the appropriate tax computation. This would have given me a maintenance problem that the solution using virtual functions avoids.

▷ Even rather obvious applications of enumerations, such as defining the set of states of a finite state machine, might be better done using objects of a suitable class, so that operations such as finding the next state or writing an output symbol could be made into member functions. (Come to think of it, modem return codes could usefully be objects belonging to classes derived from a ReturnCode class, with a virtual function to be called in connect.) Enumerations have their uses, though. An interesting example is in simulating a control structure known as Zahn's device, a form of multiple-exit loop which enjoyed a certain vogue in the mid 1970s, without making it into any widely used programming language.

Zahn's device was proposed as a way of neatly and efficiently expressing those troublesome loops you run into occasionally which repeat a certain action until one of a number of different conditions is satisfied. For each possible terminating condition, some particular action must be taken after the last loop iteration. After this action, computation proceeds in the same way, no matter what caused the loop to terminate. Conceptually, the terminating actions are part of the loop, but including them in the loop body can clutter up what should be simple code and may lead to inefficiencies from multiple testing of the same condition. (These inefficiencies might matter inside a frequently executed inner loop.) Zahn proposed a special syntax for this sort of loop where the terminating actions are cleanly separated. We can simulate it neatly in C++ using an enumeration to represent the set of different termination conditions (or *situations* as they are called in this context). While not quite as efficient as what a compiler could do if the Zahn loop was actually part of the language, this is an improvement on using multiple Boolean flags to distinguish between the situations.

The construct can be illustrated by an example. One sometimes encounters software that demands that data be stored in the form of fixed length records. For example, a database system may require that the length of text fields be declared and that any text stored into such a field is padded to the appropriate length with some null character; some data transmission formats require similar fixed length records padded with nulls. Where data is normally stored in text files consisting of lines of different lengths with a terminating newline character, there will be a need to convert from such "variable length" records to fixed length ones. You can carry out this conversion by copying each line into a record. This can be done in a loop that copies one character at a time, counting each character copied, until one of three things happens:

- A newline character is encountered when the number of characters copied is equal to the record length. Good; copying should stop and nothing else needs doing.

- A newline is encountered, but the number of characters copied is less than the record length. Copying should stop, and sufficient padding characters should be added to the record.

- The required number of characters has been written into the record, but no newline has been encountered. Copying should stop, the rest of the line should be discarded, and a warning about a truncated record should be issued.

This isn't difficult to write as a loop with the terminating actions embedded, but it is messy and, since getting the tests right is a little tricky, it's better to keep it clean. Here's how.

First, define an enumeration with four elements, one for each termination condition, and an extra one to represent the fact that none of these situations has yet occurred.

```
enum situations  { copying, exactline, shortline, longline };
```

We'll wrap the whole copying operation up into a function; this can take the streams the input is coming from and the output is going to, the padding character and the record length as arguments, for generality.

```
void copy(ostream& os, istream& is, char padchar, int reclen)
{
```

We need an integer to count the number of characters read, a character variable to hold a current character, and, most significantly, a variable of type situations to record the current state, initially copying.

```
int i = 0;
char c;
situations situation = copying;
```

Now the loop body. All this does is read a character, count it and write it, as long as the situation is in the copying state. It must look at each character and check the count, so that the situation is set appropriately if one of the three conditions just described occurs. The ordering of the tests here is crucial and easy to get wrong.

```
while (situation == copying)
{
  is.get(c);
  if (c == '\n')
    if (i == reclen)
      situation = exactline;
    else
      situation = shortline;
  else
    if (i == reclen)
      situation = longline;
    else
    {
      os << c;   ++i;
    }
}
```

On exit from the loop, we know that one of the situations holds: depending which one, we have to take different actions to tidy up the record, so we switch on situation.

```
switch (situation)  {
case exactline: break;
case shortline:
  while (i < reclen)
  {
    os << padchar;   ++i;
  }
  break;
case longline:
  cerr << "Warning: a long line has been truncated" << endl;
  while (c != '\n') is.get(c);
  break;
}
```

We have now written a record of length `reclen`, so we need only take whatever action is required to terminate a record.

```
    endrecord(os);
}
```

◁

An enumeration may be anonymous—the name following `enum` is omitted— in which case it provides an alternative to a collection of `const int` variables for declaring a set of related symbolic names.

No operations can be applied directly to values of an enumeration. However, if an integer operation is applied to a value of an enumeration type, the value is converted to an integer and the operation is applied to that. The result has one of the integer types and must be explicitly converted back with a cast before it can be assigned to a variable of the enumeration type. There is, however, no way of guaranteeing that the result of the operation corresponds to one of the values of the enumeration, so care should be exercised when doing that sort of thing.

More About Classes

9

If you begin to feel yourself flagging, and your enthusiasm for knowing more about C++ is waning, then you can do without this chapter and get straight on to the advanced stuff in the next part of the book. The features to be described next are more concerned with *finesse* than with necessity. By using them, you will be able to do some things more elegantly, perspicuously or efficiently than you would without them. Unless you are a hopeless oaf, you will find programming with *finesse* more satisfying than programming without it. In the end, it will be easier too, but it may be advisable to come back to this chapter when you feel more comfortable with C++ programming at a ruder level.

FINE POINTS OF INHERITANCE

Inheritance, as I said in chapter 5, is often considered to be the defining feature of object-oriented programming languages. In pure object-oriented programming languages, it is more or less the only means of combining classes. C++ provides other mechanisms, which are often more appropriate, but inheritance is still central. In this section, we shall look at a couple of ways it may be used to achieve something other than the class extension and sub-typing we looked at previously.

Abstract Classes and Interfaces

It is common to find class hierarchies with a class at the base implementing some functions common to all its derived classes. Often, as in the case of the Building class from chapter 5, it makes no sense to create objects of that base class. Abstract classes—classes with at least one pure virtual function—provide a very natural implementation for these classes without objects. There is a different way of using abstract classes that is at least as important. Abstract classes, mixed with a suitable amount of cunning, permit a more thorough

222

separation between the interfaces and implementations of abstract datatypes than occurs when these are mapped onto classes in the obvious way.

The problem with C++ classes is that the class declaration includes implementation details—the private members—as well as an interface specification—the public members. Although the private members are protected from interference, they are still visible; this is done to allow the compiler to allocate the right amount of space for objects; not doing it usually entails using extra pointers. The visibility of private data means that users of the class know how the datatype is implemented—not a great problem in itself, although possibly one with commercial implications in the case of proprietary software. It also means that whenever the representation of a type is changed, every other class that uses it must be recompiled. Every class or program which uses a class that has been recompiled must be recompiled in turn, after which... you know the story. If class declarations are composed in a naïve way, it is quite likely that a minor change to a member function of one class will cause the recompilation of your entire system.

It's quite easy to see, in general terms, how abstract classes can be used to get round this problem. You declare an abstract class consisting entirely of public virtual functions that provide the operations on your abstract datatype. You then declare a second class, derived from this abstract base class, which adds private members for the representation of the type, and provides definitions of the member functions. Programs can be written in terms of (pointers and references to) objects of the abstract base class; these can be manipulated using the functions in the interface specified by its definition. Only functions that create objects need to know about the derived class. Provided the creation of objects can be isolated into a separately compiled function, programs that use them need only include the declaration of the base class, so they won't need to be recompiled if the representation in the derived class is changed.

As an example, consider the time setting abstract datatype from chapter 3; there, two separate implementations were provided, but switching from one to the other meant changing the header files declaring the class `TimeSetting`, and therefore recompiling any program that included it. To avoid this, we begin by making `TimeSetting` into an abstract class.

```
class TimeSetting {
public:
  void set();
  virtual void hrs_up() = 0;
  virtual void hrs_down() = 0;
  virtual void mins_up() = 0;
  virtual void mins_down() = 0;
  virtual void display() const = 0;
  virtual int secs_after_midnight() const = 0;
};
```

This `TimeSetting` class is no use on its own, because the functions are purely virtual, so we can't create any `TimeSetting` objects—that's one reason why there are no constructors. But we can use it as a base for a class that isn't abstract: this one, for example, that stores every time as a number of clock ticks.

```
class TimeSettingTicks: public TimeSetting {
public:
  TimeSettingTicks(int = 0, int = 0);
  void hrs_up();
  void hrs_down();
  void mins_up();
  void mins_down();
  void display() const;
  int secs_after_midnight() const;
private:
  int ticks ;
} ;
```

The definitions of the member functions are just the same as the ones provided in chapter 3, for the version of `TimeSetting` based on this representation of the data, with the obvious constructor. The member function `set` is not virtual—it is the same for any implementation of `TimeSetting` because it is defined in terms of other member functions—so it is not redeclared in `TimeSettingTicks`.

The creation of objects can be isolated into a single function. The return type of this function is `TimeSetting*`, but the actual allocated object is of type `TimeSettingTicks`. Thus, the type checker will be satisfied if the pointer is used as if it pointed to a `TimeSetting` object, while the virtual function mechanism will ensure that the functions defined for the `TimeSettingTicks` class will be invoked through it. The abstract base class has provided an interface, and the class derived from it an implementation.

```
TimeSetting* new_time_setting(int h, int m)
{
  return new TimeSettingTicks(h, m) ;
}
```

This function can be put into its own file, and declared as

```
TimeSetting* new_time_setting(int = 0, int = 0);
```

in the header file for the `TimeSetting` class. Any program that uses `TimeSetting` objects must be written to work with pointers, so the `TimerEvent` class would be changed like this:

```
class TimerEvent {
public:
  TimerEvent();
  ~TimerEvent();
  void set();
  void confirm() const;
private:
  bool valid() const;
  TimeSetting *time_on, *time_off;
};
```

with corresponding changes to its member functions' definitions.

```
TimerEvent::TimerEvent() :time_on(new_time_setting(0, 0)),
                          time_off(new_time_setting(0, 0))
{}

bool TimerEvent::valid() const
{
  const int diff = (time_off->secs_after_midnight()
                     - time_on->secs_after_midnight())/60 ;
  return (0 < diff && diff <= 12*60)
         || (-24*60 < diff && diff <= -12*60) ;
}
```

... and so on. The destructor is now needed to dispose of the pointer members.

If I now decide to switch to the representation of times with separate hours and minutes members, I need not change the declaration of `TimeSetting`, nor any class or program that uses pointers to `TimeSetting` objects. All I have to do is define a new derived class, change the definition of `new_time_setting` to go with it, recompile that and relink. Similarly, if it turns out I need yet another representation, perhaps one based on some manufacturer's proprietary time codes, I need only derive a new class from the abstract `TimeSetting`, without making any further changes to `TimerEvent`.

Things don't always go this smoothly. If a member function takes an object of its own class as an argument, and accesses its data members then some subterfuge is needed to make a scheme such as the one just described work. As is often the case, you need to plan ahead to make these inheritance manoeuvres work.

▷ Using derived classes to implement an abstract datatype whose interface is specified as an abstract base class means manipulating objects through pointers. An alternative scheme for decoupling the interface and implementation relies on putting a pointer to the representation inside the class. In this scheme `TimeSetting` is no longer an abstract class. It contains a single data member, `the_time_setting`, which is a pointer to an object of some type that actually contains the data. I'll call the type of this object `TS_rep`, a contraction of time setting representation. Because `the_time_setting` is only a pointer, it is not necessary for a complete definition of the `TS_Rep` class to be in scope where `TimeSetting` is declared; only the name is required. `TimeSetting` has the same member functions as ever. This time, all they do is call the corresponding `TS_rep` member through the pointer `the_time_setting`. A good optimizer will make these calls disappear.

```
class TS_Rep;

class TimeSetting {
public:
  TimeSetting(int = 0, int = 0);
  ~TimeSetting();
  void set();
  void hrs_up();
  void hrs_down();
  void mins_up();
```

```
    void mins_down();
    void display() const;
    int secs_after_midnight() const;
private:
    TS_Rep *the_time_setting ;
} ;
```

The member definitions look like this:

```
void TimeSetting::hrs_up()
{
    the_time_setting->hrs_up();
}

void TimeSetting::hrs_down()
{
    the_time_setting->hrs_down();
}
```

…and so on.

What is TS_Rep? For maximum flexibility, you can use as TS_Rep the abstract class that, until now, we have been considering as TimeSetting itself, with a suitable implementation class derived from it. An easier choice is to use the implementation class directly as the TS_Rep, so, for example, it could be defined exactly as TimeSettingTicks was.

The definition of TimeSetting's constructor is all that needs changing when the representation is changed, because it actually has to allocate an object to represent the time. Its declaration is unaltered. If we had chosen to make TS_Rep abstract, and use TimeSettingTicks as its implementation, the definition of the constructor would be as follows:

```
TimeSetting::TimeSetting(int h, int m)
{
    the_time_setting = new TimeSettingTicks(h, m);
}
```

This method actually makes it possible to support multiple implementations of a type in the same program. I leave the details to intrepid readers.

There is some jargon which is thrown around near these techniques. An abstract class which defines an interface of pure virtual functions is called a *protocol class*; classes which contain a pointer to a representation are often called *handles*, their member functions which just call member functions of the representation are called *forwarding functions*. The trick of only declaring the name of a representation class is called the *Cheshire Cat*, although the name is sometimes applied to the class, sometimes to the handle, and sometimes to the whole technique.

◁

Private Inheritance

Most of the time, dividing a class's members into private and public, and using a style of inheritance where public members of the base class become public members of the derived class, is what you want to do. The derived class extends the base class because an object of the derived class is a kind of object of the base class. However, other arrangements are possible, and sometimes appropriate.

The presence of the apparently superfluous keyword `public` in the declaration of a derived class might make you suspect that the keyword `private` could be put in its place. Indeed it can, and, if you have an eye for a pattern, you can probably guess what it means: the public members of the base class become private members of the derived class. (*Not* the private members of the base class become private members of the derived class—that would still be a fatal blow to the access controls.) We distinguish between the two kinds of inheritance by referring to public inheritance and private inheritance, and to public and private base classes. It's not so easy to guess that, with private inheritance, a pointer or reference to an object of a derived class can only be used in place of a pointer or reference to an object of its base class inside member functions of the derived class, but this is what is meant by a private base class: the fact that it is a base class is private, and can only be used by the same functions that can use private members.

Although the only difference between private and public inheritance lies in which functions can access members inherited from the base class, an apparently minor difference, it greatly affects the way in which inheritance is used; it almost creates a new feature. Suppose we have

```
class Person {
public:
  void speak();
private:
  float cash;
  void count_cash();
};

class Waiter: private Person {
public:
  void serve();
private:
  float tips;
  void count_tips();
};
```

The effect is summarized in Table 9.1. Is a `Waiter` still a kind of `Person`? One of the things a `Person` can do is speak. The `speak` member function is public, so a person can speak to anybody. In the `Waiter` class, `speak` is private, so a waiter can only speak to himself or other waiters. Not everything that is true of a person is now true of a waiter—a waiter won't give you the time of day—so a waiter is not a kind of person if private inheritance is used.

	members	public	member function...	...can access
Person	speak()	speak()	speak()	speak()
	cash			cash
	count_cash()			count_cash()
Waiter	speak()		serve()	speak()
	cash	serve()		serve()
	count_cash()			tips
	serve()			count_tips()
	tips			
	count_tips			

Table 9.1   Private inheritance

Surely, nobody would think that private inheritance is an accurate model of the relationship between waiters and other people. What, then, is private inheritance for? Its commonest use is when a base class object is used to implement the abstract datatype specified by a derived class, but even for this purpose private inheritance is only sometimes the most appropriate use. An example will illustrate this. No computing book is complete without its stack example; this is mine.

To make things concrete, suppose you needed a stack of floating point numbers, possibly as part of an expression evaluator. A good way to implement a stack is as a one-way linked list, especially if you have an implementation of a linked list of floating point numbers left over from a previous project. It might be declared with public member functions like this:

```
class FloatList   {
public:
  FloatList();
  ~FloatList();
  void insert(float, int);
  void hdinsert(float);
  void remove(int);
  void hdremove();
  float head() const;
  float nth(int) const;
  int length() const;
    private members
};
```

The writer of this class has included member functions for the efficient special cases of insertion, removal and inspection at the head, as well as general operations to insert, remove or retrieve the nth element, and compute the length. This is convenient. The simplest way to use a FloatList to make a stack is to define a `FloatStack` class with a private `FloatList` member; the stack operations are little more than forwarding functions that use the relevant list operations, ignoring the rest.

```
class FloatStack  {
public:
  FloatStack();
  ~FloatStack();
  void push(float x);
  void pop();
  float top() const;
  bool empty() const;
private:
  FloatList rep;
};

void FloatStack::FloatStack()
{}
void FloatStack::push(float x)
{
  rep.hdinsert(x);
}
void FloatStack::pop()
{
  rep.hdremove();
}
float FloatStack::top() const
{
  return rep.head();
}
bool FloatStack::empty() const
{
  return rep.length()==0;
}
```

But what if something goes wrong? In particular, what about stack underflow—trying to look at the top of or pop an empty stack? With `top` and `pop` implemented simply as forwarding functions, if underflow occurs, you will get an error message (assuming the writer of `FloatList` wasn't totally out to lunch) about some sort of operation on an empty list, which might seem odd to someone thinking exclusively about stacks. (It would seem even odder to an end user, but, since underflow always results from an error in program logic, end users will never see such messages, will they?) You can get round this, by doing the check in the stack member functions.

```
float FloatStack::top() const
{
  if (rep->empty())
  {
    cerr << "stack underflow";
    return 0.0;
```

```
    }
    else return rep->head();
}
```

but this is a bit silly, because `rep->head()` will start out doing the same check, and more efficiently at that.

Consider, then, a less obvious implementation strategy: use private inheritance to derive `FloatStack` from `FloatList`.

```
class FloatStack : private FloatList {
public:
    void push(float x);
    void pop();
    float top() const;
    bool empty() const;
};
```

There are no private members—the data is in the `FloatList` part of a `FloatStack` object—the automatically generated default constructor does the right thing and the forwarding functions are even simpler:

```
void FloatStack::push(float x)
{
    hdinsert(x);
}
void FloatStack::pop()
{
    hdremove();
}
float FloatStack::top() const
{
    return head();
}
bool FloatStack::empty() const
{
    return length()==0;
}
```

Because the inheritance is private, the unstacklike operations on the list are hidden, and the `FloatStack` still presents a purely stacky interface. And it still has the same problem with underflow producing an error message that comes from the wrong place.

But suppose whoever wrote `FloatList` had thought it might one day be used as a base class and had provided a virtual function to be called for errors:

```
virtual void empty_error() const;
```

The function `empty_error` would be defined in `FloatList` to produce meaningful messages about lists. Any class, such as `FloatStack`, derived from `FloatList` can override this definition with one that does something meaningful in the context of the derived class, such as:

```
void FloatStack::empty_error() const
{
  cerr << "stack underflow";
  abort();
}
```

This is what private inheritance is for. If *A* is to be implemented as a *B*, and if class *B* has virtual functions that *A* can usefully override, make *A* a private base class of *B*. This is only likely to happen in an environment where people who write classes think in advance about the possibility of their being used as base classes.

This example can also be used to illustrate why you can't use a pointer to a derived class where a pointer to a private base class is required. The following is a perfectly reasonable definition of a function to add up all the elements of a FloatList.

```
float sum(FloatList *a_list)
{
  float tot = 0.0;
  for (int i = 0; i < a_list->length(); ++i)
    tot += a_list->nth(i);
  return tot;
}
```

If it was permissible to use a pointer to a derived class in the place of a pointer to its private base class, then it would be all right to call sum with a pointer to a FloatStack as its actual argument. But this would be nonsense—a Float-Stack object hasn't got an accessible length or nth member. Static binding has got us again, but this time virtual functions don't offer any way out. The conversion must be banned.

▷ If you don't like forwarding functions, you can grant public access to a base member that is privately inherited by including its fully qualified name (just the name, not a complete declaration) among the private members of the base class. So, if you weren't particular about giving things their conventional names, FloatStack could be declared like this:

```
class FloatStack:private FloatList {
public:
  FloatList::hdremove;
  FloatList::hdinsert;
  FloatList::head;
  bool empty() const;
```

and you could push items onto a FloatStack called a_stack with the statement
◁ a_stack.hdinsert(3.14159), and so on.

You can omit the keyword public or private when you declare a derived class, but the default is private, which is less helpful than it could have been. Since it could confuse someone reading your program, it's always better to explicitly specify the kind of inheritance.

Protected Members

I can now tell the truth about the different kinds of class members. In chapter 3, I described public and private members, but admitted there was a third kind. The third kind are *protected* members. Public members are accessible anywhere the class is in scope; private members are only accessible inside member functions of the class they belong to; protected members are accessible inside member functions of the class they belong to *and* any class derived from it. If the inheritance is public, they are protected in the derived class, too; if it is private, they are private in the derived class, so access to them cannot be inherited any further.

Protected members are identified by the keyword `protected`, which is used like `public` and `private`. Since the amount of protection offered to protected members is in between that of public and private ones, I like to put the protected members in between the other two, though this is just a convention. They can appear in any order.

Protected members sound like a good idea, since derived classes quite often need to access base members that you don't want to make public, but they should be used with caution. The truth is, protected members are not really protected at all; all you have to do to access some protected member of a class is derive a class from it, which you can always do.

It's tempting to consider this obsession with protecting data from interference as unduly proprietorial, or perhaps deeply Freudian, but consider this: if you want to know which functions may have changed the value of a private data member, unless you've done something really stupid, like pass a pointer to a private member out as the result of a public member function, all you have to look at is the class declaration. That lists all the functions which have access to the private members. With protected members, you need to look at the declarations of all derived classes, too. And with public members, you need to look everywhere in the program where the class is in scope. So keeping as much private as possible simply makes it easier to reason about your programs. And to debug them, if it should ever come to that.

If you do decide that derived classes need special access to base members, see whether a protected member function will do the job before making any data member protected. A typical example of the use of protected member functions is provided by the `NetResource` class of chapter 6. I declared inspection functions `machine` and `path` to allow the `connect` function of derived classes to find out the values of the corresponding data members. By making these public, as I did originally, I made the information available to everybody. It would have been better to declare them protected:

```
class NetResource  {
public:
  NetResource(const char*);
  virtual void connect() = 0;
protected:
  const char* machine() const;
  const char* path() const;
private:
```

```
    char* the_machine;
    char* the_path;
};
```

▷ Seeing as there are public, private and protected members, and public and private
  inheritance, you would probably expect to find protected inheritance, too. There
  is such a thing, but there is a very strange problem with it. Here are some C++
  experts on the subject: "No one seems to know what protected inheritance ... is
  supposed to mean."[1] "I have never heard of [it] being used on a real project."[2] And,
  in earlier days, Stroustrup wrote that the concept of protected base classes was
  among several not introduced into C++ because they "caused total confusion among
  users". Protected inheritance is not in the ARM, but, presumably after a hard day's
  standardizing, the standard committee agreed that "A base class may be protected.
  Access to a protected base is the same as to a protected member." And that, really,
◁ is all there is to say.

DECLARATIONS IN CLASSES

As well as all the other right-on things it does for you, a class establishes a
scope—a region of program text within which names defined in the class can
be used without qualification. A class scope comprises the text of the class
definition together with the bodies of all member function definitions. Outside
this scope, the names of class members can only be used either in conjunction
with an object of that class (that is to say, an expression denoting such an object
or a pointer to one) as an operand of one of the member selection operators,
or in fully qualified form, prefixed with the class name and a pair of colons.
These scope rules are orthogonal to the access restrictions imposed by the
`public`, `protected` and `private` keywords: a name can be in scope but still
inaccessible because it is private, for example.

A class definition can introduce other names besides those of the class itself,
its data members and member functions: enumerated types, type synonyms
and classes can be declared locally, and so can "members" that behave as variables global to the class. The use of any of these names will be restricted to the
class's scope. The main virtue of declarations inside classes is that they enable
you to keep your program tidy, by incorporating into the class definition all the
names that logically belong to the class. As well as preventing possible name
clashes with names declared elsewhere in your program, the use of declarations within classes allows you to control access to these names, with `public`,
`protected` and `private`.

---

[1] Scott Meyers, *Effective C++* , see page 346
[2] Robert B. Murray, *C++ Strategies and Tactics*, see page 347

Enumerated Types

One of the first things they taught me about programming was to use symbolic names for constants, and not to sprinkle magic numbers throughout the code. I don't suppose anyone would argue with that. It is the reason behind my use of constants like `prefix_len` in the examples in Chapter 6, such as

```
if (strncmp(u_string, "http://", prefix_len) != 0)
```

and so on. Good, but still not as good as I would like, because the constants are defined at the file level. Conceptually (if you'll pardon the expression), they belong to the various network resource classes. However, you are not allowed to initialize constant members in a class definition, only in a member initialization list in a constructor. Anyway, if I added constant members to the classes, every object would have to carry them around. Some other expedient is needed to define constants that are specific to a class. Enumerated types can be hijacked for this purpose.

An anonymous enumerated type declaration that supplies values for the elements of the enumeration is one way of giving names to constants—even if the enumeration only consists of a single element:

```
enum { prefix_len = 7 };
```

The type of this name is the anonymous enumerated type being declared, but since enumerators are automatically converted into integers when necessary, it can be used as if it was an integer constant. Declarations of enumerated types are among the things that can appear in a class definition, so they can be incorporated in the relevant class, for example:

```
class WebPage  {
public:
  WebPage();
  WebPage(const char*);
  WebPage(const WebPage&);
  ~WebPage();
  WebPage& operator=(const WebPage&) ;
  operator const char*() const;
private:
  enum { prefix_len = 7 };
  void error(char*, char*);
  char* the_machine;
  char* the_path;
};
```

The enumerators' names are in scope in the class, so they can be used as required in the constructors. Outside the class scope, they would have to be qualified with the class name, as `WebPage::prefix_len` and so on. Whether the use of such qualified names is allowed depends on whether the `enum` declaration appears among the private, protected or public members. Here, since the declaration appears after the keyword `private`, the name `prefix_len` can only be used within the bodies of member functions.

You can also define named enumerated types within a class, allowing variables of that type to be declared inside the class scope. It might, for example, be appropriate to define the type `ReturnCodes` from page 217 within the definition of a `Modem` class, if the return codes were only to be used inside member functions such as `connect`.

```
class Modem {
public:
  int connect(int max_retries);
  other public members
private:
  enum ReturnCodes  {
    no_carrier = 3, error = 4, connect_1200 = 5,
    busy = 7, connect_2400 = 10, connect_9600 = 13,
    connect_4800 = 18, connect_7200 = 20, connect_12000 = 21,
    connect_14400 = 25, connect_28800 = 107
  };
  ReturnCodes get_rc();
  other private members
};
```

The hack, for that is what it is, of using enumerated types to declare constants local to a class only works for integer constants, but this is the most common type you will encounter.

The technique of defining local enumerated types is used to good effect within the iostreams library. As well as holding a stream buffer, as explained in chapter 8, an `ios` object (or rather the `ios` part of any object belonging to a class derived from `ios`) records information about the state of a stream (whether it is good, bad, failed or at the end of file following the previous operation on it), the open mode and the current format; the `ios` class provides low-level functions for interrogating and setting this information. Normally, you would use manipulators that affect the state variables indirectly, but sometimes it is more efficient or convenient to access them directly.

In a manner reminiscent of bygone days, the state information is encoded by setting and clearing individual bits in a status word. Enumerated types are used to provide a named flag corresponding to each bit that can be set. The actual values are implementation-dependent (as indeed, strictly speaking, is the use of enumerated types instead of any other device). This is a typical definition:

```
enum _Fmtflags {skipws = 0x0001, unitbuf = 0x0002,
  uppercase = 0x0004, showbase = 0x0008,
  showpoint = 0x0010, showpos = 0x0020,
  left = 0x0040, right = 0x0080, internal = 0x0100,
  dec = 0x0200, oct = 0x0400, hex = 0x0800,
  scientific = 0x1000, fixed = 0x2000,
  adjustfield = 0x01c0, basefield = 0x0e00,
  floatfield = 0x3000, _Fmtmask = 0x3fff, _Fmtzero = 0};
enum _Iostate {goodbit = 0x0, eofbit = 0x1,
  failbit = 0x2, badbit = 0x4, _Statmask = 0x7};
```

```
enum _Openmode {in = 0x01, out = 0x02, ate = 0x04,
   app = 0x08, trunc = 0x10, binary = 0x20};
enum seekdir {beg = 0, cur = 1, end = 2};
```

Note the use of type names beginning with an underline: the definition is taken verbatim from the library header, and such names are reserved for internal use by the library.

These `enum` declarations are local to the `ios` class, but public. The flag names can be used outside the class scope but only by qualifying them with the class name. You should now be able to see that was going on on page 212 when I opened a stream for both reading and writing.

```
ifstream istr(filename, ios::in|ios::out);
  etc.
```

The constructor is taking a second argument formed by the logical OR of the flags `ios::in` and `ios::out`, signifying the open modes for the associated stream buffer.

A function `setiosflags`, which can be used as a manipulator, is provided for setting flags. In fact, most of the manipulators in Table 8.1 are implemented by setting appropriate flags; `hex` is equivalent to `setiosflags(ios::hex)`, for example. Typical explicit usage of `setiosflags` involves defining a constant as the bitwise OR of a collection of flags, then using the manipulator to set all of them at once.

```
const int hex_options = ios::right|ios::hex|ios::showbase;
cout << setiosflags(hex_options) << n;
```

The value of `n` will be printed in hexadecimal, preceded by `0x` indicating the fact, padded on the left to whatever field width has been specified.

Setting flags this way can be more convenient than chaining together individual manipulators, because a variable such as `hex_options` can be passed to a function to specify a format, where passing a set of arguments to choose a set of manipulators for each call would be intolerably clumsy.

Static Members

An object is a region of store; within each object there is a field corresponding to each data member of the class to which the object belongs. Looking at this from the other end, whenever you declare a data member in a class definition there will be a field corresponding to that member in every object belonging to the class. Unless, that is, the member is declared static. A static member, designated by prefixing its declaration with the keyword (guess) `static`, is a bit like a static variable, in that it has only one fixed storage location allocated to it. Put another way, there is only one copy of a static member and it is shared between all objects of a class.

Unlike a static variable, a static member is a member of some class; it is in scope in the class scope and must be qualified with the class name outside that region of program text. Additionally, a static member is subject to access restrictions: just like any other member, it may be private, protected or public.

Knowing that much about static members, you can see that they are appropriate for storing information that logically belongs to a class as a whole, not to individual objects, but not to the entire program either. If you prefer to be pragmatic, you could say that static members reduce the need for global variables (widely, if not universally, deemed a bad thing) and the possibility of name clashes between globals declared in different files.

For a slightly contrived example of data that is specific to one class, we can return to the FTP class on page 140. Given the amount of excellent Internet software available, the only reason I might have written this class would be to support some aspect of my own peculiar interactions with the Internet. That is, it would most likely be part of a custom-built package. Under those circumstances, I could choose to provide default arguments to the FTP constructor, corresponding to the anonymous ftp convention: the name would be anonymous and the password my email address. I could use a symbolic name for the latter, since it might change, but only rarely. Rather than using a global variable initialized with the appropriate value, I should add a declaration of a static member to the FTP class:

```
class FTP: public NetResource {
public:
  static const char* my_email_address;
FTP(const char*, const char* = "anonymous",
    const char* = my_email_address);
  other members as before
};
```

I am only allowed to *declare* the member inside the class definition, not define and initialize it. That must be done at the file level and such initializations are usually put with the definitions of member functions. Like member functions, a static member must be fully qualified in its definition.

Not the author's real email address

```
const char* FTP::my_email_address = "president@whitehouse.gov";
```

▷ The previous paragraph contains a fib—besides the one about my email address. You can initialize a static member when you declare it, but only if it is an integer or enumerated type, and only if your compiler vendor keeps up with the C++ standard.
◁

How do you refer to a static member? Within the class scope, just like any other member: by its unqualified name. Outside the class scope, if the static member is protected or private, you cannot refer to it. If it is public, you have a choice (this is C++, after all). You can either refer to it through some object of its class or a pointer to one, using the . or -> operators, or you can access it without reference to any object by using its qualified name. Since my_email_address is public, if f was an object of type FTP and fp was a pointer to such an object (any such object, not necessarily f) then all the following produce the same output.

```
cout << f.my_email_address;
cout << fp->my_email_address;
cout << FTP::my_email_address;
```

:-)

▷ The ARM says that if you use the e.f form to access a static member, then the expression e is never evaluated. The draft standard says it is always evaluated. So, in the world, I guess the truth is that it is sometimes evaluated. If you don't rely on ◁ side-effects, you won't care much.

Besides holding constant values which are specific to a class, as in this example, static members are most often used to keep track, in some sense, of some subset of all the objects of a class, usually by either counting them or chaining them together in a linked list, or both. Static members can be used to hold the count or point to the head of the list.

The network resource classes provide an example that is not too far fetched. It might be useful to keep track of all the resources that are currently connected. This can be done by maintaining a list of connected resources and modifying the connect functions so that objects add themselves to the list when they are connected. We might as well keep a count of connected resources, so declare two static members of the class NetResource.

```
static int open_count;
static NetResource* open_list;
```

We also need to add a link field to all these objects so a new data member is declared in NetResource—privately, of course—which also acquires a protected member function to add an object to the list.

```
protected:
  void add_to_list(NetResource*);
private:
  NetResource *next_rsrc;
```

Definitions of all these new members must be provided.

```
int NetResource::open_count = 0;
NetResource *NetResource::open_list = NULL;

void NetResource::add_to_list(NetResource *nbp)
{
  nbp->next_rsrc = open_list;
  open_list = nbp;
  ++open_count;
}
```

Constructors and the assignment operator must set next_rsrc to NULL, and the connect functions for classes derived from NetResource must call add_to_list(this) when a connect operation is performed. I leave the messy business of closing connections and deleting objects from the open list to you.

Member functions can be static, as well as data members. At first, this seems to be a redundant feature—after all, there is only one copy of each member function per class. A static member function has the advantage that it can be called without using an object and a member selection operator. Its advantages over global functions are the same as those of static data members over global variables: a static member function is defined in the class scope, is subject to access restrictions and has access to private data members. Note, though, that a static member function does not have an implicit declaration of a `this` pointer. (What would it point to?).

A function to print some details of all connected resource objects would be suitably declared as a static member of `NetResource`.

```
static void print_connected_resources(ostream&);
```

It could be defined like this (finessing about a bit with the count):

```
void NetResource::print_connected_resources(ostream& os)
{
  switch(open_count) {
  case 0:
    os << "There are no open resources" << endl;
    break;
  case 1:
    os << "There is one open resource" << endl;
    break;
  default:
    os << "There are " << open_count << " open resources" << endl;
    break;
  }
  NetResource *p = open_list;
  while (p)
  {
    os << p->the_path << " on " << p->the_machine << endl;
    p = p->next_rsrc;
  }
}
```

▷ The extent of the usefulness of static member functions to you depends on how up-to-date your compiler is. A class consisting of nothing but public static member functions is a good way of wrapping up a function library as a single entity. For example, you might have written a replacement for the standard C library's set of functions operating on C-strings. You could define a class `MyStringLib` as follows:

```
class MyStringLib {
public:
  static int strlen(const char*);
  static int strcmp(const char*, const char*);
  etc
}
```

Your functions can be referred to as `MyStringLib::strlen` and so on. Using this mechanism, programmers can develop and use separate libraries without worrying too much about the possibility of unrelated functions being declared with the same *Unless* name. A new feature, namespaces, described briefly at the end of the book, has *they all* recently been added to C++ and supersedes this trick with a facility specifically de- *call them* signed for the purpose. Namespaces are part of the draft standard, but, at the time *MyLib* of writing, have not been universally implemented in all C++ compilers, so there is ◁ life in classes of static member functions yet.

Nested Class Definitions

When one class exists only to serve the needs of another, you have the precondition for a revolutionary class struggle...No, that can't be right, we don't do that stuff any more. Start again.

If you define a class `inner` which is used in such a way that every object belonging to `inner` is a member of some other class `outer`, then it makes a lot of sense to define `inner` locally within `outer`, and you are allowed to do so.

There are two layers of access restriction involved in a local class definition. Suppose that `inner` is local to `outer`. The class `inner` itself can be public, protected or private. If it is private, `inner` objects can only be created within the scope of `outer`, because the name `inner` can only be used there to refer to this class; if `inner` is protected, they can be created within `outer` and classes derived from it; if public, then `inner` objects can be freely created, but because `inner` is local to `outer`, the type of objects defined outside the scope of `outer` is `outer::inner`, not just plain `inner`. As well as these considerations there is the question of where it is possible to access the members of `inner`. These may also be private, protected or public—within the definition of `inner` this time— and the access rules apply in the usual way. In particular, if a member of `inner` is private, it can only be used within the scope of `inner`, nowhere else, not even in the member functions of the enclosing class `outer`. Furthermore, `inner` has no special access to the members of `outer`. Putting it another way, although the name `inner` is defined with the scope of `outer`, the member functions of
Got that?   `inner` are not part of the scope of `outer`.

Commonly, the local class *is* there to serve the needs of the enclosing class, and the latter needs access to its members. In such a case, the local class can, as it were, hide behind the protection of the enclosing class. If the local class is private to its enclosing class, and the members of the local class are all public, then the member functions of the enclosing class can use the members of the local one, but no other function can. This is probably the only circumstance under which public data members are sensible—for the locally defined class, that is, of course.

▷ The keyword `struct` is a synonym for `class` except that all members of a class declared with `struct` are public unless specifically declared otherwise. Some programmers prefer to declare their local classes with `struct` when they want all the members public.

All members of a class declared with `class` are private unless specifically declared otherwise. In this book I always declare my classes using `class` and specify
◁ all access constraints and privileges explicitly, a practice I commend to you.

Enough of `inner` and `outer`! The ability to nest class definitions can be exploited to implement a popular version of a linked list in a way that demonstrates how local definitions can make your programs neater and add a bit of that *finesse* I mentioned earlier.

A one-way linked list can be built out of a collection of nodes, each comprising a stored value and a pointer to the next node in the list. The entire list is just a pointer to the first node. Lists and list nodes are different sorts of things—consider the operations—but list nodes are only ever used within lists, therefore the list node class should be local to the list class; by making its definition private, list nodes become inaccessible outwith the list class.

A linked list is certainly an abstract datatype, although there is no consensus on exactly which operations it should supply. A popular set, treating the list as a dynamic sequence, is: count the number of elements, insert an object after the nth element of the list, remove the nth element, return the value stored in the nth element—all of these assume that the nth element exists. Here is a definition of a List class that provides these operations and defines a class Node locally to build lists of strings out of. (Lists are too big and full of pointers to copy safely, so I have made the copy constructor and assignment operator private—see page 156.)

```
class List   {
public:
  List(): the_head(NULL) {}
  ~List();
  void insert(const string&, int);
  void remove(int);
  string nth(int) const;
  int length() const;
private:
  List(const List&);
  List& operator=(const List&);
  class Node   {
  public:
    Node(const string& a_val, Node* whats_next):
      the_val(a_val), next(whats_next) {}
    string the_val;
    Node *next;
  };
  Node *the_head;
};
```

Anyone who hasn't should do so now

Anyone who has read their data structures books or been to their data structures lectures will know how to implement the list operations. Although it adds little to the present discussion, here are my versions, to demonstrate how what is hopefully a familiar set of operations are implemented in C++, and to show a possible pitfall.

The automatically generated destructor for Node will delete the string the node contains as it is destroyed, which is all it needs to do. The destructor for List itself has to explicitly chain down the list deleting each node.

```
List::~List()
{
  Node *n = the_head;
  while (n)
  {
    Node *nn = n;
    n = n->next;
```

```
        delete nn;
    }
}
```

▷ Beware of being too slick. I came close to doing this:

```
List::Node::~Node()
{
   delete next;
}
```

!

```
List::~List()
{
   delete the_head;
}
```

See? The Node destructor works by deleting next; this has the effect of calling the destructor for the Node object that this->next points to, which in turn will delete its next pointer, so the deletions ripple down to the end of the list. Deleting the null pointer found there has no effect, so the destructor recursion unwinds, returning the space occupied by each Node to the free store. The destructor for List itself thus only has to delete the head pointer.

Very smart... the trouble is, if I remove an element from a list, but don't set its
◁ next pointer to null before deleting it, it will take the remainder of the list with it.

Now for the familiar operations, all based on chaining down the list to get to the right place, pausing only to make a special case of operations at the head and to make sure that we don't fall off the end of the list. Counting the elements is the easiest.

```
int List::length() const
{
   int n = 0;
   Node *p = the_head;
   while (p)
   {
      ++n;
      p = p->next;
   }
   return n;
}
```

Nothing hard there, except remembering to update p inside the loop—who hasn't forgotten to do so at least once in their career?[3]

Next easiest is the member to get the value of the nth element. Here we have to make sure it is there (but *not* by counting first).

---

[3]So use a for-loop, say the C experts. Please yourself.

```
string List::nth(int n) const
{
  int i = 1;
  Node *p = the_head;
  while (p && i < n)
  {
    ++i;
    p = p->next;
  }
  if (p == NULL)
  {
    cerr << "Error: "
         << "Attempt to retrieve non-existent list element"
         << endl;
    abort();
  }
  return p->the_val;
}
```

There are those who would have given this member a different name:

```
string List::operator[](int n)
```

Insertion is another operation that chains down to the right point, but here it is necessary to make a special case of insertion at the beginning of the list, after element zero, because there you have to update the head pointer of the list, not the next pointer of a node.

```
void List::insert(const string& x, int n)
{
  assert (n >= 0);
  if (n == 0)
    the_head = new Node(x, the_head);
  else
  {
    if (the_head == NULL)
    {
      cerr << "Error: Attempt to insert an element "
           << "beyond the end of a list" << endl;
      abort();
    }
    else
    {
      Node *p = the_head;
      int i = 1;
      while (i < n)
      {
        ++i;
        p = p->next;
        if (p == NULL)
        {
```

```
            cerr << "Error: Attempt to insert an element "
                 << "beyond the end of a list" << endl;
            abort();
        }
    }
    p->next = new Node(x, p->next);
    }
  }
}
```

Notice how much error checking code there is: first the assertion to make sure nobody tries to look for an element at a negative position, and then the checking to make sure we don't drop off the end of the list. Failure to perform these tests could be catastrophic. Removing the nth element needs even more care.

```
void List::remove(int n)
{
  assert (n > 0);
  if (the_head)
  {
    if (n == 1)
    {
      Node *temp = the_head;
      the_head = the_head->next;
      delete temp;
    }
    else
    {
      Node *p = the_head;
      int i = 1;
      while (i < n-1)
      {
        ++i;
        p = p->next;
        if (p == NULL)
        {
          cerr << "Error: "
               << "Attempt to delete a non-existent list element"
               << endl;
          abort();
        }
      }
      Node *temp = p->next;
      if (temp == NULL)
      {
        cerr << "Error: "
             << "Attempt to delete a non-existent list element"
             << endl;
        abort();
```

```
        }
        p->next = temp->next;
        delete temp;
      }
    }
    else
    {
      cerr << "Error: "
           << "Attempt to remove an element from the empty list"
           << endl;
      abort();
    }
}
```

All good computer science, but we were considering nested classes. You don't have to put the definition of a local class inside that of its enclosing class, you can just declare its name and put the class definition at file level elsewhere. That way, the details are not visible from the header for the enclosing class, and compilation dependencies are cut down. So, for example, in the definition of List, you could have just had:

```
private:
  class Node;
```

Elsewhere, probably in another header file, could have been the class declaration. The only messy bit is that, naturally, outside the scope of List, the name of the local class is List::Node.

```
class List::Node  {
public:
  Node(const string& a_val, List::Node* whats_next):
    the_val(a_val), next(whats_next) {}
  string the_val;
  List::Node *next;
};
```

Type Synonyms

Local type synonyms barely deserve a section to themselves. One of the things you can include within a class definition is a typedef. The type synonym it declares is local to the class, meaning that it is in scope within the class scope and must be qualified outside, and that it is subject to access restrictions, like class members and locally defined classes and enumerated types. You make a type synonym local for the same reasons as you make an enumerated class or type local: because it logically or conceptually belongs with the class and so you want to restrict the use of the name. What more do you want me to say?

FRIENDS

So far as we have yet seen, C++ functions come in two varieties: member functions, belonging to some class, and global functions. These two classes of function are invoked using different syntax and, more significantly, their ability to access members of objects differs: member functions can access private members of their class and protected members of its base class, global functions cannot. The distinction is simple, easy to understand, clean, and not always adequate.

Sometimes it is necessary, or at least more efficient or convenient, to allow global functions or member functions of another class to have access to private members. Friend functions, as they are suggestively known, are the means used in C++ to access private members from outside a class, as it were. Your first reaction to this news may be along the lines of "What is the good of all this data hiding if friends can just come along and get at private members?" It's all right—the declaration of a class's friends are part of the class definition. The class (that is, the designer of the class) decides who its friends are.

Warning: The author is riding a hobby horse. ▷ The trouble, if there is one, lies with the object metaphor and the way the first argument of a member function is distinguished as "the receiver of the message". Strong typing doesn't require this; algebraic data type theory doesn't require it; effective information hiding doesn't require it. Implementors find it easier—especially if there are virtual functions afoot—but the main requirement for it is the programming and design method based on the anthropomorphic metaphor of objects sending each other messages. Taken to the extreme, this method limits the structures available to the programmer. Friend functions provide an extra degree of flexibility, equivalent to letting a function be a member of more than one class, and a message have more than one receiver. It is probably worth emphasizing again that this flexibility is achieved without violating strong typing or encapsulation. ◁

Friend Functions

A global function may use the names of the private members of a class (for that is what granting access entails) if a declaration of that function preceded by the keyword `friend` is included in the class definition. The keyword `friend` is not an access specifier like `public`; there is no colon after it, and it must precede the declaration of every friend. The friend function is not a member; it does not have an implicit declaration of a pointer called `this`. Presumably, it will have at least one argument that is an object of the class in question, or a pointer or reference to one. (Accessing the private members of a global object through a friend function whiffs of the unacceptable face of anarchy.) It is the private members of such arguments that can be accessed within the body of the friend function,[4] using the usual member selection notation. None of this tells you why you might need friend functions. METAFONT provides an example of one situation where friends come in useful.

---

[4]The terminology may give rise to sniggers, but at least it makes a change from the violent metaphorical language you usually find in computing. (Kill! Zap! Abort!)

You will recall that the class MFVec, which has appeared in several examples, is supposed to implement the two-dimensional vectors used in the METAFONT language to represent points and displacements. When you are specifying the shape of a character in a font you are designing with METAFONT, it is often useful to transform a vector, by scaling, shifting or rotating it. The METAFONT language defines these individual transformations in terms of a *portmanteau* transform, which takes a vector and an object called a transformation, consisting of six values, and combines them as follows. If $z = (x, y)$ is a vector and the sextuple $t = (t_x, t_y, t_{xx}, t_{xy}, t_{yx}, t_{yy})$ is a transformation, then z transformed by t is the vector $(t_x + xt_{xx} + yt_{xy}, t_y + xt_{yx} + yt_{yy})$. Now, for example, if you want to scale up both the x and y components of z by a factor f, you can transform it by the transformation $(0, 0, f, 0, 0, f)$; if you want to shift it by (a, b), transform it by $(a, b, 1, 0, 0, 1)$; to rotate it through an angle θ (a bit tricky), transform by $(0, 0, \cos\theta, -\sin\theta, \sin\theta, \cos\theta)$; to do nothing to it (always handy) use the unit transformation $(0, 0, 1, 0, 0, 1)$. You should be able to see how a single transformation can represent any combination of shifting, scaling and rotation.

This is so nifty that anyone who has implemented an MFVec class will want to have an MFTransformation class and a transform operation to go with it. Defining the data members and constructor for MFTransformation is trivial—the default assignment and copy constructor even do the right thing—but what about the transform operation? If it is a member of MFTransformation we must supply member functions that return the values of the data members of an MFVec, for which there is otherwise no need. In the same way, if transform is a member of MFVec, functions to provide the values of all the individual members of an MFTransformation are needed. You can do it that way if you like, but by making transform a global function that is a friend of both classes you allow it to access the values needed to compute the transformed vector, but keep those values hidden from any other functions. By keeping tight control over the accessibility of information in this way, you make it easier to reason about your program's behaviour.

The definition of MFTransformation can look like this:

```
class MFTransformation {
public:
    MFTransformation(float x, float y, float xx,
                     float xy, float yx, float yy):
                     tx(x), ty(y), txx(xx),
                     txy(xy), tyx(yx), tyy(yy)
                     {}
friend
    inline MFVec transform(const MFVec& z,
                     const MFTransformation& t);
private:
    const float tx;
    const float ty;
    const float txx;
    const float txy;
    const float tyx;
```

```
      const float tyy;
};
```

The declaration of `transform` must also be added to the class definition of MFVec, preceded by `friend`, exactly as it is here. The definition of `transform` comes directly from the equation defining the corresponding METAFONT operation.

```
MFVec transform(const MFVec& z, const MFTransformation& t)
{
  return MFVec(t.tx + z.xcoord*t.txx + z.ycoord*t.txy,
               t.ty + z.xcoord*t.tyx + z.ycoord*t.tyy);
}
```

We can now apply transformations to vectors.

```
MFVec q(7, 7);
const MFTransformation scaled6(0, 0, 6, 0, 0, 6);
MFVec fortytwo = transform(q, scaled6);
```

Declared and defined this way, `transform` constructs a new vector from its arguments. As an alternative, you could apply the transformation to a vector in place, changing the values of its data members, in the fashion of an assigning operator. (If you liked, you could use operator notation for `transform`, but you would have to choose a suitable operator symbol. METAFONT uses the name.) The aesthetics of syntax suggests that such an operation should be a member of MFVec. Let's call it `transformedby`, so I can say, for example `q.transformedby(scaled6)`. The definition is trivial

```
MFVec& MFVec::transformedby(const MFTransformation& t)
{
  xcoord = t.tx + xcoord*t.txx + ycoord*t.txy;
  ycoord = t.ty + xcoord*t.tyx + ycoord*t.tyy;
  return *this;
}
```

but, as you can see, still requires access to the data members of an MFTransformation object. Such access is granted in the definition of the latter class by adding a friend declaration for the `transformedby` member of MFVec, using its fully qualified name:

```
friend
  MFVec& MFVec::transformedby(const MFTransformation& t);
```

A friend function was needed to combine MFVec and MFTransformation objects because `transform` needed access to the data members of both classes. There are other predicaments a friend might be able to help you out of. It may be, for example, that an operator function needs access to an object's members, but making the operator a member function is syntactically inappropriate. Although this description may sound esoteric, everyone comes across it quite early in their C++ programming career, in the guise of `operator<<`.

The story usually goes like this: You've defined the MFVec class, or something like it, and overloaded lots of operators to make it comfortable to use.

You find that you need to print the value of an MFVec object; doing so is easy, because the components of a vector are objects of a built-in type, for which operator<< is defined. We defined a member function in chapter 8 and then overloaded the global operator<< function to apply it. This doesn't seem very elegant to you, so you think you'll change the name of MFVec::print to MFVec::operator<<, only then you remember that cout << v is equivalent to cout.operator<<(v) and your operator<< is a member of MFVec, not ostream so you will have to write v << cout, which won't do at all. You could, I suppose, press on regardless:

```
v << (cout << "The value of the vector v is ") << endl;
```

but that is probably worse than going back to v.print().

To get the effect you want, since you cannot add members to the ostream class, you must define a global operator<< taking two arguments, as before, and returning a reference to the ostream as its result. If you are to eliminate the superfluous member function print, the operator function needs access to the components of its second, MFVec, argument, which means, since it has to be global, it must be a friend of the MFVec class. A suitable declaration should be included in the definition of MFVec:

```
friend
   ostream& operator<<(ostream& os, const MFVec& z);
```

and now its definition looks like this:

```
ostream& operator<<(ostream& os, const MFVec& z)
{
   os << "(" << z.xcoord << ", " << z.ycoord << ")";
   return os;
}
```

You may find many of your classes declare operator<< as a friend, although you should perhaps consider the alternative of keeping the print member and the unfriendly operator<<. It depends whether you find friend functions more congenial than one superfluous member function.

A third reason for sometimes preferring global friend functions to member functions concerns implicit type conversion of their arguments. Again, an example is the quickest way to explain things, and again we can adapt the MFVec class for this purpose.

In my original version of MFVec, I included assigning operators += and -= as members, and defined + and - as global functions in terms of them. At the time, I omitted any discussion of type conversions, but consideration of them did affect the design. What happens if operator+ is a member of MFVec? Nothing controversial, if I leave the constructors alone. The operator function is trivially implemented.

```
MFVec::operator+(const MFVec& z)
{
   return MFVec(xcoord + z.xcoord, ycoord + z.ycoord);
}
```

Suppose, though, I get carried away with the desire to make life convenient for users of this class and provide a default value for the second argument

Contrived?
Surely not

to the constructor, on the assumption that vectors along the x-axis are quite common.

```
MFVec::MFVec(float x, float y = 0):xcoord(x), ycoord(y)
{}
```

The constructor can now take a single argument and so I can initialize MFVec objects with a single float value, which will be converted into an MFVec using the constructor.

```
MFec x_one = 1;     x_one = (1.0, 0)
```

Similarly, if I provide a single numerical argument to a function where it expects an MFVec, implicit conversions will be applied to construct one. So, if mv is an MFVec, the expression mv + 1.5 is legal and equivalent to mv + MFVec(1.5). Why then does the expression 1.5 + mv cause the compiler to complain about an "illegal operand"?

Because operator+ is a member function, mv + 1.5 is equivalent to mv.operator+(1.5)—no problem—but 1.5 + mv is 1.5.operator+(mv)—some problem. Implicit type conversion is never applied to the object through which a member function is called. It's the asymmetrical treatment of the "receiver of the message" again. Symmetry can be restored by making operator+ a global function, but, to be able to do its work, it must be a friend of MFVec.

```
class MFVec  {
members as before
friend
  MFVec operator+(const MFVec& z1, const MFVec& z2);
};
```

defined as

```
MFVec operator+(const MFVec& z1, const MFVec& z2)
{
  return MFVec(z1.xcoord + z2.xcoord, z1.ycoord + z2.ycoord);
}
```

Whenever a binary operator may need to perform implicit type conversions on its operands it should be a global friend function, not a member, so that conversions may be applied to either argument, not just the second one. Assigning operators are still best implemented as member functions: you would probably not want to be able to write 2.4 += mv, especially since it would only update the temporary object created by converting 2.4 into an MFVec, which would then be discarded.

Friend Classes

A slightly different use of friends occurs when two classes, while conceptually distinct, are nevertheless closely intertwined in their operations. It is quite possible to find that the first class must declare all the member functions of the second to be its friends. As a shorthand, the second class itself can be declared a friend, by adding

```
friend class classname;
```

to the definition of the first class. You might well wonder why, under such circumstances, the two classes are not amalgamated into one. The answer is that you might want to create more than one object of the friend class for each object of the class granting the access.

This is all getting very vague, so we should look at a classic example by going back to linked lists. Abstract datatypes can be deceptive. With the interface provided by the List class defined on page 241, it seems reasonable to write code like this:

```
void print_list(const List& a_list)
{
  for (int i = 1; i <= a_list.length(); ++i)
    cout << a_list.nth(i) << endl;
}
```

Such a loop is hopelessly and needlessly inefficient: to obtain the ith element, the member function nth must chain down i list nodes. On the next iteration, it must do exactly the same and then follow one more pointer to get to the $i+1^{th}$ element. If the previous position could somehow be stored between iterations, only this last pointer-following would be required each time round the loop, making the complexity of the operation $O(n)$ instead of $O(n^2)$, for a list of length n.

Naturally, I could overload operator<< as a friend of List and internalize the iteration, but it is impractical to define members to perform all conceivable iterative operations on a list. As we saw in chapter 7, it would be possible to supply a general iteration operation, taking a pointer to a function as its argument, but not every iterative algorithm can be conveniently expressed through this mechanism, and the argument types can give us a headache. Sometimes, you just have to be able to look at each list element in turn in a loop outside any member function of the List class.

One approach is to add a current position indicator as an extra data member of a list, with operations to reset it, move it on to the next node, return the value it points at, and determine whether it is off the end. The drawback of this approach is that it is only possible to carry on one iteration over any list at one time. If you need several iterations going on at once, for example, a loop within a loop used to construct all possible combinations of pairs of list elements, you are stuck.

The means of providing for arbitrary separate iterations over a list has been discovered independently many times—probably by every decent programmer who has ever encountered the problem. Define a separate class of objects, we'll call them list iterators, that represent a position in a list. A list iterator is initialized by passing a list to its constructor. The operations needed to iterate over that list are member functions of the class, ListIterator, of list iterators. Obviously, all of ListIterator's operations need access to the data members of a List and the privately defined local class Node, so ListIterator is a friend class of List. We declare this fact by adding the following to the definition of List.

```
friend class ListIterator;
```

A simple version of `ListIterator` can now be defined as follows (for a full industrial strength list iterator see the section on the STL in chapter 10):

```
class ListIterator {
public:
  ListIterator(const List& lis):the_list(lis), current(lis.the_head)
  {}
  void reset()
  {  current = the_list.the_head;  }
  string next_val();
  bool finished() const
  {  return current == NULL; }
private:
  const List& the_list;
  List::Node* current;
};
```

The member `the_list`, which is used to hold the list being iterated over, is a reference to a `List`. This is not done for efficiency—a `List` object only has the one data member—but because iterators over the same list must all share the same copy of it to preserve the semantics of simultaneous iterations; if you prefer, you can use a pointer equally well.

The only non-trivial member function is `next_val`.

```
string ListIterator::next_val()
{
  if (finished())
  {
    cerr << "Trying to iterate off the end of a List" << endl;
    abort();
  }
  string s = current->the_val;
  current = current->next;
  return s;
}
```

which is *almost* trivial.

List iterators can be used like this:

```
void print_pairs(const List& x)
{
  ListIterator it1(x);
  ListIterator it2(x);
  while (!it1.finished())
  {
    string s1 = it1.next_val();
    while (!it2.finished())
    {
      string s2 = it2.next_val();
      cout << "(" << s1 <<", " << s2 << ")" << endl;
```

```
      }
    it2.reset();
  }
}
```

You can use operator overloading to make `ListIterator`s as cute as you like. I could easily be tempted to add the following to the `ListIterator` definition.

```
operator bool() const
{  return !finished();  }
string operator++(int)
{  return next_val();  }
void operator()()
{  reset();  }
```

Then I could write the double loop in the form

```
ListIterator it1(x);
ListIterator it2(x);

while (it1)
{
  string s1 = it1++;
  while (it2)
  {
    string s2 = it2++;
    cout << "(" << s1 <<", " << s2 << ")\n";
  }
  it2();
}
```

▷ If you like the idea of iterators you can define them for many sorts of data structure. You need to think carefully about the semantics of any iterator operations that change the state of the object being iterated over. For example, you might find an operation to delete the current object useful. Is it necessary to ensure that all iterators active on the structure then remain valid? If it is (and it probably is) how ◁ do you ensure this?

You should also note that friend classes offer an alternative to nested classes, in case you don't like these or find that your compiler doesn't support them too well. Instead of declaring a local class with all public members, declare a friend class, defined at global level, with all private members—including its constructors and destructor. Recast in such a form, with the node class renamed `ListNode` in keeping with its new position as a global name, the linked list classes look like this:

```
class List   {
friend class ListIterator;
public:
```

```
    member functions as before
private:
  ListNode *the_head;
};

class ListNode  {
friend class List;
friend class ListIterator;
public:
  ListNode(const string& a_val, ListNode* whats_next):
    the_val(a_val), next(whats_next)
  string the_val;
  ListNode *next;
};
```

ListIterator remains as before, except that its data member current is of type ListNode, unadorned.

Whereas the original formulation, with Node local and private, made the name Node and all its operations inaccessible outside the scope of the enclosing class List, this version makes the name ListNode accessible, but none of the operations, so in either case node objects can only be created and used by member functions of List, which is as it should be. Local class definitions are marginally to be preferred, since there is no risk of any confusion arising if a different ListNode type is defined elsewhere.

▷ Finally, a couple of tedious details must be mentioned. When you include a declaration of a friend function inside a class definition, you are not only declaring the friendship, you are also declaring the function—it doesn't necessarily need any other declaration to be in scope, the effect is the same as declaring the function just outside the class definition. By default, functions whose first or only declaration occurs as a friend inside a class definition have external linkage. This can be embarrassing if you want your friend function to be inline: inline functions have default internal linkage and the linkage implied by every declaration of a function must be the same. If you add inline to any later declaration or definition of your friend function, the implied internal linkage will conflict with the implied external linkage from the friend declaration. Everyone agrees this is all a bit odd, but, as usual, the reason is a technical one required for compatibility with C. The easy fix is to add the inline specifier to the friend declaration.

Friendship is not inherited, nor is it transitive. Succumbing finally to the seductiveness of the metaphor, we can express these rules memorably by saying that your parents' friends are not necessarily your friends, nor are your friends' friends.

◁

Late Night C++

Late night is for getting serious. The efficient general-purpose programming language with sophisticated object-oriented features you have seen so far is enough for the humdrum things. Supporting object-oriented programming on the grand scale and producing large libraries of re-usable classes requires more.

Templates

10

We have seen extensive use being made of abstraction by parameterization. Almost every function I have defined takes one or more arguments. Within the function's body, the name of an argument stands for any of a potentially infinite set of actual values which may be supplied when the function is called. Arguments can be simple values, aggregates, objects belonging to user-defined classes, or functions. Each of these categories provides different opportunities for building and using abstractions.

Templates take abstraction by parameterization in a new direction by allowing you to use types themselves, as well as the values belonging to types, as parameters. This sort of abstraction is immensely useful in allowing you to capture patterns of computation that can be applied to objects of different types, and data structures that can contain objects of different types.

The number of forward references I have had to make to this chapter reflects the importance of templates to serious C++ programming. The patterns which templates express are among the easiest to re-use, but they can only be captured awkwardly and artificially using inheritance or higher-order functions.

It is being claimed in some circles that the use of templates to provide abstraction over types is a major new contribution made by object-oriented programming to software engineering—a claim which is, frankly, exaggerated. Functional languages have been providing similar facilities for years, and in a better way than C++ does. Importing type abstraction into C++ was a significant development, though, since it has freed programmers from an over-reliance on inheritance by providing other means of making new data types from old ones.

A measure of the importance and utility of templates is provided by the extent of their use in the C++ standard library. As the library is presently defined in the draft standard, templates are ubiquitous. A major part of the standard library is the so-called Standard Template Library, which consists of nothing but templates. In addition, templates have been put to use to abstract local dependencies, such as character sets, from the iostream library, making it easier to adapt to different languages and alphabets.

FUNCTION TEMPLATES AND TEMPLATE FUNCTIONS

Sooner or later, every programmer has to write a sort routine, whether in earnest or for the educational value of the experience. No matter whether you use the crudest slowest algorithm or one of the slick sophisticated methods, provided you want to sort in place without using any additional storage, you will have to exchange pairs of elements of the array being sorted. If you've taken the concept of abstraction to heart, you will want to encapsulate this exchanging operation in a function. Supposing your project requires you to sort an array of integers, you would write this function to do the job.

```
void exchange(int* a, int i, int j)
{
  int t = a[i];
  a[i] = a[j];
  a[j] = t;
}
```

What if, elsewhere in the same program, you had to sort an array of strings? A new sort function, and a new exchange:

```
void exchange(string* a, int i, int j)
{
  string t = a[i];
  a[i] = a[j];
  a[j] = t;
}
```

And characters? And then floating point numbers? Eventually, if you needed enough exchange functions for different types, you would probably hack out an Awk or Perl script or a little C++ program that would generate these functions for you, so that you could write an outline, using some placeholder symbol for the type of objects being sorted, and then generate a specific version just by running your script and providing a specific type name to replace the placeholder.

```
void exchange(#1* a, int i, int j)
{
  #1 t = a[i];
  a[i] = a[j];
  a[j] = t;
}
```

All very ingenious, but you've had to step outside the C++ language; an extra phase has been introduced into the procedure for generating an executable program. The process of generating specific function definitions (and declarations in the right places) from their outlines probably doesn't involve much checking—this will be done on the generated function, by your C++ compiler—so error checking has been decoupled from the actual code (the outline) you wrote. Your processor doesn't know anything about the context in which your function is going to be used, so it can't warn you about potential context-sensitive problems resulting from your specification. Unless you and your Awk script are very good, you probably have to patch together the final program from the generated output and some hand-written code. And, of course, the process is not portable: your processor of function outlines probably doesn't accept the same outline format as mine does.

By providing a linguistic facility for generating families of functions, differing only in the type of some arguments and variables, C++ saves you from having to resort to home grown function generating tools, with all their attendant drawbacks. It saves you some work into the bargain.

Function Templates

The C++ construct corresponding to our function outlines is called a function template. It can be declared or defined in the following way (remember that a function definition is also a declaration):

```
template <template-args> function-declaration
```

where `template` is a reserved word and *template-args* comprises a list of template arguments, separated by commas. A template argument can take several forms, but the commonest is

```
class template-arg-name
```

The keyword `class` here indicates that the *template-arg-name*—syntactically, a name like any other—is going to be used within the function definition as a placeholder for the name of some type, either a user-defined class or a built-in type. The use of `class` does not restrict you to the former, it is merely a bit of ecologically sound keyword recycling.[1] A template argument behaves as if it were indeed an argument, but one of type `type`, as it were. We are abstracting the type of the argument to a function by using a name to stand in for a potentially infinite number of types. However, the mechanism whereby this sort of abstraction is implemented is different from that used for functional abstraction: template arguments are substituted by the compiler; there is no way of computing types at runtime, but equally, there is no runtime overhead associated with using templates.

Here is a template for our exchange function.

```
template<class alpha>
  void exchange(alpha* a, int i, int j)
  {
    alpha t = a[i];
    a[i] = a[j];
    a[j] = t;
  }
```

The `exchange` functions generated from this template can be called just like any other function.

---

[1] A recent addition to the standard allows you to use `typename` instead. This new keyword is actually required for a much more esoteric purpose, which I have no intention of describing, but, if your compiler supports it, `typename` offers a readable alternative to `class` in this context.

```
float fa[10]  =  { 1.1, 2.2, 3.3, 4.4, 5.5, 6.6, 7.7,
                   8.8, 9.9, 10.0   };
exchange(fa, 3, 7);
```

By examining the types of the actual arguments supplied to the function, the compiler can deduce an actual value for the template argument `alpha` and generate an appropriate version of `exchange`. For this deduction to be possible, all the template arguments in a function template must be used at least once as the type of at least one of the formal arguments to the function being defined.

▷ For all practical purposes, anyway, the condition just stated is a necessary and sufficient one, which is easily satisfied. What the draft standard actually says is that a function generated from a template

```
template < class α, class β, ... > fn ( formal args )
```

can be called as

```
fn<Tα, Tβ,...>(actual args)
```

where T_α, T_β,... are the names of actual types. Whenever the values of these types can be deduced from the actual arguments supplied, they can be omitted. "Whenever" is "most of the time", in particular, whenever all the template variables α, β, ... are used as types of formal arguments. The commonest reason for having to specify types when you call a function generated from a template is when you want to define a family of functions differing only in their return types. For example, in chapter 3, I defined functions `prompt_for_a_char` and `prompt_for_a_float`, and could easily have needed more functions of the same sort, differing only in their return type and the type of the temporary variable used to hold the value read. I would now use a template:

```
template <class alpha>
alpha prompt_for_a()
    body of the function
```

and call it as `prompt_for_a<char>` and so on.

It is also possible to conceive of applications where you want functions differing only in the type of some local variable.

◁ Whenever all the template parameters can be deduced, the < and > can be omitted, as well as all the type values, giving the syntax I originally described.

A function that is generated (or "instantiated") from a function template is called a template function. (Terminological economy. Or something.) You can think of a function template as being a way of writing down an infinite collection of overloaded functions, since all the template functions generated from it have the same name, but differ in the types of their arguments. Such a family is a special case of the general overloading mechanism; because the family's members differ only in respect of some types, the form of the code is always the same.

▷ Implicit type conversions do not complicate template instantiation as much as might be feared. To simplify slightly, implicit conversions are not taken into account when deducing types for template arguments. (This isn't so much a simplification as a lie, but the special cases where conversions are allowed as part of the type deduction don't seem worth mentioning.) Once the template argument values have been deduced, the ordinary overloading resolution process is used for any arguments that aren't fixed by the template argument values. For example, suppose I define two classes:

```
class BaseClass {
public:
  void f()
  {  cout << "I am base"  << endl; }
};

class DerivedClass: public BaseClass {
public:
  void f()
  {  cout << "I am vile" << endl; }
};
```

and a function template

```
template <class alpha>
void t(alpha* x, BaseClass* bcp)
{
    x->f();
    bcp->f();
}
```

If `d` is a pointer to an object of type `DerivedClass`, when I call the function `t` as follows:

```
t(d, d);
```

The following output is produced:

```
I am vile
I am base
```

The template is instantiated with `alpha` replaced by `DerivedClass`; the second argument is converted to `BaseClass*` using the standard conversion from a pointer to a derived class to a pointer to its base class. (The member function `f` is statically bound.) If the template function had been called with an explicit type argument:

```
t<BaseClass>(d, d);
```

◁ then the standard conversion would have been applied to both arguments.

You can use templates to overload operators. A useful example is the following collection of templates.

```
template <class T>
inline bool operator!=(const T& x, const T& y)
{
  return !(x == y);
}
```

```
template <class T>
inline bool operator>(const T& x, const T& y)
{
  return y < x;
}

template <class T>
inline bool operator<=(const T& x, const T& y)
{
  return !(y < x);
}

template <class T>
inline bool operator>=(const T& x, const T& y)
{
  return !(x < y);
}
```

These provide definitions of the comparisons !=, >, >= and <= in terms of ==
and <, preserving the conventional relationships between the six operators. If
you define a class of objects which it is meaningful to consider as being ordered,
you need only provide explicit definitions of the last two. By including these
templates for the rest of the operations, you will be able to use any comparison
operators, with the expected effect.

I have to admit I didn't make this up. The templates are taken from the
Standard Template Library. If you have access to this (which you should, since
it is part of the draft C++ standard library) you can incorporate the comparison
templates by including the header file utility.[2]

Specialization

If you were really writing a general purpose sort routine—everybody's favourite
function template example—you would only want to exchange array elements
if one of them was in the wrong place. This is not the book to describe specific
sorting algorithms, so let's look at a simplified operation that encapsulates the
relevant part of such a routine: a template for functions that exchange a[i]
and a[j] if, and only if, a[i] > a[j].

```
template<class alpha>
  void exchange_if_greater(alpha a[], int i, int j)
  {
    if (a[i] > a[j])
    {
        alpha t = a[i];
```

---

[2]As always, since the standard is only a draft, the name of the relevant header may be different
on your system. Check your local documentation. For pre-standard versions of the Standard
Template Library, function.h is a good place to look.

```
        a[i] = a[j];
        a[j] = t;
    }
}
```

What will this do?

```
char* a[7] = { "apple", "banana", "cherry", "damson", "quince",
                "fig", "gooseberry" };
exchange_if_greater(a, 4, 6);
```

The effect is implementation-dependent; on my machine, it does nothing at all. The reason is simple: the call of exchange_if_greater with a first argument of type char*[] causes an instantiation of the template with alpha replaced by char*, exactly as you would expect. The trouble is, when you compare two char* objects, the comparison is made between the pointers themselves, not the characters pointed to, so a[i] > a[j] is only true if the pointer a[i] points to a higher location in memory than a[j] does. It is unlikely that this is what you meant.

You can't get out of this one by overloading operator> to do what you want on C-strings—overloading operators on built-in types is one of the ways you are not allowed to change C++. No, if you want to compare two C-strings lexically, you must use the library function strcmp, or a home-grown equivalent. This doesn't mean that you should avoid templates involving comparisons, just in case someone calls a template function with char* arguments. You are allowed to produce a definition of a function with the same name as a template, with specific argument types and no template arguments, whose body consists of code to handle any special case for those argument types.

Here, for example, I could add

```
void exchange_if_greater(char* a[], int i, int j)
{
    if (strcmp(a[i], a[j]) > 0)
    {
        char* t = a[i];
        a[i] = a[j];
        a[j] = t;
    }
}
```

and exchange_if_greater will work as expected: for char*[] arguments, the explicit definition using strcmp will be used; for any other type, a template function will be generated and called.

Template Instantiation

A function template defines an infinite collection of template functions. A compiler can only generate code for a finite subset of that collection. In any given program, there is everything to be said for generating code only for the template functions that are used. In the absence of separate compilation, this is easy enough to arrange, but any C++ program of sufficient complexity to be making much use of function templates will almost certainly be constructed as a number of separately compiled pieces. How is the compiler to determine, when it translates one of those pieces in isolation, which functions to generate from a template?

The simple solution would be to give all template functions internal linkage like inline functions. Then, by insisting that template definitions were included in every file that used the templates, it would be straightforward to produce exactly the right template functions for each file, without having to bother about any other. This is not what is done. Instead, a template function is supposed to behave like any other function: to call such a function, only a declaration of the function template need be in scope, and template functions have external linkage by default. The reason for this is to prevent excessive code size: if templates were generated for each file, a copy of a template function's definition would be produced in every file that used it. It is easy to imagine a program where a sorting function was called only once in several source files, with arguments of the same type. If each file generated its own copy of `sort` for these argument types, there wouldn't be much point in making it a function, as far as code size is concerned.

So, there's a good argument for generating only one copy of each template function required in an entire program. But it cannot be known which template functions must be generated from a function template until the whole program is available. In conventional systems, this isn't until link time. In order for the generation of template functions to be done automatically, it has to be possible for the compiler to be called again after an attempt has been made to link the program, with some form of instruction to generate the missing template functions. This process may have to be iterated, if the newly-generated template functions call others that were not previously required. This iterated compilation can be very inefficient, and may be beyond the capabilities of some programming environments, so a facility is provided in C++ for explicitly instructing the compiler to generate template functions.

An instantiation request, as it is called, for a template function looks like

```
template res-type fn-name<actual-template-args>
    ( formal-arg-declarations );
```

For example,

```
template void exchange<int>(int*, int, int);
```

The effect is to generate a template function definition from the function template. A good strategy in a program making heavy use of templates is to construct a file consisting of instantiation requests for those template functions you know are going to be needed. When the compiled version of this file is linked with the rest of your program, all calls of template functions will be matched up with these definitions.

There remains the general problem of how the compiler is to find template definitions when it only has declarations. For ordinary functions, this is part of the job done by the linker, but with templates it must be done by the compiler. How it is done depends on how sophisticated an environment the compiler runs in. A common expedient is to require template definitions, not just declarations, to be available wherever templates are used.

The underlying trouble is that a template definition is neither a declaration, just specifying how to use something, nor a real definition, consisting of actual code. It is something new, and it doesn't fit in to the traditional model of generating executable code from source by compiling and then linking. To deal with template instantiation properly, a more elaborate translation system is required, which keeps more information about the source available after individual files have been compiled, and blurs the distinction between compilation and linkage. (Other languages have their own problems which also require this distinction to become blurred.) Various optimizations then become available, notably the opportunity to cache commonly generated template functions. One of C++'s major advantages would be lost, though: it would no longer fit into the venerable pattern of compilers and linkers but would demand its own compilation environment. This could present portability problems and make C++ less acceptable to traditionalist programmers.

TEMPLATE CLASSES

The little story about exchange functions that led up to the introduction of function templates could be repeated with relatively minor changes as a story about range-checked arrays. There is, after all, an air of unreality about all these examples using the class `MyIntArray`—why single out integers for special treatment? One might just as well need a range-checked array of strings or of METAFONT vectors or of range-checked arrays or of...just about anything. Each time you found a new type for which a range-checked array was needed, you would have to define a new class and you would rapidly find that they were all just the same except for the type of the elements.

The same story could be repeated again for linked lists and, in fact, for any class that implements a data structure to hold a collection of objects of the same type: sets, trees, tables, and so on. Such classes are called "container classes". (I don't think anyone has ever produced a precise definition of a container class; the assumption is that if you're a programmer you'll know one when you see it.)

To prevent you reaching for your favourite text manipulation language or macro processor, C++ provides class templates to allow you to define generic classes parameterized in some types, just as function templates allow you to define generic functions.

Simple Use of Template Classes

A class template looks like a class definition preceded by

```
template <template-arg { , template-arg }>
```

where, as in a function template, each *template-arg* usually takes the form

```
class template-arg-name
```

with each *template-arg-name* standing in for the name of some type wherever it is used within the class definition. The template describes a potentially infinite set of class definitions, each one formed by substituting a particular type name for each *template-arg-name*. As a particularly simple but useful example we can abstract out the `int` type from the `MyIntArray` class, replacing it with a *template-arg-name* `alpha`, to produce a template for a whole set of range-checked arrays, with elements of any type.

```
template <class alpha>
class MyArray   {
public:
  MyArray(int lower, int upper, alpha initial);
  ~MyArray();
  int lwb() const;
  int upb() const;
  const alpha& operator[](int i) const;
  alpha& operator[](int i);
private:
  MyArray(const MyArray<alpha>&);
  MyArray<alpha>& operator=(const MyArray<alpha>&);
  int lower_bound, upper_bound;
  alpha *the_array;
  void check_index(int i) const;
  void bounds_error() const;
  void deleted_error() const;
  void range_error(int i) const;
};
```

▷ There are those—most notable among them, Bjarne Stroustrup—who like the syntax of templates. And there are those who do not. You may find it helpful to read `template <class alpha>` as "for all types α", or $\forall\alpha$:, if you are comfortable writing upside-down. ◁

An infinite set of classes needs an infinite set of names. You form the name of a particular template class produced from a class template by following the template name by a type name enclosed in angle brackets. Thus, from the `MyArray` template we can produce `MyArray<int>`, `MyArray<string>`, `MyArray<MFVec>`, `MyArray<PartiallyAppliedFunction>` and so on (forever). The template class `MyArray<int>` can be used exactly like `MyIntArray`. In particular, its name can be used to declare variables.

```
MyArray<int> mai(0, 99, 0);
```

With template classes no automatic deduction of template arguments is done; you must always specify the particular type when you use a specific version of a template class.

Each member function declared in a class template can be thought of as a template function, parameterized in the same template arguments as the class is, and their definitions look like function template definitions. The class name used to qualify the member name has the template argument names in angle brackets. For example

```
template <class alpha>
alpha& MyArray<alpha>::operator[](int i)
{
  check_index(i);
  return the_array[i - lower_bound];
}
```

You can see that whatever type is substituted for alpha this member function performs the same computation, only the type of the array element returned changes. Such behaviour is characteristic of the generic classes described by class templates, which you should learn to distinguish from families of classes derived from a common base class, where behaviour is added or modified in each of the derived classes.

The fully qualified names of the constructor and destructor for MyArray are MyArray<alpha>::MyArray and MyArray<alpha>::~MyArray, respectively, and not MyArray<alpha>::MyArray<alpha> and MyArray<alpha>::~MyArray<alpha>. Convincing yourself that this is as it should be is quite painless.

▷ Member functions of a template class can themselves be templates, but only according to the Draft Standard, not the ARM. That is, you can have something like

```
template <class alpha>
class X {
public:
  template <class beta>
  bool cmp_with_other_type(beta);
};
```

◁

The List class and its associates can be made into templates in a useful fashion.

```
template <class alpha>
class List   {
friend class ListIterator<alpha>;
public:
  List();
  ~List();
  void insert(alpha, int);
  void remove(int);
  alpha nth(int) const;
  int length() const;
private:
  List(const List<alpha>&);
  List& operator=(const List<alpha>&);
  class Node  {
```

```
    public:
      Node(alpha a_val, Node* whats_next):
        the_val(a_val), next(whats_next) {}
      alpha the_val;
      Node *next;
    };
    Node *the_head;
};

template <class beta>
class ListIterator {
public:
  ListIterator(List<beta>& lis): the_list(lis),
                                 current(lis.the_head) {}
  void reset()
  {  current = the_list.the_head;   }
  beta next_val();
  bool finished() const
  {  return current == NULL; }
private:
  const List<beta>& the_list;
  List<beta>::Node* current;
};
```

The member functions' definitions are easily modified. Now you can have lists of integers, lists of strings, lists of METAFONT vectors and so on. Note that the friend declaration of `ListIterator` is parameterized in `alpha`; this means that `ListIterator<int>` will be a friend of `List<int>`, `ListIterator<string>` will be a friend of `List<string>`, and so on.

Fancier Use of Template Classes

I have been careful to say that template arguments are *usually* type names. They can also be constant expressions of any type except one of the floating point numerical types.[3] The corresponding template argument name is declared in the template header just as the formal argument to a function is. The difference between template arguments that are not types and function arguments is that template arguments are substituted at compile-time, not at run-time.

Probably the most useful sort of value you can use to parameterize a class is an integer denoting the size of some container. The range-checked arrays we have seen so far have their size determined at run-time from the arguments to the constructor. This provides maximum flexibility, but at the expense of run-time efficiency—space for the array must be allocated dynamically using `new`. Where efficiency is critical we may prefer an array whose bounds are fixed at compile time. By making the lower and upper bounds into template arguments

Measure, don't guess

---

[3]You can never be sure when two floating point numbers are equal.

we can achieve this.

```
template <class alpha, int lower, int upper>
class FixedSizeArray  {
public:
  FixedSizeArray(alpha initial);
  int lwb() const;
  int upb() const;
  const alpha& operator[](int i) const;
  alpha& operator[](int i);
private:
  FixedSizeArray(const FixedSizeArray<alpha, lower, upper>&);
  FixedSizeArray<alpha, lower, upper>&
    operator=(const FixedSizeArray<alpha, lower, upper>&);
  alpha the_array[upper - lower + 1];
  void check_index(int i) const;
  void range_error(int i) const;
};
```

The array itself is allocated as part of the FixedSizeArray object, and no call to new is needed. There is now no need to check that the upper bound is greater than the lower bound: any attempt to instantiate a FixedSizeArray with paradoxical bounds will result in a compiler error. The constructor need simply set the initial value of each element:

```
template <class alpha, int lower, int upper>
FixedSizeArray<alpha, lower, upper>
  ::FixedSizeArray(alpha initial)
{
  int size = upper - lower + 1;
  for (int i = 0; i < size; ++i)
    the_array[i] = initial;
}
```

The loss of flexibility required to achieve the extra efficiency resulting from computing the size at compile time may be higher than you think. As far as the compiler is concerned, there is no relationship between different classes generated from the same template using different template argument values, so the types FixedSizeArray<string, 0, 100>, FixedSizeArray<string, 1,101> and FixedSizeArray<float, 0, 100> are all different types. You cannot write a function that will accept an argument even of either of the first two—you will have to write a template function and generate two separate versions. Does this remind you of classic Pascal or aren't you that ancient?

Once you have got the hang of defining template classes, you will want to go further with them. The first thing you might think of trying in this context is using a class generated from a template as an argument to another template. For example, a common data structure for representing a directed graph or network is an array of linked lists—each entry in the array corresponds to a vertex of the graph and holds a list of the vertices to which it is connected by an edge. Assuming you have defined a class `Vertex` to hold whatever information pertains to each vertex, you would declare a data member in your `DirectedGraph` class

```
MyArray<List <Vertex> > vertex_array;
```

If you prefer a list of lists, no problem—templates can be generated recursively:

```
List<List <Vertex> > vertex_list;
```

There is a lexical ambiguity when templates are nested like this: two consecutive >s look like the operator >>, hence the unsightly spaces between closing angle brackets. If you put one in front of the opening bracket, it looks less silly.

▷ It's hard to imagine this happening, but never let it be said that a Late Night Guide doesn't cater for the strangest of programmers... Suppose your template takes a boolean argument:

```
template <bool flag>
class Unlikely {
```

etc. Instantiating it with

!
```
Unlikely< a>b > u;
```

will produce a syntax error: the first > is taken as the closing angle bracket for the template argument. Brackets fix the problem:

```
Unlikely< (a>b) > u;
```

◁

You can continue using template classes as template arguments for as far as you like:

```
List< List< List< List< Vertex > > > > the_llll_vertices;
```

And so on... Judicious use of `typedef` is probably advisable.

If you want a *template* for, say, a list of lists, you need to be a bit devious and use a degenerate form of inheritance, where the derived class doesn't add or override any members. In effect, it just renames the base class, which will be a template, like this, for example:

```
template <class alpha>
class ListofLists: public List< List < alpha > > {};
```

Certainly a `ListofLists<T>` is a kind of `List< List <T> >`.

▷ `ListofLists<T>` isn't actually a synonym for `List< List <T> >`; it is a derived class and the usual conversions between derived and base classes apply. It is prob-
◁ ably best for your sanity not to mix the two.

As you see, it is possible to combine templates and inheritance. Often, the pattern of combination is one in which the template argument of the derived template class being defined is just passed on to the base class so that a family of classes is derived from a family of base classes with corresponding template arguments.

We can use this technique to construct a family of list classes, where each class in the family is characterized by its insertion strategy (e.g., ordered/unordered, with/without duplicate entries). To do this, we start with a base class AbstractList, which does everything any kind of list should, except for insertion of a new element. The insert members of derived classes will have to take different types of arguments, so it is not appropriate to put a pure virtual insert member in this base class. Instead, each derived class will add its own.

I will make the destructor purely virtual to ensure that no objects of type AbstractList can be created. Unless you are obsessive about information hiding, you will want classes derived from AbstractList to have access to the definition of Node and to the head of the list, so these formerly private members should be protected only. The copy constructor and assignment operator remain private to prevent potentially expensive copying of these structures. I have dispensed with iterators, to avoid the extra clutter in the declarations.

```
template <class alpha>
class AbstractList    {
public:
  AbstractList();
  virtual ~AbstractList() = 0;
  void remove(int);
  alpha nth(int) const;
  int length() const;
protected:
  class Node   {
  public:
      Node(alpha a_val, Node* whats_next):
        the_val(a_val), next(whats_next) {}
      alpha the_val;
      Node *next;
    };
  Node *the_head;
private:
  AbstractList(const AbstractList<alpha>&);
  AbstractList<alpha>& operator=(const AbstractList<alpha>&);
};
```

I could easily produce a class template equivalent to List, by deriving it from AbstractList and adding its insert member. Instead, though, I will derive an ordered list, by adding an insert which takes a single argument and puts it in its proper place. This is achieved with the following definition of an ordered list class OList.

```
template <class alpha>
class OList:public AbstractList<alpha> {
public:
  void insert(alpha x);
};
```

A corresponding definition of insert is as follows:

```
template <class alpha>
void OList<alpha>::insert(alpha x)
{
  if (the_head == NULL||the_head->the_val > x)
    the_head = new Node(x, the_head);
  else
  {
    Node* q = the_head;
    Node* p = the_head->next;
    while (p != NULL && p->the_val < x)
    {
      q = p;
      p = p->next;
    }
    q->next = new Node(x, p);
  }
}
```

It's good, but not good enough. An Olist<int> will work beautifully, but Olist<MFVec> will fail to compile, while Olist<char*> will behave incorrectly. Why? The insertion algorithm hinges on comparisons performed with the operators < and >. The pre-defined meaning of these operators causes them to do the right thing for integers, but the corresponding operator functions have not been overloaded for the class MFVec, hence the template cannot be successfully instantiated for MFVec objects. On the other hand, < and > do have a pre-defined meaning for objects of char*—they compare the pointer addresses, which, unfortunately, isn't what you want to do.

▷ Ideally, perhaps, one would like to be able to associate a declaration of some constraints with a template, saying, in effect, "Only instantiate this template if the type arguments have the following properties...". However, to be really effective, you need semantic constraints equivalent to statements like "operator< is defined and reflects a total ordering on objects". The technology required to specify and check such constraints is at a much higher level than C++ aspires to. You can devise hacks to ensure that all necessary operations (including subtle ones, like default and copy constructors) are defined without having to wait until link time, but they hardly seem worth the effort. You will document any such constraints, so you will just
◁ have to hope your documentation gets read.

There is a second weakness in the implementation of the member function Olist<alpha>::insert just presented. Even if the comparison operators are defined for all the types you might instantiate it with, there is no way to accommodate alternative orderings. As a trivial example, if you want to order lists in descending order instead of ascending order, you would need a new template, even though only two symbols need changing in the function's definition. More convincingly, you might sometimes need to order strings strictly alphabetically, sometimes ignoring spaces, and sometimes in the order they appear in telephone directories and other lists of names, where Mac and Mc,

Saint and St prefixes appear together. You can use templates to accommodate alternative orderings.

If you've ever written or used a general-purpose parameterized sorting function, such as qsort from the standard C library, you will see that what is needed is a way of passing the ordering relation as a parameter. The most flexible and efficient way is to define a comparison class whose members are static functions gt, lt, eq and so on, providing the comparison operations, and pass this class as a template argument. For example, the OList template class would have been better defined like this:

```
template <class alpha, class comparison>
class OList:public AbstractList<alpha> {
public:
  void insert(alpha x);
};
```

with insert defined as follows:

```
template <class alpha, class comparison>
void OList<alpha, class comparison>::insert(alpha x)
{
  if (the_head == NULL||comparison::gt(the_head->the_val, x))
    the_head = new Node(x, the_head);
  else
  {
    Node* q = the_head;
    Node* p = the_head->next;
    while (p != NULL && comparison::lt(p->the_val, x))
    {
      q = p;
      p - p->next;
    }
    q->next = new Node(x, p);
  }
}
```

(Notice that no object of type comparison is ever created.)

To instantiate the template, a suitable comparison class must be provided. For example, if you want to create a class of lists of integers in ascending order, the following comparator class can be used.

```
class IntCmp {
public:
  static bool lt(int i1, int i2)
  {
    return i1 < i2;
  }
  static bool gt(int i1, int i2)
  {
    return i1 > i2;
  }
};
```

The required class is OList<int, IntCmp>. To reverse the ordering, just change the comparison class.

```
class RevIntCmp {
public:
  static bool lt(int i1, int i2)
  {
    return i1 > i2;
  }
  static bool gt(int i1, int i2)
  {
    return i1 < i2;
  }
};
```

Now, OList<int, RevIntCmp> is a class of lists of integers in descending order.

Since many types have ordering operators built into them, it might be sensible to use a template for comparisons.

```
template <class alpha>
class Cmp {
public:
  static bool lt(alpha i1, alpha i2)
  {
    return i1 < i2;
  }
  static bool gt(alpha i1, alpha i2)
  {
    return i1 > i2;
  }
};
```

The ordered list of integers is now OList<int, Cmp<int> >. For types such as char*, where the default meaning of the operators is wrong, a specialized version can be implemented, just as we did with function templates.

```
class Cmp<char*> {
public:
  static bool lt(char* s1, char* s2)
  {
    return strcmp(s1, s2) < 0;
  }
  static bool gt(char* s1, char* s2)
  {
    return strcmp(s1, s2) > 0;
  }
};
```

▷ According to the Draft Standard, you can supply default values for template arguments, just as you can for function arguments. Using this feature, you could define the ordered list class as follows:

```
template <class alpha, class comparison = Cmp<alpha>>
class OList:public AbstractList<alpha> {
member declarations
};
```

Instantiating it as, for example OList<int> would be sufficient to generate a list of integers in ascending order, using Cmp<int> as the comparison class. Default template arguments are not widely implemented at the time of writing.

You can extrapolate from these examples to see that the potential for combining classes offered by the template mechanism in C++ goes well beyond their mundane use in parameterized containers. But just as you are beginning to appreciate how useful template classes are, do you wonder about their price? Have you thought about the size of the generated code?

Take another look at the definitions of the member functions of the List class in chapter 9, with all their error checking. Reflect that every time you generate a List class for a different type of element you effectively produce a new copy of all that code. Linked lists are useful data structures; if you had the template available, the chances are that you would use it quite a lot. When you saw the size of the generated code you might become disillusioned about templates and resort to more primitive methods.

For example, if you only needed lists of pointers to various sorts of object, the type void* might very well flutter into your mind. Since any pointer can be implicitly converted to this type, a list of void* can serve as a list of any pointer type. There's a double drawback: you have lost type checking, so a mixture of pointers could end up on your list. (I assume that isn't what you want. If it is, then the chances are that the ones you want to insert have something in common and should therefore have a common base type, but that belongs in another story.) Even if you don't care about type checking, the second drawback remains: you will have to use a cast whenever you access a list element, because you aren't allowed to do anything to or with a void* pointer unless you first convert it (back) to some other pointer type.

Suppose you had defined a ListOfVoid class like this:

```
class ListOfVoid   {
public:
  ListOfVoid();
  ~ListOfVoid();
  void insert(void*, int);
  void remove(int);
  void* nth(int) const;
  int length() const;
protected:
  class Node   {
  public:
    Node(void* a_val, Node* whats_next):
      the_val(a_val), next(whats_next) {}
    void* the_val;
    Node *next;
  };
```

```
        Node *the_head;
    private:
      ListOfVoid(const ListOfVoid&);
      ListOfVoid& operator=(const ListOfVoid&);
    };
```

with suitably adjusted definitions for the member functions (instantiating the template class List<void*> by hand, as it were). You could store, for example, pointers to FTP objects.

```
    ListOfVoid x;
    FTP* f1 = new FTP("ftp://research.att.com/dist/c++std/WP/");
    FTP* f2 = new FTP("ftp:/ftp.std.com/AW/stroustrup2e/");
    x.insert(f1, 0);
    x.insert(f2, 0);
```

This is OK, because the pointers to FTP objects are implicitly converted to void* to match the first argument of ListOfVoid::insert. However, the reverse conversion is never done automatically, so an attempt to retrieve an element from the list without a cast fails:

!
```
    FTP* f = x.nth(1);
```

The value returned by x.nth(1) is of type void*, and so cannot be assigned to a variable of type FTP*. You can only retrieve the list elements with an explicit cast:

```
    FTP* f = (FTP*)x.nth(1);
```

▷ Incidentally, casts from void* to another pointer type are re-interpreting casts, so the new way of performing this retrieval is

```
        FTP* f = reinterpret_cast<FTP*>(x.nth(1));
```

◁

To avoid scattering casts all over the place, you could define a special interface class for lists of FTP objects, hiding the cast inside:

```
    class ListOfFTP    {
    public:
      void insert(FTP* f, int i)
      {   the_v_list.insert(f, i); }
      void remove(int i)
      {   the_v_list.remove(i); }
      FTP* nth(int i) const
      {   return (FTP*)the_v_list.nth(i); }
      int length() const
      {   return the_v_list.length();   }
    private:
      ListOfVoid the_v_list;
    };
```

All the forwarding functions are small and inline, so there is no overhead to speak of in using a `ListOfFTP` instead of a `ListOfVoid`. You could use the same technique for, say, a list of pointers to strings, or a list of pointers to METAFONT vectors, at which point a sense of *déja vu* may burst upon you: each time you have a new sort of list, you define a new interface class to hide the cast and serve as a front for a list of `void*` pointers. By now you know what to do...use a template.

```
template <class alpha>
class ListOf {
public:
  void insert(alpha* f, int i)
  { the_v_list.insert(f, i); }
  void remove(int i)
  { the_v_list.remove(i); }
  alpha* nth(int i) const
  { return (alpha*)the_v_list.nth(i); }
  int length() const
  { return the_v_list.length();  }
private:
  ListOfVoid the_v_list;
};
```

Provided you only want to have lists of pointers, this template can be used as conveniently as the original `List`, but without generating unreasonable quantities of code.

```
ListOf<FTP> x;
FTP* f1 = new FTP("ftp://research.att.com/dist/c++std/WP/");
FTP* f2 = new FTP("ftp:/ftp.std.com/AW/stroustrup2e/");
x.insert(f1, 0);
x.insert(f2, 0);

FTP* f = x.nth(1);
f->connect();
```

No, I didn't invent it

This little manoeuvre of using `void*` to obtain an efficient generic data structure and then hiding it and the casts it requires behind a collection of interface classes generated from a template is pretty smart. It can be made even tastier by making all the member functions of `ListOfVoid` protected and building the interface classes with private inheritance. That way, the ideologically unsound list of untyped pointers can never be used directly, only as a base class.

I know you aren't likely to implement a linked list class template yourself unless it be for the educational experience—there are plenty of them out there in libraries already—but the techniques illustrated in this homely example can be applied to a wide range of generic data structures.

THE STANDARD TEMPLATE LIBRARY

Object-oriented programming is supposed to be primarily about constructing reusable software components, they say. Many of the features of C++ are present to make it possible to write such components. So where are they?

Probably too many programmers have spent time using fancy features of C++ to re-implement low-level data structures when the idea is to re-use those structures and get on with something more interesting. Unfortunately, C++ was released into the world without an adequate library of general-purpose classes, but now a number of class libraries are available, some commercial, others public domain. One of these, the Standard Template Library, or STL, has recently been incorporated into the C++ draft standard. As a result, STL implementations should become generally (in fact, universally) available, and it seems likely that this will have a considerable impact on the way C++ programmers go about writing programs.

As its name implies, the Standard Template Library relies heavily on class and function templates, from which you can infer that it includes a collection of generic container classes. It goes further, though, by providing iterators and a collection of algorithms, all designed to fit together comfortably.

▷ It is clear that the design of the STL and its style of program composition have been heavily influenced by developments in functional programming stemming from the use of higher order functions to provide combining forms, a trend that probably ◁ originates with John Backus's FP Systems.

Because of its structure and the higher level datatypes it makes available, the STL goes quite a long way towards transforming C++ into a different language. It isn't possible to do justice to that language here. You should be able to appreciate its flavour from a brief outline and a couple of examples.

Containers, Iterators and Algorithms

There are three main components of the library: a collection of generic containers, a collection of iterator classes to go with them, and a collection of algorithms. Considerable effort has gone into the design of the interfaces between these components. Algorithms are designed to accept iterators over any sort of container as their arguments; it is even possible to construct iterators over ordinary C++ arrays, so the algorithms can be applied to them. Whenever an operation can meaningfully be applied to several sorts of container, it is applied in the same way, irrespective of the specific type of the container involved. Similarly, all types of iterator present the same interface whenever they have operations in common.

We can conveniently begin by describing the containers. Most of the usual suspects have been rounded up: dynamic vectors and bit vectors, lists, deques,[4]

---

[4]A deque or double-ended queue is a sequence which supports efficient insertion, deletion and inspection operations at either end.

sets, multisets,[5] maps and multimaps. The last four are grouped together as *associative containers*, the others are *sequences*, although inheritance is not used to capture this commonality. Some notorious data structures escaped the net, notably hash tables and trees (which *are* there, but are only used internally), so the STL is not a complete substitute for a careful reading of a good data structures book. Templates called *adaptors* are supplied for constructing certain higher-level data structures—stacks, queues and priority queues—as specializations of the sequence classes. Adaptors are templates that take a container class as an argument and use it as the type of a data member that implements the abstract data type.

Iterators are arguably the most important component of the STL. They effectively determine the programming style used to manipulate containers and are the means of providing a uniform interface between the library's algorithms and containers. Iterators are broadly classified into five sorts: input and output iterators behave much like the corresponding stream types, allowing a sequence of values to be read or written in a single pass. Forward iterators allow multiple passes over the values of a container. Bidirectional iterators permit backing up in addition, while random access iterators allow efficient access to elements in any order. The selection of algorithms on offer is fairly limited. A sorting operation is available and a few specialized operations for numerical containers but most of the so-called algorithms are powerful operations expressing patterns of processing and combination on containers. For example, `foreach` applies a function, passed as an argument, to each element, `remove` removes all the elements satisfying a specified condition, `transform` applies an operator to each pair of elements of two sequences and constructs a new sequence from the result.

Vagueness is setting in... Let's look at some aspects of the interfaces so that we can use classes from the STL in an example.

Each container is a class template, taking the type of its elements as a template argument. A list of strings is of type `list<string>`,[6] for example, a vector of integers is `vector<int>`, a deque of vectors of floating point numbers is a `deque<vector <float> >`. Each template locally defines a public type name `iterator` to stand for iterators over objects of that container type, so an iterator for a list of strings has type `list<string>::iterator`. Before describing how to create iterators of such types, I had better explain the STL's interpretation of the concept of iterator, since it differs slightly from mine.

In the STL, an iterator is a generalization of a pointer. That is, it is an object belonging to a class with the prefix operator * defined on it so that if p is an iterator over a container, *p is an object in the container. You can think of the iterator as pointing to a current object at any time. The increment operators ++ are defined to move the iterator to point to the next object, using some suitable ordering to determine which is next. For bidirectional iterators, the decrement operators -- are defined to back up to the previous object. Any container type has member functions `begin()` and `end()` that return an iterator that points to the first element and an iterator that points one past the last element,

---

[5] Sets with duplicate members, also known as bags.
[6] The STL `list` template should not be confused with the `List` template I developed earlier.

respectively. If an iterator is initialized to point to the first object, a sequence of increment operations will make it point to each object in the container in turn, until eventually it points to the value produced by end(). So, one way of writing out every element of a vector of integers v is

```
for (vector<int>::iterator p = v.begin();
     p < v.end(); ++p)
  cout << *p << endl;
```

which you could profitably compare with the following loop for writing out the elements of an array v[N] of integers.

```
for (int *p = v; p < v+N; ++p)
  cout << *p << endl;
```

Most of the STL algorithms take a pair of iterators *first* and *last* and apply some operation to every element $*p$ for *first* $\leq p <$ *last*. Iterators are also sometimes used as place markers. For example, the general insert operation on sequences takes an iterator and an object, and inserts a copy of the object into the sequence in front of the element the iterator is pointing at.

The STL's associative containers have some special operations defined on them. We will consider maps as an example. The objects stored in a map are instances of the template class pair, which is defined in the STL's header files as follows:

Public data members!

```
template <class T1, class T2>
class pair {
public:
  T1 first;
  T2 second;
  pair(){}
  pair(const T1& a, const T2& b) : first(a), second(b) {}
};
```

In a map, the first element of each pair is used as a key, with its associated value being stored in the second. The map template is parameterized in the types of keys and values and in a comparison—a class of function objects defining an ordering of keys. By convention in the STL, a comparison class overloads operator() to mean less than. For example, I might have

```
class CharStarLess {
public:
  bool operator()(char* x, char* y) const
  { return strcmp(x, y) < 0; }
};
```

as a comparison class for C-strings. I could use it to declare maps whose keys were C-strings, for example, a map we will meet again shortly:

```
map<char*, float, CharStarLess> r_map;
```

The map template locally defines the name value_type as a synonym for the pair type of its elements, so the objects in the map just declared are of type map<char*, float, CharStarLess>::value_type.

Among its members, `map` includes the characteristic operations `find` and `insert`. The first of these takes a value of the key type and returns an iterator pointing to the entry with that value as its key if it exists, or `end()` if not. The second takes a `value_type` object (i.e., a pair consisting of a key and a value) and inserts it into the map.

We'll use maps to solve a mundane but slightly messy problem: totting up the slate. Privileged customers in bars and cafés can "put things on the slate", that is, consume them without actually paying at the time. Instead, the proprietor notes down the price of the items and at some future date (for example, the day after pay day) adds up the total owed by each customer, who must then pay the lot (or possibly not). There probably aren't many places left where these records are chalked up on a piece of slate. It's depressingly easy to imagine a time when waiters and bartenders come equipped with electronic notepad devices and the slate is actually a data file. When that time comes, the totting up will best be done by a program.

Assuming all the data entry and communications stuff goes all right, the proprietor will end up with a file consisting of lines, each of which contains a customer's name and an amount owed for a particular round of drinks or meal. We may as well suppose a colon separates the name from the amount. The individual lines will have been added as and when the food was eaten and the drinks were drunk, so the records for any one customer will be scattered through the file. A program must bring them together and calculate the totals owed.

There are two strategies you can adopt: tabulate or sort. Tabulation means maintaining a table with entries whose key is a customer's name and whose value is a running total of the amount they owe. When you read a line from the slate file, you look up the name in the table and, if it is there, add the amount to the running total, otherwise create a new entry with the total initialized to the amount. Obviously, STL maps can be used to implement a program along these lines.

I will use a map with entries of type `pair<const char*, float>`, so, in order to instantiate the map template I need a class of comparison objects for the keys of type `char*`. The class `CharStarLess` defined on page 280 is exactly what is needed. As well as its definition, I also need the map template and its associated iterators; these are included in some system header files.[7]

```
#include <map.h>
#include <iterator.h>
```

To make the program easier to read, a couple of type synonyms can be defined.

```
typedef map<char*, float, CharStarLess>::value_type Record;
typedef map<char*, float, CharStarLess>::iterator MapIterator;
```

The logic for processing the file is simple and just follows the outline given above. More interesting is the method of reading the records. The STL provides a handy means of processing formatted files: special sorts of output and input

---

[7]As ever, the names of the headers may be slightly different on your system. Check the documentation.

iterators called *stream iterators*. A stream iterator template is parameterized in the type of objects you want to read.[8] If i is an istream iterator for objects of type K, the effect of i++ is to read (the textual representation of) an object of type K into *i using operator>>(istream&, K&) (a suitably overloaded version must be available) and move the input stream on to the next object. An istream_iterator object is constructed from an istream by passing the stream to a constructor; the default constructor for istream_iterator produces the end iterator, so you can test whether an istream_iterator<K> is exhausted by comparing it with istream_iterator<K>().

If we are going to use the stream iterator approach to processing the slate file, we need to overload operator>> for the type Record, which we are going to insert into the map. This is relatively easy to do with a bit of low level mucking about with arrays of char and strsteams—especially if you omit any validity checking, as I have done here.

```
const int record_length = 50;

istream& operator>>(istream& is, Record& r)
{
  char rec_buffer[record_length];
  is.get(rec_buffer, record_length, '\n');
  is.ignore(1, '\n');
  char temp_buffer[record_length];
  istrstream iss(rec_buffer);
  iss.get(temp_buffer, record_length, ':');
  iss.ignore(record_length, ':');
  iss >> r.second;
  r.first = new char[strlen(temp_buffer) + 1];
  strcpy(r.first, temp_buffer);
  return is;
}
```

The net effect is to read everything up to a colon into r.first and the rest of the line into r.second. At the risk of stressing the obvious, a serious program would have to check that the input was a line consisting of a string followed by a colon then a floating point number representing the amount, and take appropriate action if it was not. But this is just an example.

We can now write a function to tot up the slate.

```
void process_map(istream& fin, ostream& fout)
{
  map<char*, float, CharStarLess> r_map;
  istream_iterator<Record>i = fin;
  while (i != istream_iterator<Record>())
  {
    Record r = *i++;
    MapIterator p = r_map.find(r.first);
    if (p != r_map.end())
      (*p).second += r.second;
```

---

[8]If your C++ compiler does not yet support default template arguments (see page 274) you may need to supply extra ones. Consult your local documentation.

```
        else
          r_map.insert(r);
    }
    copy(r_map.begin(), r_map.end(),
         ostream_iterator<Record>(fout, "\n"));
}
```

The last function call needs some extra explanation. The STL function `copy` takes three arguments: the first two are a pair of input iterators denoting the start and end of a range, the last is an output iterator. The effect is to copy all the items in the range to the output iterator. Here, the range covers the entire map and the output iterator is an `ostream_iterator` constructed from the output stream `fout`. The second argument to the constructor for `ostream_iterator` is a string which is written after every record, so the effect of this call of `copy` is to write each pair from the map which tabulates the slate to the output stream `fout`, following each with a newline. Objects are written to `ostream_iterator`s using `operator<<`, which I overloaded for `Record` objects.

```
ostream& operator<<(ostream& os, Record& r)
{
    os << r.first << ":" << fixed << showpoint
       << setprecision(2) << r.second;
    return os;
}
```

Each record is written out to look like an input record—handy if impecunious customers need to carry over their debts. Given the input file

```
Arthur:2.40
Bjarne:1.25
Arthur:2.40
Arthur:2.40
Orinoco:0.35
Bjarne:17.95
Arthur:2.40
Lois:1.23
```

the output

```
Arthur:9.60
Bjarne:19.20
Lois:1.23
Orinoco:0.35
```

can be produced by wrapping `process_map` in a simple main program.

```
int main()
{
    ifstream ffin("slate.dat");
    process_map(ffin, cout);
    return EXIT_SUCCESS;
}
```

The alternative way of totting up the slate is to read all the records into a sequence, sort them so that all the records for any individual customer fall together, and then scan the sorted sequence from beginning to end, totting up as you go. (It is reasonable to assume, as I did in the previous version, that the entire slate will fit into memory at once. You wouldn't stay in business long if you let it grow too big for that.)

We may as well use the same Record type. I'll use a list<Record> to hold the data. (A vector<Record> would do at least as well, since vectors are dynamic in the STL.) I'll also choose a version of the sorting routine that relies on operator< as a change from a comparison object, so I need to overload it.

```
bool operator<(Record& x, Record& y)
{ return strcmp(x.first, y.first) < 0; }
```

An istream iterator can be used to scan the data file. As each record is read, it is added to the back of the list using the member function push_back.

```
list<Record> r_list;
istream_iterator<Record>i = fin;
while (i != istream_iterator<Record>())
   r_list.push_back(*i++);
```

Lists know how to sort themselves; all that is needed is

```
r_list.sort();
```

Now we just need to scan the sorted list using an iterator. For this, a type synonym is advisable.

```
typedef list<Record>::iterator RlistIterator;
```

The loop works like this: a variable current_punter holds the value of the name most recently read. Records are read from the list; as long as the name matches current_punter, the amounts are added in to a running total. When the name changes, we know that all the transactions for that punter have been seen because the list is sorted, so a record is written to the ostream_iterator, by assigning to the object it points to. The cycle is repeated for the new name. Careful use of prefix and postfix incrementing of the list iterator makes everything work neatly.

```
RlistIterator it = r_list.begin();
ostream_iterator<Record> oi(fout, "\n");
while (it != r_list.end())
{
  Record r = *it++;
  char* current_punter = r.first;
  float total = r.second;
  Record rr = *it;
  while (it != r_list.end()
         && strcmp(rr.first, current_punter) == 0)
  {
    total += rr.second;
    rr = *++it;
```

```
        }
        oi++ = Record(current_punter, total);
    }
```

That's all there is to it...the processing must be wrapped up in a function called from a main program. The output is the same as before.

Programming with the Standard Template Library

To illustrate my point about the STL turning C++ into a different language, I will show how, using stream iterators and some of the STL algorithms, it is quite easy to set up a framework for file processing programs that allows you to use C++, in a manner reminiscent of Awk or Perl, to write short and snappy text transforming programs.

I based my program on Awk's processing model: an input file consists of records, which consist of fields. The main execution loop repeatedly reads the next record, splits it into its fields and applies the programmer's code to the record. Within a program, the fields of the current record are referred to as $1, $2...$NF, where NF is a variable magically set to the number of fields in the current record. Awk supplies built-in regular expression pattern matching, text substitution, associative tables, and a fairly conventional set of low-level control structures, all of which can be simulated in C++, for use in the programmer's code.

The only creative part in implementing such an execution loop in C++ with STL is in defining classes for records and fields. Everything else falls out after that. Feasible class definitions are shown in Figures 10.1 and 10.2.

The basic idea behind the `Record` class is to use a `vector<Field>` to hold the fields of the current record. An integer `nf` records how many of them there are. As in the slate totting program, a static array of `char` is used for record buffering—nasty limits on record sizes and the number of fields in a record ensure compatibility with real Awk implementations. By default, records are separated by newlines, but the record separator can be changed by assigning to the variable RS; the separator written between records when they are output is similarly recorded in ORS. Here, I have made both of them public static members of the `Record` class. (Awk purists will object that they should be strings, not single characters, but Awk purists won't like this program anyway.) Awk also allows you to enquire how many fields are in the current record (NF) and how many records have been read (NR). I have provided member functions for these enquiries and made the corresponding data members private, since it doesn't seem to make sense to assign to them. The field variables $1, $2...$NF have been simulated by a member function, wittily called `dollar`, which returns a reference, because Awk lets you change the value of a field by assigning to one of the $i variables.

The operator >> is a friend function. It has to do the hard work of reading a record and splitting it into fields. I use `istream::get` to read up to the record separator and then turn the C-string just read into an `istrstream` so that the task of extracting fields can be left to `operator>>` overloaded for arguments

```
class Record {
public:
  static int NR;
  static char RS;
  static char ORS;
  enum { default_max_fields = 25, max_record_size = 300 };
  Record(int max_fields = default_max_fields)
                         :the_fields(max_fields) {}
  int NF() const {  return nf; }
  Field& dollar(int n)
  {  return the_fields[n-1];  }
private:
  static char record_buffer[max_record_size];
  vector<Field> the_fields;
  int nf;
friend
  istream& operator>>(istream&, Record&);
};
```

Figure 10.1   Definition of the class Record

of type Field. Before doing any of this, I call the function erase, which is a member of the vector class and deletes any old entries in the_fields.

```
istream& operator>>(istream& is, Record& r)
{
  r.nf = 0;
  r.the_fields.erase(r.the_fields.begin(),
                     r.the_fields.end());
  is.get(Record::record_buffer, Record::max_record_size,
                                Record::RS);
  is.ignore(1, Record::RS);
  istrstream rec(Record::record_buffer);
  while (rec)
  {
    Field f;
    rec >> f;
    r.the_fields.push_back(f);
    ++r.nf;
  }
  ++Record::NR;
  return is;
}
```

Now let us turn to the definition of Field. The characters of the field will be stored in a C-string pointed to by a data member the_field. A constructor is provided to build Field objects out of C-strings; the default and copy

```
class Field {
public:
  Field():the_field(NULL) {}
  Field(const char* s);
  Field(const Field& f);
  ~Field();
  Field& operator=(const Field& f);
  static char FS;
  static char OFS;
private:
  enum { max_field_size = 55 };
  static char field_buffer[max_field_size];
  char* the_field;
  int field_length;
friend
  istream& operator>>(istream&, Field&);
friend
  ostream& operator<<(ostream&, Field&);
friend
  bool operator==(const Field&, const Field&);
friend
  bool operator!=(const Field&, const Field&);
};
```

Figure 10.2   Definition of the class `Field`

constructors, the destructor and assignment operator do all the good things described in chapter 6 to ensure that `Field` objects can be passed around and assigned in a sensible way. Public static members hold the field separator FS and the output field separator OFS. A buffer will be needed to read fields; this is a private static member `field_buffer`, whose size, and hence the maximum size of a field, is defined by a local constant. The definition of `operator>>` for `Field` objects is simple.

```
istream& operator>>(istream& is, Field& f)
{
  is.get(Field::field_buffer, Field::max_field_size, Field::FS);
  f.the_field = new char[strlen(Field::field_buffer)+1];
  strcpy(f.the_field, Field::field_buffer);
  f.field_length = is.gcount();
  is.ignore(1, Field::FS);
  return is;
}
```

It shouldn't be *that* simple. Like the input operator for records, it should perform more validity checks on the input stream. I could write the code, you could write the code, he, she or it could write the code, but we, you and they wouldn't want to read it, so I've left it out, "without loss of generality", as mathematicians like to say.

To simulate the Awk execution loop, I can use the STL function `for_each` to apply a function corresponding to the user's Awk script to each record in an `istream_iterator<Record>`. This application is wrapped up in a function that takes a pointer to a function of a suitable type and passes it on to `for_each`.

```
void run(void (*script)(Record&))
{
  for_each(istream_iterator<Record>(cin),
           istream_iterator<Record>(),
           script);
}
```

Awk programs consist of a series of actions, each associated with a condition. An action is a section of code that is applied to every record read from the input if the corresponding condition is true. C++ already has command structures that can simulate these, so simple programs to perform the kind of text processing normally done by short Awk scripts can be written as equally short C++ functions that can be passed to `run`, with perhaps a little initialization and finishing off code.

Counting the number of records in an input file can be done using a function that does nothing at all. The value of `nr` will be set as a side effect and can be printed out at the end.

```
void nullfunction(Record&) {}

int main()
{
  run(nullfunction);
  cout << Record::NR() << endl ;
  return EXIT_SUCCESS;
}
```

A program to examine the slate file from the previous examples and pick out all the entries for one particular customer can use a function that applies a suitable test to `dollar(1)`, the first field of each record. Before running this script over the input file, the field separator must be set to a colon.

```
void find_arthur(Record& r)
{
  if (r.dollar(1) == "Arthur")
    cout << r;
}

int main()
{
  Field::FS = ':';
  run(find_arthur);
  return EXIT_SUCCESS;
```

```
}
```

As a final example, here is a simple program to tabulate the data in the slate file. It assumes that the file has been sorted by customer's name—something easily achieved using the STL's built-in sorting function, whereas in Awk one would normally use an external sorting utility. A block of entries is printed, one for each customer, with the name included only on the first line. Most of the difficulty in this program lies in using stream manipulators to tabulate the data nicely. A global variable prev is used to remember the name in the previous record; a name is only printed when it does not match the value in prev. The use of globals is typical of Awk scripts.

```cpp
static Field prev = "";

void tab(Record& r)
{
  if (r.dollar(1) != prev)
  {
    cout << endl;
    prev = r.dollar(1);
  }
  else r.dollar(1) = "";

  cout << setw(10) << left << r.dollar(1)
       << fixed << showpoint
       << setprecision(2) << r.dollar(2) << endl;
}

int main()
{
  Field::FS = ':';
  run(tab);
  return EXIT_SUCCESS;
}
```

Run on a sorted version of the sample input we had before, this program will produce the following output.

```
Arthur    2.40
          2.40
          2.40
          2.40

Bjarne    1.25
          17.95

Lois      1.23

Orinoco   0.35
```

 You might like to compare this code with the following Awk program, which is based

on an example in *The AWK Programming Language* by A.V. Aho, B.W. Kernighan and
P.J. Weinberger (Addison-Wesley, 1988).

```
BEGIN  {  FS = ":"  }
{  if ($1 != prev)  {
      print ""
      prev = $1
    } else
      $1 = ""
    printf("%-10s %5.2\n", $1, $2)
}
```

The Awk output statement is less verbose, but, I would contend, no less obscure
◁ than the C++.

The STL's maps can be used to simulate the tables provided in Awk. Although not part of any standard library, there are regular expression pattern
matching and replacement routines widely available that could be used to
achieve the same effects as Awk's built-in mechanisms. It is probably not a
good idea to pursue this line too far, though. Awk encourages programming
habits such as the extensive use of global variables that are not necessary or
desirable in C++. What this example demonstrates is that the combining forms
provided by the STL algorithms and iterator types and the template mechanism
itself make it relatively easy to transform C++ from a low-level system programming language into a much higher level language, suitable for quite different
sorts of programming.

The style of programming induced by the STL will not suit everybody, and
the range of data structures supported does not provide a complete solution
to every information storage problem. There are other class libraries available,
which may suit you better. Nevertheless, the STL is part of the C++ draft standard so you can expect it to be available wherever a C++ compiler is. (That is,
approximately everywhere.) It is only prudent to be familiar with its capabilities for those occasions when it can save you some work, time or money—
whichever of these is most important to you. One cloud on the horizon is that,
since the range of data structures has gaps and since some of the interfaces are
inconvenient, commercial library vendors are designing their own conflicting
extensions to the STL, which rather destroys the point of standardization.

I have only provided a sketch of the main features of the Standard Template Library. There are many details which I have simplified or omitted, and
as the standardization process inches towards ratification the library's specification may be changed. If you intend to use the STL you should read any
documentation that came with your copy of the library.

Exceptions

11

There is a saying in compiler writing circles that "any fool can write a compiler that only handles correct input". It isn't true, of course—it takes a special kind of fool to write a C++ compiler—but it contains an important insight: when a program has to cope with events that, in some sense, aren't supposed to happen, the programmer's job becomes a great deal harder.

What sort of events, and in what sense are they "not supposed to happen"? The short and easy answer is "Oh, you know—indexes out of range, tables overflowing, running out of heap space, things like that...", and you probably do know, but perhaps we should try a little bit harder to characterize them. We can begin by analogy with a situation that may be more familiar to some of you than you would like.

Mail order suppliers of personal computer equipment have a procedure for dealing with orders an algorithm, we might call it. The prospective purchaser rings up and tells them what they want, the salesperson checks the items are in stock, takes a credit card number and dispatches the goods with an invoice. The courier delivers them next day and the delighted punter plays with their new kit and everybody is happy. Only, sometimes the equipment turns out to be faulty, and the last step in the algorithm is never reached. On closer examination, you can see that most steps in the procedure rely on certain conditions being satisfied if they are to be successful: the items must be in stock, the salesperson's computer must be up and able to handle the stock enquiry, the customer's credit card must be able to bear the cost, the courier must drive safely, and so on. If any of these conditions fails to be satisfied, the orderly progress of the transaction is disrupted. We hope and expect that a mail order supplier will be able to recover from any such disruption, for example, by sending out a replacement for a faulty keyboard. In practice, we probably all have evidence that organizations find difficulty in handling exceptional events as smoothly as ones that fall into the expected pattern. Invoking a suitable response to the problem may require intervention by the customer in the form of irate telephone calls. Attempts to revert to the established algorithm after some special action has been taken may go awry, so that, for example, customers may receive a whole series of invoices for replacements that are supposed to be free. We often judge the quality of a supplier by their ability to deal with complaints and mistakes at least as much as by the way they handle straightforward orders.

If we stand back and think in abstract terms about how a program executes, we will find a similar situation. We can begin by considering a C++ program as a series of statements to be executed in sequence. Loops and function calls mean this sequence is not linear and may not be finite, that doesn't matter. You write your program so that, in the normal course of events, execution of the sequence performs the computation you require. In general, if any individual statement is to play its part in the grand sequence, certain conditions must be satisfied before its execution. For example, if your program includes the assignment

```
y = 2/r;
```

and your intention is that, after its execution, the variable y should hold the quotient 2/r, then you are assuming, at the very least, that r is not equal to zero when the division is carried out. Similarly, the expression a[i] will only denote the ith element of a if i is greater than or equal to zero and less than the number of elements of a. The events that are not supposed to happen are those that violate the assumptions under which each statement in your program achieves its desired effect. I will call such occurrences *exceptional events*.

There are some events over which you can have no control: power failures, users pressing interrupt keys or pouring beverages into their keyboards, and other events totally external to your program. I assume that nothing can be done about these, although you may find that there are system-dependent facilities that enable you to respond to certain unprovoked external events. Exceptional events that occur inside the program can be dealt with more systematically. You may find that the quality of your programs is judged by how well you do so, at least as much as by its performance the rest of the time.

COPING WITH EXCEPTIONAL EVENTS

The possibility of exceptional events occurring presents you with a series of choices, the first being whether to let them happen or not. Since we have excluded external events beyond your control from consideration, in principle you can insert code in front of any statement depending on a non-trivial condition, to test that the condition is satisfied and only execute the statement if it is. This doesn't mean you have to sprinkle validity checks between every statement. Many statements don't depend on any pre-condition for their successful outcome, and it is often the case that satisfying the pre-condition for one statement can be shown to ensure the satisfaction of that for the next. It is believed, though not usually by C++ programmers, that there is a class of useful programs for which it can be proved that the necessary pre-conditions are always satisfied.

In the everyday world, you can't prove your programs are correct, certainly not in practice and probably not in theory, so should you insert validity checks? It sounds as if this is a set-up rhetorical question that only admits the answer

"Yes". Who would be so irresponsible as to leave out *validity checks*? Well, I might, for one, but I would only do so deliberately under certain special circumstances. Specifically, if I was writing a program that was going to be used by nobody but myself and perhaps a close associate, I knew what I was doing and I or we were prepared to live with the consequences. Although C++'s strong type checking helps prevent many potential runtime errors and exceptional events caused by erroneous program logic occurring, it is impossible to guarantee that a program will run without anything exceptional happening, so for any other case, it is necessary to insert at least some elementary validity checks if you wish to avoid the possibility of a crash. Even where the input of one program is the output of another which is known to be reliable, there is always going to be someone who tries to run it on some other input, or tinkers with the output of the first program to improve it. Tempting though it is to leave such tinkerers to their fate, it isn't very kind or professional or smart... they'll only send in a bug report.

Nearly always, then, your programs will include validity-checking code. The next question is: "What happens if a validity check fails?"—and what a good question that is! Taking the broadest view, you again have only two options: curl up and die, or don't. The easiest option is always to do as I have done in all my examples: when an exceptional event occurs, write an informative message and terminate execution. Sometimes this is too pessimistic—it may be possible to fix matters up and continue. Here we come to the interesting and difficult case, where, yet again, we can consider two possibilities.

The first possibility is to try and patch things up on the spot. If the exceptional event is detected at a point in the program where it is possible to make changes that will make the assumption which was violated valid again, then in many programs you will want to do so. An example that will probably be familiar is a function that accepts input interactively. If only certain values can legitimately be handed on to other parts of the program the function will check whatever value is provided from the keyboard and, if it is not valid, ask for another. The code always comes out so untidy, but it does what is required:

```
char yes_or_no()
{
  char c;
  cout << "Enter Y or N: ";
  cin >> c;
  while (c != 'Y' && c != 'N')
  {
    cout << "I said enter Y or N, dimwit.\nTry again: ";
    cin >> c;
  }
  return c;
}
```

It's a joke. Don't send for the HCI inspectors

I guess we've all done plenty of that sort of stuff in our time, but it's not just the character-oriented input and output that is old-fashioned. When programs are assembled out of separately written components, it is increasingly likely that a different possibility will arise: the exception cannot be fixed up at the point where it occurs. The epitome of this possibility is a range error in a range-checked array. If `MyArray<int>::operator[]` is called with an index outside the subscript range of its left hand operand, nothing can be done inside the operator function that will always be an appropriate response, because the "error" has really occurred in the calling function where the value of the duff argument was computed. Expecting every user of an array to perform a range check every time the array is accessed is unreasonable and inefficient. The check does belong inside the subscripting operation, but the response to its failure doesn't, just as it is the customer who must find out whether their new keyboard works, but the supplier who must replace it. In my examples of array classes a range error always causes immediate program termination. Imagine the frustration this could cause if the offending index had been generated as a result of a spurious signal from a sensor, which could have been reset and interrogated again, if only the program hadn't stopped, leaving a paralyzed robot, a hundred and forty two million miles from the nearest service engineer.

There are several established techniques by which a function that detects an exceptional event can communicate the fact to its caller, giving it the chance to recover. None of them is very satisfactory.

If the function returns a value, it can sometimes indicate that something has gone wrong by returning an extraordinary value that could not normally occur. Have you ever tried to do this? First find your extraordinary value. The elements of an object of type `MyArray<int>`, for example, can be used to store *any* value in the range of the type `int`; its `operator[]` returns an `int`, so any value it can return might have been stored in the array. There is no room in the range of `int` for an error indicator. You tend to resort to stretching the type system, declaring functions to return an `int` when they can only legitimately return a `char` just so that you can have them return minus one as an exception indicator. This sort of thing can seriously undermine the type relationships in your program.

The only safe way to communicate information about exceptions through a function's return value is by having every function that might detect an exceptional event return a pair comprising its real return value and a state indicator. The awkwardness and overhead of packing up the returned value in such a pair and then taking apart the package to get at the real value is almost never going to be acceptable. A popular and more practical alternative is to leave the return value alone and use a global variable as a state indicator. Sometimes, an extra reference argument could be used to hold the state information, but not, I think, for operator functions.

Once you've found an error value to return, or provided a global state indicator, and written your code so that it is set consistently, you are left with the problem of making sure that every call of your function is followed by a test of the return value or global. More precisely, you have left everybody who uses your function with that problem.

I have no doubt that somewhere there are programmers so steeped in discipline and self-control that they will always insert the necessary tests, but most of us can't be bothered to put in the tests, or forget sometimes, or reckon that the program will go twice as fast if we leave them out, and so we just hope for the best. We have to hope quite hard, because if the best fails to happen, that error value, or the undefined value that was returned when the global state indicator was set to FAIL will propagate as if it was a legitimate value, invalidating all assumptions and leading to entirely unpredictable results. Really, something better is required.

How about a nice jump? Counter-revolutionists who would rehabilitate the goto statement and overturn the reforms of Structured Programming often appeal to the needs of exceptional events to justify their demands. Jumping away from an exceptional event is superficially appealing: because the event has occurred, you can't carry on with what you were about to do; the point at which remedial action is possible is elsewhere in the program; an exception, by definition, disturbs the normal flow of control, so why not a jump?

First, a simple jump (i.e., the high level equivalent of reloading the program counter) won't do, because we need to be able to jump out of a function, so we must remove activation records from the stack until we find the one corresponding to the function we are jumping back into, and we ought to call the destructors of all the local variables in the discarded activation records.[1] We also need to be able to choose the destination of the jump dynamically. Even with a powerful enough goto to achieve all this, we would still not be able to communicate any information about the exception to the point we jumped to and would have to resort to globals if we wished to convey any. Finally, as ever, any unstructured jump facility is open to abuse.

A better solution takes the form of a new structured control statement that achieves the effect of a non-local jump, unstacking activation records and calling destructors on the way, and allows you to transmit information from the point where the exceptional event is detected to the point where it is dealt with. To minimize the potential for writing confusing or incorrect code, the control structure should maintain a clear logical connection between the code that deals with an exception and the nature of the exception that caused it to be invoked.

THROWING AND CATCHING EXCEPTIONS

The exception handling mechanism of C++ is designed to fulfil the rather tall order at the end of the last paragraph.

An exception in C++ is just an object, usually one belonging to a class specially defined to hold information about the circumstances surrounding an exceptional event. In a refreshingly non-violent metaphor, free of *double entendre*, a function that detects an exceptional event can *throw* an exception, which may be *caught* somewhere else in the program, where remedial action can be taken. To throw an exception means initiating a transfer of control, possibly requiring the unstacking of some activation records and the calling of destructors. Catching an exception means providing a destination for that transfer and initializing a variable with the object thrown as the exception.

To make this account concrete, we need some syntax and some more jar-

---

[1] In case you are a C expert and think setjmp and longjmp would do the trick, don't forget about those destructors.

gon. Throwing an exception is done using a statement resembling a return statement, except that the keyword `throw` is used instead of `return`.

```
throw expression;
```

Throwing is a much more rewarding activity if someone catches the thing you throw. Sadly, the things that catch exceptions are not called fielders, they are called *handlers*. A handler has the syntactical form

```
catch ( (type | variable-decln ) ) { statements }
```

The handler is introduced by the keyword `catch`. The typename or declaration inside the following brackets indicates the type of exceptions that this handler can catch—remember, an exception is just an object. If a variable is declared, when the handler catches an exception, it is initialized with the object that was thrown, just as if the name was that of a formal argument to a function. As with function arguments, the type can be a reference type, so that the exception variable is initialized by reference.

▷ More precisely, when a `throw` statement is executed, a temporary variable is created (somewhere) to hold the exception object, and this temporary is used to initialize
◁ the variable named in the handler.

The statements inside the curly brackets will be executed when an exception is caught by the handler. Even if there is only a single statement, the brackets are required.

A handler may also have the form

```
catch ( ... ) { statements }
```

A handler of this kind will catch exceptions of any type.

If I had thrown an exception of type `Caber`, it could be caught by any of:

```
catch (Caber the_caber)
catch (Caber& the_caber)
catch (Caber)
catch (...)
```

The first two of these forms would cause the variable `the_caber` to be initialized with the thrown object or a reference to it.

You need to arrange for your handlers to be in place to catch exceptions. You do so with a construct called a *try-block*, which is a compound statement tagged by the keyword `try` and followed by some handlers.

```
try { statements } handler { handler }
```

The effect is most easily understood from the inside out. When an exception is thrown, it will be caught by a handler in the most recently entered try-block that has one that can deal with that type of exception. That is, if the statements in a try-block include a throw, the exception will be caught by any of that try-block's handlers that can deal with it. If none can, any enclosing try-blocks in the same function are looked at from the inside outwards. If there aren't any, or a match is still not found, the activation record for the currently executing function is popped off the stack, once destructors for its locals have been called, and the search for a handler continues outwards from the point where the function was called. If no handlers are found in the caller, its locals are destroyed, its activation record is popped and the search continues in its caller, and so on. If the entire stack has to be popped and no suitable handler is ever found, a void function with no arguments called `terminate` is called. By default, it calls `abort` to terminate the program's execution without further ado.

Once the code in a handler has been executed, control passes to the statement following the try-block, unless the handler explicitly transfers control elsewhere, for example, by calling `abort`.

▷ Sometimes, a handler is only partially able to fix things up after an exception is thrown. It can do what it can and then throw the exception out again to be caught by a handler further back in the stack, using the unadorned statement

```
throw;
```

◁

My array types are crying out to be rewritten to throw exceptions instead of calling the private error functions that have been used hitherto. I first need to define classes to represent each type of exception that may occur within the member functions of `MyArray`. Both classes have a `message` member function that produces an appropriate diagnostic string, should a handler choose to use it as a dying message, and functions to return the values of their data members, which record information about the exception.

```
class BoundsError {
public:
  BoundsError(int lo, int upp) : low(lo), up(upp) {}
  const char* message() const
  {
    return "lower bound of array exceeds upper bound";
  }
  int lower() const
  {   return low;   }
  int upper() const
  {   return up;   }
private:
  const int low, up;
};

class RangeError {
public:
  RangeError(int idx, int lo, int upp)
              :index(idx), low(lo), up(upp) {}
  const char* message() const
  {
    return "array index is not in range ";
  }
  int badindex() const
```

```
  {  return index;  }
private:
  const int index, low, up;
};
```

▷ Often, a class of exceptions will only be thrown by member functions of one particular class. In such cases, it is sensible to provide public local definitions of the
  exception classes within the class that throws them. In this case we don't want to
  do that, because MyArray is a class template and we don't want separate exception
◁ classes for each class generated from it.

The calls of error functions that terminate execution can be replaced by
statements to throw exceptions with only small changes to the constructor
and the check_index function.

```
template <class alpha>
MyArray<alpha>::MyArray(int lower,  int upper, alpha initial)
{
  lower_bound = lower;
  upper_bound = upper;
  if (lower > upper)
    throw BoundsError(lower_bound, upper_bound);
  else
  {
     as before
  }
}

template <class alpha>
void MyArray<alpha>::check_index(int i) const
{
  if (the_array == NULL)
    throw DeletedError();
  if (i < lower_bound || i > upper_bound)
    throw RangeError(i, lower_bound, upper_bound);
}
```

Meanwhile, on the surface of Mars, there is a robot. To orient itself, this
robot must periodically take readings from an array of digital sensors. The
robot's designers know that every legitimate sensor reading is a whole number
lying between a pair of known values, designated sensor_min and sensor_max.
Any reading outside the range sensor_min...sensor_max must be a spurious
signal caused by a sensor malfunction. Such malfunctions are relatively rare
and usually only transient. Inside the robot's control software, a count is kept
of the number of occurrences of each discrete value that may be read from a
sensor. The template class MyArray<int>, generated from MyArray, is being
used to record these counts. After the values of the whole sensor array have
been read, the array of counts is passed to another function that carries out
a co-extension analysis of the field flux parameters obtained. If a sensor fault

causes a spurious value to be read, an attempt will be made to increment a non-existent array element. With `MyArray` as it is now re-written, this will cause an exception to be thrown. We must arrange for it to be caught and the offending sensor reset. We will keep a count of the number of times sensors are reset; if it exceeds a preset limit, it looks as though the sensor array has a serious fault. We all know that any fault can be cured by re-routing the primary EPS circuits, so we will do that and make another attempt. Naturally, if the re-routing fails, we will be obliged to switch to the secondary systems, but once that has been done we will have no further recourse and any sensor fault will be fatal.

You can learn a lot about Science by watching Star Trek TNG

We begin by defining some constants.

```
const int sensor_min = -5;      minimum and maximum sensor readings
const int sensor_max = +5;
const int sensor_count = 10;    number of sensors in array
const int max_exceptions = 4;   maximum allowable exceptions
```

Assume definitions to go with the following function declarations

```
void co_analyze(const MyArray<int>& ma);    perform the
                                            co-extension analysis
int read_sensor(const int i);    obtain and return the reading from
                                 sensor i
void reset_sensor(int i);     reset sensor i
void re_route(float percent);     reroute percent% of the circuits
void secondaries();    switch to secondary systems
```

In the absence of exception handlers, a function to read the sensors and record the flux parameters could be written as follows:

```
void read_flux()
{
  MyArray<int> flux_parameters(sensor_min, sensor_max, 0);
  int i = 0;
  while (i < sensor_count)
  {
    ++flux_parameters[read_sensor(i)];
    ++i;
  }
  co_analyze(flux_parameters);
}
```

If this function was called in a straightforward way, without any try-block, any range error resulting from spurious sensor readings would cause the program to halt with an uncaught exception. To prevent this doleful occurrence we must add try-blocks, with handlers to perform the recovery actions just outlined. Something must be done about the possibility of too many sensor errors being detected. I will count the number of times `reset_sensor` is called, and if it exceeds the limit I will throw another exception. I need to define a class for that purpose. The definition is at file level.

```
class SensorFault {
public:
```

```
    SensorFault(int n): fault_count(n) {};
    float rate() const
    {   return (100.0*fault_count)/sensor_count; }
  private:
    int fault_count;
};
```

The class holds the count of faults detected, and has a function to return it as a percentage of the size of the sensor array, to guide the re-routing process.

The `read_flux` function now looks like this:

```
void read_flux()
{
  int ex_count = 0;
  MyArray<int> flux_parameters(sesnor_min, sensor_max, 0);
  int i = 0;
  while (i < sensor_count)
  {
    try
    {
      ++flux_parameters[read_sensor(i)];
      ++i;
    }
    catch (RangeError&)
    {
      reset_sensor(i);
      ++ex_count;
      if (ex_count == max_exceptions)
        throw SensorFault(ex_count);
    }
  }
  co_analyze(flux_parameters);
}
```

Because the increment of i is done after the call to `read_sensor` which might throw the exception, the offending sensor will be read again after being reset.

Since `read_flux` can throw an exception I want to surround its call with a try-block. The handler for `SensorFault` must re-route the sensors using an al-

Yes I know gorithm based on the percentage failure rate passed in the exception object and
it's always read the flux again. The new call to `read_flux` from the handler lies outwith
the same. the try-block, so what happens if the sensor array fails and throws a `Sensor-Fault` exception again? It will not be trapped by this handler. According to the scenario, a second occurrence of sensor failure should cause control to switch to the secondaries. We can put a try-block round the first try-block and equip it with a handler to achieve this end.

```
void run()
{
  try
  {
    try
```

```
      { read_flux(); }
      catch (SensorFault& sf)
      {
        re_route(sf.rate());
        read_flux();
      }
    }
    catch(SensorFault&)
    {
      secondaries();
      read_flux();
    }
  }
```

If a `SensorFault` exception is thrown after we have switched to secondaries, we are doomed. I will surround the call of `run` with a try-block and a handler that sends a message back to Earth (`cerr`). I will add a catch-all handler in case my logic is awry and any other exception is thrown.

```
try
{ run(); }
catch(SensorFault&)
{
  cerr << "Damn! Irrecoverable sensor fault" << endl;
}
catch(...)
{
  cerr << "Surprising internal error" << endl;
}
```

The Methodology Police have asked me to say a few words at this point on the subject of exception abuse. It is understandable that programmers faced with the complexities of today's software systems and bewildered by the vast number of choices that C++ presents them with will sometimes be tempted to seek an easy way out. Escaping your responsibilities through exceptions may seem like an easy way out. You don't know how to cope? Throw an exception and let someone else handle it. Can't work out how to formulate the right loop condition? Throw an exception when you want to get out. We shouldn't dwell on this sort of behaviour, but it won't help to avert our eyes from a growing menace. Here is a case that is far from uncommon.

```
int sum(const MyArray<int>& ma)
{
  int n = 0, i = ma.lwb();
  try
  {
    while (true)
      n += ma[i++];
  }
  catch (RangeError)
  { return n; }
```

```
    return 0;
}
```

A sad sight and easy to condemn, but exception abuse can take more subtle and insidious forms. Did I really need to throw that `SensorFault` exception earlier? Could I not have patched things up on the spot and resumed with a conventional control structure? Hasn't the code become obscure and convoluted with those nested try-blocks and their handlers? Can I really control this thing?

Using them for kicks in private is something else

Exceptions should not be used as an easy escape route from tricky situations. Exceptions can make reasoning about your code easier if they are reserved for genuinely exceptional events, but if they are used routinely as loop exits or multi-level returns they become little more than fancy `goto`s, with all the attendant obscurity and instability. And if you use an exception as a superficially nifty way of transferring control under normal circumstances, what have you got left to deal with exceptional events?

Unfortunately for the writers of homilies and sermons, reducing practices to the category of "abuse" and condemning them is not an adequate response to a complex situation. It is easy to say that "exceptions should be exceptional" and that "exception handling should be error handling", but the concepts of error and exceptional event are elusive ones. If I have written my robot's software so that spurious sensor readings don't cause a crash, why is a spurious reading any more of an error than a valid one is? In either case, specific code has been written to cope with it. You might appeal to statistics and say that exceptional events are those that happen relatively rarely. And yet, in a compiler, syntax errors might reasonably be considered exceptional events, even though a compiler will detect errors on more runs than it doesn't. An empty queue would not seem to be an exceptional event, but what if the queue was used as a communication channel between two processes executing quasi-synchronously in such a way that you knew an item should always be placed in the queue by one process before any attempt was made to remove it by the other?

As you probably know from experience, handling exceptional events is difficult, no matter what language facilities and programming techniques you employ. Exceptions, try-blocks and handlers don't make it any easier. Using them effectively to produce robust readable code that is easy to maintain calls for considerable skill and judgement. It may help if you bear one more thing in mind: exceptions are an inefficient way of transferring control in a program. Their implementations are designed on the assumption that throwing an exception will be a relatively rare occurrence. You would do well to minimize the use of exceptions, for this reason if for no other.

ORGANIZING EXCEPTIONS

If an exception is thrown but not caught, the program will crash reasonably gracefully and you will hardly be in any better a position than you would have been if the exceptional event itself had caused an immediate crash. Therefore, if you want to prevent crashes caused by events inside code that throws exceptions, you must provide handlers for all the types of exception that might be thrown. This is a bit tough: it not only means that you must meticulously read the documentation of any library to find out what exceptions it throws, it means that, if a new release of the library adds another type of exception, you must add a new handler and recompile all your code that uses it.

Leastways, that would be the case if the writers of the library in question had not used inheritance to organize their exception classes. If, on the other hand, every class of exception thrown by a particular library is derived from a common base class, guaranteeing that your code will not drop a catch is much easier. The resemblance between the declaration that appears in brackets after the `catch` keyword and a formal argument's declaration is more than syntactic. Exception variables are initialized in the same way as function arguments, so a handler for a base class of exceptions will also catch exceptions of any class derived from that base.

When I added exceptions to my array classes, I should have begun by defining a base class

```
class ArrayError {
public:
  virtual const char* message() const = 0;
};
```

My specific exceptions would be derived classes that overrode the pure virtual function `message`.

```
class RangeError: public ArrayError ...
class BoundsError: public ArrayError ...
```

A handler introduced by

```
catch (ArrayError& ae)
```

would catch any exception of type `RangeError` or `BoundsError` and could access the exception's error string as `ae.message()`, taking advantage of having caught the exception by reference to invoke the right virtual function.

When a handler is being sought to catch an exception, the handlers attached to a try-block are considered in turn, in the order they appear. Therefore, if you want to provide some specific actions for certain types of exception only, the handlers for the derived classes corresponding to those exceptions should appear before the handler for any base class they are derived from. (Similarly, any handlers that name a type of exception should appear before a handler with three dots.) Even if you want to provide specific handlers for each derived exception class it is a good idea to put a handler for the base class after them to ensure you catch any new exceptions that might be added in a later version of the throwing code.

As an instructive example of how exception classes can be organized, Figure 11.1 is a schematic representation of the hierarchy of exception classes defined for use by functions and classes in the C++ standard library.[2] Derived

---

[2]Beware of old library versions. You may find a hierarchy of classes all having names beginning with the letter x, derived from a base class called xmsg. This arrangement is obsolete.

```
exception
    logic_error
        domain_error
        invalid_argument
        length_error
        out_of_range
    runtime_error
        range_error
        overflow_error
    failure
    bad_alloc
```

Figure 11.1   Standard exceptions

classes are shown indented below their base classes. You ought to be familiar with these exception classes so that you can catch exceptions thrown from within the standard library.

At the base of the hierarchy is the imaginatively named class `exception`. It has a default and a copy constructor and an assignment operator, so exceptions can be created and copied. Its distinctive member function is declared as

```
virtual const char* what() const;
```

The contents of the string it returns are implementation-dependent, but presumably they are of an informative nature concerning the event that caused the exception to be thrown. The `what` function is overridden in classes derived from `exception` to provide specific information about specific types of exceptional event.

A distinction is made between logical errors, runtime errors and input/output failures. Failure to meet a request for heap space is treated separately; I will look at exceptions and space allocation later. Logical errors are, in theory, preventable by suitable checks inserted in the program. It may not be feasible to insert these checks, perhaps because of information hiding, or it may be felt preferable to allow the errors to occur and rely on exceptions to recover from them. Runtime errors are genuinely unpredictable in advance and leave no alternative to runtime error handling. The distinction is perhaps a bit arbitrary, as consideration of the types of errors placed under these headings will show.

The exception classes have self-explanatory names: `logic_error` and the classes derived from it correspond to logical errors; runtime errors are represented by the classes derived from `runtime_error`; failures in input and output operations by `failure`; and heap exhaustion by `bad_alloc`. It should be noted that an `overflow_error` exception will not be thrown automatically if hardware detects an overflow fault. It may be that such a fault will cause an interrupt and that the interrupt handler may set things up so that an exception can be thrown, but exceptions cannot be thrown safely from within interrupt handlers.

In order to take account of `exception::what`'s being virtual, handlers should be written to catch library exceptions by reference. For example, if you wanted to catch any exception thrown from the standard library and diagnose it accurately, you could write the program by putting everything that you would have put in `main` in another function, say `real_main`, and using a try-block as the body of `main` itself, with a handler that caught `exception` objects by reference.

```
int main()
{
  try { return real_main(); }
  catch (exception& e)
  { cerr << e.what() << endl; }
  return EXIT_FAILURE;
}
```

A class with a virtual function returning an error message as a string provides a minimal interface for a hierarchy of exception classes. The very least a handler will want to do is print a message and give up. Normally you will be able to augment such a function with others specific to the exception in question, but you should always aim to provide the minimum.

▷ A further aid to organizing exceptions and handlers takes the form of annotations that may be added to function declarations, specifying which classes of exception that function may throw. The argument list in a function declaration may be followed by `throw` and a list of exception types in brackets, for example

```
void read_flux() throw(SensorFault)
```

The specification is part of the declaration of, and hence the interface to, the function, making it easier for the user of a library to determine which exceptions must be caught. A function with no throw specification may throw any exception; one with an empty list in the brackets may not throw any.

The weakness of these specifications is that they are only checked at runtime. If an exception not in the list is thrown from within a function, the function `unexpected` is called. By default, this calls `terminate`. (Presumably, if it was possible to check at compile-time that no unexpected exception was thrown, it would be equally possible to determine automatically which exceptions could be thrown, so the specification would be redundant anyway.) ◁

LIVING WITH EXCEPTIONS

Now that exceptions are part of C++, your programming practice must take account of the possibility of their being thrown. In particular, the possibility of abrupt non-local transfers of control means that you have to be very particular about how to allocate and release system resources, if you are to be sure that everything will always be cleaned up and put away tidily.

Space Allocation

Everybody knows it can happen, but nobody likes to think about it much: the drunk driver on the wrong side of the road, the engine bursting into flames on take-off, the call to new that cannot find enough space on the heap. When I mentioned the possibility in chapter 4, I told you that normally the program is terminated. My bringing up the subject again in this chapter should suggest that the full story involves exception throwing, and so it does.

If the heap becomes used up so that space to create an object cannot be found when new is called, an exception of type bad_alloc is thrown. What happens then is up to you. If the exception is not caught anywhere, the program will indeed terminate. Whether it is useful to catch the exception depends on how you are organizing space allocation and de-allocation in your program and on the runtime environment. If you have managed to cobble together a limited form of garbage collection, a bad_alloc exception could trigger it, for example. If your system allows you to expand the memory region allocated to your program as it runs, a handler for bad_alloc might try to do so. Generally, handlers for space allocation exceptions will be most effective if you have taken control of the allocation and deletion operators yourself, as described in chapter 12.

▷ Before exceptions were added to C++, a different strategy was needed for dealing with exhaustion of the heap. The default implementation of operator new would return zero (i.e., a null pointer) if it failed to find any space. This led to much code like

```
root = new TreeNode;
if (!root)
{
  cout << "!!Out of memory, giving up" << endl;
  abort();
}
```

(and also much code that omitted the test and worked fine…until it didn't).

This default behaviour could be modified. By calling a library function called set_new_handler, taking as its argument a pointer to a void function with no arguments, a programmer could set the value of a function, confusingly called a *new handler*, which would be called after operator new had tried and failed to find some memory. The new handler could terminate the program or take some positive action to find more memory, just as a handler for a bad_alloc exception would do now. If the new handler returned, another attempt would be made to find the requested memory. It was only when the new handler was null, as it was by default, that a null pointer was returned.

The relevance of this is that you might find that your C++ system still behaves in the old way. If it nevertheless supports exceptions, it is very easy to persuade it to behave the way the draft standard says it should, by setting a new handler that throws an exception. (You may have to provide your own definition of the bad_alloc class.) First define a function of the right type.

```
void new_thrower()
{  throw bad_alloc(); }
```

then, at the beginning of main, set the handler function.

```
set_new_handler(new_thrower);
```

◁

Constructors and Destructors

If an exception is thrown and causes activation records to be popped off the stack, you are assured that destructors will be called for all objects stored in discarded activation records, which is to say, all the locals of all the functions which are prematurely terminated. Only objects have destructors; if a function allocates any resource that is not associated with an object, it will not be correctly released.

Consider, for example, the programming idiom known as a "frame" in Macintosh circles, which consists of some code bracketed by statements to save and restore some component of the graphic state. For example, a function to send some graphic output to a graphic port associated with a window would take the form of a "port frame". If the low level toolbox routines were used for this purpose, it would take this form:

```
void g(WindowPtr w)
{
  GrafPtr save_port;        save the old state
  GetPort(&save_port);
  SetPort(w);       set up the new

    do the graphics output to w
  SetPort(save_port);       restore original state
}
```

(I don't intend to go into details of Macintosh toolbox programming here. I hope the general idea is clear.)

If an exception is thrown while g is performing its output and not caught inside the function body, the statement SetPort(save_port) will never be executed, and when the program continues after the handler, output may go to the wrong window.

To prevent such an accident, the state should be saved by the constructor of a local variable and restored by its destructor. We need a special class to do the saving and restoring with a data member to keep the old state in.

```
class PortSaver {
public:
  PortSaver()  {  GetPort(&save_port); }
  ~PortSaver()  {  SetPort(save_port); }
private:
  GrafPtr save_port;
}
```

Now a function with a port frame can look like this.

```
void g(WindowPtr w)
{
  PortSaver s_p;
  SetPort(w);
   do the graphics output to w
}
```

The original state is saved in `s_p.save_port` when the default constructor for `PortSaver` is called to initialize `s_p` on entry to g. The state is restored when `s_p` is destroyed as control returns from g, whether normally or as a result of throwing an exception.

One of the places where it is worthwhile making sure that resources are allocated in a constructor is…in a constructor. This is not as paradoxical as it sounds. Remember that constructors typically initialize the data members of the object being constructed. Like local variables of a function, data members can hold resources that must be released—most commonly, but not exclusively, they are pointers to heap storage. Destructors will usually release these resources. What happens, then, if a constructor throws an exception?

If an exception is thrown before a constructor finishes its work, it is not going to be sensible—it may be disastrous—to call the destructor on the partially constructed object. Instead, something that *is* sensible is done: destructors are called for every member whose constructor has been executed when the exception is thrown. This isn't going to help you with, for example, a pointer to a heap object, though. Pointer types don't have destructors; they must be explicitly deleted in order to cause a destructor to be called on the object they point to, and to free the space it occupies.

To make sure that everything is cleaned up and tidy after an exception is thrown in a constructor, you must make sure that every data member has a destructor. Putting this another way, you must put all your pointers to dynamically allocated storage and other resources that must be released inside classes that do nothing but allocate and release those resources.

Consider, for example, the `WebPage` class from chapter 6. It has two pointer members, both initialized in the constructor by calls to new (see page 137). If the second fails and throws an exception that is not caught immediately, the space allocated for `the_machine` will never be reclaimed. To ensure that it is, we can define a class with a single data member, the actual pointer, which is initialized by its constructor and deleted by its destructor. For example, I might define the following class (privately within `WebPage`).

```
class CharPtr {
public:
  CharPtr(): the_ptr(NULL) {}
  CharPtr(int n): the_ptr(new char[n]) {}
  CharPtr(const CharPtr& p);
  ~CharPtr()
  {
    delete [] the_ptr;
  }
```

```
    CharPtr& operator=(const CharPtr& p);
    char* the_ptr;
};
```

(The copy constructor and assignment operator have the usual sort of definitions.)

The data members of WebPage are of type CharPtr. If the original assignment

```
the_machine = new char[i+1];
```

is replaced by

```
the_machine = CharPtr(i + 1);
```

everything appears to work as before. In fact, the_machine is first initialized by the default constructor for CharPtr, then updated by its assignment operator. At all times it is a valid CharPtr object, so if an exception is thrown at any point, the destructor will be invoked and will do whatever is necessary. In particular, if an exception is thrown after the assignment, the string the_machine.the_ptr will be deleted.

Perhaps this strikes you as a lot of trouble to reclaim a little heap space on rare occasions, and so it is. The technique can be applied to any resource acquired in a constructor, though, and for some, for example locks on shared devices, it is important that destruction be accomplished in an orderly manner, even under exceptional circumstances.

▷ My example is a little bit too glib. Getting the semantics of a pointer-holding class like CharPtr right if you want to be able to assign such objects and return them from functions without ending up with shared pointers is quite tricky, especially if you also want to overload operators * and -> to make a smart pointer class. The draft C++ standard library defines a class template auto_ptr<class I>, which is intended as an abstraction of such classes. Who knows? By the time you read this
◁ someone may have sorted out how it should behave.

Finally, what happens if a destructor throws an exception? Normally, nothing special, the exception is treated like any other. However, if the exception was thrown from a destructor that was being executed while activation records were being popped because an exception had already been thrown, terminate is called.

▷ If you don't like what terminate does by default—call abort—you can substitute your own function in its place, by calling a library function declared as

```
PFV set_terminate(PFV);
```

where the name PFV is a type synonym for a pointer to a void function with no arguments:

```
typedef void(*PFV)();
```

Your substitute function must be of this type. It must never return to its caller, but must indeed terminate execution somehow or other.

Similarly, if you don't like the behaviour of the function `unexpected`, which is called when a function throws an exception that is not on the list of exceptions it admits it may throw, you can replace it using `set_unexpected` in the same way. Your unexpected function should never return either.

◁ Both `set_terminate` and `set_unexpected` return the previous value of the corresponding function as their result, allowing you to save and restore them.

Further and More

12

And some stay to the end and have to hear all the stories and know *everything*.

MULTIPLE INHERITANCE

Lois Lane and Clark Kent are discussing multiple inheritance, as young people will when they need something to take their minds off their complicated personal relationships.

CLARK   I never actually *lied* to you. I just... omitted to mention certain things.

LOIS   Like how a derived class can have *more than one* base class?

CLARK   That *is* one thing.

LOIS   (*Brightly*) Well, you can tell me now.

CLARK   It's just a simple generalization...

LOIS   No it's not! Inheritance is useful because it's simple: if A is derived from B it means that every A object is a kind of B object. If A can be derived from B *and* C, what does that mean? Inheritance has got to have a tree structure; arbitrary digraphs don't make sense.

CLARK   Digraphs?

LOIS   Directed graphs. You know, points connected by arrows. Networks.

CLARK   *I* know. (*Shamefaced*) I just didn't think *you* knew.

LOIS   I may know more than you think I do. Anyway, what *is* your multiple inheritance a model of?

CLARK   Well, when something is a kind of this *and* a kind of that, say.

LOIS   (*Puzzled*) Such as?

CLARK   Such as... such as a toy truck. A toy truck is a kind of toy and it's a kind of truck.

LOIS   (*Incredulous*) You think a toy truck is a kind of truck?

311

CLARK   Sure…it's got four wheels and a body and…and an engine. (*Sheepish*) Maybe.

LOIS   Maybe. Can you do the things to it you can do to a truck? Can you fill it with furniture and drive it across town? All you can do with a toy truck is play with it. Maybe you should.

CLARK   OK, OK…Then what about the duck-billed platypus?

LOIS   *What* about the duck-billed platypus?

CLARK   The duck-billed platypus is an oviparous mammal—it lays eggs but, apart from that, it has all the characteristics of a mammal: it suckles its young, it has fur, it's warm-blooded…

LOIS   Everybody knows that. So what?

CLARK   So, suppose you built a class hierarchy to model the classification of animals. You could start by defining two sub-classes, oviparous and viviparous, for animals that laid eggs or gave birth to live young. Mammals would be a sub-class of viviparous and platypuses a sub-class of mammal, but platypuses lay eggs…

LOIS   So platypus should be a sub-class of oviparous, too. Is that what you're saying?

CLARK   Right—multiple inheritance!

LOIS   Wrong—an example of a wrongly constructed hierarchy. Some mammals, namely platypuses, lay eggs, so mammal shouldn't be derived from viviparous. In fact, all you've shown is that oviparous/viviparous is not a good basis for classification. *Precisely* because it puts platypuses into two different classes.

CLARK   Erm…perhaps that wasn't a good example, but you have to concede that things can belong to more than one category. Take me, for instance. I belong to the class of mild-mannered bespectacled reporters, and…

LOIS   (*Interested*) Yes?

CLARK   …and, uh, to the class of…coffee drinkers.

LOIS   Aren't you getting a bit desperate? Those two classes don't belong to the same domain. For any practical purpose, only one of them could be of interest. Unless, of course, every mild-mannered bespectacled reporter drank coffee, but then you'd be back with good old-fashioned single inheritance. But, *even if* I was to grant you that some situations might be modelled by multiple inheritance, I still wouldn't want to, because of paradoxes. Don't you know about the King of Siam's elephants?

CLARK   No, but I'm sure you can tell me about them.

LOIS   Every elephant is grey. Every present given to the King of Siam must be white. So what colour is an elephant that you give to the King of Siam as a present? (*Looks perkily triumphant, in an irritating way.*)

CLARK   But it isn't true.

LOIS   (*Deflated*) What isn't true?

CLARK   That every present given to the King of Siam must be white. It's just a set-up. It isn't even a logical paradox, because you can always conclude that the set of elephants given to the King of Siam as presents is empty. Which isn't a problem, because there's no such country as Siam any more.

LOIS   (*Not without a hint of petulance*) This is a stupid conversation. Multiple inheritance isn't anything to do with philosophy or classification. We might as well start saying method*ology* when we mean method, if we're going to bring all that stuff in. Multiple inheritance is just a method of organizing programs. And *I* don't think it's a very good one.

CLARK   Yes it is.

LOIS   No it isn't.

CLARK   Is.

LOIS   Isn't.

CLARK   Listen...I found a good example in this software catalogue. (*Picks up glossy catalogue and begins to read.*) "MegaProg's Popup directory lets you view the contents of a directory just like a popup menu.[1] This easy-to-use navigation aid..."

LOIS   OK, I get the picture.

CLARK   Now, suppose you want to implement something like that.

LOIS   As ace investigative reporters will.

CLARK   You start with established classes directory and menu, and then a popup directory is a kind of directory and it's a kind of menu.

LOIS   No it isn't. It's a kind of menu that has a directory as a data member.

CLARK   But wait. "View directories hierarchically up to sixteen levels deep."

LOIS   Why not seventeen? Are they amateurs or what?

CLARK   Maybe, but if you have hierarchical menus, you're saying that menus can contain other menus. So, if a menu is made up of menu item objects, you need a class of...I don't know, menu item menus, to represent menus that can appear as items in other menus. The menu item menu class must be derived from menu *and* from menu item.

LOIS   Just derive menu from menu item—then any menu can appear in any other. Full generality, no multiple inheritance.

CLARK   But what if you are given separate menu and menu item classes and you want to combine them afterwards?

LOIS   Aha! Now we have it—multiple inheritance is for patching up faulty program structures. Come to think of it, that fits in with your other examples.

---

[1] Any resemblance to any real software product is unintended.

CLARK It doesn't have to be a question of "patching up". If you've got multiple inheritance, you can use it to combine features from lots of small classes so you avoid having to add things to any one class to cope with all the possible uses it may be put to.

LOIS That begins to sound sensible at last.

CLARK It's called the "mix-in" style.

LOIS (*Looks at him suspiciously*) Why?

CLARK It's *supposed* to be evocative. I actually read in one of Bjarne Stroustrup's books that it originates with the practice of adding nuts, raisins, gummy bears, cookies, etc. to ice cream in an ice cream shop somewhere near MIT.

LOIS Sounds absolutely revolting.

CLARK Mmm, you could have a point when it comes to ice cream...

LOIS (*Dreamily*) Double chocolate...

CLARK ...but it's just an analogy. You use multiple inheritance to put together features from a selection. Actually, iostreams can be done like that, you know.

LOIS Nope. I didn't know.

CLARK Yes. You start with a base class, stream. Actually, you don't, it's more complicated than that, but let's pretend you do.

LOIS (*Beginning to get bored.*) Must we?

CLARK (*Carrying on regardless.*) *And* you derive two classes, istream and ostream, for doing input and output. Then you find you need streams that you can both read to and write from, so you define iostream as a sub-class of both istream and ostream.[2]

LOIS (*Decidedly unimpressed.*) You've just done it upside-down. Each of istream and ostream is a specialization of iostream, so iostream should be the base and you can derive istream and ostream by single inheritance.

CLARK Uh, well, it not really that simple...

LOIS No? Well, it's not that simple the way you've done it. If istream and ostream are both derived from stream, and iostream is derived from both of them, then iostream is indirectly derived from stream twice, so in practical terms every iostream object will contain two stream sub-objects. Which is ...ridiculous.

CLARK (*Impatiently.*) Don't you think maybe that little problem has been thought of? You can declare stream as a virtual base class...

LOIS "Virtual" again?

CLARK ...and you only end up with one stream sub-object in each iostream.

---

[2]Clark's information is out of date, see chapter 8.

LOIS   And what happens when your virtual base classes get involved with virtual functions?

EDITOR   (*Faintly.*) Help, help! I'm drowning in a vat of silly dialogue.

CLARK   (*Picking up this cry for help with his super hearing.*) Uh...I have to rush off right now and...uh...witness somebody's will. Several of them. I'll be right back. (*Rushes off.*)

LOIS   Not again. I suppose that means it's time for me to fall off the top of another tall building...

Technical Details

Multiple inheritance has been the subject of much debate and controversy, both in the abstract, as a feature of object-oriented programming in general, and in the particular guise in which it appears in C++. Right now, though, multiple inheritance is a feature of C++, it is not going to be removed, and it is being used, especially to construct class libraries intended to be used in a mix-in style. Even if you are convinced by the arguments against multiple inheritance you may find yourself using it, so you had better know how multiple inheritance works in C++.

Syntactically, everything *is* very simple. We already know that when you declare a class derived from a base class you put the base class's name, preceded by one of the qualifiers `public` or `private` (or even `protected`) after a colon which follows the derived class's name. If there is more than one base class, you just put a list of base class names with qualifiers, separated by commas. That is, the syntax of a class declaration is:

```
class name [ : qualifier name {, qualifier name }]
{ member-declarations };
```

Each *qualifier* is `public`, `protected` or `private`; single inheritance is just a special case of multiple inheritance (as is no inheritance). It is quite legitimate and sometimes useful to mix public and private base classes. Protected base classes are still a mystery.

Multiple inheritance tends to be most useful in fairly complex systems. Rather than drag in extraneous details or produce unconvincing small examples, in this section I have mainly stuck to schematic outlines of the classes involved, in the hope that you can extrapolate from these. An unconvincing small example can be found in the next section.

Leaving aside Lois's objections, let's consider that class of popup directories, which have the properties of both directories and menus. Putting it another way, popup directories constitute the intersection of the classes of directories and menus—they are the things that can behave like both. Assuming that classes `Directory` and `Menu` already exist, the class `PopUpDirectory` should have both of them as public base classes.

```
class PopUpDirectory: public Directory, public Menu {
    members unique to PopUpDirectory
};
```

Alternatively, you may want a popup directory to behave like a menu and to be implemented like a directory. In that case, the derivation from `Directory` is private.

```
class PopUpDirectory: private Directory, public Menu {
    members unique to PopUpDirectory
};
```

In either case, a `PopUpDirectory` object has all the data members and member functions of both a `Directory` and a `Menu` object, as well as any members declared in the `PopUpDirectory` class itself. Access to inherited members depends on the qualifiers, exactly as it does when there is only one base class. If both bases are public, public members of `Directory` and `Menu` can always be accessed through a `PopUpDirectory` object; if `Directory` is a private base class, its public members can only be accessed through a `PopUpDirectory` object within the scope of the `PopUpDirectory` class.

▷ As ever, if you omit the qualifier, it defaults to `private`. The omission is ill-advised: if you write

```
class PopUpDirectory: public Directory, Menu {
    members unique to PopUpDirectory
};
```

you may know what you mean, but you have to admit that it looks as though you have specified a list of public base classes. You haven't. ◁

A pointer or reference to a derived class can be used whenever a pointer or reference to any of its accessible base classes is specified. For example, if both of `PopUpDirectory`'s base classes are public, a `PopUpDirectory` object can be passed to either of these functions:

```
void menu_f(const Menu& mp);
void dir_f(const Directory& dp);
```

Virtual functions work just as you would hope and expect. Abandoning for a moment all pretence that this example has anything to do with reality, suppose that the base classes were defined like this:

```
class Menu {
public:
  Menu(const string& n):menu_name(n) {}
  void p_menu() const
  {   cout << menu_name ;   }
  virtual void mf() const
  {
    cout << "A menu ";
    p_menu();
    cout << endl;
  }
private:
  string menu_name;
};
```

```
class Directory {
public:
  Directory(const string& n):dir_name(n) {}
  void p_dir() const
  { cout << dir_name; }
  virtual void df() const
  {
    cout << "A directory ";
    p_dir();
    cout << endl;
  }
private:
  string dir_name;
};
```

Suppose PopUpDirectory overrides both of the virtual functions.

```
class PopUpDirectory: public Directory, public Menu {
public:
  PopUpDirectory(const string& m, const string& d):
    Directory(d), Menu(m) {}
  void mf() const
  { pudf(); }
  void df() const
  { pudf(); }
private:
  void pudf() const
  {
    cout << "A PUD ";
    p_dir();
    cout << "/";
    p_menu();
    cout << endl;
  }
};
```

Finally, assume that menu_f and dir_f each call the appropriate virtual function.

```
void menu_f(const Menu& mp)
{ mp.mf(); }

void dir_f(const Directory& dp)
{ dp.df(); }
```

The following program

```
int main()
{
  PopUpDirectory pud("PM", "PD");
  Menu m("MMM");
  Directory d("DDD");
```

```
        menu_f(m);
        menu_f(pud);
        dir_f(d);
        dir_f(pud);
        return EXIT_SUCCESS;
    }
```

produces this output:

```
A menu MMM
A PUD PD/PM
A directory DDD
A PUD PD/PM
```

It can sometimes be helpful to draw diagrams of the relationships between derived and base classes, with arrows running from derived classes to base classes. In keeping with computer science tradition, these diagrams are usually drawn upside down, with the bases at the top (just as trees have their roots at the top and leaves at the bottom). The diagram for a `PopUpDirectory` is shown in Figure 12.1.

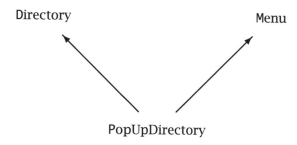

Figure 12.1   Multiple base classes

It is also sometimes helpful to imagine an object of a derived class as containing sub-objects of each base class, so, for example, a `PopUpDirectory` object contains within itself a `Directory` and a `Menu`. These sub-objects are parts of the complete object, not members. (Using set notation, we would say the relation holding between sub-objects and objects is ⊂ not ∈.) Thinking about sub-objects and drawing diagrams can help you understand some of the difficulties associated with multiple inheritance. In particular, there is this business of virtual base classes.

If the contents of a directory are normally displayed in a window, as they are on a Macintosh, for example, it would be quite natural for both `Directory` and `Menu` to be derived from a common base class, say `InterfaceComponent`. The derivation would be indirect most probably but we'll ignore that and assume we have

```
class Menu: public InterfaceComponent ...
```

```
class Directory : public InterfaceComponent ...
```

Since class `PopUpDirectory` is derived from both `Menu` and `Directory`, it is indirectly derived from `InterfaceComponent` twice. Graphically, the situation looks like Figure 12.2.

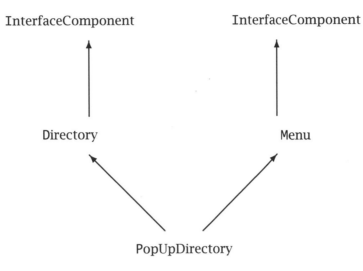

Figure 12.2 Duplicated bases

If you believe that public inheritance is a way of modelling the relationship embodied in the phrase "is a kind of" then this situation is weird: a `PopUpDirectory` is a kind of `InterfaceComponent` twice, or, perhaps more accurately, in two ways. If you forget about that and just think about sub-objects you will sometimes find that this situation is useful. Say, for example, that the `InterfaceComponent` class includes a link field, used by an interface manager routine to maintain lists of displayed objects. With two sub-objects, a `PopUpDirectory` could be on two lists at the same time—say a list of menus available and a list of open directories.

More likely, you won't want duplicate sub-objects. To prevent duplication you use the keyword `virtual` as an additional qualifier when you declare a base class, thus:

```
class Directory: virtual public InterfaceComponent ...
class Menu: virtual public InterfaceComponent ...
```

The effect is that, whenever an object has both `Directory` and `Menu` sub-objects, there will only be one shared `InterfaceComponent` sub-object. Graphically, the situation can be depicted as in Figure 12.3.

An immediate difficulty with virtual base classes is the apparent need for second sight on the part of the programmer. I have to specify `virtual` when I declare `Directory` and `Menu`, but only because I am going to use them both as

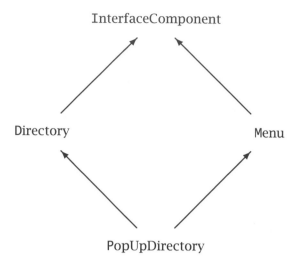

Figure 12.3   Virtual base class

base classes of `PopUpDirectory` later. In the real world, this problem is more apparent than real, I suspect. If you start out designing a library with multiple inheritance in mind, intending your classes to be combined in a mix-in style, you will construct it accordingly, using virtual base classes where necessary. This doesn't mean all the time—using virtual base classes is marginally less efficient than using non-virtual ones, and rules out the possibility of having duplicate sub-objects when you do want them.

Virtual base classes prevent unwanted duplication of sub-objects, but the presence of shared sub-objects brings its own problems. For example, how do you assign a `PopUpDirectory` object when it has `InterfaceComponent` as a virtual base class? Generalizing the old method (page 183) in the obvious way leads to the `InterfaceComponent` sub-object being copied twice. If we just provide token data members for the classes, assume that constructors do the right thing, omit the safety checks for the sake of conciseness and replace them with some tracing code, the effect is easy to see.

```
InterfaceComponent&
InterfaceComponent::operator=(const InterfaceComponent& ii)
{
  ic = ii.ic;
  cout << "copying " << ic << endl;
  return *this;
}
```

The name `ic` is a data member of `InterfaceComponent`, of type `string`. Assume that the constructor for `InterfaceComponent` will set it to the concatenation of the menu and directory names when a `PopUpDirectory` is created.

```
Menu& Menu::operator=(const Menu& m)
{
  InterfaceComponent::operator=(m);
  menu_name = m.menu_name;
  cout << "copying " << menu_name << endl;
  return *this;
}

Directory& Directory::operator=(const Directory& d)
{
  InterfaceComponent::operator=(d);
  dir_name = d.dir_name;
  cout << "copying " << dir_name << endl;
  return *this;
}

PopUpDirectory& PopUpDirectory::operator=(const PopUpDirectory& p)
{
  Directory::operator=(p);
  Menu::operator=(p);
  return *this;
}
```

An assignment of a `PopUpDirectory` shows the effect.

```
int main()
{
  PopUpDirectory pud;
  PopUpDirectory pp("MP", "DP");
  pud = pp;
  return EXIT_SUCCESS;
}
```

The program yields the output

```
copying MPDP
copying DP
copying MPDP
copying MP
```

In this case, the behaviour is merely inefficient, but it is possible to generate examples where it would be fatal. To prevent the double copying, we must take explicit control over the assignment of sub-objects in derived classes, instead of just letting the assignments ripple down to the base. It is necessary to allow assignments of objects of any class in the program, so the `operator=` function still has to be defined for all classes. The trick is to provide a protected function that does the actual assignment, and, for each derived class, call these functions explicitly, only as often as needed.

The protected member of `InterfaceComponent` would be defined like this:

```
InterfaceComponent&
InterfaceComponent::assign(const InterfaceComponent& ii)
```

```
    {
      ic = ii.ic;
      cout << "copying " << ic << endl;
      return *this;
    }
```

Its actual assignment operator is just a forwarding function.

```
    InterfaceComponent&
    InterfaceComponent::operator=(const InterfaceComponent& ii)
    {
      return assign(ii);
    }
```

For the classes derived from `InterfaceComponent`, things are more interesting. We must split the assignment of the class's own data members from the assignment of the sub-object. The protected member function for `Menu` only assigns its data member; `operator=` explicitly calls the `assign` function of the base class.

```
    Menu& Menu::assign(const Menu& m)
    {
      menu_name = m.menu_name;
      cout << "copying " << menu_name << endl;
      return *this;
    }

    Menu& Menu::operator=(const Menu& m)
    {
      InterfaceComponent::assign(m);
      return assign(m);
    }
```

`Directory` is similar—isomorphic, even.

When we come to `PopUpDirectory`, there are `assign` functions available in its various base classes to copy all the requisite data members.

```
    PopUpDirectory& operator=(const PopUpDirectory& p)
    {
      InterfaceComponent::assign(p);
      Directory::assign(p);
      Menu::assign(p);
      return *this;
    }
```

This time, the driver program gives the right trace output:

```
copying MPDP
copying DP
copying MP
```

The technique of using a protected member function to carry out the part of an operation that involves only the members of a sub-object, and allowing derived classes to synthesize a complete operation on the complete object is a generally applicable one where virtual base classes are being used. It avoids duplicated operations on the shared sub-object, which can not only be wasteful but sometimes positively incorrect or dangerous.

The spectre most likely to haunt novice users of multiple inheritance is that of ambiguity. Two classes might use the same name for completely different operations. If these two classes are used as base classes for a third class which does not redefine the name in question, then that class will have two members of the same name in scope at once. Letting our imagination run riot (or at least engage in a bit of minor civil commotion), let's suppose that the Menu class has a member function erase that removes the menu from the display, and that the Directory class has a member function erase that deletes all the files in a directory. If pud is a PopUpDirectory, what should pud.erase() do? A mistake here could be unfortunate.

In C++, the use of a member name that does not refer unambiguously to a single member is an error that is detected at compile-time. It is only the *use* of the name that is an error, not the presence of the two homonymous members. You can always distinguish between two members with the same name in different base classes by using a fully qualified member name. Often, as in this example, you will always want to refer to just one of the members. In such a case, the best thing to do is redefine the name in the derived class as a suitable forwarding function.

```
void PopUpDirectory::erase()
{  Menu::erase();  }
```

This brings us obliquely back to our lovelorn superhero, who wrote the following C++ program.

```
#include <iostream>

class B {
public:
  virtual void f() {  cout << "She loves me" << endl; }
};

class D1: public virtual B {
public:
  void g() { f(); }
};

class D2: public virtual B {
public:
  void f() {  cout << "She loves me not" << endl; }
};

class DD:public D1, public D2 { };

int main()
{
```

```
    DD me;
    me.g();

    return EXIT_SUCCESS;
}
```

Imagine his perplexity and disappointment at the output:

```
She loves me not
```

"Well," he thought, "Whatever's going on here, I'm not using any member of D2, so if I make `D2::f()` private, it can't get called". So he did, and...

```
She loves me not
```

So what's happening? Well, the thing is, she's hung up on his superhero persona, or thinks she is, and she's too dim to see that they're both the same person, so, even though...Oh, the *program*? That's not so simple.

The apparently bizarre behaviour of Clark's program results from the way in which uses of a name are connected to its declaration when virtual base classes are present. If any class can have only a single base class, a straightforward way of looking up names is possible (leaving aside considerations of template arguments): if a member `x` is accessed through an object of class K, first you see whether `x` is a member of K, if not, look in K's base class, and so on, until you find a declaration of `x` or run out of base classes. If K has more than one base class, you must, in effect, go back up through base classes via more than one route. You may well find more than one `x` declared *en route*. This would constitute an error—any use of `x` is ambiguous—if no virtual base classes were involved, but in their presence the ambiguity can be resolved. If a name `x` is declared as a member of a class B and of a class A, then, provided B has A as a base class, the use of `x` is resolved as `B::x`. The jargon is: `B::x` *dominates* `A::x`, and, as we all know, the dominant prevail. If you read it several times and think for a while, you'll see that this rule is entirely consistent with the behaviour in single inheritance and in multiple inheritance with no virtual base classes.

In our example, `D2::f` dominates `B::f`, which is why it is called. Figure 12.4 may help clarify who dominates whom. Class names have been decorated with their members' names in curly brackets.

The name resolution process takes no account of access controls. Although this is surprising, as Clark discovered, it is not half so surprising as some of the effects that could be achieved if it did.

Is it meaningful to talk about intuition in such an artificial context as multiple inheritance in C++? I don't know, but I'm still inclined to say that there is something counter-intuitive about this behaviour. Since the call to `f` is made from a member of D1, you would expect it to be resolved as a call to `B::f`, since B is a direct base of D1. (I would, anyway.) Indeed, in the paper that first described the multiple inheritance mechanism when it was introduced in C++, an example equivalent to the one just given is annotated with no fewer than three exclamation marks. Nevertheless, if you are going to have virtual base classes, it is the right decision. One way to think of it is as a generalization of the rule for resolving the use of virtual functions' names. Another is to think about the

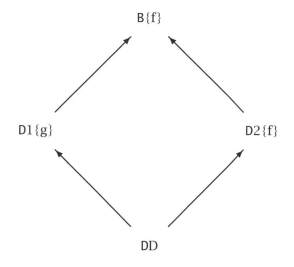

Figure 12.4 A hopeless case

layout of a DD object. It contains a D2 sub-object. Since f is overridden in D2, the only version of f available within a DD object is D2::f—she loves me not.

The behaviour of virtual functions with virtual base classes has been claimed as a virtue. It allows information and behaviour to pass sideways between classes, like D1 and D2, at the same level in a class hierarchy, instead of requiring all information to flow down from a common base class.

There is one more important thing you need to know about multiple inheritance. Initialization of virtual base classes works differently from initialization of other base classes. To quote the ARM, "Virtual base classes constitute a special case". Normally, (unless you think virtual base classes are normal) the constructor for a derived class can pass arguments to the constructor for its immediate base classes by using their names in a member initialization list. The immediate base classes can pass values to constructors for *their* immediate base classes, and so on. Values pass to the base of the inheritance hierarchy and objects are then constructed base upward. This isn't going to work with virtual base classes—the virtual base sub-object is shared, so there is more than one derived class that could pass arguments to its constructor. Some extra rule is needed to determine how virtual bases are initialized. The rule is that the virtual base sub-object is initialized via the member initialization list for the complete object.

Going back to PopUpDirectories, let us suppose that the constructors for all the base classes are trivial ones that just use an argument to initialize data members.

```
InterfaceComponent::InterfaceComponent(const string& s):ic(s) {}
Menu::Menu(const string& n):menu_name(n), InterfaceComponent(n) {}
Directory::Directory(const string& n):dir_name(n),
                         InterfaceComponent(n) {}
```

When we write the constructor for `PopUpDirectory`, the argument for the `InterfaceComponent` constructor must be included in the member initialization list.

```
PopUpDirectory::PopUpDirectory(const string& m, const string& d):
              Directory(d), Menu(m), InterfaceComponent(m+d) {}
```

Although `Menu` and `Directory` also initialize `InterfaceComponent`, they are ignored when a `PopUpDirectory` object is created.

Don't ask me why this rule is used, I don't know. I suspect it is the only rule that can be made to work consistently, but it is nasty for all that. The initialization of a virtual base class is done in the constructor for the class furthest removed from it in the inheritance structure, and adding a new class still further removed changes the effect of the constructors for the old classes.

There's another consequent piece of nastiness. If you fail to initialize a virtual base class in the complete object's constructor, the virtual base class's default constructor will be used if it has one. This is reasonable, but it can cause unexpected surprises. Consider the following changes to `PopUpDirectory` and its base classes. First, add a default value to the constructor for `InterfaceComponent`.

```
InterfaceComponent::
InterfaceComponent(const string& s = "untitled"):ic(s) {}
```

The constructor can be called with no arguments, so it is the default constructor for this class. Do the same for the `Directory` class.

```
Directory::Directory(const string& n = "untitled")
          :dir_name(n), InterfaceComponent(n) {}
```

Now remove the initializations of `InterfaceComponent` and `Directory` from `PopUpDirectory`'s constructor.

```
PopUpDirectory::PopUpDirectory(const string& m, const string& d)
                                                       :Menu(m){}
```

Presumably, the intention is to use the menu name to initialize `ic`, by passing it back through the member initialization list of `Menu`, cavalierly ignoring `Directory`. This is not what happens: the virtual base class is initialized in `PopUpDirectory`. Since no constructor arguments are specified, the default constructor is used, and every object has its `ic` member set to the string `"untitled"`.

Innocuous Multiple Inheritance

The preceding few pages might make multiple inheritance sound thoroughly terrifying—a feature to be used only by the most foolhardy and adventurous of programmers. There is some truth in this impression, when it comes to virtual base classes and all that, but it is possible to use multiple inheritance in harmless ways, fit even for the most timid. If all you want to do is combine two otherwise separate classes to produce a composite with the properties of both, which can be used as either one or the other as circumstance requires, you won't run into the oddities described in the previous section. Provided you keep an eye out for potential ambiguities, everything will be plain sailing.

To illustrate the positive side of multiple inheritance, I will combine two examples from earlier chapters. In chapter 5, I introduced you to the use of inheritance, with a program to assist a fictional system administrator to maintain a collection of compilers and produce executable versions when required. In setting up the scenario for that example, I postulated that most of the sources for compilers come from archive sites on the Internet. Let us suppose now that our system administrator finds disk space is getting tight and decides that compiler sources will no longer be routinely fetched over the network. Instead, a database of remote compiler sources and their locations will be added to the records for locally maintained compilers. New compilers will be fetched only when necessary.

In chapter 6 I introduced classes for representing network resources identified by Uniform Resource Locators. A remote compiler source is a kind of compiler source—one that happens to be somewhere else—and it is a kind of network resource—one that happens to be a compiler. A class to represent remote compiler sources can be constructed by using multiple inheritance to combine the two existing classes for compiler resources and remote files accessible by FTP. The new class `RemoteCompilerSource` will be derived from both `CompilerSource` and `FTP`. (For the definition of `CompilerSource` see page 112; for that of `FTP` see page 140.) For this example, it is enough just to add a constructor, which initializes the base classes, and to override the `connect` member function so it not only makes a connection but also stores the retrieved file—or at least says that it does so.

```
class RemoteCompilerSource: public CompilerSource,
                            public FTP {
public:
  RemoteCompilerSource(char* u, char* fn, char* il, char* sl):
      FTP(u), CompilerSource(fn, il, sl) {}
  void connect()
  {
    FTP::connect();
    cout << "Saving as " << filename() << endl;
  }
};
```

Knowing what we now know about constructors, virtual functions and overloading, the `CompilerSource` class and the program that uses it could be cleaned up and simplified, but I'll leave that to you and just re-use what I've got—much of the point of using multiple inheritance is that I don't have to touch the definitions of the existing classes.

To keep track of remote compiler sources I will just add a third array and counter to the ones I am using to keep track of the local compiler sources and binaries.

```
static RemoteCompilerSource* RCSs[max_files];
static int nRCSs;
```

The program behaves just as before until an attempt to find the source of a suitable compiler in the function `findcompiler` fails. Instead of giving up and returning a null pointer, we now try to find and retrieve a suitable remote compiler, by calling a function `fetchcompiler`. If this succeeds, then we compile the source that it has fetched. Cheerfully omitting the checks for overflow of the various arrays, the new version of `findcompiler` looks like this:

```
CompilerBinary* findcompiler(ProgSource *prog)
{
  string pl = prog->language();
  cout << "Seeking a " << pl << " compiler to compile" << endl;
  int i = 0;
  while (i < nCSs)
  {
    if (CSs[i]->filename() != prog->filename()
        && CSs[i]->compiles() == pl)
    {
      CompilerBinary * xc = cc(CSs[i]);
      if (xc)
      {
        CBs[nCBs++] = xc;
        return xc;
      }
    }
    ++i;
  }
  CompilerSource *remote = fetchcompiler(prog);
  if (remote)
  {
    CompilerBinary * xc = cc(remote);
    if (xc)
    {
      CBs[nCBs++] = xc;
      return xc;
    }
  }
  cout << "Given up" << endl;
  return NULL;
}
```

The new function `fetchcompiler` is quite simple. It is basically just a linear search of the RCSs array. Whenever it successfully fetches a compiler, the pointer in this array is copied into CSs, since we now have a compiler source. It can be left in RCSs safely, and why not do so? The local copy might have to be deleted. Notice that while I am searching the array, I treat the entries as pointers to `CompilerSource` objects and use the `compiles` member function to find out which language they accept as input. Once I have found a suitable entry, I treat it as an FTP object, using its `connect` function to do the actual fetching. Finally, I return a pointer to it as a `CompilerSource*`. This is what multiple inheritance is all about.

```
CompilerSource* fetchcompiler(ProgSource *prog)
```

```
{
  string pl = prog->language();
  cout << "Trying to FTP a compiler for " << pl << endl;
  int i = 0;
  while (i < nRCSs)
  {
    RemoteCompilerSource *r = RCSs[i];
    if (r->compiles() == pl)
    {
      r->connect();
      CSs[nCSs++] = r;
      return r;
    }
    ++i;
  }
  return NULL;
}
```

It should be clear that the same effect can be achieved without using multiple inheritance, by deriving RemoteCompilerSource from CompilerSource only, providing it with a data member of type FTP and writing a forwarding function to do the connection. If the job was done that way, though, it would not be possible to pass a pointer to a RemoteCompilerSource object to any function expecting an FTP, or to store it in a data structure of pointers to FTP objects. Additional interface code would have to be added. Multiple inheritance allows a RemoteCompilerSource object to be treated sometimes as a CompilerSource, sometimes as an FTP and sometimes as a complete RemoteCompilerSource, provided you access it through a pointer or reference. This ability to use the same object in different roles is sometimes convenient, whether or not you are entirely happy about exactly what sort of relationships are modelled by multiple inheritance.

The duality that multiple inheritance permits is often used to advantage in graphical user interface programming. It is common to describe such interfaces in object-oriented terms: every component in the interface is an object that can display itself in one or more ways and can respond to certain events such as mouse clicks or the pressing of command keys. When it comes to implementation, these two aspects of an object are separate. Displaying is a graphical operation, under the control of a display manager that deals with output to the screen and treats the object as passive data—a description of the displayed item as it is to appear on the screen. In order to be able to respond to input, though, the object must be a process. Its execution is under the control of a task manager, and this is not interested in its graphical properties, only its status. In a sophisticated system, there will be several sorts of displayed item: windows, menus, dialogue boxes, alerts, icons, and so on. There can be several sorts of process, too: ones that track a mouse, or respond to a selection of command keys, or wait for keyboard input, for example. One approach to constructing a tool kit for building interfaces of this sort is to provide separate class hierarchies for these aspects: a range of displayed elements and a range of processes with different capabilities. A programmer can put together a selection of specialized facilities from the tool kit, using multiple inheritance. The resulting object can be treated as a graphical item by the display manager and as a process by the task manager. Constructing a tool kit with single inheritance is said to lead to large classes overburdened with facilities, since every class has to be capable of functioning in both roles.

SPACE ALLOCATION

Here is a different story. There was a programmer (and a jolly one, too) who wanted to do something really clever. Not just anything really clever, you understand, but a specific Something Really Clever (SRC) that he needed for a reason. Being a humble programmer, he started out by looking up SRC algorithms in academic computer science journals, until he found one devised by some people who were cleverer than he was, which seemed to be just the thing. The computer scientists who had devised the algorithm had also analysed its complexity and shown, with the aid of two theorems and a lemma, that their algorithm was optimal in speed and had acceptable worst-case space requirements. Brilliant!

So the programmer made a photocopy of the clever computer scientists' paper and studied it. He had to teach himself some extra mathematics to follow the notation, but that was OK. He looked in Knuth's *Art of Computer Programming* to find some good ideas for implementing the data structures needed by the SRC algorithm. Then he wrote a program and it ran... like a three-toed sloth.

"Why? This is a demonstrably highly efficient algorithm. These are classic data structures. It must be my coding". So he re-wrote the program, using all the hand optimization tricks he knew. For good measure he switched on the compiler's heaviest duty optimizer. All of this made no measurable difference. Only then did the word "profiler" enter his mind. Better late than never, he set to with a will, profiled his SRC program and discovered the sad truth. It was spending all its time in the system's space allocation routine.

OK, it *was* me, and I just learned to live with it. A more determined (and less jolly?) programmer could have done something more positive. Usually in such cases, it turns out that a small number, often only one, of different sorts of object are being used, but there are a lot of them. The system's allocator is being called many times, but it is being asked to allocate only a few different sizes of block. System allocators have to be written to accommodate requests for any number of blocks of arbitrary sizes. Inevitably, an allocation routine which must be sufficiently flexible to deal with any pattern of requests that any program may throw at it will be less efficient—possibly much less efficient—than one which just has to dole out chunks of memory that are all the same size, which can be anticipated in advance.

Writing your own free space allocator for fixed size blocks is easy. Fitting it smoothly into a statically typed language with constructors can be tricky, but a neat mechanism is available in C++. You can overload an operator function and have it called when you use new to create an object. Because new isn't a conventional operator, the function operator new has some slightly strange properties, but, in a broad sense, it behaves like any other overloaded operator. In particular, you can define a member function called `operator new`, to provide space allocation specific to a class, or you can define a global `operator new` with extra arguments, which will be called instead of the standard one when suitable argument values are supplied. The second option is a good deal more adventurous than the first.

Naturally, you can write your own `operator delete` to go with your `operator new`. Since the two are interdependent, you better had.

Allocators for Classes

The first question that must be answered is: What is the type of `operator new`? Don't try to guess. The version normally used is declared as

```
void* operator new(size_t);
```

(If you've forgotten about `size_t`, read the section on the `sizeof` operator on page 196.) Both argument and result types are a little odd, at first sight, but they could hardly be anything else, it's just that the syntax of expressions using `new` is misleading.

Suppose you write

```
Womble* orinoco = new Womble;
```

If being able to define a function `operator new` makes you willing to believe that the keyword `new` is an operator symbol, it looks as though its argument is a type name (`sizeof` sets a precedent for this) and its result is a pointer to an object. In reality, the creation of an object on the heap is composed of two distinct actions. First, sufficient space for the object is obtained from the free area of the heap. Second, a constructor is called to convert this storage into a correctly initialized object. It is only the first of these operations which is performed by `operator new`. As with other operators, the C++ compiler transforms the expression you write into a function call, only here, as well as moving the arguments about, it does a further transformation and calls

```
operator new(sizeof(Womble))
```

The usual rules are used to find a definition of the operator function, so if you have declared it as a member function of the `Womble` class it will be used to do the allocation part of creating new Wombles. The `void*` pointer returned is used as the pointer `this` inside the constructor, where type rules are stretched a bit.

In a similar way, `operator delete` is called after a destructor has done its work, to return the memory remaining after an object has been dismantled to the free area. It is therefore declared as

```
void operator delete(void*);
```

The next question is: How is the space actually allocated? A footnote in the draft standard admits that the semantics have been defined so that the system's `operator new` can be implemented using the allocation function `malloc` from the C standard library, and this is how it usually is implemented. (It doesn't *have* to be, though, and you would be very unwise to depend on it in any way.) It is `malloc` that does all the work of keeping the heap in shape (with the aid of its partner `free` that returns storage to the free area and is usually used to implement `delete`). It is `malloc` that uses up all the processor cycles.

If you want to save those cycles, it is not a good idea to try and replace `malloc` with something else operating at a similar low level doing general purpose allocation. Instead, you can ensure that calls to `malloc` are infrequent, by using it to allocate space for many objects at once and then using your own code to dole them out one by one. The `ListOfVoid` class is a perfect example, both of when this might be worthwhile and of how easy it can be.

I will provide the list node class with its own simple space allocation routines. The strategy is to use the system `operator new` to get enough space for a large number of list nodes. I will then allocate single nodes by carving them off this chunk, keeping a pointer `free_p` to the first available and another `free_lim` to the top of the chunk. I increment `free_p` whenever I hand out a node and when it reaches `free_lim` I need to allocate a new big chunk. At the same time, I will re-use any nodes that are deleted by maintaining a linked list, to which they are added on deletion. My `operator new` makes three attempts to find a list node. First, it looks at the free list; second, it checks whether there is any space left in the large chunk; finally, it tries to get a new large chunk off the system.

To clarify the presentation, I will assume there is a class `ListNode`, which is a friend of `List`, rather than `Node` nested within it. I must add some private static data members to `ListNode`.

```
static ListNode* free_list;
static ListNode* free_p;
static ListNode* free_lim;
```

I also need to declare the space allocation operator functions as members.

```
void* operator new(size_t);
void operator delete(void*);
```

▷ If they are members of a class, `operator new` and `operator delete` are always static members, whether you declare them as such, or not. They must be, because ◁ when they are called there is no object to call them through.

Static members must be defined outside the class definition.

```
ListNode* ListNode::free_list = NULL;
ListNode* ListNode::free_p = NULL;
ListNode* ListNode::free_lim = NULL;
```

The code for `operator new` is straightforward, apart from a safety check at the beginning. The argument supplied is the size of the object requested. You might think this is redundant. Since `operator new` is a member of `ListNode` it can only be called to allocate space for `ListNode` objects, can't it? No, because `operator new` functions are inherited. If someone derives a class from

ListNode and fails to redefine it, ListNode::operator new might get called to allocate space for some object of a derived class with extra members. It is wise to check that the argument is the expected size and to pass the request on to the global operator new if it isn't. After that, everything proceeds as outlined above.

```
void* ListNode::operator new(size_t sz)
{
  if (sz != sizeof(ListNode))
    return ::operator new(sz);
  if (free_list)
  {
    void* t = free_list;
    free_list = free_list->next;
    return t;
  }
  if (free_p < free_lim)
  {
    void *t = free_p;
    free_p += 1;
    return t;
  }
  char* new_chunk = new char[chunk_size * sz];
  free_p = (ListNode*)new_chunk;
  free_lim = free_p + chunk_size;
  void *t = free_p;
  ++free_p;
  return t;
}
```

The constant chunk_size specifies the number of ListNodes that the big chunk of memory should be able to accommodate. We get this chunk as an array of char because we know that sizeof(char)==1, so it will be the right size. It would not be a good idea to ask for an array of ListNodes, because that would cause their constructors to be called, totally unnecessarily. If the global operator new is unable to allocate new_chunk, it will throw a bad_alloc exception. Since I have not put any handlers in my code, the exception will propagate outwards, so it will appear to have been thrown just as if the system operator new had been used.

The deletion operation is very simple, it only needs to put the deleted node on the front of the free list. It is necessary to use a cast to convert the void* argument back to a ListNode*. This is safe, because we know it used to point to a ListNode before the destructor was called. Since allocation and deallocation functions are working with actual memory, not constructed objects, casts are inevitable.

```
void ListNode::operator delete(void* d)
{
  ((ListNode*)d)->next = free_list;
  free_list = (ListNode*)d;
}
```

As a crude measure of the effectiveness of customizing space allocation for this class, I ran a program that built a linked list using the following "two steps up and one step back" method.

```
ListOf<int> L;
int xx = 99;
for (int i = 1; i <= N; ++i)
{
  for (int j = 1; j <= M; ++j)
    L.insert(&xx, 0);
  for (int j = 1; j <= M/2; ++j)
    L.remove(1);
}
```

Using the custom allocation routines cut the runtime by about 35% over using the standard ones, a worthwhile improvement, if not a spectacular one. (The precise improvement depends on the values of N and M.)

Arrays of objects are allocated and deallocated using `operator new[]` and `operator delete[]`, which can be overloaded too, although the exercise is less likely to be worthwhile.

Allocator Classes

There are only a few effective techniques for building free space allocators, so if you get into building them you will find that all your `new` and `delete` operator functions look pretty much the same, and where's the fun in that? You would do better to build an abstract version in the form of a space allocator class, which could be re-used whenever some critical class had to do its own storage management.

A simple version would consist of a class of objects that allocate and deallocate blocks of a size specified as an argument to the constructor. That is, we can abstract the block size out and re-use the algorithm. We might end up with a class `Allocator` with the following interface:

```
class Allocator {
public:
  Allocator(int s);
  void* allocate(size_t);
  void deallocate(void*);
private:
    implementation details
};
```

This class could be used to provide `ListNode` with its `new` and `delete` operators. A static member of type `Allocator` does the store management for all `ListNode` objects; the operator functions just forward requests to it.

```
class ListNode  {
private:
  static Allocator a;
```

```
    ListNode(void* a_val, ListNode* whats_next):
      the_val(a_val), next(whats_next) {}
    void* operator new(size_t s)
    {  return a.allocate(s);  }
    void operator delete(void* p)
    {  a.deallocate(p);  }
    void* the_val;
    ListNode *next;
  };
```

An `Allocator` object could be used in the same way for any class that needed its own version of these operators.

A simple implementation of `Allocator` uses the same allocation regime as we used in the previous section. The use of list nodes in that section as elements of the free list as well as the objects returned was a sort of programming play on words and we cannot really get away with it again. Instead, a special class is declared, purely to hold the links in the free list. We will depend on arithmetic to make sure that the links are in the right places and the blocks that are allocated are the right size. This time, I will link together all the blocks in a newly allocated chunk, just to make a change. All the available store can thus be found on the free list. This is a popular variation that doesn't seem to make any difference to the performance, but saves you a couple of members.

The private part of the `Allocator` class needs to declare the local class to hold the links, and data members to remember the block size and to point to the free list. This time, the free list is not a static member—different `Allocator` objects should not share their free lists, especially if they are allocating objects of different sizes.

```
  class Allocator {
  public:
    Allocator(int s);
    void* allocate(size_t);
    void deallocate(void*);
  private:
    class Node {
    public:
      Node* next;
    };
    int block_size;
    Node* free_list;
  };
```

The `allocate` and `deallocate` members resemble the code we saw before, except for the variation just mentioned and the way in which arithmetic is used to find the start of each block. Notice all the nasty casts to and from `char*`: everything depends on the fact that `sizeof(char)==1`.

```
  void* Allocator::allocate(size_t sz)
  {
    if (sz != block_size)
      return ::operator new(sz);
```

```
      if (free_list)
      {
        void* t = free_list;
        free_list = free_list->next;
        return t;
      }
      char* new_chunk = new char[chunk_size * sz];
      Node *new_list = (Node*) new_chunk;
      Node *p = new_list;
      char* q = new_chunk + sz;
      for (int i = 0; i < chunk_size-1; ++i)
      {
        Node *pp = (Node*)q;
        p->next = pp;
        p = pp;
        q += sz;
      }
      p->next = NULL;
      free_list = new_list->next;
      return new_list;
    }

    void Allocator::deallocate(void* d)
    {
      Node *dd = (Node*)d;
      dd->next = free_list;
      free_list = dd;
    }
```

The `Allocator` class needs a constructor. The truly cautious programmer will make sure that the objects being allocated are big enough to double as `Nodes`. It may seem unlikely that anyone would want to allocate objects smaller than a pointer, but there would be an awful tangle if they tried. If such an attempt is made, the size is reset to the minimum feasible.

```
    Allocator::Allocator(int s)
    {
      if (s < sizeof(Node))
        s = sizeof(Node);
      block_size = s;
      free_list = NULL;
    }
```

To get everything moving, the static member of `ListNode` must be initialized with an `Allocator` for the right size of block.

```
    Allocator ListNode::a = Allocator(sizeof(ListNode));
```

There are many variations in the way allocator classes can be used. By fixing the size of block and making the data members static, all classes allocating blocks of a certain size can share one free list—useful if you have many different classes of the same size but only need a few objects of each. The size of block can be an argument to a class template instead of to a constructor, so that a family of allocator classes for different sizes can be generated. An allocator class can be passed as a template argument to another class, allowing you to generate different versions of the same class using different space management algorithms. Use your creativity to devise different ways of organizing space allocation.

▷ I have omitted any mention of alignment. On some machines, objects occupying more than one byte can only be accessed if they start at an even address, or an address divisible by four, or satisfy some other whim of the machine's designer. A space allocation routine ought to be written to take such restrictions into account. Alignment considerations are highly machine-specific and you will have to consult your machine and compiler documentation to discover what is required on your ◁ system.

Placement of Objects

As I remarked earlier, you are allowed to overload `operator new` so that it accepts extra arguments, although in all cases the first arguments must be of type `size_t` and `void*`, respectively, and you can't overload on the return type. The additional actual arguments are supplied as an argument list in brackets after the keyword. If you can think of a good reason to define such overloaded operators and feel you understand what you are doing, let no-one stand in your way.

There is one overloaded version of `operator new` declared in the standard library header `new`, which you are not allowed to replace. It is equivalent to

```
void* operator new(size_t size, void* p)
{  return p;  }
```

Curious, eh? Its primary function is to allow you to create an object in a specific location. You might want to do this if you are writing low-level software on a system that performs memory-mapped input and output.

Going back to our very first example of a class, suppose `TimeSetting` objects are being used by software that controls devices attached to a computer, and that the software that communicates between the computer and one particular device makes it possible to write a time value into a timer register on the device by writing to the memory location, with address 0x142. By using the placement form of `new`, I can create a `TimeSetting` object (presumably using, and justifying, the version of that class which stores times as a number of clock ticks) at that address.

```
TimeSetting *dev_time = new ((void*)0x142) TimeSetting;
```

This ruse enables me to use the member functions of the `TimeSetting` class to manipulate the device's timer. Using this interface will be safer and more convenient than writing bits to crude memory.

If you make a mess of object placement, it will be a truly frightful one.

End of the Night

You've had enough. Let's just finish off the leftovers and tidy up.

End

It's just about time to go. Before we leave, I'd like to give you some pointers to further directions, both deeper into C++ and off into new territory.

THE LATEST THING

You could be forgiven for thinking that enough C++ is enough, and that what you've read about is too much C++ already. Nevertheless, the language continues to evolve and to acquire new features. The ANSI/ISO standardization process is exerting a stabilizing influence—the extensions sub-committee has shut up shop, so there should not be any further new features in the standard—but, even as it proceeded, new features were designed and incorporated into the standard. I have described some of these in earlier chapters. Two more features deserve mention, although neither will be described in detail since their availability is presently still patchy.

The first is simple and long overdue. A set of declarations may be grouped together into a named collection, called a *namespace*. A namespace declaration has the form

```
namespace name { declarations } ;
```

The *declarations* can declare anything which could be declared at file level, including classes, functions, variables and even namespaces. I might choose to group together all my Internet resource classes, together with a useful function, into a namespace:

```
namespace InternetResourceLibrary {
  class NetResource {
    member declarations
  };
  class FTP:public NetResource {
    member declarations
  };
  class WWW:public NetResource {
```

341

```
      member declarations
   };
   NetResource* decode_URL(const char*);
};
```

Namespaces, like classes, are scope regions from which names can be exported. One way they differ from classes is that a namespace's declaration does not have to be all in one place. For example, if I implemented a class for gopher resources, I could add it to the namespace `InternetResourceLibrary` with the declaration

```
namespace InternetResourceLibrary {
   class Gopher:public NetResource {
      member declarations
   };
};
```

This extends the namespace, it doesn't redeclare it.

Names declared in a namespace can be defined either inside or outside it, just as member functions can be defined inside or outside the class declaration. If the definitions are outside the namespace, then the members' names must be fully qualified, as described next.

If `N` is a namespace, then programs wanting to use the names declared in `N` can do so in one of three ways. A name `n` belonging to `N` may be referred to as `N::n`. The similarity to the fully qualified name of a member `m` of a class `K`, `K::m`, emphasizes their similarity as scope regions. A convenient alternative to using fully qualified names is to insert the *using declaration*

```
using N::n;
```

into your program; subsequently the name `n` on its own will be taken to mean `N::n`. Finally, a *using directive*

```
using N;
```

makes all the names in `N` available without qualification. For example, I might refer to the class of ftp resources as

```
InternetResourceLibrary::FTP
```

or, by adding a using declaration of its name

```
using InternetResourceLibrary::FTP;
```

I could use it as if `FTP` had been declared where the `using` declaration appeared. If I added instead

```
using namespace InternetResourceLibrary;
```

all the names from the namespace would be available without qualification. The three methods allow me to choose how many of the names belonging to a namespace I import into my program, and over how large a region.

One of the reasons for using namespaces is to help cut down the risk of name clashes between entities declared in separately developed libraries. Prudence suggests that namespaces should have long descriptive names, to avoid clashes between namespace names. However, using long names is a drag. You can therefore define a synonym for a namespace, to give it a more convenient name, The syntax is:

```
namespace name = namespace-name;
```

where *namespace-name* is the name of a namespace that is in scope. For example, if I had included the declaration of the namespace `InternetResourceLi-brary`, I would probably add:

```
namespace Net = InternetResourceLibrary;
```

and refer to `Net::FTP`, and so on.

Namespaces are a systematic and flexible alternative to the use of static members to partition the global namespace described in chapter 9 on page 222, which finally provide C++ with the basis for a proper module structure.

▷ You can omit the *name* in a namespace declaration, giving an anonymous namespace. Its members can be referred to by their unqualified names wherever the namespace is in scope. This superficially pointless feature provides a preferred ◁ alternative to the use of `static` to declare names local to a file.

The introduction of namespaces into C++ will have an immediate impact on everybody, because the standard library is being reorganized to take advantage of them. Each of the standard library header files declares its names within a namespace called `std`. Thus, if you want to access, say, the standard iostreams, you must, as ever, have the directive

```
#include <iostream>
```

at the head of your program, but then you must do one of three things: use fully qualified names, such as `std::cout`; provide using declarations such as

```
using std::cout;
```

for all the names you want to use; or follow the include directive with

```
using namespace std;
```

which will allow you to refer to any name in the standard namespace without qualification—even those in headers you `#include` later.

There is an extra complication where those headers which provide C++ programs with access to the standard C library are concerned. Whereas previously these headers had names ending in `.h`, which they shared with the corresponding C header, now there will be headers beginning with the letter `c`, with no extension—like the C++ standard headers—which declare the appropriate names within the namespace `std`. Thus, where before we had `stdlib.h`, now there is `cstdlib`, and the names it declares can only be accessed if they are qualified by `std::`, unless a using declaration or directive is provided. To ease the transition, though, the draft standard provides for a collection of headers with the old names, which simply include the new headers, and then add a using declaration for each name declared. So, for example, `stdlib.h` now contains

```
#include <cstdlib>
using std::abort;
    etc.
```

so you can go on using it as before, if you wish.

These "compatibility headers" are supposed to get phased out, and are only stipulated for the C library. On the other hand, the standard permits compiler vendors to provide any additional headers they wish, and it seems pretty certain that most will also provide similar compatibility headers for the rest of the standard C++ library, with whatever extension they were using before, so that if you are used to

```
#include <iostream.h>
```

the chances are you will be able to go on using it. Compatibility headers for anything except the standard C library are not specified in the standard, though, so the usage will not be portable. Anyway, you will have to feel guilty about not using `using` like a good software engineer should.[3]

The second extension is more complex and much more controversial. It concerns polymorphism based on inheritance. We have seen how it is possible to declare a function taking an argument of type `C*`, where `C` is some class, and that the function will accept arguments which are pointers to objects of type `C` or any class derived from `C`. What if you need to know the exact type of the pointer passed as an argument to your function? For a long time, the OK response among C++ experts was: You *don't* need to know. Designing your class to use virtual functions meant the argument could take care of its own operations, so what did you need the exact type for? However, it has now become accepted that you sometimes *do* need to know. In particular, if you have derived a class of your own from some library class, you may not have access to the base class, so you can't add the necessary virtual functions. You really do need to know, sometimes, whether the pointer you've just been passed points to one of your objects, or just any old standard library object.

The mechanism proposed to deal with run-time type information (RTTI, for short) is based on the observation that usually, as soon as you have determined the actual type of a pointer, you will want to use a cast so you can assign it to a variable of that type. The testing and casting have been combined into a single operation called a *dynamic cast*: this is parameterized in a type and takes a pointer argument. If the dynamic type of the pointer matches the type parameter of the cast, it returns its pointer argument cast to that type, otherwise it returns a null pointer. The syntax is the same as the new notation for other casts: the type parameter is enclosed in angle brackets following the keyword `dynamic_cast`, with the pointer being tested and cast enclosed in brackets after this, as in `dynamic_cast<dwelling*>(bldg_p)`. A dynamic cast can only be used with a type that has at least one virtual function.

It is widely believed that testing runtime types and selecting an action based on the result is poor programming practice. It has the effect of scattering type

---

[3] And if your compiler uses `.h` as the extension for its compatibility headers, there is the interesting question of what the header which includes `string` should be called, since `string.h` is already taken for `cstring`. Expect incompatible resolutions to this one.

information widely through a program and making it harder to change or add types—the very maintenance problems that virtual functions are supposed to eliminate. However, it has been accepted that sometimes type interrogation really is necessary. Of course, it is not difficult for programmers to encode their own type information and make it available. The reason for including RTTI in the language is to avoid a situation where different libraries used different encodings and different interrogation techniques. By putting the facility in the language, compatibility is ensured.

The dynamic cast is the preferred way of using RTTI, because it does the necessary job most of the time and minimizes the temptation to revert to a style of type-switching programming. Behind the dynamic cast, there has to be a mechanism for getting hold of information about an object's type. In keeping with the C++ philosophy of trusting programmers to know what they are doing, it is possible to gain access to this explicit information if you really feel you need it. What is actually available is implementation dependent and could range from an encoding of the type name to a complete description of the object's members, member functions and storage layout.

Where will C++ go next? The most likely direction is into the field of distributed computing. It is still unclear what form this development will take and whether an extended C++, or any language based on C++, will actually be suited for distributed computing or will become accepted by the distributed computing community. Meanwhile, the developments most likely to affect programmers will be in the area of libraries, both general purpose alternatives to the standard library, and specialized libraries for areas such as graphical interface programming, numerical computation and simulation.

MORE THINGS TO READ

If you want to know more about the intimate details of C++, or its history and background, or the pragmatics of C++ programming, you will have to do some more reading. Here are some suggestions.

Reference Material.

Margaret A. Ellis and Bjarne Stroustrup. *The Annotated C++ Reference Manual*. Addison-Wesley, Reading, Mass., 1990 (reprinted 1994).

If you are serious about C++ you will need this; it forms the basis of the standard, and includes a great deal of informative commentary, explaining some of the reasoning behind the design and describing possible implementations of some features. Recent reprints include the text of ANSI/ISO resolutions made since the ARM itself was written. It is not, of course, easy reading and, because it is a language definition, it is greatly concerned with marginal cases and pathological behaviour. Still, if you want most of the answers, you must have it.

You only get most of the answers in the ARM, because the standard has added some new questions. Nevertheless, the draft standard itself is not a document I would recommend anybody to read, especially not before it has been revised and ratified. If you must read it, see the section below on Internet resources.

The standard library has acquired a new importance with the incorporation of the STL. Books have been slow to catch up with this development, and most available books about the library describe out-of-date versions. You may have to rely on your system's documentation for definitive descriptions of the current library. You may find it useful, nevertheless, to consult either of the following, bearing in mind that they are not up to date.

P.J. Plauger. *The Draft Standard C++ Library.* Prentice-Hall, Englewood Cliffs, N.J., 1995

Steve Teale. *C++ IOStreams Handbook.* Addison-Wesley, Reading, Mass., 1993.

I would not be surprised to see revised versions of these, or even a *Late Night Guide to the C++ Standard Library*, appear when the standard is finished.

Books about the STL are beginning to appear, although they tend to discuss only that part of the library. The best is probably

David R. Musser and Atul Saini. *STL Tutorial and Reference Guide: C++ Programming with the Standard Template Library.* Addison-Wesley Professional Computing Series. Addison-Wesley, Reading, Mass., 1996.

Advanced C++ Programming and Design.

Scott Meyers. *Effective C++: 50 Specific Ways to Improve Your Programs and Designs.* Addison-Wesley Professional Computing Series. Addison-Wesley, Reading, Mass., 1992.

This is a very good book, which deals with using C++, as it says, effectively. It takes the form of fifty aphorisms, each followed by a lengthy explanation and rationale, advising you how to make best use of various C++ features. A sequel, with the wittily ambiguous title *More Effective C++* deals with more advanced topics and recent additions to the language.

Bjarne Stroustrup. *The C++ Programming Language.* Addison-Wesley, Reading, Mass., 2nd edition, 1991.

This, on the other hand, is only a good book in parts. Stroustrup is really too deep into C++ to write a useful tutorial, which this is intended to be. However, it does have some value as a halfway house between the *Late Night Guide* and the ARM, being detailed but not pure reference. It has some useful chapters on program design and the design of libraries, and includes the reference manual, without annotation, for the truly intrepid. Make sure you get the second edition. As with the ARM, recent reprintings incorporate new ANSI/ISO resolutions in an appendix.

Robert B. Murray. *C++ Strategies and Tactics.* Addison-Wesley Professional Computing Series. Addison-Wesley, Reading, Mass., 1993.

Although not as good as Meyers' books, this is another helpful guide to using C++. This one is more concerned with higher level design decisions. Most books on object-oriented design are pretty worthless, unless you like being told how to draw diagrams by people who can't write programs. Murray's book is valuable in this company because he obviously does know how to write programs, and concentrates on C++.

One other, more general, design book that isn't entirely worthless is:

Timothy Budd. *Object-Oriented Programming.* Addison-Wesley, Reading, Mass., 1991.

which is an exposition of the object-oriented philosophy, with examples from other languages besides C++. It thus provides some perspective; it mostly deals with what I have called the romantic view of object-oriented programming, so it may provide some counterbalance to my own largely classical preferences.

Background

Bjarne Stroustrup. *The Design and Evolution of C++.* Addison-Wesley, Reading, Mass., 1994.

Here you'll find lengthy discussions of the decisions that made C++ what it is. If you don't like C++, reading this might make you more sympathetic, since it gives a clear picture of what Stroustrup was and wasn't trying to achieve. The book also includes descriptions and discussion of all the major language features introduced since the ARM was published—and some that were considered but not introduced—although there is nothing worth mentioning on the standard library. On occasion it is perhaps too self-congratulatory, but I suppose he can be let off under the circumstances.

Data Structures

I have referred you to a good book on data structures on several occasions, so I had better suggest a couple. Not many such books are based on C++, and some of those that are are not actually very good. One I quite like, despite some peculiar quirks and an unsound attitude to `const`, is

Mitchell L. Model. *Data Structures, Data Abstraction: A Contemporary Introduction Using C++.* Prentice-Hall, Englewood Cliffs, N.J., 1994.

When it comes to data structures, though, you still can't really beat

Donald E. Knuth. *The Art of Computer Programming, vol 1 Fundamental Algorithms and vol 3 Sorting and Searching.* Addison-Wesley, Reading, Mass., 1973.

The presentation, with flowcharts and assembly language programs, is hopeless, but the information is priceless. A new edition, using his Cweb system for the programs, is said to be "in preparation".

Internet Resources

If you believe in the Internet, you can find a fair amount of material related to C++ out there. Starting at the bottom, the newsgroup `comp.lang.c++` is dedicated to discussion of C++ and C++ programming. Like most Internet newsgroups, it has a low signal to noise ratio. A better class of newsgroup is `comp.lang.c++.moderated`. Since, as its name implies, this newsgroup is moderated, less complete dross appears on it. Another group which may be of interest is `comp.std.c++`, which is devoted to the draft standard and its implications. Much of the discussion on this group is incredibly pedantic and obscure, but various people actively involved in the standardization effort regularly contribute, and announcements about its progress are posted to this group.

Because of the nature of the Internet and the way it is (dis)organized, any information about the location of specific files, directories and web pages is unreliable. The following references are accurate, to the best of my knowledge, at the time of writing, but I offer absolutely no guarantee (express or implied) that they will still be accurate when you read this—or even tomorrow—or that anything you find there will be up to date.

If you *really* want it, ISO document WG21/N0687, also known as ANSI document X3J6/95-0087, *Working Paper for Draft Proposed International Standard for Information Processing—Language C++*, the first committee draft of the C++ standard,[4] can be found in (at least) these places.

```
ftp://research.att.com:/dist/c++std/WP/
ftp://ftp.maths.warwick.ac.uk/pub/c++/std/WP/
ftp://ftp.su.edu.au:/pub/C++/CommitteeDraft/
```

Use the site nearest to you, and read the README file before you attempt to fetch anything else. Within these directories are versions of the documents in several formats, including PostScript and PDF (Acrobat). It is not small—over two megabytes and about seven hundred and twenty pages when printed. It is also virtually unreadable. Think at least twice before getting it.

The appendix to Stroustrup's *The C++ Programming Language* summarizing the resolutions passed by the standards committee since the ARM was written is available for FTP from

```
ftp://ftp.std.com/AW/stroustrup2e/new_iso.ps
```

It is a PostScript file, so if you haven't got access to a PostScript printer or

---

[4]The second committee draft is scheduled to appear for comment in late summer 1996, with an official draft international standard at the beginning of the following year, provided it is acceptable to the ISO member nations. Ratification is expected to take a further year, although the only changes allowed between the draft and final stages are to fix errors and typos, as I understand it.

something that can simulate one you won't be able to print it. (You didn't think there was anything democratic about the Internet, did you?)

The ANSI has set up a World-Wide Web page for news on the C++ standard. Its URL is

```
http://www.x3.org/tc_home/x3j16.html
```

The last time I looked, there wasn't much there, except a message telling you that the page was under construction and a list of the committee members' affiliations.

For information about the Standard Template Library, try

```
http://www.cs.rpi.edu/~musser/stl.html
```

You can obtain a copy of Hewlett-Packard's public domain implementation of the STL itself from

```
ftp://butler.hpl.hp.com/stl/
```

DIFFERENT DIRECTIONS

There will always be some programmers who find C++ too much to cope with, or too complex to be worth learning, or just too much of a dog's breakfast to bear. Sometimes, there may not be a choice if they want to use a particular library or application framework, or get a job, so they will just have to live with it. Many programmers still have some control over what language they use, though, so what can they do? Well, there are plenty of viable alternatives. Don't let the attention which C++ is attracting make you forget that if there's one thing the computing community isn't short of, it's programming languages.

The first alternative to C++ to consider is whatever you are using already. Although many programmers come to find object-oriented programming a comfortable and effective style of programming, no matter what size of system is being developed, the significant advantages of this style and the languages that support it only really relate to large-scale systems, particularly evolving systems built by groups of programmers over time. If you are not involved in that sort of scene—maybe you just write shareware in your own home—then perhaps it isn't worth mastering a language of the size and sophistication of C++. Despite the impression you may get from some self-professed software engineering gurus, the old methods of program design—top-down construction and stepwise refinement—haven't suddenly become wrong, nor have languages like Pascal and Modula-2 worn out or gone senile. It's just that the limitations of these methods and languages for producing large software systems and reusable components have been acknowledged. If these methods and languages work for you on the programs you want to write, then carry on.

The only exception to the advice that you might as well stick with what you know unless you want or need to change is that it doesn't apply to C. Anything you can do in C can be done in C++. Some of it can be done more safely, some using more convenient notation, some without resorting to tricks. Why go on making life hard for yourself?

A more radical alternative is to move away from general-purpose programming languages altogether. Many day to day tasks can be accomplished perfectly well using special-purpose little languages. The best known of these are probably the various UNIX shell languages and their cousins Awk, Perl and Tcl. In effect, these are very high level extensible languages, providing flexible facilities for combining programs to achieve a particular end. Although they provide control structures similar to conventional languages, the operations which are treated as primitive are actually performed by other programs, often system utilities, each of which may carry out a highly complex task. The user of one of these languages need never worry about low-level details or data structures. Conventional programming is replaced by a process of putting tools together to carry out the desired job. An increasingly important development in this area are the visual application-building systems, which let you produce graphical user interfaces by a similar process of combination, without writing any code at all.

If you still have a yen for programming, but feel dissatisfied both with established programming languages and object-oriented programming, then look at functional languages. These are languages where all computation is specified by the application of functions to arguments. There are no updateable variables, no assignment and no sequencing of instructions. Radical enough for you? Examples of such languages include Miranda, which is arguably the most elegant design, but suffers from a poor implementation; ML, which is widely known and available in several dialects; Haskell, which is intended as a standard for functional languages, and is consequently over-elaborate; and Gofer, a subset of Haskell, which is available free (not to be confused with Gopher, the Internet thingy). All of these modern functional languages support abstract data types in some guise. In theory, functional languages are a good thing, because it is easier to reason about functional programs than about imperative ones, and to carry out systematic program transformation. Furthermore, because there is no inherent sequencing in the execution of functional programs, they hold the promise of being able to take advantage of parallelism to increase their efficiency much more readily than conventional languages. (I oversimplify here, but the consequent is true.) The problem here is that this promise has been held out for years, with little sign of its fulfilment. For the moment, serious use of functional programming languages is limited by their poor performance and the difficulty of interfacing them to conventional operating systems. Working programmers tend to dismiss them as academics' curiosities, but if you are interested in other new approaches to programming besides object-oriented languages, functional languages will repay your attention, especially in view of their evident influence on the STL.

If you don't want to be so radical and do want to write object-oriented programs, but don't care for C++, there are still alternatives. Probably, if programming languages were judged only on their intrinsic merits, without reference to the wider technological, economic and social context, we would all be using Oberon-2. This is a language with a high-class pedigree, being descended from Pascal via Modula-2 and plain Oberon. The Oberon design philosophy has been summarized as: simplicity, flexibility, efficiency, and elegance. In contrast to C++'s development from C, the evolution from Modula-2 to Oberon was achieved by the addition of a few features and the removal of rather more—Oberon-2 is actually a smaller language than Pascal. Minimalists will be disappointed that the progression from Oberon to Oberon-2 introduced three new features and reintroduced one more, but the language remains very sparse. It still provides fully adequate support for object-oriented programming. The Oberon-2 reference manual is thirty-four pages long; the unannotated C++ reference, written in a similar style at a similar level of detail, is one hundred and fifty seven pages (and the draft standard is five times that length). The Oberon-2 system occupies little disk space, has no need for gigantic amounts of memory and is very fast. It is a possible runner in the Next Big Programming Language race, as C++ grows ever more obese.

As a language, Oberon-2 is probably the best vehicle for object-oriented programming presently around, but there are plenty of others. Modula-3 is another serious contender. If Oberon-2 is sort of Modula-2−−, then Modula-3 is Modula-2++, as it were. That is, it is an extension of Modula-2, providing not only object-oriented features, but also exception handling and concurrency. Eiffel is more dogmatically object-oriented. Beta, which is designed by some of the same people who started it all with Simula, is also worth looking at. For the real hardliners, there is still Smalltalk, but, to be honest, I have trouble taking it seriously, and even its enthusiasts tend to think of it as a prototyping system.

None of these languages is Lisp, though, but Lisp programmers need not feel left out. CLOS is the Common Lisp Object System. It is identifiably object-oriented, it's different from anything else, has been adopted as a standard, has minimal syntax and uses lots of brackets. "People who like this sort of thing will find this the sort of thing they like". (Not my joke, Abraham Lincoln's. Really.)

All of these alternatives have their merits. Even if you have become wildly enthusiastic about C++, you ought to be aware that there are other programming languages and other approaches to programming.

PARTING WORDS

Perhaps the best way to say farewell is by looking again at some of the criticism stated or implied at the beginning, to see whether a closer acquaintance with C++ has diminished its force.

C++ is ugly. You might well claim that this is in the eye of the beholder, so let's say C++'s neglect of established notations seems wilful and perverse. Judging from recent developments, it will ever be so, but it doesn't really matter. "Notions are more important than notations"—and you can largely disguise the notation. In time, you may never even see it, as programming systems that separate the programming language from the user interface are developed.

C++ is based on C. Nobody can deny it, and it is noticeable that the most serious deep defects in C++'s syntax and semantics are actually left over from C. However, compatibility with C was the secret of C++'s initial success; probably, only a language based on C could have brought object-oriented programming out of research laboratories and into widespread use. It is a tribute to Bjarne Stroustrup and the other people who have developed C++ that so much has been salvaged, and that enough facilities have been provided to allow you to bring the low level features of C under control by hiding them inside more attractive data types.

C++ is big and complicated. Undeniably, but if you want to say *too* big and *too* complicated, you have to answer the question "Too big and complicated for *what*?" Certainly, C++ is too big and complicated for comfort or ease of learning. The big question is: "Are the size and complexity necessary for the tasks facing modern programmers?" I don't know. I suspect not, but the pressure from programmers for new features to be added to C++ suggests that the perception among people who are actually writing big programs, and not just books about programming languages, is that contemporary systems require complex languages.

A positive aspect of the complexity of C++ is that it enables the language to support a wide range of programming styles. I can use abstract datatypes, you can use multiple inheritance, someone else can use procedural abstraction, but we all share a common language. We can share libraries and exchange programs, without any need for the monstrosities that surface when mixed-language programming environments are called for.

In the end, the debate about C++'s virtue is irrelevant. I can only repeat something I said at the outset: C++ is here. It's up to you what you make of it.

Index